IN MY TIME

IN MY TIME

AN AUTOBIOGRAPHY

Lord Elwyn-Jones

WEIDENFELD AND NICOLSON · LONDON

The supporters of the author's coat-of-arms
represent his father and mother

First published in Great Britain by
George Weidenfeld & Nicolson Limited,
91 Clapham High Street, London SW4 7TA
1983

The drawing on p. 274 is by Dan Jones;
all the others are by Pearl Binder (Lady Elwyn-Jones)

ISBN 0 297 78159 6

Text set in 10½/12 pt Linotron 202 Baskerville, printed and
bound in Great Britain at The Pitman Press, Bath

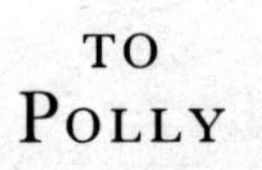
TO
POLLY

Contents

Illustrations

Acknowledgements

My daughter Josephine helped me with the initial planning of this book and my son Dan and younger daughter Louli refreshed my memory about their childhood. Fiona Sosnow, my research assistant and archivist, undertook the formidable task of putting the accumulated mass of my papers in order. Christine Salmon also helped with research.

Mrs Pitt, my Private Secretary when I was Attorney-General, helpfully collated sources for me from my ministerial days, as did David Owen, my first Private Secretary when I was Lord Chancellor, and other members of the staff of the Lord Chancellor's office. The Library staff of the House of Lords, particularly David Jones and Ken Woods, tracked down parliamentary and political sources. Harold Prescott, Llanelli's Librarian, and Alun Bowen-Thomas, its Chief Executive, enlightened me about various facets of Llanelli's history.

Susan Haylock, Gladys Cremer and Kim Chisholm undertook the deciphering of my handwriting and typing.

Alex MacCormick edited the book with skill – and patience.

To all those who have helped me so much I give my most grateful thanks.

I

Growing Up In Wales

> You must know that there is nothing higher and stronger and more wholesome and good for life in the future than some good memory, especially a memory of childhood, of home. People talk to you a great deal about your education, but some good, sacred memory, preserved from childhood, is perhaps the best education. If a man carries many such memories with him into life, he is safe to the end of his days, and if one has only one good memory left in one's heart, even that may sometime be the means of saving us.
>
> *The Brothers Karamazov*, Fyodor Dostoyevsky

Waking up in my bedroom in the Lord Chancellor's residence in the House of Lords to watch the glorious sunrise flooding the sky, I would hear the river sounds beneath its tall windows, the hooting of tugs hauling laden barges on the broad Thames, the crying seagulls and the quacking ducks in the winter, and once or twice high in the sky the beating wings of white swans. All the year round these were the regulars of the Palace of Westminster: the cooing pigeons, the sparrows, the starlings, the sweet melancholy aria of the blackbird. I had often heard the blackbird's song at the other end of the Palace of Westminster when there were all-night sessions in the Commons. When the weary custodian shouted, 'Who goes home?' I would escape out of the stale air of the Commons into the freshness and silence of a deserted Whitehall.

Other recurring sounds were the chimes of Big Ben, loud enough to disturb the sleep of Mr Speaker Thomas in his bedroom at the other end of the Palace, but far enough away from me to blend harmoniously with the different sounds of the morning. At my bedside I kept the notes of my day's engagements: a cabinet committee, swearing in a new judge, attending a Privy Council in Buckingham Palace, the Lord Chancellor's procession to open the day's proceedings from the Woolsack, official dinners, clearing from the red boxes the unending flow of papers and correspondence arising from my three jobs as Head of the Judiciary, Speaker of the House of Lords and member of the Cabinet.

Waking up as a child in Wales, in my small bedroom in 132 Old Castle Road, Llanelli, where I was born in 1909, I heard river sounds too. The narrow Afon Lliedi flowed right in front of our house. It was a tidal river. When the tide receded, fresh water flowed down from 'Swiss Valley' and from the green hills above it, where my mother used to take me to pick blackberries and bilberries in the fall. In those unpolluted days it was possible to catch 'silcots', sticklebacks, minnows, and plenty of elvers and eels that came in with the tide, and sometimes even a trout.

There were other morning sounds. Filled coal trucks from the mines outside the town were marshalled at the bottom of our road before being taken to the docks at Llanelli, then a busy little port sending Welsh anthracite and steam coal to the Continent. Loudest of all, when shifts changed, was the scream of the hooters of the Llanelli Steel Works and the Old Castle Tinplate Works, where my father worked, just a few hundred yards from where we lived.

Ours was one of two houses built by my mother's grandfather of stone from the local quarry. It was a well-equipped little house: it even had a bathroom, but like all the other houses there was no inside lavatory. There was one outside – we called it *Y Ty Bach*, the small house. There were four bedrooms. The bedstead in my small bedroom had beautiful round brass knobs, which I enjoyed unscrewing, taking care to put them back before my mother found out. The wallpaper had a twirly blue floral design which, endlessly repeated, had a curiously mesmeric effect on me. On the right-hand wall there was a framed, richly illuminated Lord's Prayer in Welsh. On the wall opposite was a coloured print with 'The Lord is my Shepherd' in large letters below Jesus, surrounded by little lambs, which I took for granted must be Welsh lambs.

The front parlour of the house was rarely used. The principal purpose of front parlours in our road seems to have been to house the coffin when a bereavement occurred. Happily there was no death in my family while we lived there. We moved to another part of the town when my sister married, so that my parents could live near her, and in the sad fullness of time my parents, sister and brother were buried from there.

Our parlour in Old Castle Road was enlivened for me by a very large, handsomely framed coloured print of a gondolier serenading two buxom Venetian girls leaning over a balcony above the canal, one dark, the other blonde. I thought they were wonderfully beautiful.

My mother was born in No 132. Her parents had come from a small farm outside the town. My father was one of the five sons of Henry Jones, a farm labourer, who, like many farm workers of his time, sought work in industrial Llanelli, becoming a copperworks rollerman. When my father left school at the age of fourteen, his predestined career was to work in one of the mills of the town. First he learned to be a 'monkey shiner' at the Morewoods works at one shilling and fourpence a day. Then he progressed to being a 'splatcher' in the copperworks where his father worked. He went from there to the Old Castle steel works as a 'behinder', graduating finally to rollerman. He worked as a rollerman for thirty years.

The rollerman was in charge of the shining steel rolls in his part of the mill. His team consisted of a 'doubler', a 'furnaceman', and a 'behinder'. Their job was to roll out the thick steel plates until the metal became thin enough to be used for tin cans and saucepans. Saucepans were important for Llanelli. They inspired Llanelli's famous song, '*Sospan Fach*' (Little Saucepan), now more a hymn than a folk song and a joy to sing in a mighty chorus at the international rugby matches at Cardiff Arms Park. The rollerman's work was hard: he was always near the red hot furnace. My father was a small, muscular man, strong and skilled at his work. His team always had the best output. At work he wore a *crys bach*, a short-sleeved Welsh flannel shirt, which absorbed the sweat – his shirt was white with body salt at the end of the shift. My father was a tea-totaller: he relied on large quantities of tea that he took to work with him in a *stên*, a blue enamel lidded tin can that had a wire handle and was kept hanging against the furnace wall to keep it warm.

Occasionally father would let me go with him to the mill. He would lend me tinted glasses so that I could look at the red hot flaming interior of the furnace and the glaring steel plates being brought up to the right heat to be rolled. After this I always doubted the story of Shadrach, Meshach and Abednego surviving in the fiery furnace. Fires have fascinated me since those days. I remember when I was a small boy greatly enjoying watching Pugh's timber yard on fire with huge flames lighting up Old Castle Road like daylight.

Father worked in the Old Castle works until 1937, when he was sixty-eight. Cataracts caused by the glare of the furnace and the steel plates clouded his eyes. Happily a brilliant Llanelli eye surgeon, Dr Healy, operated on them successfully and Father was able to continue reading right up until he died. We had tried to persuade him to retire from work long before he did, but he would have none of it. He himself never made heavy weather of his work; indeed he made fun of those who did. When he was eighty-eight he appeared on a BBC television programme. I have a recording of his comment on one of his less enthusiastic workmates: 'If you saw him going to work, always at a crawling pace, you would think he was on his way to the gallows.'

My father was a happy man, trim, moustached and always with a welcoming face. He enjoyed playing merry little tunes to us on his small brass fife. He was a fine speaker and was often asked to be master of ceremonies in chapel concerts and at the Whitsun eisteddfod in the Market Hall.

He was a man without gall. On his retirement from the works after forty years of unstinting service, he was given no recognition from the management: not even a gold watch, and of course no pension from his employers. Fortunately by then his sons and daughter were able to help and he lived a cheerful life, giving service to the chapel and the folk round him until he died peacefully at ninety-one.

I was the last-born of the family – *y cyw melyn olaf* (the last yellow chick) as mother used to say. Three of the seven children to whom my mother gave birth – William Henry, Aneurin Glyndwr and Elizabeth Gertrude – only lived for eleven, five, and eight months respectively. That was the pattern of infant mortality in working-class homes in those days. My mother used to say sadly that the two boys who died were brighter babies than the three boys who survived: Idris, Gwyn and me. I myself was often ill and only survived the dreaded diphtheria and rheumatic fever because my mother was a superb nurse and we had a devoted family doctor, Dr Davies ('G.L.' as he was fondly called). He came to us under the provisions of a limited insurance scheme providing medical care for my father only. Dr G.L. ignored this and looked after us all, as did his son who succeeded him. They also performed surgery. I remember the day my mother brought me home from Llanelli General Hospital in a black, bumpy, horse-drawn cab after having my tonsils out. My family and I have always been fortunate in the doctors who have looked after us wherever we have lived: in Llanelli, in Middlesex and London, and in Brighton. They all became family friends.

During the first years of my life South Wales was in the grip of industrial conflict. There was a bitter railway strike in 1911 when the Riot Act was read in Llanelli. There was arson and there was looting. Armed soldiers marched through the town. A railway worker was shot dead. Then came the Cambrian Combine strike and the riots at Tonypandy, where soldiers were brought in again. There was a national strike of miners for a minimum wage. When a strike took place in my father's union, he took part in it. As a boy I was told of the day when, along with his workmates, my father lay across the railway line on which trucks brought supplies to the works, to stop them from going in.

Llanelli had a strong radical tradition. One of my school teachers at Lakefield Elementary School was Dan Griffiths, a powerful socialist orator. The local dentist who treated me was another socialist, Farley Neft. Keir Hardie, whose first parliamentary constituency, Plaistow, I later had the honour to represent in Parliament, was campaigning in South Wales at the time for an independent Labour Party freed from Liberal dependence.

My father, whose activities centred on Tabernacle Congregational Chapel, was not involved in this political ferment, but he was an early member of the Iron and Steel Trades Federation and a loyal trade unionist. Like most South Wales working men of his time, he transferred his support early from the Liberals to the Labour Party and bridged the gulf that had separated the Nonconformist chapels from the Labour movement. But the chapel remained my father's main commitment. One relic of the Liberal tradition survived in our home: the large black-framed portrait of the Grand Old Man, Mr Gladstone.

I was never beaten by either my father or my mother; our punishment as children was to be sent upstairs to bed. Mother would speed the process by banging her hands on the lowest tread of the stairs and shouting, '*cer i'r gwely*' ('get to bed') and pretending to be in hot pursuit. My father left all discipline to her.

I do not recollect much political discussion at home, and we had only one political quarrel that I can remember; during the General Strike in May 1926, when I was in my last year at school. The strike started with the miners coming out. 'Not a penny off the pay, not a minute on the day,' was their reply to the mine owners' demands for cuts in their pay. When the General Strike was called, my father, like the rest of his workmates, came out on strike and my mother supported him. Gwyn, then a student at Aberystwyth University College, was a socialist and supported the strike. Idris was working for his Ph. D. in Cambridge. Over half the undergraduates of Cambridge registered for emergency duty, and Idris went with his Gonville and Caius contingent, most of whom were sent as special constables to Whitechapel. I remember the day when he brought a policeman's truncheon home with him. This division in the family disturbed me greatly while it lasted, for I respected my father and admired both Idris and Gwyn. Time healed the breach, however, although it did not heal the industrial conflict.

After the TUC called off the General Strike, the miners continued the strike alone. There was much suffering. The miners set up soup kitchens in the miners' halls. My old friend Jim Griffiths, with whom I was later to sit in Cabinet, was then one of the miners' leaders and told the bitter story in his book *Pages from Memory*: 'When winter came we had to give in and return on the owners' terms. Alas, not all who came out could get back, for the managers took it out on the activists. When we appealed to the coal owners to reinstate the men they had victimised, our appeal fell on deaf ears. It was beyond them to be generous even in their hour of triumph.' These events were neither forgotten nor forgiven in the mining community of South Wales.

Most of the families who lived in the terraced houses of Old Castle Road were Welsh. There were a few English like our nextdoor neighbours, the Pedleys and the Bodmans. The Irish O'Sheas lived two houses away. A pious Jewish family lived at the other end of the road. One Friday evening when I was walking home from school an elderly Jew asked me to come into his house to light the gas lamp in his kitchen. It puzzled me greatly. I had no knowledge then that on their Sabbath pious Jews forswore all such activities.

I never sensed any racial animosity in Llanelli. I do not recollect any anti-semitic feelings in either of the two schools to which I went. Harold Benjamin was one of my friends at school. His older brother Isaac had been a friend of my older brother Gwyn. Harold won a scholarship to Oxford and took a brilliant First there. He became a solicitor and sent me some briefs when I started at the Bar, when briefs were most welcomed, as did R.I.Lewis, another Jewish schoolmate. Like the Welsh, the Jews believed in education and, however poor, made sacrifices to give their children this start in life.

There were marked class differences in the town, though no one asked you who your father was. The assumption that every person is as good as another was at the heart of our social behaviour. In moments of exaltation in Wales, I have felt that Thomas Traherne in the seventeenth century expressed its essence when he wrote: 'You never enjoy the world aright, till the sea itself floweth in your veins, till you are clothed with the heavens, and crowned with the stars: and perceive yourself to be the sole heir of the whole world, and more than so, because men are in it who are every one sole heirs as well as you.'

Our family income was small, especially during the recurring bouts of unemployment, when all my father got was a pittance of dole money. But my parents were able to supplement it in various ways. We had a fair sized garden at the back of the house where we grew vegetables and flowers. In the field behind the house we had a large allotment on which we grew most of the vegetables we needed, storing the potatoes in sacks in the garden shed.

At the bottom of the garden we kept chickens. Occasionally, in hard times during the 1914–18 War, my mother sent me to the better off streets on the other side of the park to sell eggs on the doorstep. When a hen went broody – we kept Rhode Island Reds, which laid lovely brown eggs – we made a comfortable nest for her on straw in an empty barrel in the garden, in bushes sheltered from the wind and the rain. Sometimes I used to check whether the eggs were addled by floating them in a bowl of warm water. If there was life in the egg, it would move vigorously. When the time came to watch the chicks breaking out of their shells, it was happiness for me : a kind of spring. Once, during the First World War, my father bought a gosling to fatten for Christmas. He got it cheap at the market because it had a squint. We fed it lavishly, proudly watching it grow to a majestic size. Alas, on the morning of Christmas Eve it was stolen. We searched high and low for it and always suspected that the thief lived at the bottom of the road, for we found a heap of goose feathers in the lane at the back of his house.

Between our allotment and the back lane behind our home, we had a pigsty. Each year, four or five piglets would be fattened there: one was kept for the family, and the others were sold. Rarely were we without bacon or ham. The problem about keeping pigs, especially in wartime, was how to feed them. Pig-meal was always supplemented by boiled potato peelings. When they were old enough, Idris and Gwyn would go round the back lanes to collect peelings from kitchen waste dumped there.

When fuel was dear, my own modest contribution to the household as a young lad was to clamber over the municipal waste tip at the back of the field behind our house to collect bucketfuls of coal or coke.

Another occasional source of family income was keeping a lodger. One was a friendly Irish labourer named Dan Moriarty. He took me to the Llanelli photographer one day and I have a photograph of myself as a small boy sitting on his knee. He taught me an Irish song:

I went down the lane to buy a penny whistle,
A copper came behind and stole my penny whistle,
I asked him for it back, he said he hadn't got it.
Ai, Ai, you curly wib, you got it in your pocket.

But he never told me what a 'curly wib' was.

My mother was always full of zest, energy and shrewdness. Her rosy face was oval and her hair, parted in the middle, was combed smoothly back into a bun. Her blue eyes were discerning. She was a good neighbour. She nursed those who were sick and helped local women in childbirth. There seemed to be nothing she could not do. Once there were gypsies living in a caravan in a field behind our house. When one of their children died, I remember my mother collected enough black mourning clothes to enable the family to have a proper funeral : in those days, no matter how poor you were, black mourning clothes were indispensable. She cared for others. On one occasion, when she was shopping in town she came across people who were laughing and jeering at a woman staggering about and somewhat the worse for drink. My mother went up to them and told them they should be ashamed of themselves. She took hold of the woman's arm and escorted her home : a Christian act, for my mother disapproved of alcohol.

My mother ran our home cheerfully and efficiently. Everything was cleaned and scrubbed and polished, from the brass knocker on the front door to the fancy silver-plated tea-pot, cream jug and sugar basin that were kept for Sunday best and for the social teas in the chapel schoolroom that the ladies of the chapel provided twice a year. All our clothes as well as all the household laundry, blankets, sheets and all, were washed in the back scullery. My mother hung it out hopefully to blow dry on the washing line in the garden. She did the washing in a large wooden tub with a wooden dolly and a scrubbing board. She ironed the clothes with a flat iron heated on the fire. For my father's fly-away starched Sunday collars of the kind preachers wore, and his sham (a small starched dickie he wore over the front of his Welsh flannel shirt), my mother used a heavier 'box' iron. She baked our bread in the kitchen oven and Welsh cakes on an iron griddle over the fire. Her apple tarts were famous. We all had a hand in preparing the huge Christmas pudding and after Christmas I used to enjoy going to the pantry to eat it cold. I loved the smell of baking bread, and on washing and ironing days the fresh clean smell of the clothes.

I made several contributions to the household chores. We had no bookcase in our house and I kept my school books on the tiled floor, as my brothers and sister had done before me, under a small table in a corner of the kitchen. Once a week it was my task to sort them out, dust them and pile them tidily. If my mother was needed in chapel sometimes on Sunday morning, when normally she would be at home cooking the dinner, I was allowed to be the cook. My father would have prepared the vegetables the night before, as he always did. My main job was to keep an eye on the roast joint in the oven which was a once weekly treat. Save in the direst times of unemployment, we would eat the joint hot for Sunday lunch and cold for Sunday supper. What was left we ate in a stew the next day. My mother excelled in the preparation of the economical *cawl*, that admirable Welsh broth with *trollies* (oval pellets of delicious stuffing with chopped sage).

Despite the struggle my parents had to bring up and educate their four children to the level they did, I do not recollect that they worried about money. Nor was I ever aware that we were poor: compared with our neighbours, we were not. My parents never drank, not only from Nonconformist conviction but also because they needed the money to keep the home going. They never got into debt. That was a cardinal principle, a moral imperative. My mother used to keep her money in a leather purse with concertina compartments. On pay day, my father, confident in her good management, handed over the whole of his wage packet to her. But apart from his wages, he earned a few shillings a year as secretary or treasurer of more than one Friendly Society. He kept their limited funds in small tin money-boxes that he concealed in a wardrobe or in a chest of drawers.

The Friendly Societies developed before the National Insurance Act of 1911. The names of the Ivorites, the Oddfellows and the Rechabites come to mind. Hatred of the cruelties of the Poor Law led British working people to join these Friendly Societies as a small insurance against sickness and to provide for funeral benefit. The latter was the most popular: for a penny or tuppence a week one could be insured against a pauper's burial – the final humiliation.

All of us were good at exams and won scholarships at every stage of our careers. One of my mother's regular bits of advice was *gwna dy orau*, do your best. I was fortunate in being the youngest of the family. By the time I went to school my sister Winnie had graduated from Aberystwyth University College and become a schoolteacher and Idris was leaving Cambridge to be a scientist with ICI. Both Idris and Winnie sent money home regularly to my mother as soon as they were earning, and Winnie delayed her marriage for this reason. As a result of their contributions, Gwyn, like Idris, was able to complete his education at Gonville and Caius College, Cambridge, after graduating from Aberystwyth. Idris may well have sacrificed his own personal happiness in keeping the family going. Six foot two, extremely handsome, sociable and very popular, a distinguished scientist, a Cambridge blue and the Welsh rugby captain, he was the only one of us not to marry. He gave me his unfailing support and affection till the day he died.

A constant factor in my young life was the Tabernacle Congregational Chapel. My father was senior deacon and Sunday School superintendent there for sixty years. Sunday was chapel day, morning, afternoon and evening. At morning service at 10.30 the children recited verses from the Bible from the front of the *sêt fawr* – the deacons' pew. It was my earliest experience of public speaking. On Sunday afternoons at Sunday School we were taught the Scriptures. In the winter my father would delight the chapel children by telling us Bible stories with the aid of brightly coloured lantern slides and a 'magic lantern'. Daniel in the lion's den and David and Goliath were the most popular stories. That was before I ever went to the cinema.

My mother also taught at the Sunday School. Like my father, she followed what we did closely. If we were given anything to learn by heart for Sunday or day school, she was always ready to test us, whether it was poetry or even Latin declensions.

The Sunday night service in chapel started at six o'clock. When I was small, I sat in the second pew from the front with my mother. I enjoyed cleaning her spectacles so that she could follow the hymns. Father faced us from the deacons' pew. He had a fine baritone voice: I have a record of him singing a hymn at the age of eighty-eight. After I was thirteen, I sat in the gallery with the other boys, widely separated from the girls in the choir. But after chapel we took them for walks up to the Furnace Pond and the country lanes in the green hills above the town.

In those days you could count on about sixty voices in the chapel choir, large enough to sing one of the great oratorios once a year – Mendelssohn's *Elijah* or Handel's *Messiah*, or the *Hymn of Praise*. We sang the Halleluia chorus then as children nowadays sing pop songs.

Our chapel was dominated by the formidable preacher, the Rev. Gwylfa Roberts, and his sermon was the linchpin of the service. The Welsh language is a powerful vehicle for emotional oratory, for *hwyl*. And how they preached in those days!

Sunday was not all solemn, save in the chapel itself. I remember my father telling a story about me which made him think I would go far. Walking across People's Park with him one Sunday night on the way to chapel, I found a sixpenny bit: a fortune for a boy in those days. After the service, my father told one of his fellow deacons and workmates, Sammy Daniels, of my find. As we left the chapel Sammy came up to me and said: 'Your father has told me you found a sixpence.'

'Yes, I did,' I replied.

'There's glad I am because I think it's the one I lost on the way to Chapel.'

'Oh do you?' I answered; 'Well what's the date on it then?' Sammy Daniels, chuckling, gave in.

Apart from Sunday services there were also weekday functions in chapel. Thursday night was Band of Hope night. On Friday night we often had rehearsals for the children's choir. The conductor was a large, moustached Llanelli draper, Mr L. W. Adams. I used to be taken to his shop to buy a new Sunday suit when I grew out of my old one. I would then appear proudly in chapel in my new suit: knickerbockers, a navy blue jacket with a wide sailor collar, a lanyard and a whistle. Mr Adams, as our conductor, was respected but feared. His prowess enabled the choir to win many an eisteddfod contest. Our choir song was '*Côr Adams yw y gore, y gore, y gore*' ('Adams's choir is the best, the best, the best'). When I was about eleven, the choir competed in an eisteddfod in the Rhondda Valley which we won with our rendering of 'Little Lamb who made thee, Dost thou know who made thee?'

Choral competitions were fought with as much passion as the rugby contests in Cardiff Arms Park. Wynford Vaughan Thomas relates that after such a battle, one conductor told his rival: 'You beat us hollow in "Lift up Your Heads Ye Gates of Brass", but we gave you hell in "Love, perfect love".

The chapel children also performed operettas from time to time. A stage would be erected over the *sêt fawr* and the chapel would be turned into a theatre. I remember playing the title role in *The Rajah of Rajahpore*, dressed up in my mother's idea of oriental costume, red turban and all. I cannot remember what it was all about, but I do remember some lines I sang:

Suffragettes you all must be
If you dare disturb the peace so
Off to prison you all must go.

I had no idea what a suffragette was. I sang a lot as a child: in the choir, and at home after chapel around the organ in our 'middle' room between the kitchen and the front parlour. I sang a solo from the pulpit once in a crowded chapel – a sad hymn about Cain and Abel – with my mother and sister both in proud tears in the family pew. I dared not look at them or I would have been in tears myself.

I am especially indebted to my father for teaching me how to recite. He taught other children as well: boys and girls would come to our house and rehearse their recitations with him. When he was teaching me, he would walk to the bottom of the garden and get me to recite from the doorstep of the back kitchen. If he failed to hear me, he would shout, '*Rwy ddim dy glywed ti*' ('I can't hear you'). I then had to speak up louder and clearer – an important lesson for my later activities. Once, I even recited Mark Antony's oration, 'Friends, Romans, Countrymen . . .', from the stage of the Market Hall. Most recitations were in Welsh – often very solemn for a small boy to cope with. One I remember was entitled: '*Beth ddaw o honno Fi?*' – 'What will become of me?'; I cannot remember the answer, although at one point I had to say 'perhaps I will become a preacher.' That was a tremendous aspiration for a young chapel boy in those days.

My parents were deeply religious. But they were tolerant and believed that the message of Christ was, above all, the message of love. This is certainly what they communicated to their children. They lived by what they taught. They accepted fully the Nonconformist rules of personal conduct. Honesty was one. One of my mother's constant reminders was:

> It is a sin
> To steal a pin
> Much more to steal
> A greater thing.

I remember being told a family horror story about Idris 'stealing' a handful of threepenny bits from chapel. He was not yet four, and was allowed into the *sêt fawr* where the deacons were counting the money after a special 'silver collection'. He innocently helped himself to a handful of those pretty baubles from a collection plate. Fortunately father spotted him, recovered the loot and restored it to the collection plate, horrified lest Idris's 'theft' had been noticed.

I never heard either of my parents swear. They did not drink or smoke. We did not whistle in our home on Sunday, but there was no show of solemn piety. On the contrary, there was much fun and laughter in the house. On Sunday evening, we would gather around the organ and sing Welsh folk songs and hymns and Negro spirituals and even 'Clementine'. When I was a boy the organ was festooned with little silk coloured prize bags made by the ladies of the chapel: our reward for winning singing or recitation contests. Winnie played our organ with vigour, and later her husband, Glyn Evans, joined in the singing. I have the organ in my own home now and my grandsons play 'Boogie Woogie' on it.

Singing and acting were not confined to our houses or chapel or school. The games we enjoyed in the streets often involved a lot of play-acting and singing. One game was 'Jack Y Lantern'. One of us would have a bicycle lamp run on smoky paraffin. When it was lit and could be seen by the searchers it gave special excitement to what was no more than playing hide and seek in the dark. A popular sport was to run along with steel 'washers' (hoops) controlled by a long metal hook – both made in the steel works. In the summer we played cricket in the road alongside the tinplate works with the cricket stumps and bails chalked on the wall. In the winter we played soccer in one of the less busy streets. But the winter favourite was rugby.

New Year's Eve was always an exciting time. As soon as midnight struck, children would go from door to door and hail the New Year through the letter-boxes. Sometimes the reply from the other side of the letter-box was less than benevolent. But often you would be invited into the house to be given a *calennig* – a threepenny bit if you were lucky – for your good wishes. On New Year's mornings the Llanelli Tramways Department gave us a special treat. We could travel anywhere we liked on the Llanelli trams for a penny.

While most of my childhood memories are happy, there was a phase when awareness of death troubled me. Llanelli was a neighbourly place and I had many relatives. Mother was often in mourning. Indeed black was her normal Sunday attire. When a death occurred in the street, the front blinds in the house of mourning were drawn for weeks. Neighbours would draw their blinds too until the funeral was over. When a relation or a neighbour died, I would be taken along with my parents to see the body in its coffin in the front parlour and be lifted up to see the dead face. This distressed me especially when I was taken to see my aunt Sarah's marble white face in the coffin. I carried a bunch of hyacinths with me. It took me a long time to stop associating their scent with death.

On one occasion I saw a drowned boy being dragged out of the sea on Llanelli beach and men trying in vain to revive him. At about this same time I also saw a drowned man being pulled out of the pond at the back of our house. I don't think I confided my fears to my parents, but in due course I conquered them. Funerals in those days in Llanelli were big occasions for the display of public grief. Family and friends gathered around the graveside. There would be prayers and a tribute to the dead and a great Welsh hymn would be sung, and mourners would throw a little bunch of flowers over the coffin in the grave. As has been said, grief locks the English heart, but it opens the Welsh one. All our sweetest songs are sad and in the minor key.

One other troubled memory comes back to my mind. That was the cold winter night when my brother Gwyn, who must have been brooding over some grievance, disappeared from home. He vanished after nightfall. There was a great search for him all round the house, all down the street. My father was at work. Auntie Jane, who lived down the street at No 113, anxiously joined in the search. She was small and wore a grey shawl over her shoulders. At the back of our house the field led down to the pond which received the waste from the steelworks. It came in steaming before it cooled. Swans nested where the water was cool. There were reeds and bulrushes. We used to catch small fish there. It was a favourite place to play when I was a boy. Auntie Jane, pessimistic as she always was, took a lighted candle to the water's edge searching for Gwyn. I remember seeing her pointing the guttering candle towards the water. Mercifully, Gwyn wasn't there. The neighbours searched the rest of the field and the People's Park. No sign of him. Then my mother decided that father should be told 'Gwyn is lost'. A neighbour went to the works to tell him and he came rushing home and joined the search for Gwyn. There was no trace of him. We were in despair. Suddenly there came a knock at the front door. Standing there was a workman from the steelworks with Gwyn asleep in his arms. He had run off to the works and fallen asleep near the large warm furnace.

2

SCHOOLDAYS

My schooldays began in Lakefield Elementary School where my sister and my two brothers had been before me. There was no field anywhere near its playground, which was an asphalt yard amidst rows of small terraced houses. There were no trees and no grass.

I walked to school through a lane alongside the Lliedi river to a narrow footbridge across the river and then through five streets. As I walked one morning singing to myself, a smiling housewife threw a penny from her doorstep to me. I was puzzled, for I had done nothing to deserve it. I picked it up. I was too embarrassed to thank her but I spent it on home-made *loshins du* (black lozenges) in one of the small front-parlour sweetshops that flourished in those days.

We were taught to read and write and do sums quite early. Much of the teaching was done in chorus. We loudly chanted the multiplication tables, the alphabet, and the days and months of the year. We were taught in English. We spoke Welsh at home, but English was our second language. We sat at small wooden desks and learned to write on a slate: no paper and pencils, no pen and ink. We sang every day and had performances on spccial days such as St David's Day and at Christmas. I was thc pagc in Good King Wenceslas. When I got to the top form I played the king and my mother made me a cardboard crown painted in gold. I remember two of the teachers particularly well. One was Edgar J. Rees, whose teaching got me through the entrance scholarship examination to the intermediate school. When I was appointed attorney general fifty years later, he wrote to me that he remembered me singing in a St David's Day concert at Lakefield school:

> ' *'R' oedd menyw fach ym Mhenfro*
> *a'i enw ydoedd Non'*

['There was a little woman in Pembroke whose name was Non': Non was the mother of St David.] You were a fair-haired, frail and delicate looking little boy in those days – but you have certainly weathered the storm of life in no uncertain fashion.'

The other teacher I liked was Dan Griffiths, a warm, eloquent socialist orator, famous in the public meetings of the time. He was interested in how we lived. He would ask us during his class what we ate, how we spent our Bank Holidays and so on. I remember he once asked each of us what we had had for breakfast that day. The first boy said he had had bacon and eggs, tea, toast and marmalade. All the rest of us who followed also said we had had bacon and eggs and tea and toast and marmalade too. The reality for most of us was bread and butter and jam. I am sure Dan Griffiths was not taken in. We were more truthful about how we had spent our Bank Holiday. Some had gone in a horse-drawn brake for the day to Mumbles. Others, like me, had tobogganed on a tin sheet down one of the works slag tips, our local pyramid. That was great fun – but punishing on the trousers. It also involved trespassing within the works perimeter and keeping a watchful eye for the foreman.

In the autumn we wandered in the green hills above the town to pick blackberries and cob-nuts from the hedges. We had the long Llanelli beach and the sand dunes to play in. A big adventure was to pick the succulent cockles from the shoals on the sands when the tide went out. It needed careful watching – you could easily get cut off by an incoming tide. We took the cockles home in a sack and soaked them in a bucket of water to get the sand out of them. Mother would boil them for supper. Delicious. Another delicacy was *bara lawr* (black lava bread), an edible seaweed mother used to fry with bacon. In Llanelli in my childhood, our 'dark satanic mills' were surrounded by lovely countryside and a wide seashore. Not that the mills ever seemed satanic to me, fascinated as I was by the furnace fires. My uncle, William Henry (Auntie Jane's husband), was a volunteer fireman in the local fire brigade and one of my heroes. His gladiatorial brass fireman's helmet hung glittering on his kitchen wall.

The 1914–18 War broke out just as I entered Lakefield school. I cannot recollect that it affected school life but I do remember the occasion when one of the Bodman boys who lived next door at No 130 came home on leave straight from the trenches. His boots and puttees and uniform were thick with Flanders mud and my mother invited him to use our bath. I shall never forget the terrible day in September 1918, during the last weeks of the war, when the news came that my cousin, Albert John, a bombardier in the Royal Garrison Artillery, the only child of Auntie Jane, had died at the age of twenty-one in Boulogne in the Spanish flu epidemic on his way home. I went over to her house just after the telegram had come from the War Office. Poor Auntie Jane was lying on the tiled kitchen floor writhing and wailing. She never recovered from that shock. Some years later I went with her and my parents on a sad pilgrimage to the British military cemetery at Terlincthun near Boulogne, where Albert lies alongside thousands of his comrades.

The same flu epidemic struck down Idris in army training just before he was due to be sent to France. Summoned by a War Office telegram Mother hastened to the military hospital at Brighton. Years later Idris told me that he was floating into unconsciousness when he suddenly felt the grip of Mother's hand pulling him back into life.

When I was eleven I sat the entrance scholarship exam of the County Intermediate School, as it was then called. Until the end of the nineteenth century, for the vast majority of the people of Wales education was limited to a few years at an elementary school. This was my father's experience. As the century progressed, however, so did the growth of Welsh university colleges – Aberystwyth was opened in 1872, Bangor in 1878 and Cardiff in 1883 – and a new vista of university education was opened to the youth of Wales. The old 'higher grade' schools (there was one in Llanelli called 'Coleshill') could not promise the right qualifications to get into university and a new type of school was urgently needed. In addition, industrial expansion demanded technical and scientific education. The 1889 Welsh Education Act was the Government's response to these pressures. The Llanelli Intermediate School came into being five years later. The school was fee-paying. There was no free secondary education but sixteen entrance scholarships for the boys of the borough, which the winners held throughout their stay at school, were awarded to pupils of 'proven ability'. They were of the value of £4 10s 0d: sufficient to pay the annual school fees. But little in the way of academic achievement was expected from education in the school. When the new school building was opened in 1897, in welcoming it, the Llanelli *Guardian* wrote: 'Education is not supposed to make a gentleman in the sense of abstinence from manual labour; but it should dignify and improve the labour of the workshop, the counting house, manufacturing, the warehouse and all other departments of trade and labour in which the nations of the world are now competing with us so earnestly for supremacy.' However, although most of the pupils of the school took the *Guardian*'s path, a few did go on to enjoy higher education. Many more would have done so had today's possibilities been open to them. But even if a lad had the ability to win a scholarship to university, money was needed for food and clothing during the years of study. Poor families with several children could not afford this: an injustice which was not put right until after the 1945 election.

There was intense competition between the local schools for entrance scholarships. Publication of the names of the successful scholars in the Llanelli *Guardian* was our local equivalent of the Birthday Honours List and there was much happiness in my home when my name appeared eighth in the 1921 list of sixteen names of Llanelli's 'borough boys'.

There was no school uniform but we had to wear the green school cap and badge. Getting to *Yr Ysgol ar y Bryn* – the school on the hill – from Old Castle Road was an adventure. It was over a mile from my home and was finally reached by a very steep hill known as Marble Hall Road. It housed no marble hall, but there was a fine pillared chapel at the foot of it – *Capel Als*. I had learned to ride the push bike which I had inherited from Gwyn, and I rode off happily to school, pushing the bike slowly up the steep hill but speeding down joyfully on the way home.

The school's amenities and equipment were modest. There was no gym. The assembly hall consisted of two schoolrooms made into one when the partition between them was drawn back. There was no sixth form study or reference library. The school cloakroom, or in winter the boiler room, came in useful for quiet reading. The teachers made up for these shortcomings, and I was greatly helped by the librarian and staff of the Llanelli Public Library.

My favourite subject was history, which Lewis Griffiths taught. He was also the school rugby coach. Our French language teacher was Mr Stockton, sedate and elegant in Edwardian collars. Mr D.T. Roberts, who taught English, was a different character. He wore a pair of old plus-fours and lived like a gypsy in a caravan near Ashburnam golf course in the summer. In the winter it was horse-drawn to shelter behind the school pavilions. Although he stammered, D.T. communicated wonderfully his own love for English and French literature. Mr T.V. Shaw, a quiet, modest man, who later became headmaster of the school, was another fine teacher of English.

I was in some awe of the headmaster, Mr Griff Thomas, a classics graduate from Jesus College, Oxford. He caned me once for being late for school. On that occasion I was late because my mother was ill and I made her breakfast, but I never told the headmaster this. As he swished the cane down on to my outstretched hand, I fixed my eyes on the plaster bust of Julius Caesar beneath which was an inscription: 'It is better to wear out than to rust out.' Come to think of it, Julius Caesar did neither. Discipline in the school was not oppressive and prefects had no power of punishment.

Serious music was introduced into the school with the appointment of Frank Phillips in 1921. Thanks to him there was a good school choir and supporting orchestra.

It was the Debating Society which attracted me most, however. I have often wondered why, in a politically conscious community such as ours, politics made no impact on the school or on our debates. The General Strike, the League of Nations, parliamentary elections – I cannot remember any discussion of these. If members of the staff had any political opinions, they did not communicate them to us.

There was also a Dramatic Society and in my last year at school a revolution took place when we did *Pygmalion* as a joint production with the girls' school. It adjoined the boys' school, but rarely did the twain meet. Indeed the headmistress of the girls' school did all she could to prevent this. A girl was not allowed to walk to school with a boy even if he was her brother. When one of the mistresses saw my sister Winnie walking with Idris, she was sent for and reprimanded. When she explained that it was her brother and surely it was a natural thing to do, the headmistress did not accept that: 'Other people would not know it. You must not do it again.' Happily, this sexual segregation did not apply after school hours.

Schooldays ended when I was seventeen. Only a few of my school colleagues were able to go to university. I had not formed any clear ideas of what I would like to be. My recurring Walter Mitty dream was to be an eye surgeon saving a brilliant artist's sight. I was not good at science and there was little encouragement to boys at our school to take up medicine. Later, when I practised at the Bar, I enjoyed doing medical negligence cases. This was the nearest I came to medical practice.

Our family never had holidays. My parents married on a Christmas Eve because tinplaters had a holiday the next day and they could celebrate the wedding by going on a day excursion together. When I was a boy I enjoyed the chapel excursions by horse-brake to the Gower coast. We could swim when the tide was in on the Llanelli beach or in the Llanelli dock itself. My brother-in-law Gwyn Evans, who was like a brother to me, taught me to swim there. Gwyn was an expert swimmer and would do high dives from the masts of ships in the dock. My mother was appalled when she heard this and hid his bathing costume for a while, until he found it above the cistern in the *ty bach*.

The favoured recreation when I was at school was rugby: playing it and watching it. Father always managed to find the money to get into Stradey Park to see the Llanelli Scarlets playing and he used to take me with him. Rugby was like a religion in Llanelli. It is said that a Llanelli vicar was worried that the people of his parish were getting too obsessed with rugby. His verger told him 'Don't worry about it. Just mention Albert Jenkins once or twice in your sermon and you'll be all right.' The devotees worshipped stars like Albert, the Llanelli and Welsh rugby captain. He was the hero of my childhood, and he lived in Old Castle Road quite near our house.

My own enthusiasm for rugby was heightened when Idris became one of its stars. He was tall, strong and powerfully built and played hooker for Llanelli, Cambridge, London Welsh and finally for Wales, which he captained in 1925. He followed in the tradition of my uncle Elias Jones. When Idris died and left me his personal belongings they included Uncle Elias' Llanelli cap: scarlet with a silver tassel and dated 1895.

Although rugby was in my blood, alas I was not strong or skilful enough to follow in Idris' footsteps, although Gwyn got pretty near to doing so.

My mother did not share my father's enthusiasm for the game although she did accompany us to Twickenham once when Idris invited us to see the Oxford versus Cambridge match. Mother had never seen a match before and was appalled to see Idris leading the pack into the scrum and the fierce long rucks of those days. She demanded anxiously: 'Idris *Bach*, where is he? Is he all right?' She did not enjoy the match. I did. It was when the Light Blues, led by Wakefield, beat the Dark Blues by thirty-five points to three.

The people of the little town of Llanelli have a great sense of belonging. The greatest compliment that one Llanelli man can say of another is that he is '*un o ni*' ('one of us'). The greatest compliment that can be paid him is to make him an honorary Freeman of Llanelli, an honour I myself prize greatly, as I do the fact that the Llanelli Borough Council named a new civic building *Ty Elwyn* – Elwyn's House – in my honour. It is this sense of belonging which has enabled the town and its people to survive, indeed to excel, in so many fields – even in dark years like 1929, when so widespread was the unemployment and hardship that Llanelli was classed as a distressed area and shared in the Lord Mayor of Cardiff's distress fund.

When I was growing up there the town was full of rich characters. The robust individuality of some of them was reflected in their *figenwe* (nicknames). Dai Bendigedig (Blessed Dai) was a deacon. Dai Gang went from one communion to another, not from devotion but because of an acquired taste for communion wine. The organ blower of the Welsh Congregational Chapel, *Capel Als*, was more discriminating. He refused to blow the organ in the All Saints Church because 'he couldn't blow English'. Dai Rwsh was an eloquent local politician, ready to hold forth on any subject and so called because he 'rwshed in where angels fear to tread'.

One of my father's workmates was known as Dai Substantial. His real name was Dai Jones. When he started work his foreman was told his name and said, 'That's no good. We've got dozens of Dai Joneses in here.' Dai said: 'I don't mind what you call me as long as it is something substantial.' So he became Dai Substantial. A member of the Tabernacle chapel congregation was a reformed alcoholic who used to proclaim the three stages of his salvation. The first, when he was drunk: *Nynd a ffaelu gweld* – able to go, but unable to see where he was going; the second stage was *gweld a ffaelu mynd* – able to see but unable to go, when he had been arrested and locked up in the police station; the final stage was seeing the light, sobriety and reformation. *Mynd a gweld* – going *and* seeing. He was a persistent prompter of the preacher's sermon with 'amen' and '*felly wir*' (truly so) and 'halleluia'.

Local pride is inherent in Wales. I remember speaking for Megan Lloyd George in the Carmarthen by-election campaign. It was in a small village in the heart of the country called Llanfihangel-ar-Arth. After the meeting in a small schoolroom lit by oil lamps I walked out with the chairman into the brilliant moonlight. I told him: 'I've never seen a moon like this in my life before.' 'Oh,' he said proudly, 'you've never been to Llanfihangel-ar-Arth before.'

3
University Years

The high summer of 1927 brought with it the testing time of A-level exams, or Higher Certificate as it was known in those days. I gained a distinction in History, which was what I wanted to read at university. The Welsh quarrymen, farmers, miners who wanted a university of their own had largely paid for the University College of Wales at Aberystwyth and they are proud of it. I went there in the fall of 1927, after winning the £10 'Visitor's' entrance scholarship to the college, enough to pay the fees for a year in those days. I had difficulty in persuading my father not to wheel my trunk to Llanelli station in a wheelbarrow, as he had done for my sister and brothers before me.

I did not stay in Aberystwyth long, greatly as I enjoyed it. At the end of my first term, Idris and Gwyn urged me to try for an entrance scholarship into Gonville and Caius College, Cambridge. They had both been post-graduates there, winning Rhondda research studentships, founded by Lord Rhondda to help Welsh students. I had visited them when they were students and enjoyed my time with them there. Many Welshmen had been admitted to the college over the centuries even though the original college statutes of Dr Caius provided that 'no scholars are to be elected who are deaf, dumb, deformed, lame or Welshmen'. I got an exhibition to Caius in December 1927 and went up the following October. This meant that I had no exam worries during the rest of my academic year in Aberystwyth. The Professor of History, Stanley Roberts, took me in hand. In addition to attending his lectures I wrote weekly essays for him which I researched under his direction in the magnificent National Library of Wales on the hillside above the town. He knew that would stand me in good stead when I got to Cambridge.

At Aberystwyth at that time the head of the Law Faculty was 'Tommy' Levi, who allowed me to attend his lectures, although at that time a career in the law was not in my mind. He was entertaining and much loved despite, or perhaps because of, his heavy nasal accent and his deaf aid, which he switched on and off during his lectures. He was a brilliant teacher. Some of his pupils became leading figures in the law as practitioners or academics. An eloquent lay preacher on Sundays, he enjoyed a little fun in his lectures. 'I am often asked,' he said once, 'what is the maximum sentence for bigamy? The answer, of course, is two mothers-in-law.' He had a soft spot for the girls and was very popular with them. When one of them fell out of his favour and complained that she did not like playing second fiddle, he retorted, 'Second fiddle, indeed – you are very lucky to have a place in the orchestra.'

College lectures were held in the main college building on the sea front. It is a remarkable gothic fantasy, looking, as H.V.Morton described it, 'like an illegitimate child of the London Law Courts'. So far from being purpose built as a college it had been built as a hotel in the middle of the nineteenth century by a railway promoter, to encourage travellers to come to Aberystwyth by train from Euston. The scheme foundered and the college bought the building for a song in 1870. It had a great hall which became the college quad. During each morning break the students would walk round and round quad, the bravest males sometimes joining up with the girls. The college had an active social life. It was there that I learned to dance, after my fashion. There was a good Literary and Debating Society, in which I frequently took part. Although at that time I had never tasted liquor, my maiden speech was against prohibition, the side I was asked to take for the debate.

My year at Aberystwyth was one of the happiest of my life: I had time to read without examination pressures, I had the guidance of Professor Roberts and I made friendships which have endured. Curiously enough, in my year there was very little political activity in the college. Welsh nationalism had made no apparent impact as yet. Students worked pretty hard. Many, as I did, went to chapel on Sundays. We played rugger in the winter, tennis in the summer, and swam in the sea when the sun was warm. We sometimes went on expeditions to the lovely country outside Aberystwyth to places such as Devil's Bridge. The girl students were allowed to come with us, although in Aberystwyth itself they had to keep within certain bounds. Even a pleasant walk called Plas Grug (Heather Palace) was out of bounds to the girls, but there was always the long promenade and the sea shore itself where we were allowed to escort them. The sea air set me up and I grew several inches taller during my year in Aberystwyth.

I had gone to Cambridge in December 1927 to sit the scholarship examination, wearing for the first time the then fashionable plus-fours, soon briefly to be replaced by grotesquely wide, light grey Oxford bags, which Herbert Farjeon once described as 'maternity trousers'. Dr Zachary Brooke interviewed me in his book-lined room in Caius. He was a great medievalist and editor of the *Cambridge Medieval History*.

A few days after the exam at Cambridge the postman delivered a telegram to 132 Old Castle Road. It said that I had been awarded an exhibition and asked whether I would accept it. There was much happiness at home at the news until it was realized that the exhibition was only worth £60 a year. In those days a year in Cambridge even for a prudent undergraduate cost about £250. There was no help from the Carmarthenshire Education Committee. Although there were nine grammar schools in the county, they only awarded two exhibitions of £25 each. However my parents and brothers and sister resolved that I should take the exhibition. By then Winnie was teaching in a grammar school in Milford Haven, Idris was a research scientist with ICI in Billingham and Gwyn was starting in industry. They decided to see me through.

The cultivated serenity of Cambridge was a long way from the staid sea-front and wild surging seas of Aberystwyth. Whenever I return to Cambridge now, over half a century later, this first impression of perfection floods back to me, as well as gratitude that for three precious years I was a small part of it: the college buildings, the emerald velvet lawns of the Backs, the walks beside the slow-moving, willow-veiled river Cam.

The atmosphere in college was totally monastic. It was a sad contrast with Aberystwyth, where there were always female students about; there were few women in Cambridge then. Newnham and Girton, the women's colleges, were remote. I was invited to tea in both, but only once – and had to be out by five o'clock sharp. It was a world where the learned Professor Winstanley, who taught us Constitutional History, continued to pretend that women students attending his lectures were not there and to address his class as 'Gentlemen'. Two years later, when I became President of the Union, my proposal to install the first women's toilet in the Union faced strong opposition. I was warned: 'This is the thin end of the wedge. It will end with a woman occupying your Presidential chair.' They were right. It happened. The first woman president was Ann Mallalieu. Thirty years later I had the pleasure of welcoming her as a fellow member of my chambers in Lamb Building in the Temple, another male preserve which only slowly opened its portals to women.

Although there were 'sets' in Cambridge such as the Pitt Club and in those days public schoolboys were overwhelmingly in the majority, nobody asked me what school I had been to nor what my father did – nor did I ask them. In fact most of my closest friends at Cambridge had been grammar school boys like me, so some degree of class identification was clearly at work.

I had rooms in college in my first year, high up in the attic in Tree Court. My senior tutor was Arnold McNair, who later, as Lord McNair, became President of the International Court of Justice at the Hague and was one of the greatest international lawyers of his time. He was also one of the kindest and most modest of men. It was he who first suggested to me, when I was in my last year at Cambridge, that I might do well at the Bar and that he would sponsor me if I applied to join his own Inn, Gray's Inn.

My own kindly tutor at Caius was Francis Bennett. When I was elected Secretary of the Union the required dress was white tie and tails. He knew I could not afford this and told me to go to his own tailor, Whybro and Walker, to get fitted up. Later I had the pleasure of repaying that debt and I received a note from him saying this was the kind of experience that made tutoring a pleasure. My cheerful and encouraging History supervisor was Michael Oakeshott, later Professor of Political Science at the London School of Economics.

I had the good fortune to be reading History during the great professorial triumvirate of G.M. Trevelyan, J.H. Clapham and Sir Ernest Barker. I attended Trevelyan's lectures on the reign of Queen Anne, a special subject in my last year. Trevelyan, the most lucid and readable of all historians, was shy and hesitant as a lecturer. Economic History was a new subject in Cambridge and was taught by Clapham, appointed the first Cambridge Professor in Economic History in 1928. Unlike Trevelyan he was an eloquent communicator. Professor Barker was another first, the first Cambridge Professor of Political Science. He was the son of a miner and a man of warm geniality. I remember the occasion when, in 1931, he and Harold Nicolson came to lunch in my rooms in Caius with the officers of one of the undergraduate societies. Nicolson asked Barker whether he had read any good poetry lately. The Professor, who had just got married, said in his strong North Country accent, 'Ah don't read poetry now. Ah live it.'

It was the impact of these teachers which, as T.E.B. Howarth has written in his fascinating study, *Cambridge Between The Wars*, caused the emphasis in Cambridge History 'to move somewhat away from politics, war and diplomacy to institutional and social change'. It was a change of emphasis I greatly enjoyed.

Constitutional history was taught by determined traditionalists. I have already mentioned Winstanley. He had a curious inability to say 'King Charles'. He always called him 'Ching Carles'. Kenneth Pickthorn was a don in the then High Tory and High Church citadel of Corpus Christi. Our paths crossed again in the House of Commons when I was Attorney General, particularly during the debates in 1965 on the Southern Rhodesia Act which I steered through the Commons. He informed the House he had made 'some attempt' to teach me history.

Professor G.C.Coulton, the passionate anti-Catholic medievalist whose lectures I attended, added much colour to the academic scene. He was a powerful polemicist, Hilaire Belloc's 'remote and ineffectual Don, that dared attack my Chesterton'.

I kept to a steady timetable of work in my studies at Caius and did well enough to get firsts in my preliminary examination at the end of my first year and in Part 1 of the History Tripos at the end of my second – efforts which were rewarded by the college with a minor scholarship in my second year and a major scholarship in the third, which considerably reduced the financial burden on my family.

My studies did not prevent me from taking an active part in the social life of the university. I joined the Union Society as soon as I went up, Idris paying for my life subscription. The Union became a major commitment and I was elected President in the Michaelmas Term 1931. I joined the Marshall (Economics) Society, the League of Nations Union, the Welsh Society (of which I was President) and the Anglo-German Association. In the years after the 1914–18 War there was sympathy, and not only in radical circles, for the view that the Treaty of Versailles had been too harsh on the German people and had put at risk any prospect of reconciliation between Germany and her former enemies. I became Secretary of the Anglo-German Association. The Association's officers once entertained Baron von Neurath, the then German Ambassador in London, to lunch in my rooms in Caius. I next saw him fifteen years later in the dock at the Nuremberg Trial, at which I was one of the prosecuting counsel. He sent a message to me through his German counsel that he was glad to see me again after all the intervening years since I had entertained him at Cambridge. During those years however he had been Hitler's Reich Protector for Bohemia and Moravia, holding the formal rank of Obergruppenfuehrer in the S.S. and lending aristocratic cover to the brutal Nazi regime in Czechoslovakia. I informed his counsel that I could not communicate with an accused in the dock.

Student politics in Cambridge in the 1930s have acquired notoriety since the exposure of the treason of Philby, Burgess and Maclean and the confessions of Blunt. At Cambridge in my time (1928–31) I came across little intense party political activity, although there was already concern about the economic crisis, growing unemployment, the impotence of the League of Nations and support for the Movement for Colonial Freedom. It was the challenge and threat of Fascism that changed the political mood. Hitler did not come to power until 1933; the Spanish Civil War did not break out until 1936, the year the hunger marchers came to Cambridge. Those were the years of political commitment.

I began to take part in debates in the Union in my second term and thereafter spoke regularly, undiscouraged by President Lord Pentland's good-natured comment on one of my early speeches, that 'Elwyn Jones made a charming speech, but his Welsh accent amounted to an impediment in it.'

My maiden speech was in support of a motion, which was defeated: 'That all forms of literary censorship are highly undesirable.' Curiously, Hugh Foot (later Lord Caradon) deserted the liberal tradition of the Foot family and spoke against the motion. Later in the year his brother John, with whom I was to debate in the House of Lords in due course, spoke as I did against another motion: 'That the policy followed by Great Britain in Palestine has been grossly unjust to the Arab race.' A debate against fox hunting was interrupted by an invasion from the members of the Pitt Club blowing hunting horns. Kenneth Adam, later the Director-General of BBC Television, wrote in the *Cambridge Review* of my speech in the debate: 'Mr Jones, whether as politician or agitator or Evangelical preacher, clearly has a remarkable future before him.'

In 1931 the debates became more political. President John Green, a staunch Tory, began the year with a memorable debate on the motion: 'That the immediate return to power of a Conservative Government is essential to the social and economic welfare of the country.' At that time there was a Labour Government in office under Ramsay MacDonald. The Union chamber was packed. I was Secretary of the Union then and had to clamber over members sitting on the floor in order to get to my seat and to make my speech, following the Tory opener, Baron de Rutzen. I was followed in the debate by Edward Marjoribanks MP (a stepson of Lord Hailsham), whom the President wrote 'would be a great Parliamentary debater'. Tragically, he died at an early age.

Oliver Baldwin MP, the socialist son of Stanley Baldwin and a vigorous, irreverent character, spoke after him and delared, 'Economy that starts, not on Lord Chancellors' pensions but on the unemployed dole, will bring about Socialism in five years, instead of thirty.' Sir Austen Chamberlain MP followed. He had last spoken at the Union forty years earlier. Before dinner he had told me that he was in favour of a republican form of government – but he asked me not to mention it in the debate. He spoke with great eloquence, ending in a peroration on imperial unity and protection. Finally a fourth MP, Geoffrey Shakespeare, wound up the debate, which the Conservatives won by the narrow margin of three votes: 338 against 335. There were cheers and counter cheers when the President read out the result. Ten years later these same young men were involved together in the Second World War and Baron de Rutzen, who had opened the debate, was killed in action.

Taking part in debates like this stimulated my own growing interest in political affairs, for which the Union was an admirable training ground.

The final debate in John Green's term as President was on a motion 'Disapproving of all Hereditary Titles and Places amongst His Majesty's subjects'. Lord Ponsonby, then Labour Chancellor of the Duchy of Lancaster, supported the motion. Forty years later his grandson, Tom Ponsonby, sat with me on the Opposition Front Bench in the House of Lords.

That term ended with a motion moved by Karl Britton, the retiring President, later Professor of Philosophy: 'That this House no longer has faith in youthful idealism.' Young Randolph Churchill marked the occasion by turning up very late for the President's dinner, smoking a cigar.

I spent the 1931 long vacation in Cologne. A German contemporary at Cambridge had arranged for me to tutor the younger son of a leading Rhineland industrialist in their palatial mansion overlooking the Rhine. Their affluence had not apparently been diminished by the great depression which had cast its shadow over Germany and all Europe since 1929.

One day towards the end of my stay in Cologne, my friend asked me to go with him to a meeting of the Nazi Party. It was a packed meeting addressed by one of the local Nazi leaders. His demagogic and fanatic oratory roused the audience to shouts of '*Zieg Heil*' and aggressive Hitler salutes. This, my first encounter with Nazi demagogy and the mob aggression it stirred up, disturbed me greatly. It was a warning sign that an aggressive, violent, racist political force could well achieve a mass following in the prevailing conditions in Germany. It was a political development that was going to affect my generation profoundly. Exposing it and resisting it dominated much of my life for the next fifteen years. My alarm at the effectiveness of its appeal was made all the greater when, after the meeting, my friend raised the lapel of his coat and to my astonishment revealed his Nazi Party swastika badge. My friend was to come into my life again on two further occasions. Not long before the outbreak of war in 1939 he visited London and called on me. He had, so he claimed, been taking soundings of British opinion on Hitler's foreign policy. He said he had found much support for it in the circles in which he had moved. I told him that this did not reflect British public opinion and that unless there was an end to Nazi threats and aggression and a change of course in Germany, the outcome would be war. I next heard from him in very different circumstances in 1945 in Nuremberg. After publicity had been given in the press to my part as counsel in the Nuremberg trial, I received a letter from him, telling me that he had been in command of a German army unit in northern Italy and had arranged for his unit to surrender to the allied forces as the war ended and thereby saved a lot of lives.

I had been elected Secretary of the Union in the Hilary Term of 1931. In those days progression to Vice-President and then President followed without further election and I was installed as President in October 1931. My father and mother came for the occasion. From the Presidential Chair I looked up to them in the Gallery, my father listening critically to my utterances, no doubt wondering whether I remembered what he had taught me, my mother expressing herself simply as she always did in important moments of joy – she quietly shed happy tears.

My term as President began at a time of political crisis. The National Government had been formed in August 1931 with a coalition cabinet led by Ramsay MacDonald. The economy measures it announced in September cut unemployment benefit from seventeen shillings to fifteen shillings and threepence a week for an adult man – paid only after a means test. Unemployment was soaring to the peak of $3\frac{3}{4}$ million out of work reached in 1932. I remember a sad line of Welsh miners with collecting boxes singing hymns in Chancery Lane, London.

My first debate as President was on a motion: 'That this House condemns the policy pursued by the National Government.' I had by then become a committed supporter of the Labour Party. The motion was defeated by 257 votes to eighty-three.

The Government announced that the General Election would take place on 27 October. We had an eve-of-the-poll debate on the motion: 'That this House would welcome a triumphant Labour victory at the polls'. It was heavily defeated and was a foretaste of what was to come. In the General Election the next day the National Government won 554 out of the 615 parliamentary seats.

The Government Round Table Conference on India was held in November 1931. I brought forward a motion: 'That this House would welcome the immediate establishment in India of a representative Constitution based on full Dominion Status'. I had been friendly with a number of Indian students at Cambridge. One was Honi Bhabba, who became a distinguished nuclear scientist. His death in an air crash was a grievous loss to India. Another was Shanti Dhavan, who opened the debate powerfully. He became the first Indian President of the Union, later a judge in the Allahabad High Court and a popular Indian High Commissioner in London.

The Indian debate took place during the second Round Table Conference. Mahatma Gandhi had been let out of prison in order to take part in informal preliminary meetings with Lord Irwin, then Viceroy of India. Winston Churchill opposed such attempts at conciliating Indian nationalism and made his notorious statement: 'It is alarming, and also nauseating to see Mr Gandhi, a seditious Middle Temple lawyer, now posing as a fakir of a type well known in the East, striding up the steps of the Viceregal Palace, while he is still organizing a campaign of civil disobedience, to parley on equal terms with the representatives of the King Emperor.'

In fact Gandhi had never been a Middle Temple lawyer. After his conviction in India in 1922 on charges of sedition, for which he was sentenced to six years imprisonment, his Inn, the Inner Temple, removed his name from the books and disbarred him. It was not until 1971 that the Inn made some amends when a commemorative plaque, a gift from the Calcutta Art Society, was unveiled by Lord Gardiner on the staircase of the Inn Library to commemorate the centenary of Gandhi's birth. The Treasurer of the Inner Temple, Sir Cecil Havers, attended, along with Lord Denning, the Master of the Rolls, the Indian High Commissioner and me.

During his visit to England Gandhi visited Cambridge. He was sixty-two, with mind and body in full vigour. My Indian friends honoured me by bringing him to tea in my rooms in Caius. It was a typical bleak November day. Gandhi, small, very thin and shaven headed, was wearing his simple white homespun dhoti. His bare feet were in sandals. His eyes behind round glasses were extraordinary. He was courteous and friendly and seemed very happy to be with us. He radiated goodwill. Listening to his passionate creed of non-violence, love of the human race and liberation of India from colonial rule, made clear to me his hold over the hundreds of millions of his followers in India. Few men have made as great an impression on me as did Gandhi at that time.

A succeeding debate was on a motion: 'That this House disapproves of dons'. Jacob Bronowski, already a significant figure in Cambridge in those days as poet and controversialist, spoke in favour of it. Despite his powers of persuasion, the motion was defeated; dons were still admired by students in those days. Bronowski was to come into my life again later. When Idris was Director-General of Research of the Coal Board, Bronowski was one of his colleagues in the research establishment at Stoke Orchard. Later, when Bronowski undertook the brilliant *Ascent of Man* series for BBC Television, my daughter Josephine worked with him in its production and co-edited his book on the series.

In his book T.E.B. Howarth refers to the 1920s as 'the age of exclusivity *par excellence*'. I did not encounter it. I once read a paper on Leonardo da Vinci to the 'Sheba Club' in King's, a small group of historians. I knew nothing of the 'Apostles' at King's, nor did I ever come across the 'Heretics'. I spoke once to the Magpie and Stump, a Trinity debating society, which had a stuffed magpie in a glass case on the President's table. We debated irreverently the motion: 'That the League of Nations is a damp squib'. In none of the societies to which I belonged did I come across anything faintly conspiratorial. As far as the Union debates were concerned, I do not recollect any expression of views from the radical left. They may of course have taken the view that the Union was not worth taking seriously. The Tories did.

One of my particular pleasures was to see – from the 'gods' at a cost of less than a shilling, – the memorable productions by Tyrone Guthrie in the Festival Theatre. Superb Flora Robson and Robert Donat were among the regular performers.

Cambridge was then a quiet place. Undergraduates were not allowed to have motor cars or motor bicycles. Young Conan Doyle, who was at Caius and whom I coached at one time, got round the difficulty by engaging a full time taxi for himself.

To me the great joy of Cambridge was the endless talk that went on in our rooms until the small hours of the morning. We truly 'tired the sun with talking and sent him down the sky'.

4

Austria in Turmoil

I left the cloistered world of Cambridge for London in December 1931. I had by then decided to read for the Bar, encouraged by Arnold McNair and by James Whitehead, a leading Patent Silk whose son Norman I had coached for the History tripos during a happy long vacation in 1930 at Littlestone-on-Sea. Both McNair and Whitehead were benchers of Gray's Inn, and so it was Gray's which I had the good fortune to enter in 1932 with a helpful scholarship which paid my fees.

Accommodation was easier to find in London in those days than it is now. I started in a furnished room overlooking quiet, tree-lined Torrington Square, in the heart of Bloomsbury. I next shared a flat in Mecklenburgh Square (next door to R.H. Tawney) with a Caius friend, E.V. Francis, who was a journalist, and Harvard Montgomery Hyde, biographer of Norman Birkett and others. Finally, I moved to Hampstead to share a ricketty flat above an off-licence shop with Richmond Postgate, brother of Raymond. My address there – 'The Old Brewery, Hampstead' – led to some anxious questioning from my parents in Llanelli.

My first task in London was to pay my way. I went to see the Cambridge Appointments Board, who told me of a vacancy for a part-time tutor at the home of a Mr Hale Munroe, in Hampton, Middlesex. One fine morning a week or so later, I took the train to Hampton Station to be met by a breezy, bespectacled, smiling man in an MG sports car. I had no idea who he was. He explained to me that my intended pupil was not his son, but his wife's young brother Eddie. Mr Munroe drove me to a fine old farmhouse – 'The Old House', Hampton – set in a pleasant garden and orchard. The farmhouse had been much refurbished. In the hall he had installed a small bar named 'The Spotted Cow'. After a few minutes talk with Hale Munroe, a gorgeous dark-haired young woman with sparkling eyes entered the drawing room, full of warmth and friendliness. I had no idea who she was.

After they explained to me what they wanted me to do and introduced me to Eddie, they left the room, no doubt to decide whether I would be suitable.

While they were out I noticed some press cuttings lying on the table. They were about Jessie Matthews and Sonny Hale. Thus began a warm friendship with Jessie which lasted until she died in 1981. She was the seventh of ten children of a coster in Berwick Street Market in Soho. When she became successful on the stage she decided to help Eddie, her much younger brother, further his education. I tutored him for about a year. Jessie and Sonny were then co-starring in the musical *Hold My Hand* in the Gaiety theatre. I accompanied her sometimes to the film studios to watch her filming *There Goes the Bride* and later playing Susie Dean in *The Good Companions*. Jessie thought that I would make a natural Inigo Jollifant, but I was never put to the test. The part went to John Gielgud.

This glimpse of theatrical life was a sparkling experience for me. I remember once accompanying Jessie to the London Palladium to a hilarious performance by the Crazy Gang. Jessie was summoned on to the stage and presented by Jimmy Nervo with a small pup. She came back to her seat and deposited the pup in my precious concertina top hat. Happily it did neither of them harm.

Another part-time job in London was reading *The Times* to a blind old Jewish gentleman in Portman Square. But my main source of income in the 1930s was from freelance journalism and a series of Cambridge university extension lectures I gave in different parts of the country. They were courses of twelve lectures on 'English statesmen of the nineteenth century'. It was a useful grounding for my later years in Parliament. I familiarised myself with the political struggles inside and outside the Houses of Parliament during the Victorian period and the battles in the Commons between parliamentary giants of the period. I also lectured for the WEA (the Workers' Educational Association) in London and in Wales.

When I settled in London in 1932, I became involved in politics. Richmond Postgate introduced me to Fabians such as his sister Margaret and her husband Douglas Cole, the Webbs and particularly Dick and Naomi Mitchison. In 1934, through my Fabian associations I first became actively involved in politics. This watershed in my political experience arose out of the dramatic developments in impoverished little Austria, wedged precariously between Hitler's Germany and Mussolini's Italy.

Dollfuss, a clerical reactionary and former Minister of Agriculture, had become Chancellor of Austria in May 1932, heading a coalition with a parliamentary majority of one. His power rested increasingly on the strength outside Parliament of the fascist 'private army', the Heimwehr. The following March, when three chairmen of the Austrian Chamber resigned, he suspended Parliamentary democracy. Tension was heightened when, at the end of January 1933, Adolf Hitler became Chancellor of Germany, with the avowed intention of annexing Austria. The Nazi reign of terror began. Dollfuss turned to Mussolini for help. It was given on one condition: that he would suppress 'Red Vienna', which had been governed by Social Democrats since 1918, first under Victor Adler and then Otto Bauer.

But by June 1933 Austrian Nazi terrorism and Nazi propaganda pressure, directed by radio from Munich, became so intense that Dollfuss banned the Nazi party. It was a brave but ineffective act of defiance. Then, under Mussolini's pressure, Dollfuss took the fateful step in February 1934 of banning the Schutzbund, the Socialist Republican defence corps, driving its members underground. The Heimwehr, by then in control of the security forces, had pressed for similar action. The Schutzbund leaders were arrested before they could tell their supporters where their limited supply of arms was hidden. The local Schutzbund leader in Linz, Bernascheck, resisted and urged the two Viennese leaders to take up arms. But the reluctant Bauer and Julius Deutsch tried to delay such action. By the afternoon, however, the assault by the Heimwehr, the army, the police and the gendarmerie overwhelmed them. Hundreds were killed and thousands wounded.

Fierce suppression followed. The Social Democratic Party was outlawed. Thousands of its members were imprisoned or sent to detention camps.

Hugh Gaitskell was in Vienna at this time studying economics with Professor Hayek. Hugh contacted his Fabian Society friends – the Coles, the Mitchisons and Richmond Postgate – in London to enlist help for the beleaguered Austrian Social Democrats and trade unionists. Sir Walter Citrine went out for the trade unions. Naomi Mitchison went too, with such financial help as the Fabians could muster, and linked up with the Quakers, who had been doing relief work in impoverished Vienna ever since the 1914–18 War.

Gaitskell emphasized that legal help was essential for the prisoners and detainees. Richmond Postgate suggested me. I left by train for Vienna on 6 March 1934. My first call there was on Hugh. He quickly put me in the picture and introduced me to Viennese lawyers. The next day, Naomi took me to meet some of the inhabitants of the shell-torn Gemeindehaüse, pock-marked from machine-gun fire. I was welcomed warmly with the Social Democrats' greeting *freundschaft* (friendship). I met some of the families of the people who had been killed or were in custody.

I learned that there were over nine thousand men and women in custody. The need for relief was urgent. What was available came from three main sources: a Quaker fund; money provided by the International Confederation of Free Trade Unions; and the British TUC's 'Henderson Fund'. Much legal aid had already been provided by Vienna's socialist lawyers. John Price came out from the headquarters of the Second International of Social Democrats in Zurich, along with the Belgian lawyer Somerhausen, to give what help they could.

When I returned to London, I reported the facts to Ernest Bevin, then Chairman of the National Joint Council of the Labour Party and the TUC. A few weeks later he asked me if I would return to Austria with a promise of funds to pay for the legal defence of those in prison or detention. He advised me on my way there to call on Fritz Adler, the Secretary of the Second International, in Zurich. Adler was an avuncular, grey-haired, senatorial figure. He warned me that I would come across violent extremists in Vienna and that I must be on my guard not to get involved with them. It was not until I got there that I learned from Hugh Gaitskell that Adler himself had murdered the Prime Minister in a café in Vienna in 1917.

In the meantime a deputation of lawyers consisting of Professor Basch, Dick Mitchison and others had interviewed the then Minister of Justice, Dr Schuschnigg, and asked for permission to set up a bureau in Vienna to organize legal aid and defence. The Minister suggested that this should be done under the auspices of the Austrian branch of the League of the Rights of Man. However, the Austrian Chief of Police informed the President of the League that on no account would the setting up of a bureau be permitted. We decided to continue with the arrangements that had already been made to provide legal defence discreetly and quietly.

I spent most of my time in Vienna, but I travelled to the provinces as well, to St Pölten and Graz and other places where there had been resistance and there were prisoners – to interview lawyers there. Sometimes I went with them to the prisons to meet their clients.

Naomi Mitchison came to Leoben with me on one occasion, she to distribute relief, and I to meet some lawyers. While we were there we took spring flowers to the grave of the Socialist leader Koloman Wallisch, who had been hanged after summary trial in a military court soon after the fighting. The authorities had intended it to be an unmarked grave but comrades of Wallisch followed the burial party and marked the place very carefully. It became a place of pilgrimage and when we arrived at the cemetery there were already bunches of fresh gentians on the grave.

My chief ally in the legal defence work was the able and dedicated Jewish lawyer Heinrich Steinitz. He had a delightful family. In his pleasant home in Vienna he had a fine collection of paintings. We became friends. I kept in touch with him and tried to persuade him, the nearer the Nazi seizure of Austria came, to leave the country. He refused. 'This is my home,' he said; 'this is where I am needed.' What I feared happened. Steinitz was arrested by the Nazis and killed in one of their concentration camps.

During the time I worked with him and saw him in Court, Steinitz was a fearless advocate. While several lawyers had their offices searched by the police, on the whole defence lawyers were not interfered with, although occasionally the more outspoken were threatened that they would be sent to the detention camp at Woellersdorf for their actions. This did not deter Steinitz from submitting that the members of the Schutzbund, by their resistance, were protecting the Austrian constitution against a fascist movement which had secured control of the Government, and had repeatedly broken the democratic constitution and was preparing to destroy it.

It is a tribute to the integrity and courage of Austrian lawyers that over 4,850 of those held in prisons or camps since February were legally represented, while only £5,500 was paid out in legal fees for this work. For the most part they agreed to a fee of twenty Austrian schillings a case: then worth about seventeen shillings and sixpence. Many of the lawyers were themselves socialists. The Austrian Bar acted honourably. The judges on the whole maintained the independence of the Judiciary, although there were a few exceptions. In the early days after the fighting, sentences were severe; nine men were sentenced to death and many received long terms of imprisonment. After February, save in some courts such as Leoben, sentences were milder and were normally six to twelve months' hard labour.

I found that the atmosphere in the courts I attended varied with the personality of the judge. Often judges in some of the smaller Viennese courts allowed signals to pass between the accused and their families and friends. Despite their long imprisonment awaiting trial, I could see during my prison visits that the spirits of the accused were unbroken. Friedrich Scheu, the Austrian writer, in his book *Der Weg Ins Ungewisse* wrote: 'Wherever Elwyn Jones went, maltreatment was either stopped or considerably reduced.' I hope this was true.

Our work in Vienna was greatly assisted by the distinguished team of newspaper correspondents who were there. Outstanding was G.E.R. Gedye, the correspondent of *The Times*, who was expelled from Austria as soon as the Nazis took over. His book, *Fallen Bastions*, which he wrote shortly before the outbreak of war in 1939, was a passionate warning to the West of what was to come. John Gunther, author of *Inside Europe*, and Fodor of the *Manchester Guardian* were also helpful to us. Naomi Mitchison worked ceaselessly in relief work and has described her experiences movingly in her book *Vienna Diary*. Hugh Gaitskell incurred great risks, particularly in the early days, in sheltering and smuggling across the border many of those who were in hiding from the Austrian police. Occasionally I acted as courier, taking letters to Viennese Socialists in Brno, in Czechoslovakia, where Albert Mendel had performed his famous genetic experiments in the monastery garden in the 1860s. This, like other quiet centres of European culture, was shortly to be engulfed by Nazi racism. The Czech Ambassador in Vienna gave us a great deal of help, as did Dr Ecer, a Czech lawyer with whom I worked closely. Later he assisted us at Nuremberg and for a time he was a member of the International Court of Justice in The Hague.

As the months went by, the violence of the Nazis increased as they campaigned to disrupt and sabotage the life of the community. I was present in the exquisite Vienna Opera House during a Mozart performance when tear-gas bombs were thrown and the theatre had to be evacuated.

The Dollfuss Government reacted to the Nazi campaign by giving additional powers to the Executive and to the police. In early July it promulgated a decree which undermined the independence of the Judiciary by enabling a judge to be dismissed summarily and with loss of pension if he did an act 'contrary to the political direction of the State' – that is, the will of the Executive. At the same time, the Staatsanwaltschaft (the public prosecutors of Austria) were instructed that sentences had been too mild and that they should be more severe.

Trial by jury for offences punishable by sentences of five years or more was ended and the Schoffengericht, a special court of judges and lay assessors, was created in its place. The police were given the power to rearrest persons acquitted by the courts and to detain them in prisons or detention camps. While most of this arbitrary action was directed against the Austrian Nazis (it was mild compared with what they did to their victims when they seized power in 1938), at the time I left Austria in July 1934 there were still many Social Democrats in prisons or camps without trial or in detention after having been acquitted.

I shall always remember the warm friendships established with the Viennese comrades with whom I worked. Small, civilized Austria had so much to offer: Vienna itself had lovely baroque palaces, a magnificent cathedral, delightful coffee-houses; there were the romantic Vienna woods, the green vineyards of Grinzing and the river Danube. What a relief it was to take a canvas canoe aboard a Danube steamer in Vienna and sleep on deck with my friends. We would arrive upstream in Melk the next morning, have breakfast there and visit its great cathedral. Then we would launch our canoes and drift gently on the fast-flowing Danube back to Vienna, going ashore for a swim or a picnic. There was always someone with an accordion or a guitar and there were Viennese songs to sing.

One curious episode occurred before I left Vienna. Through Hugh Gaitskell I had been in contact with lecturers at Vienna University. Some were Nazis and I had fierce arguments with them. They suggested to me in June that I should visit their leader, Theo Habicht, in Munich. After the dissolution of the Nazi Party by the Austrian Government in June 1933, many of its members fled to Bavaria, where they were organized and trained in camps as an 'Austrian legion'. Habicht himself was German and a member of the Reichstag. I thought it might be useful to learn more about the set-up there and I agreed to go to Munich on 29 June 1934 with a cryptic introduction to Habicht which one of the Vienna lecturers wrote in red crayon in my small 1934 pocket diary. I still have it. It reads: Ti/15 gibt aufschluss' (Ti/15 confirms); 'Ti geht in ordnung' (Ti is O.K.)

I found that Habicht's office in Munich was near the headquarters of the SA – the Nazi storm troopers. When I met Habicht he was obviously under some tension. That fateful Saturday, 30 June, proved to be the day when Hitler and the SS wiped out the SA leadership in spectacular style. The SA leader, Captain Roehm, was caught and murdered just outside Munich, along with six other leaders. Whether Habicht knew when I met him that these events were taking place I cannot tell. We had a brief discussion, during which he asserted that Austrian National Socialism would be more radical than its German counterpart and would begin where German National Socialism left off. I asked him whether there was any indication of a second revolution in Germany, for I had been told in Vienna that this was expected. He replied that it would be untrue to speak of a second revolution because Nazi Germany was in a perpetual state of change, of revolution. He had not been speaking for long when the phone rang. He answered it and told me hurriedly that he would now have to break off the discussion. Before leaving me he handed me a bundle of Nazi publications which I put in my rucksack, including a faked postcard showing Hitler looking down upon and laughing at a diminutive Dollfuss. The card was captioned 'Millimetternich', after the nineteenth-century Austrian statesman.

When I left Habicht's office I noticed there was a manned machine gun on the roof of the Brown House. I met one of the British newspaper correspondents shortly afterwards and he told me that many violent events were taking place and that it was fortunate that I had got away safely from the headquarters of the Austrian Nazis. It was not until the next day, when I was back in the comparative safety of Vienna, that I learned what had been happening. On the way back I was interrogated by the Austrian immigration authorities on the Austrian border as a suspect Nazi courier. I had foolishly put the Nazi publications Habicht had given me in my rucksack and forgotten them. After questioning me they confiscated the Nazi literature and let me go.

How many were murdered on that night and day of the 'Long Knives' has not been ascertained. The largest group of victims were SA men, from the rank of SA Obergruppenfuehrer down. Another group consisted of General von Schleicher and his wife, Gregor Strasser and his two assistants. Erich Klausener, the German leader of Catholic Action, was another victim. These early victims of Nazi violence and of the use of murder as a political weapon were Germans. The pattern was soon to be extended to Austria.

Austrian Nazis (in Section 89 of the SS in Germany) plotted a coup in Vienna to capture Dollfuss and his colleagues at their meeting in the Chancellery on 25 July 1934. One hundred and fifty-four Austrian Nazis who had been dismissed from the army and police marched up in their uniforms. But the Cabinet had been informed. Most of its members escaped. Dollfuss was caught and shot by an ex-policeman called Planetta. He asked in vain for a doctor and a priest. He died about three hours later in the hands of his murderers. As G.E.R.Gedye reported, this was 'less than twenty-four hours after Dollfuss had sent to the gallows the young Socialist Gerl for doing what thousands of Nazis had for months been doing almost with impunity – trying to damage railway property with explosives'.

On 30 July Kurt von Schuschnigg, a Tyrolese former clerical lawyer, was appointed to succeed Dollfuss as Chancellor.

I did not go back to Austria again until December 1935, when D.R. Grenfell, a leading Welsh Labour MP, asked me to accompany him on a mission to Vienna to urge Chancellor von Schuschnigg to grant an amnesty to the Socialists who had been imprisoned since 1934. I had become friendly with the much respected Dai Grenfell. He had worked in the South Wales coal mines for many years and his face and hands were scarred blue with coal dust impregnated in his skin. He later became a Minister in the Mines Department in Winston Churchill's wartime government. The other member of the mission, which had the backing of the National Council of Labour, was John Parker MP, who was the General Secretary of the New Fabian Research Bureau. We had a meeting with a sympathetic Anthony Eden in London before we left and another with Léon Blum in Paris.

When we arrived in Vienna our Ambassador, Sir Walford Selby, was not encouraging. However, Chancellor von Schuschnigg received us the next morning. At the massively guarded Chancellery in the Balhausplatz, over which Metternich had ruled, we were led through files of soldiers and detectives to the room where Dollfuss had bled to death. The Chancellor had a death mask of Dollfuss on his desk.

Von Schuschnigg received us courteously. We expressed the hope that the Austrian Government would grant an amnesty to the Socialists still in custody. I asked for permission for us to visit the Rossauerlander Prison, the Landesgericht Prison and the detention camp at Messendorf, about which we had received complaints, and also to interview Herr Winterstein, the Minister of Justice, in order to discuss with him complaints regarding the alleged police tyranny in Austria.

The Chancellor told us in confidence that his government did intend to introduce a wide amnesty at Christmas. This would close the February 1934 chapter, except for those persons who, he said, had been found guilty of 'individual murders', which he said meant those who had arms in their hands when arrested during the fighting. Almost all those arrested in February would be released. He said that we could visit any prison we chose and that they had nothing to hide. He kept his word. Of the 171 men from the February days, 154 were amnestied at Christmas. The Schutzbund leaders were released and the trials of Social Democrat leaders still outstanding were abandoned. It was a tragedy that the flexibility and willingness to conciliate that von Schuschnigg displayed then was not shown in the critical eighteen months after Dollfuss was murdered, so that Austrian resistance against the Nazis could have been sustained with the full commitment of the Austrian workers. Von Schuschnigg himself however, like Dollfuss, was a man of dauntless personal courage.

As the Chancellor promised, we were allowed to visit firstly the modern Rossauerlander Prison, where the conditions were good, and Landesgericht I Prison, old, musty and ill-equipped, and finally Messendorf concentration camp: Nazi propaganda had spread reports of brutality and ill treatment of the Nazi detainees there. There were 114 prisoners at Messendorf, of whom about 100 were Nazis, the rest Socialists and Communists. We were allowed to speak freely to the prisoners. There were eighteen to twenty of them in rooms fitted for thirty people. The complaints were that smoking and chess were prohibited and that visits from relatives were only allowed once a month. We talked to one of the prisoners, a trade union leader named Ditto Poeltzl from the Wagner Biro factory, who was charged with Communist activities. He said that conditions inside the camp were better than they were outside it: the food was better and greater freedom of political discussion was allowed. We saw no evidence of the brutality and ill-treatment which various reports had alleged were taking place there. The contrast with what was already known to be happening to anti-Nazis in the murderous concentration camps of the Third Reich was stark.

This was my last visit to Austria before the war broke out. The Nazi Army marched into the country in March 1938 and completed the destruction of Austrian democracy begun so tragically by the native Fascists in February 1934. Anti-Nazis were caught and shot or sent to Dachau concentration camp. A *Times* correspondent reported in the spring of 1938:

> In Vienna and Austria no vestige of decency or humanity has checked the will to destroy and there has been an unbroken orgy of Jew-baiting such as Europe has not known since the darkest days of the Middle Ages. ... There can be no Jewish family in the country which has not one or more of its members under arrest ... not a day still passes without its toll of arrests.

Throughout this period the governments of France and Great Britain stood idly by and did nothing to relieve the beleaguered Austrians. It needed the defeat of the Third Reich in a world war to bring democracy back to Austria.

One small personal memory remains from my visit. The American journalist Louis Fisher visited Vienna on his way to Moscow at this time. I gave him a small red silk handkerchief to take to my future wife, Polly, who was there. A few weeks later I got a letter from her saying, 'I will wear the hankie on special occasions, as when you are elected to parliament for the first time.' But that is another story.

5

Prelude to War

I was called to the Bar at Gray's Inn in January 1935. I had become friendly with D.N. Pritt QC, known to his friends everywhere as Johnny. He was a leading Silk and always helpful to young members of the Bar. Rosy, bald, bespectacled, he looked like Mr Pickwick. He and his wife Molly kept open house in their flat in Pump Court in the Temple and in their beautiful country home in Berkshire. Through Johnny Pritt's introduction I became a pupil of St John Field, one of the busiest libel juniors in the Temple, in his chambers in the Cloisters, alas later destroyed in the blitz.

St John Field had appeared with Sir Patrick Hastings for Princess Youssoupoff in the famous libel action which she brought against Metro-Goldwyn-Mayer. In their film *Rasputin and the Empress*, which was renamed for British showing *Rasputin, The Mad Monk*, 'Princess Natasha' was portrayed as having been ravished by Rasputin. The jury found that there were features in the film which identified 'Princess Natasha' as Princess Youssoupoff. They awarded her record damages of £25,000 : equivalent to about £260,000 today.

St John Field's chambers were run by his clerk, Mr Adam, as we pupils knew him. He wore a top hat every day. We were only allowed to see our pupil master by appointment with Adam. We three pupils, in those days each paying a pupillage fee of 100 guineas for the privilege, were not permitted to attend St John Field's conferences with his clients nor did we get the chance to discuss with him the papers and pleadings which we were allowed to study and work on. Nowadays pupils no longer pay pupillage fees and they work closely with their pupil master. St John Field took Silk half way through my pupillage and thereafter could no longer take pupils. I then became a pupil of Freddie Wallace in an immensely busy set of chambers in Crown Office Row, 'place of my gentle engendure' as Charles

Lamb described it. Glyn Jones and Stanley Rees, who both became High Court judges, were in practice there. George Baker, another member of the chambers, became President of the Family Division. I enjoyed accompanying them around the courts and it was a valuable apprenticeship.

When my pupillage was over I joined the chambers of Norman Parkes in Dr Johnson's Buildings. He was an astute and impressive advocate who would have gone to the High Court had he not died comparatively young. Ronnie Dow and Conolly Gage were also members of chambers. Both became judges, Conolly after many years in the House of Commons. He was a Unionist MP, cheerful and undogmatic, quite untypical of the other Ulster Members. I stayed in those chambers until the outbreak of war.

I earned £150 in my first year at the Bar and £230 in my second, which was quite good going in those days. To pay my way, I did a lot of writing, lecturing and tutoring. I also became a part-time law lecturer at King's College, London. Professor Potter was then Head of the Law Faculty. He gave me good advice: 'To first-year students pretend you know everything. To second-year students admit that there are some-things you don't know. To third-year students pretend that you know nothing.'

I shared the evening lectures at King's with Richard Latham, a friend who had won brilliant Firsts at Melbourne and Oxford. He had a Jewish business friend, Wilfrid Israel, who owned a department store in Berlin. Just before the war, when the persecution of the Jews became increasingly violent, Mr Israel tried to get as many Jewish children as he could out of Berlin to England. Richard organized the English end. Polly and I, – we were married by this time – chose Margit from a sheet of photographs. She was only fifteen. We agreed to be her guardians and learned her story later. Her father was a graphic designer, a Christian who refused to divorce his Jewish wife and renounce his children in compliance with Nazi decrees. When in 1939 his studio in Cologne was looted and burned and he was beaten up by the Nazis, he decided to take his wife, son and daughter to Berlin in the hope of being able to establish a new home there.

In 1938 all Jewish children were forbidden to attend German schools. Margit's parents found a place for her in a Jewish art college in Berlin where she studied design and textiles. Part of the course involved visits to Israel's store to study materials. On 10 November 1938 came the terrible 'kristal nacht' (crystal night). The Nazis looted and burned all Jewish business premises. Margit was in the Israel store at the time. I have asked her what she remembers of those events. She told me that she had tried in vain to obliterate them from her memory. She wrote: 'I escaped down a rear staircase during the fire. I ran home and looked for the "all clear" signal from my mother. A prearranged handkerchief "code" on the balcony was put up by my mother if the Nazis were in the flats. When the handkerchiefs were out we just kept on walking.' By such devices Margit survived. She wrote:

> In May 1939 I left for England. A letter came from Polly and Elwyn in April to welcome me. It was my passport to life. [Margit still has the letter.] I left on what was to be the last Jewish children's 'transport' out of Berlin and Le Havre. I remember my parents were not allowed to come to the station to see me leave and that I was permitted to take very little with me. Little else remains in my mind of the sad and miserable journey. I was met by Polly at Waterloo Station in London. Later I discovered that shortly after my departure my parents and my brother were arrested by the Nazis and disappeared into concentration camps. Afterwards I learned that my brother had been gassed in Theresienstadt Camp.

Polly remembers vividly going to meet Margit and bring her home. The arrival platform was crowded with German Jewish children. Some were extremely young, some were clutching shabby toys. All were pale, thin and exhausted. Each child bore a placard bearing identification details in large letters and the name of the sponsor. Polly spotted Margit. She bore the description 'Margit "Sara" Reiter'. The Nazis added the name 'Sara' to every Jewish girl's name, while 'Israel' was added to boys' names. They were compelled to wear a yellow star. None of the children spoke English. Margit, when she arrived at Harwich, was asked where she was born. She replied 'Köln'. The immigration officer said: 'No, not Köln, child, Cologne.' She burst into tears. Beautiful, steady and intelligent, Margit became one of our family and helped to bring up our first two children, Josephine and Dan.

She married Brian, a Catholic whom she met in the Lake District, where Polly had been sent in October 1940 to have our second baby. Brian was in the Navy during the war and served in the north and south Atlantic. In due course he became headmaster of a notable English school. Margit's father and mother survived the war although her mother had been subjected to inhuman medical experiments in a concentration camp. Margit's marriage has been a happy one. She and her husband respect each other's religion as Margit's parents did. They are now grandparents, and Margit named her first child Josephine, after our eldest.

I have related Margit's story in some detail because it tells much of Nazi Germany. Richard Latham, who rescued her, joined the RAF in 1941. In 1942 he was posted 'officially presumed to have lost his life on active service' when his plane did not return from a raid over Germany. Wilfrid

Israel, Margit's other rescuer, was in the unarmed KLM aircraft with actor Leslie Howard when it was shot down over the Bay of Biscay by a Nazi plane in August 1943.

Building up a practice at the Bar during the depressed 1930s was a slow business. Though Poor Prisoners' Defence Regulations allowed payment of a nominal fee in serious criminal cases, in those days there was no legal aid for civil cases. Many deserving cases simply went by default. I was one of several young lawyers who conducted unpaid cases for the 'Bentham Committee for Poor Litigants' in the county courts, resisting claims from some of the less reputable hire purchase and finance companies, which were based on the small print at the back of hire purchase agreements. Some judges could be persuaded to award so small a sum by way of instalment payments as to make them not worth collecting.

I fought several cases in London for the National Council for Civil Liberties. Most arose out of disturbances resulting from fascist marches and street corner meetings in the East End of London. In those days fascist provocation was directed against Jews in the Whitechapel and Stepney areas, where Jewish refugees fleeing from Polish, Russian and German anti-semitic persecution had traditionally settled.

I made my first appearance in the High Court in a divorce case. My client was the petitioner, a middle-aged man. When my clerk brought him into my room in Chambers, he looked around impatiently: 'When do I meet my counsel, Mr Elwyn Jones?' 'I am your counsel,' I said timidly. Whether my comparative youth put him off I know not. He might have been even more concerned if he had known that it was my first ever case in the High Court. Fortunately we won: his case was undefended.

In 1936 I joined the Welsh Circuit and spent many busy and and happy years in practice at the Bar alternating between work on Assizes and in the High Court in London. The fact that I was Welsh-speaking helped a good deal in many of my cases, especially at the Assizes in Carmarthen, Mid-Wales and Caernarvon.

My first important case was the mass trial at Glamorgan Assizes in Swansea in December 1936 of thirty-one men and five women from Tonypandy on charges of riot and unlawful assembly and related criminal charges. The trial arose out of demonstrations by about 1,500 Rhondda men and women who met at the De Winton Field, Tonypandy on 11 June 1936 to protest against the arrival in the town of a contingent from the British Union of Fascists led by Thomas Patrick Moran, a pugilist. He and some of his fascist supporters were wearing black-shirt uniforms. It was when the loudspeaker van carrying the Fascists arrived that the violence and disorder complained of arose.

The dock was filled with as many of the accused as it would hold. The remainder overflowed on to the press bench and the benches below the dock. Most of the accused were unemployed coal-miners. One was a postman. Another had been a special constable. One of the women was a twenty-two-year-old secretary, the others were all mothers of families.

The trial got off to a bad start when, on the first day, the judge, Mr Justice Lewis, refused bail to all the defendants. The Executive Council of the South Wales Miners' Federation, without my knowledge, sent a resolution of protest to the Attorney General urging that the decision should be reversed and that the refusal was 'without precedent in recent history in cases of this kind' and imposed 'difficulties and hardships upon the defendants and their counsel'. At the end of the day I again applied for bail and was able to say that some of the most respectable organizations in South Wales had prepared food and accommodation for the accused. This time bail was granted.

Trouble on the De Winton Field had been inevitable when the black-shirts appeared. Indeed the case for the defence was that the black-shirts deliberately provoked it. Conditions at that period in Tonypandy and the Rhondda Valley were appalling. There was massive unemployment. Most of the accused had been out of work for many years, barely surviving on a pittance of dole. Several of the older men in the dock suffered from pneumoconiosis, or 'black lung', caused by the accumulation of coal dust in the lungs. Because of the circumstances in which they lived, the first loyalty of the South Wales miners was to the organization which did most for them – the South Wales Miners' Federation. The anti-trade unionism of the Fascists was anathema to them.

As soon as the fascist van appeared on the field a serious disturbance broke out; conflict arose not only between the miners and the Fascists but between the crowd and the Glamorgan police, who (as today with the National Front demonstrations) had been sent in strength to enable the Fascists to hold their meeting. The main issue at the trial was who were the real instigators of the violence which ensued: the miners or the Fascists.

After a week's trial three of the defendants were acquitted, the remainder convicted. I had a brush with the judge when he showed impatience with the medical evidence I called on behalf of some of the defendants and with evidence about their social conditions. He sentenced seven of the defendants, one a woman, to terms of imprisonment ranging from two to twelve months. Nine more were sentenced to twenty days' hard labour, which for technical reasons they did not have to serve. Sixteen of the defendants were bound over to keep the peace. It was the first of many cases in which I represented the Welsh miners and learned their qualities of steadfastness and loyalty.

The year I started at the Bar was also the year when Polly (Pearl Binder) came into my life. We married two years later in the Registry Office in the Guildhall in the City of London with my brother Idris and an ancient mariner friend of Polly's from the the East End as our witnesses. Except for the times when our work commitments in different countries separated us (sometimes for up to six months and even longer during the war) we have been together ever since. When we were separated, we wrote to each other frequently. Going through my papers now I find that much of our correspondence has survived, more by accident than design.

We first met at a party given by Powys Mathers – famous as a translator of the *Arabian Nights* and as 'Torquemada' of the *Observer* crossword puzzles – to celebrate the success of Polly's book *Odd Jobs*. At the time Polly was living and working in a room in the Ostler's Cottage in Spreadeagle Straw Yard, Whitechapel. That summer of 1935 Johnny Pritt, whom I had helped as political secretary in his successful election campaign earlier that year in North Hammersmith, invited me to join him and his wife Molly in a villa they had rented in Vence in the Alpes Maritimes. I had been under the weather and they thought a holiday there would do me good, as indeed it did. The Pritts also felt a stay in the Midi would build Polly up – she had had tuberculosis in her younger days – before a winter in Russia: she was about to go there to gather material for a book about ordinary Russian people which publisher Victor Gollancz had commissioned. I am sure matchmaking was not in the Pritts' minds: indeed it seemed a highly unlikely match. While we were both politically minded, I was a lawyer and she an artist and writer. I like company; she was a loner and was happiest travelling on her own in cargo boats or long-distance trains.

In the winter of that year I waved Polly farewell from Hay's Wharf on her voyage in a Russian ship bound for Leningrad. We did not like being separated at a time of growing world tension. Mussolini marched into Abyssinia (Ethiopia) in September 1935. In the Far East, Japan, having already invaded Southern Manchuria, made further demands on China. Polly's letters from Moscow that winter told of the mounting anxiety there about the threat of war. After the German troops marched into the Rhineland on 7 March in flagrant violation of the Versailles and Locarno treaties she wrote: 'The League of Nations meets today. They'll sit and talk, round and round, and nothing will be done until Germany makes another spring and violates more territory so war will creep on us.'

I flew to Russia in April 1936 to meet Polly. We spent a fortnight together in Moscow. I enjoyed *Lohengrin* in the Bolshoi Theatre, visited the Kremlin Museum, and descended into the showpiece mausoleum in red granite in Red Square to see the embalmed Lenin in a glass case. Also I was invited to Bolshevo, where interesting experiments were being made in rehabilitating young delinquents.

We returned to England via Leningrad, Peter the Great's magnificent 'window on the West', where we spent a memorable May Day. The ice on the river Neva was breaking with loud crashings. In front of the Hermitage Palace huge massed choirs sang the 'Internationale' at the proper brisk tempo, guns from destroyers on the Neva thundering through the music.

The Spanish Civil War started in 1936. In November of that year there was a meeting in Cambridge to launch a 'People's Front for Britain'. Harold Macmillan and G.D.H.Cole shared a platform. Macmillan welcomed the idea as being 'the genesis of a national government of the centre and left'. It was a time of searching for a way forward. Some of my generation and friends such as Ralph Fox, with whom Polly was planning a book called 'Work', courageously made their way to Spain to join the International Brigade to defend the democratically elected Spanish Government. Ralph was killed there.

I had become increasingly involved in the activities of the Labour Party, particularly during the 1935 General Election campaign. I addressed large meetings in different parts of the country and I spoke twice for Jim Griffiths in Llanelli. The town's Market Hall was packed on each occasion: these were the days before television, when election meetings were crowded. At the eve of the poll meeting, which was attended by almost 4,000 people, the kindly, patriarchal George Lansbury preached the pacifist message. Nye Bevan's caustic wit and fiery commitment were more in accord with my views. By then I had concluded that it was crucial for Britain to build up and organize armed resistance against Nazi aggression. Pacifism was not enough; it was too late.

During 1936 I accepted invitations from the International Association of Democratic Lawyers to go as an observer to a number of political trials in Germany, Greece, Hungary and Romania and countries where dictatorial rule of different degrees of oppression prevailed. One of the purposes of these visits was to try to give encouragement to the prisoners and their defenders. The judges tended to behave a little better towards the accused when a foreign lawyer was known to be present as an observer. But the trials were a travesty of justice and the accused were never given a chance. Sentences were fierce. I remember the grimness of a trial of an anti-Nazi in a so-called 'people's court' in Leipzig: everyone entering the court gave a Hitler salute.

I went to Athens in the autumn of 1936, when General Metaxas was in power, to try to help Professor Svolos, Professor of Constitutional Law at the University in Athens and President of the Greek League for the Rights of Man, who had been handcuffed and deported to the island of Milos. His assistant, Professor Agrijay, suffered a similar fate, as did a number of Liberal, Agrarian and Social Democrat deputies. The power to send these men into exile had been given to a committee of security consisting of a prefect, the Chief of Police and the Public Prosecutor. Until 19 September 1936 there was a right of appeal to the judges of the High Court against the committee's sentences. Thereafter it was permissible to appeal only to the committee itself, on the ground that the judges were 'personalities moved by humanitarian motives, having no contact with reality nor understanding the safety of the State'. It was one of many illustrations in my experience, of the fact that the independence of the Judiciary is an early casualty of totalitarian regimes. I heard many accounts of violence and ill-treatment to prisoners.

From Athens I went to Romania, where, at the time, there were hundreds of political prisoners. The lawyers I met told me they could do little to help them . They were tried by military tribunals. Counsel who defended opponents of the Government – all dubbed Communists no matter what their political colour was – were told they would be disbarred. Here again an independent Judiciary and Bar became targets of an oppressive regime. One of the Romanian lawyers who assisted me during my investigations in Bucharest was Patrascanu, a courageous young man who risked his own liberty to save that of others. He survived the war but I was appalled to discover that he had been sentenced to death during one of the Stalinist upheavals in post-war Romania. I learned later that he had received a posthumous rehabilitation.

I went on other missions to Europe right up to 1938. That year I visited Budapest to enquire into the possibilities of setting up a legal organization in Hungary for the defence and protection of the hundreds of political prisoners there, some of whom had been tortured. But the lawyers I met believed that an organization such as I proposed was impossible. Most of them thought that to set it up would be dangerous to moderate radical movements struggling to recruit members who might like to join it: young Catholics, young peasant groups and others. One of the lawyers I met told me that the external tie-up with Rome and Berlin had made things far worse in Hungary.

Besides attending trials of political prisoners and arranging help for them in different countries, my main political activity in the immediate pre-war years was writing. I contributed political articles to various English and American newspapers and magazines including the *Manchester Guardian*, the *New Statesman* (then edited by Kingsley Martin), *Reynolds News*, the *Fortnightly Review*, the *Economist*, *Picture Post* and *Lilliput*. I also wrote three books on the fascist threat.

At the time I was acquainted with Sir Walter Layton, the chairman of the *News Chronicle*, for which I had also written some articles. His daughter Margaret and I had been friends at Cambridge. In 1938 Sir Walter asked me if I would like to be *News Chronicle* correspondent in Vienna. To be a British foreign correspondent was a tempting assignment in those days. Before I turned it down I discussed it long and hard with Polly, to whom the prospect seemed attractive. It was not an easy decision as I was only just beginning to make a living at the Bar. Although I had made good progress in writing and enjoyed the friendship of journalists such as Eric Gedye, Tom Hopkinson, James Cameron and Sidney Jacobson, I felt that journalism was not my true vocation.

In 1937 Victor Gollancz, who had heard of my legal and political experiences on the Continent, asked me to write a book about them. The outcome was *Hitler's Drive to the East*, published in 1937. I wrote:

> From Berlin the Nazis are now organising direct intervention in the internal affairs of other countries. Newspapers are being bought and propaganda freely distributed. Corrupt politicians are being subsidised. Murders and kidnappings plotted. Terrorists and reactionary groups are being trained, financed and armed.

I described conditions inside Germany:

> Anti-Fascist work inside Germany today demands little short of heroism, for the Gestapo is at once the most efficient and the most brutal secret police in the world. Suspected men and women are arrested, taken to the police station and frequently never heard of again. They are either murdered in prison or commit suicide lest under torture they betray other anti-Fascists. By October 1936 there were sixty concentration camps in Germany, in which 25,000 prisoners were being indefinitely detained.

German people themselves were the first victims of Nazi terror. In my book I quoted Winston Churchill's speech in the House of Commons on 13 November 1936: 'the testing time will come', he had said, 'when Germany reaches the culminating point of her gigantic military preparations and will be forced by financial and economic stringency to contemplate a sharp decline or another exit from her difficulties.' I added the comment: 'The Fascist way out is war.' The book concluded with an urgent call for collective action by people of all creeds and classes, all of whom were equally menaced by the threat of war.

The American edition of *Hitler's Drive to the East* was published by Dutton, as was my second book *The Battle for Peace*, which appeared in America under the title *The Defence of Democracy*. Both were more favourably reviewed by the *New York Times* and the *Herald Tribune* than they were by the London *Times*.

The Battle for Peace, which was published in 1938, gave a fuller account of the mounting crisis than the earlier book. In Chapter I I wrote:

> Since 1933 a new political dynamic has made its appearance in Europe – that is Fascism on the offensive. The Fascist attack on the key positions of European Democracy has dominated the political scene. An alliance of world-wide dimensions has come into being and has been formally embodied in the German-Japanese Pact, to which Italy subsequently adhered.
>
> This new dynamic has brought with it its own peculiar technique. Since its big offensive began in 1933 with Hitler's access to power, a King and a Chancellor, a Prime Minister and a Foreign Secretary, several Ambassadors, Generals, Members of Parliament and political leaders have fallen victim to Fascist assassination. And since July 1936 three countries, Abyssinia, Spain and China, have been subjected to this new technique of terrorism, while another, Austria, has succumbed to the threat of its application.
>
> The leaders of the 'Fascist International' (as the Berlin-Rome-Tokyo Alliance may conveniently be called) have invented a new technique of aggression: that of stirring up rebellion by a national or social minority within the territory of the proposed victim and supplying the rebellion with arms, men and money.
>
> This new technique of war is being applied to every country in the world which the Fascist powers wish to weaken or terrorise into submission. The aggressors have perfected a technique of waging war without formal declaration of war, or waging war in fact in the teeth of their own protestations of peace....
>
> The new technique of aggression does not depend on military invasion as its sole weapon. Military invasion can be dangerous in Europe, where most states are linked up in defensive alliances and where direct attack on one of them might involve the aggressor in war against overwhelming forces.

The book gave detailed evidence of these developments. In Chapter III I examined Nazi imperialism:

> Hitler's avowed intentions are, of course, pacific.... He regards his conquest of Austria as 'peaceful', although it was achieved by a military invasion, has established another reign of terror, and is accompanied by an epidemic of

> suicides. It is clear that when overwhelming force is turned against a powerless opponent resistance is hopeless. The result is victory without actual war – as in Austria. In other words it is a 'peaceful victory'. What then does Hitler mean by peace? The answer is given in Hitler's own words in *Mein Kampf*, the Nazi Bible:
>
> 'Whoever really desires the victory of pacifist thought must give his whole-hearted support to the German conquest of the world.'

(Later, at Nuremberg, I addressed the tribunal on the value of *Mein Kampf* as evidence of Hitler's intention to wage aggressive wars if he could not achieve 'peaceful' conquest.)

My book warned against appeasing Hitler and concluded by urging that: 'There is enough democratic power in Europe to change the face of Europe overnight. Democratic forces throughout the world must redouble their energies.'

That optimistic note was struck before Czechoslovakia was sacrificed at Munich and before the surrender to Hitler which took place there was acclaimed by Neville Chamberlain from a window at No 10 Downing Street with the words: 'This is the second time in our history when there has come back from Germany peace with honour. I believe it is peace for our time.'

The following year Allen Lane asked me to bring what I had written up to date in one of his 'Penguin Special' series. This was published in June 1939 under the title *The Attack from Within*. By then Hitler had overrun Czechoslovakia and Nazi troops had goose-stepped across the beautiful Charles Bridge in Prague. The book ended with the words: 'Europe has been steadily drifting towards chaos during the last seven years not because the forces of peace lacked power but because their representatives lacked the will to resist aggression. If they are found wanting now, they will not have a second chance.'

A reprint of *The Attack from Within* came out in July 1939 and a third was due to appear when Nazi Germany invaded Poland in September. The attack from without and the Second World War had begun. What I had foreseen and foretold since 1934 was now upon us.

6

To Meet My Son

The first home Polly and I had was in Goldsmith's Building in the Temple, which we moved to in 1937. Josephine, our first child, was born in the City of London Maternity Hospital in January 1938. I well remember the excitement and the joy of bringing her and her mother home to the Temple. We had a third floor three-roomed flat plus kitchen and bathroom, level with the top branches of the great plane tree alongside the round church of the Knights Templars. We could see the pigeons in their nests on the high branches. Oliver Goldsmith's plain gravestone bearing only his name and age lay below our flat in what was once the Temple churchyard, near a portentous tomb of a forgotten judge of long ago.

The rent and rates were £150 a year. I was beginning to earn more in writing and lecturing, and briefs were coming in. As much out of curiosity as to help out, Polly took a job in advertising until the advent of television with its exciting visual possibilities, lured her to Alexandra Palace, the home of BBC Television.

Our household soon grew to include a resident housekeeper and a nurse who were both paid the current rate of £1 a week. The housekeeper slept on a divan in the dining room and the nurse on another divan in the small room, which had become the nursery. Polly and I slept on a bigger divan in the living room. Overcrowded as we were, we loved the place and did not want to move. As I was working all hours, the Temple surveyor came up with the ingenious idea of partitioning a corner of our sitting room into a study where I could work in privacy. I did work there, but never in privacy.

Some of the pleasanter events in my life have been the result of accident rather than design. One January day in 1939, when Josephine was a year old, a Chinese friend dropped in on us and pointed out an advertisement in *The Times* placed by Hounslow Borough Council offering 'a large old-fashioned residence in some disrepair in Cranford, Middlesex'. Somewhat reluctantly we arranged to inspect it. Stansfield House, as it was called, turned out to be an unspoiled red brick Queen Anne house set in large, neglected grounds. It was a bitterly cold day and flakes of snow were beginning to fall. We pushed open a handsome but creaking wrought-iron gate and walked towards the front door of the house. The tangled lawn was matted with dead leaves and covered with white frost. I dug in my walking stick and lifted the frozen crust. Underneath were clusters of snowdrops in bloom. That decided us. We took the house. Hounslow Council proved admirable landlords and redecorated the house and put it in good repair for us at a rent of £150 a year including rates. We had an acre of garden and orchard with neglected but recoverable mulberry, quince, fig, plum and Cox's orange-pippin trees, and a curious greenhouse facing north. There was also a coach house and harness room. We moved in with our handful of furniture during the spring.

I had decided in the previous summer, since war seemed to me to be inevitable, to join the Territorial Army. One morning my friend Jim Rose, his brother Tom and I queued up with many other volunteers to join the HAC (the Honourable Artillery Company) at Armoury House in the City. When my place in the long queue brought me to the recruiting officer's table he declared: 'You can only join now if you are ready to go to camp tonight.' There was an air of crisis about London at the time. I explained that this would be impossible as I had a defence brief in a serious criminal case next morning and I had to be in Court. The recruiting officer said: 'Very well, fall out.' A similar experience befell Jim and Tom Rose. Each of them, too, had inescapable commitments the next day. Both joined the RAF later and served with distinction.

A few days after I had been frustrated at Armoury House, Neville Chamberlain signed the Munich agreement with Hitler. It did not bring 'peace with honour'. On 15 March 1939, the German armies occupied Prague and Hitler took up residence in Hradschin Castle. On 7 April Italy invaded Albania. The Rome–Berlin Axis was triumphant.

It was a time of despair. I remember calling on Jan Masaryk, the Czech Ambassador, at his embassy in Grosvenor Place a few days before Munich. He was grave. He already had grim forebodings of what was afoot. After seeing him I went straight across to the House of Commons and managed to get to Clem Attlee's room. I told him of my conversation with Mazaryk and of his fear of a sellout. He listened, I thought, somewhat impatiently to what I said. Later I was to have further experience of Attlee's terseness.

In the spring of 1939 I joined the Middlesex Regiment, the nearest Territorial unit to Cranford, with its drill hall in Hounslow. It had recently been converted into a Searchlight unit, anti-aircraft protection by then receiving first priority. Its young members were a cross-section of the people of Hounslow: clerks, bus drivers, factory workers. As the months went on I attended drills in Hounslow Drill Hall and a week-end camp in tents in Windsor Great Park. We also had a week-end searchlight practice in Purley. It was a theatrical experience to point the great torch into the night sky and to catch and hold a practice plane in its beam – when we finally succeeded in finding it.

Our summer camp was fixed for the latter part of August 1939. Before then Polly, Josephine and Margit and I went for a delightful, but all too short, holiday in Veules-les-Roses on the Normandy coast. It was the last holiday we were to have together for many years. On the cross-Channel steamer on the way back there was anxious talk among the passengers about the mounting tension and the threat of war. Within a year Veules-les-Roses was overrun by the Nazi Panzer divisions.

We had only been back home in Cranford a few days when I had to report to the drill hall to go to camp. I had by then been made a bombardier and was proud of my two stripes. My mother and Polly sewed them on to my uniform upside-down, but I spotted the error just in time.

The battery never went to training camp. Within a day or two we received marching orders to move to our war station in Devonport. By then the unit had changed from a searchlight battery to the 465 Light Anti-Aircraft Battery, providing protection to the dockyard, Saltash Bridge and other potential enemy targets in Devon. We drove to the south-west through the night at high speed in London buses, the top of our bus crashing through the overhanging branches on the country roads. We reached Bull Point Barracks, which was to be our base, in the small hours of the morning. The empty barrack rooms were covered with the accumulated dust of decades. We saw no newspapers. I missed the news of the Soviet-German Pact, which was signed on 23 August at about the time our buses were taking us at full speed to Devonport.

In the meantime, on 24 August, Parliament had passed the Emergency Powers Act. On 1 September Germany invaded Poland. There were forty-eight hours of agonizing confusion and delay. Finally the fateful decision to fight was taken and the British ultimatum to Germany was delivered at 9 am on 3 September. It expired unheeded two hours later. Then France declared war on Germany from five o'clock that afternoon. The Second World War had begun. I myself saw no alternative course to that which was taken by the British Government either then or in 1940, when we stood alone. Had we not resisted, England would have fallen under Nazi domination. The Gestapo and the death camps would have come to England.

At Devonport, as Bombardier, I was put in charge of a small section that was detailed to man a Lewis machine-gun on the roof of Aggie Western's, the 'sailor's rest', at the entrance to the Devonport Dockyard. On the brilliantly sunny morning when we heard the news that Germany had invaded Poland we were stationed on the roof. Our Lewis gun was supported precariously on a wooden mounting attached to a shaky post. Happily we never had occasion to fire it while I was there.

A grim reminder that we were at war happened immediately: that was the torpedoing on 3 September of the British passenger liner S.S. *Athenia* while outward bound to America. Six years later, when it fell to me to present the prosecution case against Admiral Raeder at Nuremberg, I saw a copy of the *Voelkischer Beobachter* published after the sinking, in which Goebbels proclaimed that Churchill had deliberately sunk the *Athenia* to encourage American hostility to Germany. In fact the liner was sunk by German U-boat 30 under the command of Lieutenant Lemp. After the war Admiralty intelligence experts examined its captured log book, which showed that original entries had been altered in a clumsy attempt to prove that the U-boat had not been responsible and was hundreds of miles away from the *Athenia* when it was torpedoed.

During the first few nights of our stay at Aggie Western's we slept on its top floor, just below the roof. Each of us had a small separate cubicle with wire netting over the top and each night we stayed there one or two of the sailors tried to force their way in. I complained to our Commanding Officer, who arranged for us to be moved to a nearby house. This, too, was not without an element of risk. The woman who owned it kept a pet chimpanzee in a cage on the top floor.

We never discussed politics in the unit, nor did we concern ourselves with matters outside our daily routine and our families. My promotion to Sergeant did not change this pattern: I cannot recollect any discussions in the Sergeants' Mess about what was happening in the world outside.

Polly and I had long been friends of Mary and Vyvyan Adams. Mary was a BBC Television talks executive at Alexandra Palace and Polly had been preparing some programmes for her there. Vyvyan was a member of the Bar and a Tory MP. He was also a 'premature anti-Nazi', as those of us who denounced Hitler were called before being anti-Nazi became patriotic. Vyvyan introduced me to his friend Victor Cazalet, the Tory MP for Chippenham, another prominent 'premature anti-Nazi', who had read my books.

At the beginning of August 1939, Victor, who had won a Military Cross during the First World War, was asked to form the 83rd LAA Battery of the 16th LAA Regiment in Kent. He invited me to join his battery. Until the end of December 1939 there were direct promotions from the ranks of the Territorial Army to commissioned rank. Victor applied to the War Office for me to be posted to the 83rd as a Second Lieutenant. It was not until Christmas time that my commission came through and I reported to the headquarters of the Battery in a large requisitioned mansion in spacious grounds in Sevenoaks, Kent.

The personnel of 83rd LAA Battery was a mirror of Sevenoaks, just as the 465 reflected the Hounslow community: it included young publishers, lawyers, actors, stockbrokers, architects, grooms, farm workers, gamekeepers, clerks, lorry drivers. Peter Cazalet, Victor's brother, and jockey Anthony Mildmay (who was famous for an incident in the Grand National: the horse he was riding, Davey Jones, was leading when the bridle broke at the last fence) were two of the battery captains.

When I became Troop Commander, I made regular visits to the gun sites. The character of the battery was reflected in an early visit I made when we were stationed in Chatham. I asked the NCO how his detachment were. 'Healthy but unhappy, Sir.' He complained that they didn't have enough to do, although they did not lack initiative. One night they asked me to share their dinner of roast pheasants. I learned later that the pheasants had been cleverly trapped by a gamekeeper-turned-poacher in the Admiral's grounds inside the dockyard perimeter.

The battery soon was scattered to different key positions in the south-east of England. My troop gave protection to the radar station on a high hill in wooded Dunkirk in Kent. We then moved to the Battle of Britain aerodromes, Kenley and Tangmere. For a time our guns were on the foreshore of Littlehampton awaiting the invasion.

Whenever we were separated Polly and I wrote to one another regularly. During the spring of 1940 some RAF pilots and later American pilots stationed at nearby Heston Aerodrome were billetted in Stansfield House. While I was in Littlehampton, Polly wrote to me from Stansfield:

> The war news is disquieting, isn't it, but our Air Force is so superb and the general morale seems very fine, judging by your letters and my RAF men here. They are so nice and gentle and courteous, more than ever lately. One nice Canadian hasn't returned after a raid. I pray he's a prisoner of war and no worse. A fellow officer came today to inventory his belongings ... nearly broke my heart.

In May 1940 I was sent as an instructor on predictors (a new device which enabled the anti-aircraft guns to get on target) to the Fleet Air Arm Station in Ford, Sussex. Just before our troops were rescued from the beaches of Dunkirk, an RAF Spitfire pilot made a forced landing in Ford after an air battle over Normandy. He told us about the total collapse of the British and French armies and of the massive retreat to the coast. No one would believe him. There were angry protests from the Navy that he was a defeatist and ought to be reported for spreading alarm and despondency. A day or two later the news came through of the massive evacuation of our troops from the Dunkirk beaches. By then Poland, Denmark, Holland, Norway, Belgium and France had all been conquered.

In June a letter came from an American friend in San Francisco inviting Polly and Josephine to stay with her. Polly was of Jewish parentage, and so there were good grounds for concern about her and her family should the Nazis invade Britain. My own anti-Nazi books also made me vulnerable. However, we were determined to keep together as a family in Britain. Polly wrote on 22 June:

> I should bitterly hate to leave you here and take Poppet to another Continent ... One feels curiously animal-like these days about one's young, both the born and the unborn [Polly was then pregnant] ... a primitive desire to shelter them with one's own body somehow from physical dangers ... it's curious and I suppose mother apes have the same instinct in the jungle exactly.

On 16 July Polly wrote:

> A big cheerful Lance-Corporal (an old sojer from the last war now on duty at the airport) came round to Stansfield House to confirm their intentions of setting up a sandbag outpost in the front garden. It will only be used in case of actual invasion he says and then as a second line of defence. He unbosomed himself cheerfully about the Molotov cocktails they would throw at any venturesome Nazi light tanks, etc .... He was so sweet.

Early in September 1940, my troop was stationed in Manston Aerodrome, just a few miles out of Dover. The German Panzer army was on the French coast just across the Channel. One beautiful moonlit night I was summoned to report at once to the RAF Station Commander. I chugged across the aerodrome on my power-driven pushbike. He informed me that significant movements across the Channel of enemy troops, planes, ships and barges had been reported, that weather conditions for an air and seaborne invasion were perfect and that my troops should be ready for action an hour before sunrise.

'How long can your guns fire?' he asked me.

'To the last round, Sir.'

'And how long will that be?'

'Seventy-five seconds, Sir.' I explained that I only had 150 rounds for each of my three Bofors guns and that they fired 120 rounds a minute.

Where do you get your reinforcements from?' he asked me.

'Dover Castle.'

'Do you realize that the Nazi paratroops are going to drop between here and Dover?'

'I mentioned this to a brigadier, when he came round recently,' I explained; 'but he said it was none of my business.'

We duly took up our positions before a lovely dawn in the deep quiet of Kent, waiting for the invasion, armed with three Bofors guns and about fifty rifles. I had my .38 revolver.

I recalled this experience five years later at Nuremberg when I examined the 'Operation Sea Lion' order for the invasion of Britain dated 16 July 1940. It bore Adolf Hitler's depressive signature: a big 'A' drifting sharply downwards and an equally big 'H' similarly sinking. The first paragraph of the order merits a high place in our history: 'Although the British military situation is hopeless, they show not the least sign of being prepared to compromise.' Hitler directed that 'preparations for the large-scale invasion of Britain must be completed by the middle of August'. That document now occupies a prominent place in our National Maritime Museum in Greenwich.

In early September, while we were having invasion alerts in Manston, and damaged RAF bombers limped in to land, Polly and Josephine were being subjected to the blitz in Cranford. On the 7th over three hundred German bombers covered by six hundred fighters attacked the oil installations in the lower Thames, the docks and East London. The blitz had begun.

Polly was then in the eighth month of pregnancy. She wrote nearly every day about the civilian experience of war and our forthcoming baby.

8 September

Another long night, nothing desperately near but some loud crashings ... I gather they've made a bloody shambles of the East End.... How wicked and evil this sort of thing is ... so haphazard against unarmed civilians. I shudder too at burning down the Black Forest, so lovely and gentle, all the pleasantest bits of German culture there. I remember sweet little spotlessly clean villages in Schwarzwald in 1927 with men and women peasants in native dress looking like carved wooden figures ... and such beautiful quiet little inns .... Still this is war. Pray God it's the last war or we'll have to move out and give the ants a chance, though I gather they are just as bloody minded when it comes to warfare.

10 September

Last night in the darkness of the shelter, whilst Poppet slept, I thought again especially of her being born and a tiny little moppet and you rushing up from chambers six times a day to have a peep at her and me feeding her at 6 a.m. on chilly January mornings ... and how she used to dart at the nipple like a little trout. What good memories to store up and so much nicer than just listening to the drone of Nazi planes get nearer and then crash! ... and then fade away again for a little bit.

16 September

I get a bit more sleep now as I'm relaxing my vigilance a trifle at nights and we get so many sirens I don't remember whether it's alert or all clear so raspberries to it – though I do put Poppet to sleep in the shelter well wrapped and rugged and hot water-bottled. Terrific bombardment and gunfire last night.

17 September

'*Quelle vie*! a bomb dropped immediately opposite our house last night in the garden of the little villa *en face*. It covered our windows in dirt, shook our house thoroughly and did us no hurt beyond a minor shakeup.... Poppet slept right through it though it lifted the shelter and bumped it down again.... A.R.P. lorry out all night trying to locate an unexploded bomb in the garden or round about here.... A few bombs on the airfield but I think not much damage. Today we all feel triumphant and slightly foolish at the same time.

I've been in London all day today. A bomb hit the Langham Hotel so the B.B.C. is a bit disorganized. However I did my piece all right. ... Then to Middlesex Hospital where the doctor informed me that Daniel is all in the wrong position .... He manipulated him round a bit (but very painful for me) and says I must come again in a week. There was a raid just before we were leaving and I went to the hospital basement and had a bit of a nap on the mattress there.

18 September

The fourth siren today has just sounded. Poor Poppet will get celery-coloured from living so much below ground level I fear (in the garden shelter at the back of the house). We have more hours alarm than all clear now .... Having a baby in war conditions isn't just a matter of heroics (one can easily brace oneself to Beethoven heights) it's a matter of adequate hot water, a clean safe cradle, no microbes and proper rest, in fact organisation and proper care ... just the things that are most difficult to ensure with 8 raids a day and one long one at night. *Néanmoins* I've struggled through to the end of the ninth month and with Jones's strong heart behind me I'll beat the sods yet.

22 September

These night raids are getting very difficult. Poppet wakes screaming now when the bangs get near her, though I do try to see that she doesn't get too frightened.

I saw some of the poorest slummers from Kings Cross with filthy rags to sleep on and tired dirty kids huddled up together getting ready for the night in the

Underground . . . a grey faced woman was suckling a baby of about eight weeks. They're a tough crowd. I wish the Government could organise things for them. A good intelligent social leader or a humane padre could make things so much easier for them. They are very orderly and obedient but ready to fight tooth and nail for their inches of staked claim by the wall. I have a feeling that when they pay their 1½d for the ticket to the next station they feel they are paying for their night's lodgement so they're quits.

On 19 September, written after I had had twenty-four hours' leave:

Yesterday was one of the happiest days for years, first waking up in bed with you, to find we were both alive and had several precious hours of sleep into the bargain, then seeing my husband busily pottering blissfully about, sitting in his own armchair and picking his own apple trees and playing with his Poppet, then my rather successful dinner (even if the dumplings were a bit indigestful) and you buying me sugared almonds and fetching me home in the siren.

1 October

Chaucer Avenue demolished by bombs two nights or so ago. About 100 people, homeless, are sheltering in the local Chapel and are being fed by voluntary shifts of helpers. People's kindness makes one not despair for humankind .... Wish I could find somewhere to get my family to ....

Undated

All this destruction makes me doubly grateful to be creating a new life inside me. Wish I'd been able to do it in more peace and tranquillity. Spiritually I can but the old flesh gets weary sometimes in the long night vigils.

A week before Dan was due, an old friend who was living in the Lake District arranged for Polly to have our second child in a nursing home in Bowness. I was given leave to take Polly, Josephine and Margit up there. Bombing had disorganized the train service and we had to change trains at Crewe Station. I foolishly left a cardboard box full of rations Polly had carefully saved, on the station platform alongside our other luggage. I took the family into the station buffet for a cup of tea. When I came back the cardboard box had gone. It was a nasty shock and out of keeping with the way of life in those days of struggle for survival. The trains were hours late and I prayed that Polly would not give birth on the crowded train.

On 27 October Polly wrote from Bowness: 'I am sitting up in bed now with my beautiful *son* snoozing in his crib beside me. It all seems so miraculous. He was born at 2.10 a.m. this morning . . . and what a lusty cry he greeted the world with.' I was given forty-eight hours' leave to visit Polly and the baby. On the morning I was to go, Willesden Junction was bombed out of action and the train services to the Lake District were cancelled. I was not to be outdone and hitchhiked there instead. We drank Dan's health when I returned to the Battery.

Serving in Victor's battery was a happy and stimulating experience. Through him I met his close friend Dr Chaim Weizmann, the Jewish leader and one of the most impressive men I have ever met. At one time Victor and Weizmann and our Brigade Major, Orde Wingate, planned to raise a Jewish force. Wingate visited the battery frequently. He had a passionate loathing of Nazi Germany. I remember on one occasion he came into the Officers' Mess when someone was laughing at Lord Haw-Haw on the radio. Wingate tore the plug out of the set in fury and said that never again should the voice of the traitor Joyce be heard in the Mess.

Soon after I joined the battery, Victor visited the Maginot Line. When he returned he assured us that it was absolutely impregnable and that it was to the Maginot Line that we owed our security. Through the grim summer of 1940 his confidence in our ultimate victory never faltered. Later Victor became liaison officer between the Free Poles led by General Sikorski and the British forces. This meant that he had to give up command of the 83rd Battery, which by then was scattered around south-east England. We all regretted Victor's departure. Life in the Battery was never the same again.

But Victor and I kept in contact and he sent me a copy of his private report on his three week visit with Sikorski to Russia in 1942:

> Russia is winning the war for themselves and incidentally for us. The Germans are being killed in vast numbers. If after victory, we continue to live in England in even a relatively free condition of politics and economics, it will be because millions of so-called Communists have died to help us defeat the Germans. No one has yet suggested how we should have won the war until Russia had been attacked by Germany.
>
> Very little changes in Russia. It is just different people doing the same things under different names. The Germans are being defeated by exactly the same enemies as were Charles XII of Sweden and Napoleon – the size of Russia, the coldness of the winter and the inherent bravery of her people .... What a life (in Russia)! No privacy, no comforts, cold, hungry and no liberty, and yet they fight, magnificently.

Victor continued to take an active part in the life of the Commons, in which he made his last speech on 19 May 1943. It was on the subject of refugees and was strongly critical of the Government: 'The Jews are being exterminated today in tens of thousands. The stories of the horrors of the massacres at a camp called Treblinka would put to shame the massacres of Genghis Khan, of the sufferings of the Albigenses in the past.' He referred to the 60,000 to 70,000 Jews brought into Britain before the war, 'by no means because of any action on the part of the Government'. He ended : 'I know there is anti-semitism in this country, but I am ashamed of it. The fact that anti-semitism is increasing is a measure of the victory of Goebbels. Unless our final victory includes the defeat of anti-semitism it will be a sham victory.'

Less than two months later, on 4 July, the aircraft taking Sikorski and Victor back to England from a visit to Cairo crashed into the sea after taking off from Gibraltar. Both were killed.

7
In Convoy to Algiers

In 1941 my career in the army changed course when I was appointed Staff Captain in the Department of Army Legal Services (DALS). I had earlier been summoned to an interview at the War Office (in a former hotel in Northumberland Avenue) about the possibility of serving in Intelligence, presumably because of my pre-war connections with the underground anti-Nazis, particularly in Germany and Austria. I heard no more about it – whether because of my earlier political activities or the limitations of my French and German I know not.

Service with the gunners had not totally severed my links with the law. Indeed soon after my battery arrived in Devon I was given an unexpected brief. The gunners who manned a gun protecting Saltash Bridge used to refresh themselves in a nearby pub. One morning an eager police sergeant visited a hut where they were billeted in search of a box of dominoes which the landlord of the pub had told him was missing from the night before. The dominoes were discovered among the belongings of one of my fellow bombardiers, who was promptly served with a summons to appear before the Saltash magistrates' court on a charge of stealing. My troop commander, who happened to be a solicitor, asked if I would undertake the bombardier's defence. He phoned his London Office for brief folios and red tape and a few days later, duly and properly instructed by him, I turned up at the magistrates' court accompanied by the accused, my instructing solicitor, our battery commander and our Sergeant-Major.

I walked to the front of the court and asked a police sergeant when the case was coming on. He looked somewhat contemptuously at my two bombardier's stripes and said: 'You're the bombardier, I suppose.' 'No,' I replied, 'I'm his counsel.' He asked incredulously: 'You mean you're a barrister and are going to appear for him?' The sergeant then had an anxious consultation with a police inspector. Evidence about finding the box of dominoes was given and the bombardier admitted taking it, but claimed he had only borrowed it and intended to return it. The next witness was the landlord himself. When I cross-examined him, he readily agreed that if he had known who had taken the box he would not have been at all concerned. He would have had every confidence that the bombardier, one of his regular and most obliging customers, would bring it back. My submission that the accused had no case to answer, the prosecution having failed to prove that the accused intended permanently to deprive the landlord of his dominoes, was readily accepted by the magistrates and the man was acquitted.

We duly celebrated the acquittal in the landlord's hostelry. Shortly afterwards I told the story at a dinner party in London attended by the then Director-General of the BBC, Sir Frederick Ogilvie. He observed that it was a classic example of British justice and the Territorial Army in action. He asked me to broadcast the story.

My next court appearance was far more serious. In August 1940 I was briefed for the defence in a court martial in Kent. Sir David Maxwell-Fyfe QC was Judge Advocate at the trial. It was a unique case in which the accused, a bombardier, was charged with 'cowardice and misbehaving before the enemy'. It was alleged that during a dive-bombing attack on an airfield, instead of bringing fire to bear on an enemy plane, he cowered in the corner of the gunpit. I called a psychiatrist, who said that the conduct of the bombardier was the result of a psychiatric breakdown caused by continuing stress in action and exhaustion. He was nevertheless found guilty of cowardice, reduced to the ranks and sentenced to eighty-four days' detention. However, the confirming officer remitted the sentence. I believe that this was the only cowardice charge brought during the Battle of Britain.

Before I was posted to North Africa in the latter part of 1943 I was stationed in London in the Judge Advocate General's office in Spring Gardens and then in Shrewsbury at the HQ of the North Wales District of Western Command. Polly and the two children were able to join me in Shrewsbury, where our third child Elizabeth Polly (always known as Louli) was born on 26 January. Whereas Dan had nearly been born in an Anderson shelter in our garden during the Battle of Britain, Louli, who arrived a fortnight early, had to be accommodated in a freezing greenhouse attached to a nursing home which was crammed full.

We shared a house in the village of Meole Brace outside Shrewsbury with an RAF officer and his wife and young son. It was a pleasant, old-fashioned house and among the kitchen equipment was a stately fish kettle the like of which we had never seen before. A brook which ran into the Severn flowed through our sloping garden and was crossed by a narrow footbridge. Food was rationed and scarce, so I tried to catch the occasional eel in the brook with the primitive device of line and worm. Early one morning, when I went down to the brook, to my astonishment a sizeable fish had taken the bait. I pulled it quickly to the bank and fell upon it to ensure its capture. It was a fine young salmon. I gave a shout to Polly which brought the excited family rushing down to help. The salmon, which that evening was poached to perfection, just filled the fish kettle. I regret that in catching the salmon unwittingly as I did, I no doubt broke not only the canons of fishing protocol but probably the rules of the Severn Water Authority as well. But we were at war: the two families needed protein and made a memorable meal of it. I had hoped that the village would not hear the story. However, Josephine, bubbling with excitement, told her nursery school class all about it in morning 'news class' when the children were encouraged to speak of their daily adventures. The children took the news back home and I was alternately teased or chastised about it in the village.

My new duties as staff captain were partly advisory and partly forensic – prosecuting in court martial trials in different parts of the North Wales District where troops were stationed. They were the ordinary run of the army offences: desertion, disciplinary offences, assaults, sexual offences, stealing. There were one or two cases alleging conduct unbecoming to the character of an officer and a gentleman, such as passing dud cheques. Criminal offences committed by the military against civilians were tried in the ordinary criminal courts. On the whole discipline was good.

Crimes committed by prisoners of war were also tried by court martial. I remember a rape case involving an Italian prisoner in the camp at Ruthin in mid-Wales. I had never been in a prisoner-of-war camp before; the conditions and atmosphere did not appear to be very different from any army barracks in the countryside. The handsome young Italian worked on a farm and was alleged to have raped the farmer's daughter. He was highly emotional, and swore that he and the daughter had fallen in love and that she had willingly consented to intimacy.

A new friend came into our lives at this time: my clerk Corporal Warburton, affectionately called 'Corpie Warbie' by the children. He was full of loyalty and resource.

While we were stationed in Shrewsbury we went back to Stansfield House from time to time: Polly to broadcast in London and I to visit HQ. On one such visit, I was surprised to find the kitchen door unlocked, a

Write the address in large BLOCK letters in the panel below.
The address must NOT be typewritten.

192870

TO:— MAJOR F ELWYN JONES
JAG BRANCH
NORTH AFRICA
DISTRICT
B.N.A.F.

DATE STAMP

Write the message very plainly below this line.

Sender's Address Jones Stanfield House Cranford Middlesex

17/2/44

The Jones Family (with Blimp)
The four children
and four fowls.

This space should not be used.
MAKE SURE THAT THE ADDRESS IN WRITTEN IN LARGE BLOCK LETTERS IN THE PANEL ABOVE

stack of empty wine bottles on the kitchen floor and a cheerful young black man washing up at the kitchen sink. He informed me in Ivory Coast French that he was batman to Free French pilots stationed at Heston aerodrome. When I went upstairs to my bedroom I found a young woman there dressed in what appeared to be a French officer's shirt. She told me cheerfully she was 'looking after' the officers. When I went downstairs to sort things out, the batman beamed and said: '*C'est la guerre.*'

In October 1943 I was appointed a Deputy Judge Advocate and told I would be relieving Major Hylton-Foster in North Africa, so that he could be sent from there to the Italian war zone.

I travelled by train to a misty Liverpool and found my way in the blackout to the ship which was to take me to Algiers. We sailed up the coast to the Clyde, where a large convoy was assembled. From there we sailed over a grey Atlantic on an endless zig-zag course, with a couple of destroyers keeping constant watch over us, a wonderfully reassuring presence. I shared a cabin with three other officers. By a happy chance one was an old friend, Ronald Furlong, a St Thomas's Hospital surgeon in the RAMC. Another passenger with whom I became friendly was actor Peter Ustinov.

Our convoy reached North Africa unscathed. There was no sign of the presence of either enemy aircraft or submarines. We were fascinated, as we sailed through the narrow straits of Gibraltar, to see that Tangiers was brilliantly lit while across the water Gibraltar was dark and shrouded in its blackout. The only incident of note on the voyage was when Ronald Furlong was called upon to take out an appendix at midnight. I took my turn one night as Duty Officer and noted with concern the closely packed quarters occupied by the soldiers, a discomfort they endured stoically.

Lord Russell of Liverpool and Robertson Crichton met me when our ship docked at Algiers. I did not stay long in the city, but was sent into the mountains to Sétif, a cold and grim military base in the Atlas mountain range in northern Algeria. This was my HQ for several months. I travelled long distances from there to sit as Judge Advocate in courts martial, on a continuing assize in Constantine, Bone, Carthage, Tunis and other military centres in Tunisia. On one visit in January 1944, Lionel Daiches, then Staff Captain, and I were billeted with a French–Jewish family in bomb-scattered Sousse (Susa) on the warm Mediterranean coast. As the son of the Chief Rabbi of Scotland he was given a princely reception. Our Jewish hosts were well aware that but for the defeat of Rommel and the Afrika Korps they might have suffered the fate of the Jews of Germany.

In the meantime Polly's letters to me arrived regularly. The success of the forces' postal service was an immense morale booster. I remember the almost reverent silence whenever a bundle of mail was delivered and read. Polly, who realized I was missing every fascinating stage of our children's progress, cheered me with graphically illustrated accounts of how they were doing. Many were written on official letter cards; one page per letter, which were miniaturized for air mail delivery.

Just before Christmas, when I was in Carthage, Polly wrote:

> I've made a lovely Christmas tree in the hall, all glittering with paper stars. We've had carol singers every night this week. Children made gingerbread men in the kitchen. I've just eaten one arm. . . . I waited for hours in a queue today for Christmas pork and beef. . . . Josephine said: wouldn't it be nice if Daddy were sitting there instead of his photo.

Early in 1944 I did two broadcasts to Austria for the Psychological Warfare Branch of the Political Warfare Executive at the request of Dick Crossman, who was then in charge of the Algiers branch. One was on the tenth anniversary of the February rising of the Austrian workers. I spoke about the rising and appealed to the people of Austria to join in the battle against Nazism and for the freedom of their country. The texts were translated into German, which I coped with as best I could. I had not really spoken the language for a decade.

The trials in which I took part in North Africa related to varied offences: manslaughter, robbery and stealing, fraud, desertion. Discipline was strictly enforced in sexual matters and convictions for rape were severely punished. My work attending trials took me vast distances in North Africa across the great hills and to several of the battlefields. I saw the beautifully kept lines of war graves near Medjez el Bab where many of our dead lay buried.

Polly's letters in February 1944 reported that the air raids were starting again and that she was now working for the Ministry of Information. Shortly after she had bought two Rhode Island Red hens (for thirty-five shillings each) in the hope of supplementing the egg ration, she sent me an illustrated Valentine. (We have exchanged Valentines ever since we have been together.) It read:

The Rose is Red
The Violet is Blue
Kids need eggs
What shall we do?

Off to Hounslow like a bullet
Polly flies to buy a pullet
The Rhodes are red
Their price is blue
What is that
To me and you?

Listen to the Joneses pray
Lay you devils. Lay! Lay! LAY!
On omelettes we hope to dine
So please to be our Valentine.

'We have now got our indoor Morrison shelter,' Polly wrote a little later. 'As there was a raid last night we all crawled into it when the guns started and very snug it was with a mattress and blankets etc.'

I was posted back to Algiers in February that year and there I attended the trial of officials and warders who ran the Vichy concentration camp outside Algiers and were charged with the murder and assault of camp victims, mostly Communists and Jews. Free French supporters called for death sentences on the accused. A row of black Senegalese troops stood on guard between the public and the judges.

In March at the invitation of French friends I was also able to attend the trial of Pucheux, the former Vichy Minister of the Interior. He was a character straight out of Ehrenburg's *Fall of Paris*. There was high drama in the trial when Grenier, a Paris Communist deputy, said to Pucheux:

'You're sorry you didn't have me guillotined as you guillotined so many of my comrades.' On 14 March Pucheux was sentenced to death.

The army's way of sealing itself off from everything but its military tasks and preoccupations cut us off from almost all contact with the people around us. This applied just as much to the inhabitants of Devon and Kent as it did to the people of Algeria and Tunisia and, as I was soon to discover, of Italy too. So I was not aware, during my four months' stay in North Africa, of the wide and hostile gulf between the French occupying colonial power and the people of the country.

My stay in North Africa came to a sudden and unexpected end early in April 1944 when I was instructed to meet my friend Hylton-Foster at Tunis airfield. He looked deeply worried when I met him off the plane. He told me he had been sent away from Italy under a shadow and that I was to take his place there. When we had time to talk he told me that a letter he had sent from Caserta, the Army headquarters in Italy, to an army friend in Sicily had been opened by the censor. In the letter Hylton had given an account as he saw it of the workings of Parkinson's Law in the 'A' Branch

and of how increases in staff numbers resulted in rapid promotion until a colonel soon became a general. This apparently caused deep affront at Staff Headquarters and Hylton, as a mark of disfavour, was dispatched to North Africa. He was despondent, fearing that this episode would not only damage his prospects in the Army but – at that point of time much more worrying – the prospects of a successful return to the Bar. I cheered him as best I could, assuring him that his fears were unfounded. They were. In 1945 he returned to England, took Silk, became an MP and later Solicitor-General and finally Speaker of the House of Commons.

The day Hylton arrived in Tunis I was saddened by the news that Orde Wingate, whom I had got to know well in Sevenoaks, had been killed in an air crash in the Far East.

Within a day or two of Hylton's arrival I flew to Sicily, where I attended a trial there of a number of army deserters who were charged with robberies and hold-ups, some in league with the Mafia.

I soon moved up to Naples, which became my base for several months. I was attached to what was called the 'British Increment' of the US 5th

Army. There were occasional air raids, which caused great alarm to the Neopolitans as they rushed *Al ricevero* (to the air raid shelter). There were *Al ricevero* signs in all the Italian towns. The GI jest was that Al Ricevero was a US presidential candidate.

Courts martial in Italy, where again army discipline was strictly enforced, especially if the offences were against Italians, took me to many parts of the country, sometimes to remote villages in the Apennines, sometimes to the Adriatic, to Bari and Brindisi and gradually northwards in the wake of the Allied advance. The Italian campaign was fought in mountainous terrain which gave great defensive advantages to the retreating German army. Bitter battles such as Anzio and Monte Cassino cost the lives of thousands of fine young men of many countries as well as my own: men from the Commonwealth, Americans, Poles, French, Brazilians, and a Jewish battallion from Palestine, and on the other side the Germans.

I wrote to Polly on 11 May 1944 from

> a little hill town in the Apennines with a neat little square and a small garden, small houses and narrow cobbled lanes. The country around is beautiful. Just now the blue flax flower is in full bloom and blue fields are set beside the green corn fields and the red poppies. Apple trees are in blossom and the vines are green with leaf. It is the fourth spring I have had this year, the first in Algiers in February, the second in March in the Barbary mountains, the third in April in Sicily and now this fresh loveliness in the Apennines. Yet not many miles away shells and bombs tear up the green earth. The peasants, as they have always done through history, go on tilling their fields and in the south sowing for the autumn crops in the very line of battle.

Later in the month I went from Naples to Anzio to take part in a mutiny trial in the beach-head. I sailed from Naples in an American LST (Land Ship Tank). I was greeted on the Anzio beach by the Deputy Assistant Adjutant General, Lord John Hope. It was 23 May, the day the Allied forces broke out of their encirclement and advanced through the German lines to the Alban Hills a few miles from Rome. From these hills the German artillery had been able to pound our positions for weeks and observe our movements. There were still some German air raids and shelling of our positions.

Ten soldiers were on trial for mutiny, charged with jointly refusing to obey an order to their platoon to attack a strong enemy position; they had been through weeks of shelling and bombing and fighting. Casualties in the Anzio beach-head were heavy. Before I left Naples I had been supplied by Army Headquarters with ten death sentence forms to give the accused if they were convicted and sentenced to death. In a mutiny trial, before a death sentence could be passed, it had to have the unanimous approval of all five members of the court. They were all officers with medals for gallantry.

After a tense trial, seven of the accused were acquitted. Three were convicted and sentenced to imprisonment for ten, seven and five years respectively. These sentences were reduced on review by the Commander-in-Chief. I was glad to be able to return the death sentence forms to Headquarters.

I described Anzio in a letter to Polly on 31 May:

> It is now possible to tell you that for the last 8 days I have been in Anzio beach-head. I came in the cavernous body of an LST and found Anzio the wreckage of what must have been a lovely town – a little like our nice Rimini. There are soft sandy beaches and the lovely Med. Anzio was the place where Nero fiddled while Rome burned, but there is little of the past here. Now it is a place where history has been made. I got here two days before the beach-head was relieved by our forces moving up from the South. . . .
>
> Courage is combined here with as many safety precautions as men have been able to contrive. First thing of course was to go into the earth. Dugouts of all shapes, sizes, situations have been carved out of the earth. Hospital operating theatres, Officers' Messes, small cinemas even have been dug out of the yielding soil.
>
> Anzio runs into the equally pleasant resort of Nettuno. The richer Romans had villas here.
>
> Our big push from the beach-head had started. Seldom has a Court Martial sat under such dramatic military conditions. Batteries of heavy guns behind us fired over our heads at the enemy lines beyond and we had to stop intermittently till the firing died. Out at sea, ships of the Navy hurled shells over at the enemy.

A few days later, on 2 June I wrote:

> I have just returned from Anzio. Since I wrote to you from there you will have read of our attack northward from the bridgehead. By the time this letter reaches you, Rome should be ours.
>
> Galllant men have held those few square miles against Hitler's guns, tanks, planes – and divisions, without the comfort of any natural barrier. No high hill gave them aid, no deep river stood between them and the enemy. They dug in and stood fast. The Nazis attacked them, and were hurled back. Then they tried propaganda – leaflets and broadcasts. Leaflets dropped on British lines blamed the position on the amateur Yanks. Leaflets for Americans told them this was a characteristic illustration of the Englishman's readiness to die to the last ally. But of course it failed utterly. Never have Anglo-American relations been so cordial and sincere as in that beach-head.
>
> When they went to earth our men did what they could to give the utterly unreal a sense of normality. They put English street names on communication

lines – I saw 'Fleet Street', 'Piccadilly', 'Baker Street' – and 'Rotten Row'. And into the dug-outs, which were their homes, officers' messes, hospitals, chapels, they put what touch of home they could – a piece of rug, a rescued chair, a picture.

Did I tell you that in Anzio beetle racing was a great sport. You put your selected beetle under a jam jar in the centre of a wide circle. You mark your beetle with a spot of paint. Winner is the first to reach the outside of the circle. It was a tremendous sport in the dug-outs. The black beetle, Penicillin, which was the star performer, was nurtured by the doctors. Indeed there was a general belief that some sinister medical interference made Penicillin the invariable prize winner. Next to shell holes, most familiar sight in the beach-head were football pitches. Every unit cleared a pitch out of the undergrowth and there were some terrific matches. They also had their own newspaper.

When we had pushed onwards from the beach-head I saw the battlefield. The devastation to the North was as savage and dramatic as the Ypres battlefield – so a Colonel who fought in the Ypres battle told me. Shell holes and bomb craters every two or three yards, shelled tanks (I saw three or four Nazi Tiger Tanks which had been knocked out), burned out lorries. Then dead horses, mules, oxen. And dead men.... Over from the growing corn comes on the lightest breeze the sour-sweet smell. This was the day after we took the place. Now we are cleaning the shambles and are burying the Nazi dead.

I went through Rome on my way to a court martial in Perugia of a lieutenant colonel charged with being unfit for duty because of alcohol. The Germans had just retreated from that ancient university town. The next trial, of a soldier who was charged with attempted murder, took place near Monte Cassino. I wrote to Polly on Midsummer's Night.

Cassino was once a Monastery town with the quiet charm of Cambridge. The ancient Monastery was a cradle of medieval culture. Now the whole town is an unbelievable obliteration. Nothing has survived. Not a roof, not a room, hardly a bare wall. As you approach the town from the South you don't realize you are approaching an inhabited place at all. The wreckage of grey stones and mortar has simply merged with the hill. No identifiable contours of a town remain. There are hundreds of black, dead trees. And in the wreckage many dead men. One or two of the townspeople have crept back. But they weren't even bothering to prod pathetically at their ruined homes as the Italians usually do. They just sat and stared. I doubt whether even Stalingrad presented a horror so complete.

I was very concerned about this time about the safety of Polly and the children. She had written to me on 17 June: 'Now robot planes [V1s] have kept me awake a night or two but we have our Morrison shelter and don't worry.' Two days later: 'Pilotless plane raids go on day and night. Kids all asleep in the shelter. Baby's vocabulary grows. Shelter all clear now ... siren now.'

Then on 30 June I received the very sad news that my mother had died peacefully in her sleep. I remembered when I said goodby to my parents at Cardiff Station she had said quietly: 'I will never see you again.' Polly went to the funeral and wrote that our home was heaped with flowers. A few days later I heard from Father about Mother's death. He wrote: 'We have lost a great guide in our path through life. We have prayed for your safety in that foreign land where you now abide. She never rested without commending your care to the Almighty.' In the same bundle of mail awaiting me when I returned to base was another letter from my father saying that they had received photographs of my children: 'We think Elizabeth resembles her Welsh Grandma,' he wrote. 'She is a little gem.'

Polly decided to take the children to Llanelli safely away from the flying bombs. On 20 July I wrote to her there about the news of the attempt to assassinate Hitler. 'Millions will have groaned at the news that the man still lives. He is indeed a man with the hiss of the world against him.'

Polly and the children had returned to London by the autumn and her letters described the flying bomb raids. On 5 October she wrote: 'Flying bomb fell unpleasantly near last night... knocked off an odd tile and broke odds and ends in the greenhouse.... Round Law Courts, blast has done a lot of damage and I lost myself in Fetter Lane so much is not there. Poor darling London. London is a shambles. It is sad to see it so, but grand to see the spirit of the people in the streets.' The bombing resumed and on 3 November Polly wrote of the 'intensification of rocket bombing – no warning and a hell of an explosion'. Josephine had made three wishes: 'Fly bombs stop. War over. Daddy home.' Dan had created a new word: 'Portember', an imaginary time, a dream month.

That summer and autumn I spent travelling widely, attending many court martials between Florence in central Italy and Naples in the south, staying sometimes in lovely places such as Sienna and Assisi and Perugia, which were largely intact, sometimes in shell-shattered villages near the line.

The nature of the charges was broadly the same as in the North African cases, save that in Italy I had to deal with three or four murder trials. In September I officiated in trials in an Indian Army division in the high Apennines in what had been one of the bastions of the Nazi-Gothic line. I was dismayed by the extent of illiteracy among the Indian troops, and even the NCOs. Most of these fine soldiers signed their names by thumbprints.

At the end of October I dealt with the curious case of a Basuto prisoner who was charged with attempted rape. The accused said his trouble was

that a bad devil who always sat on his left shoulder prompted him to do wicked things. A doctor was called to say that the Basuto had come to see him and had said that the devil was giving him headaches and earache. The doctor examined him and found he had some ear infection and explained to him that it was the infection that was the cause of all the aches and pains. But the Basuto put more faith in the devil than in the doctor and continued to wrestle with the demon on his shoulder.

When in due course I was stationed in Florence I was delighted to run into one of my oldest friends, Gordon Lawrence, who had been the first solicitor to send me a brief after I was called to the Bar. He was at this time a Royal Naval Volunteer Reserve lieutenant and, having taken part in naval engagements which had won him the DSC, he was posted to Florence to take part in the preparations for the Allied landings in the south of France.

I wrote to Polly on my thirty-fifth birthday on 24 October:

> The years – especially these war years – pass at a giant's pace. Five years of my life in uniform, one overseas, it's a big slice out of living.

I am spending my birthday on the banks of the yellow ochred Arno, coloured now by the white masonry of broken buildings and the grey dust of ancient plaster and mortar that workmen all along the length of the river to the very sea are pouring into it so that shattered villages may be cleared and roads made where men can walk, children play and cattle move . . .

On 21 November I celebrated America's Thanksgiving Day in an American mess with lit-up pumpkins and festoons of corn on the cob suspended over mantlepieces and lamps. I wrote to Polly about it:

This National Autumnal feast is a happy occasion. It reminded me of the harvest thanksgiving service we used to have in the Tabernacle Chapel in Llanelli. Around the pulpit would be marrows and a sheaf of corn and cabbages and apples. Father had a cousin with a good orchard and he used to get a loaded branch of red apples for the occasion. A farmer made a small hayrick and this always had the central place.

A few days later I flew to Naples again. On the flight I noticed that Mussolini's model farm land in a previously mosquito-plagued area was again under water. The pump house and a dam had been blown up and malaria was returning to the area once more.

Soon after this I took part in the trial of an officer on a serious fraud charge in the Supreme Court in Rome. It was a vast colonnaded room. Behind the Bench were draped the Union Jack and Old Glory. The lights failed on the last day and I summed up by candlelight. Richard Lloyd (author Richard Llewellyn), who was in the public gallery, said it was one of the most dramatic scenes he had ever witnessed.

In December I was President of a court of inquiry at Arezzo into allegations that three German officers had murdered eleven Italian civilians. Italian peasant women testified to the killing of these victims. They produced the bloody and bullet-holed garments of their dead men. It was a

Sender's Name & Address Josephine Elwyn Jones Sandfield House Cranford M/sex

Dear Daddy I am getting
better from measles
I have knitted
scarf for a long
is red Margret it
and white
Josephine love
19th Feb here are
Father 1945 some heghogs
Babby with
there
prickels
coming
throught there
clothes

foretaste of my later involvement in war crimes trials. The kindness of the Italian peasants and their families, in spite of their poverty and suffering, was touching. And their suffering was extreme. Salt, for instance, was almost non-existent. On my drive inland in November I went through a town where there was a natural salt water source. Peasant women were walking miles to this place to fetch some of the precious water, some carrying wine flasks on their heads and walking as erect as guardsmen.

After further trials in Florence and Tuscany, in the spring of 1945 I flew back to North Africa to try some cases there. Meantime, Polly wrote on 18 March that 'rockets are getting bad in London again'. Three days later: 'Hell of a crash – rocket on the Great West Road factory this morning – heart in my mouth.' But the family came to no harm and on 25 March Polly wrote: 'Jo says I'd rather have Daddy home even than a new puppy and a new bicycle.' She did not have to wait long.

On 3 April came the great news from Lord Russell that I had been granted leave to fly back home in time for the meeting in the Plaistow constituency of Essex to select the Labour candidate for the General Election.

8

MP for Plaistow

When I went to the Commons in the 1930s to meet Dai Grenfell, Philip Noel-Baker and other MPs I always felt a sense of excitement as I waited under the great chandelier in the famous high-domed central lobby: beneath my feet the well-worn Pugintiles, on my left the impressive marble statue of Gladstone, frock coat and all, and all around milling constituents lobbying their local Members. Ever since my Cambridge Union days I had hoped one day, with a little luck, to become an MP myself and part of the great institution of Parliament.

By the end of the war many parliamentary seats were falling vacant. I had written from Italy to Morgan Phillips, General Secretary of the Party, about my continuing interest in a parliamentary candidature. He referred my letter to George Shepherd, the Labour Party's National Agent at Transport House, who wrote to me in June 1944: 'We have added your name to our list of "possible" candidates and that list is now being circulated to constituencies where the selection of candidates is to take place.' He added: 'The position is not quite free from difficulty, quite a number of people like yourself have their names upon our lists and few of them will be able to attend Selection Conferences. We will do our best however to see that their interests are not overlooked.' He was true to his word.

Circulation of my name by Party headquarters resulted in a series of enquiries about me, with which Polly, rushing between children, chickens and jobs, endeavoured to cope. The first approach came from Twickenham, a constituency which then included Cranford where I lived. I had applied for leave to attend a selection conference there in November 1944 but the War Office ruled that 'in the case of individuals serving overseas no special leave can be granted for return to the UK'. Happily the next February the Government changed its mind and Ernest Bevin announced in the House of Commons that servicemen would henceforth be given special leave to attend selection meetings.

A number of constituencies then approached me: Stockton-on-Tees, Peterborough, Macclesfield, Wolverhampton, Newark and Dover. The only enquiry from Wales came from Caernarvon. In February 1945 suddenly out of the blue I had an excited letter from Polly saying that I had been nominated as parliamentary candidate by two wards in the Plaistow constituency of West Ham. We knew no one there and knew little then of its historic place in the history of the Labour movement. When I heard the news I talked it over with Denis Healey, who was also in the Army in Florence at that time. He told me that it was one of the finest Labour seats in the country and genially offered to go there in my place! There followed a letter from Syd Warren, the Secretary of the Divisional Labour Party, asking me whether I would accept the nomination for Plaistow. I sent him my delighted acceptance and on 5 April I informed him that I had been given leave to return home for the selection meeting. Polly was allowed to sign the nomination paper on my behalf.

By a happy and auspicious chance I flew back to London with my parliamentary sponsor, Philip Noel-Baker, then Parliamentary Secretary to the Ministry of War Transport. As we were leaving Naples Airport we were shocked to learn of the death of President Roosevelt. To avoid enemy aircraft we flew a circuitous route back to England, over the snow-capped Pyrenees, and landed in an airfield in the south of England. It was a fine spring afternoon. I found it deeply moving to be back in the lovely English countryside with its green fields and trim hedges and little back gardens full of spring flowers. Late that night, from Paddington Station in the blackout I took the Underground to Hounslow West, where I was lucky enough to get a bus to Cranford.

Very early next morning, three small heads appeared, peeping round our bedroom door: my daughters eyed me with curiosity, my son with suspicion. The image which Polly had tried to keep alive while I was away did not appear to correspond in their minds to the stranger in their mother's bed. Within a few days, however, they accepted me happily, although Dan seemed to take a little longer.

Later that day I went to meet Syd Warren, Dr Harry Boyd and Mrs Phyzaclea, a Roman Catholic school teacher, who, unknown to me, had all been working energetically on my behalf. They and other members of the constituency party had decided, having read *The Battle for Peace*, that they would like to see me – after spotting my name on the list of possible candidates circulated by Transport House. This was a great stroke of luck for me. The name Jones helped too – solid and unpretentious, it recalled Jack Jones, the popular former MP for Silvertown.

Plaistow was one of the four constituencies of West Ham which, in the second half of the nineteenth century, had been developed from fields and marshes into the scene of the largest docks in the world – the Royal Group of Docks. They in turn attracted associated industries, such as ship building and ship repairing, and industries relying on heavy and bulky imports – flour mills, for instance, and the Tate and Lyle sugar refinery. Rows of mean little terraced houses were built for workers who came from all over the United Kingdom. Living and working conditions were bad. A survey conducted by Charles Booth between 1889 and 1891 revealed that 60 per cent of the population of East London lived in degrading poverty. It was to fight against these conditions that the Labour movement grew up in East London, just as it did in industrial south Wales.

West Ham was one of the worst blitzed areas of the country. Eight hundred and forty-eight West Hammers were killed and thousands injured by the bombing. During the terrible raid on 7 September 1940, when I was stationed at Manston Aerodrome, over 100 high explosive bombs were dropped on West Ham and there were 648 casualties. Of the 51,000 houses which had existed there before the war, 14,000 had been completely destroyed and thousands badly damaged, as were many of the schools and hospitals.

It was Plaistow which in 1892 sent the first Labour MP, Keir Hardie, to parliament. The seat had been won for Labour by Will Thorne in 1906 and he represented it until I succeeded him in 1945. Thorne was a trade unionist: in 1889, with the assistance of Ben Tillett, Tom Mann and John Burns he formed the Gas Workers and General Workers Union, which was to become the National Union of General and Municipal Workers.

Will Thorne was eighty-eight years of age by the time of the 1945 General Election and the constituency had decided to seek a new candidate. The selection meeting took place in Balaam Street School on 18 April. It was a small, old fashioned, dimly lit infants' school with asphalt yard and outside toilets. There were four candidates besides me: a young Co-operative Party nominee, an elderly trade union official, Alderman Daisy Parsons, who was the first woman Mayor of West Ham and a suffragette, and Herbert Willig, a local school caretaker and President of the local trades council. Willig had notable claims on the constituency. He was self-educated, served on innumerable local committees and was a fine speaker. He would have been a good MP.

Seventy delegates attended the election meeting from the Labour Party wards, trade union branches and women's organizations. There were railwaymen, dockers, lightermen, stevedores, bargemen, seamen, building workers, Tate and Lyle workers ('treacle benders' they were called), clerks, housepainters, teachers, members of the Co-op; altogether a cross-section of the working population of Plaistow, which was just emerging from the battering of the blitz. Bob Anker, a delegate from the Painters' Union who was Secretary of the Plaistow Ward, shepherded the five candidates. Each of us spoke in turn in the absence of the others. After I had addressed the meeting I was closely but encouragingly questioned by the serious and critical audience.

On the first count I had a fair lead over the other candidates, and at the final count I won by a good margin. As Bob Anker led me back to the meeting to hear the result he whispered happily: 'You're in.' He remained my staunch supporter. During the General Election which followed I had the generous support of all the candidates, particularly Bert Willig. Will Thorne, somewhat frail by then, sat on the platform at the launching of my election campaign.

It was an exciting and invigorating campaign. There was ferment in the air and the heartening conviction that we were about to enter on a new era. Despite the admiration that was felt for Winston Churchill's wartime leadership, the mood in favour of change all over the country was overwhelming. In particular the returning members of the armed forces were strongly on the side of Labour.

We held our election meetings in school-rooms and outside dock gates and factories and at street corners. House-to-house canvassing enabled me to get to know my constituents quickly. I was told many stories of the blitz. One old granny who was rescued from the shambles of her terrace house was clutching a bottle of whisky. The air raid warden suggested, 'Hadn't you better take a drop of that?' 'Not blooming likely,' she replied; 'I'm keeping that for a real emergency.'

The packed eve-of-the-poll meeting in Canning Town Public Hall, scene of many famous trade union meetings, was tremendous. None of us who took part will ever forget it – the rows of intent, uplifted faces – dockers in their caps and white mufflers, the wives and children and old men and women who had been through so much. Someone gave me a Labour Party rosette from the Keir Hardie election of 1892.

In my election address I said:

> Our country has just emerged victorious from a bitter war in which those who kept faith on the battlefields of London displayed the same courage and devotion as those who fought on the field of battle, on the sea and in the air. But it was

not only the bravery of our people that brought us victory. We could not have won the war had not the resources of the whole country been mobilised. Now we, as a nation, must choose the way in which our resources should be mobilised for peace.

The National Interest During the war we organised for victory on the principle that private interests and private profits must give way to the vital needs of the nation. First things were put first. Necessities for all came before luxuries for the few. Distribution was organised, and so we got the food and munitions we needed. I say that if we do not now put the people first and organise industry, public utility services and financial institutions in the public interest – we shall lose the peace and we shall have lost the war.

Jobs and Houses Before you can be certain of these the whole of our national resources in land, material and labour must be fully employed. Before the war we never used the whole of our productive capacity. Secondly, a high and steady purchasing power must be maintained through good wages, social services and social insurance – particularly adequate pensions for our disabled ex-servicemen and for old age pensioners. Thirdly there must be a wide extension of public ownership and enterprise for coal, electricity, heavy industry, inland transport and the Bank of England. They must be made efficient in the service of the people.

Unless the nation can get the keys of economic power in its hands – we cannot plan for peace as we successfully planned for war. Had houses and schools been needed for war we should have had them. We need them now to win the peace. Houses – not tin sheds. Houses now – not in 20 years' time. . . .

With new houses must come new schools and a new National Health Service in which wealth must no longer be the passport to the best treatment.

The Battle for Peace The war we have just won had to be fought. The war against Japanese aggression remains to be won and the Labour Party – which has never been an apologist for Japan – will prosecute it energetically.

But wars do not end wars. I promise you to work for a world organisation based upon close co-operation between Britain, America and Soviet Russia. On the Continent the peoples are overthrowing the reactionary social and political forces which betrayed them to Hitler. These liberal movements have hitherto been our natural allies. A Labour Government will encourage them and not seek to turn the clock back and restore the old regime in Europe.

My Tory opponent in the 1945 election was a pleasant young RAF officer named Baldwin-Raper. The old hands in West Ham advised him that he would do better in the election if he dropped the Baldwin from his name and fought the election as plain 'Mr Raper'.

The count took place in Stratford Town Hall, where I went with my confident but tired supporters after the Polling Booths closed. The counting was conducted under the eagle eye of Alderman Margaret Scott. When 'spoiled' ballot papers came to be examined by the returning officer and the candidates, she was reluctant to concede even a single vote and it grieved her to see votes for me lost when in an excess of zeal a voter had written 'Good Old Jones' or 'Vote Labour' on the ballot paper, forgetting to make the cross against my name. The election result was: F.E.Jones: 17,351; J.B.Raper: 2,463. (The Conservative candidate lost his deposit.) Labour of course won a landslide victory nationwide with 393 seats against 213 Tory, twelve Liberal, two Communists and twenty others. This gave the party a powerful majority of 154.

The next morning Polly and I and the other successful candidates stood happily on the balcony of Stratford Town Hall when the Mayor of West Ham read out to a cheering crowd the election results for the four West Ham constituencies. Labour had swept the board in all of them.

9

My First Parliament

Democracy means government by discussion but it is only effective if you can stop people talking.

Clement Attlee

When the members of the Parliamentary Labour Party met in London after the election it was in a mood of confidence and exhilaration. A good many of us were still in uniform, some were old friends, many were meeting one another for the first time. With a big majority in the Commons the Labour Government had a mandate to bring about major social and economic changes. The party had long been committed to a far-reaching programme of social reform. As far back as 1942, nine months before the publication of the Beveridge Report, the Party Conference had carried unanimously a motion by Jim Griffiths calling for 'a comprehensive scheme of social security ... adequate cash payments to provide security whatever the contingency, provision of cash payments from national funds for all children through a scheme of family allowances and the right to all forms of medical attention and treatment through a National Health Service'. We were committed to provide 'a shield for every man, woman and child against the ravages of poverty and adversity'. Our goal was to create a more equal society based on social justice and to do so by parliamentary means.

During the war (which we sometimes forget that we won) the British people had all faced common dangers and undertaken common tasks together as one nation. To survive and win the war against Hitler had required utilizing our resources, planning and agreeing on priorities, and the acceptance of restrictions and sacrifices. In his book *As it Happened*, Clem Attlee wrote: 'It was clear that there could be no return to past conditions. The old pattern was worn out and it was for us to weave the new.... Our experience in the war had shown how much could be accomplished when public advantage was put before private vested interest . . . I therefore determined that we would go ahead as fast as possible with our programme.' This we proceeded to do.

Parliament met on 1 August 1945 to elect the Speaker. On the morning of this great day in my life – my entry into Parliament – Polly and the children, waving me goodbye from the garden gate of Stansfield House, inadvertently let out our three young goslings, who plodded faithfully after me in line as far as the Great West Road and refused to return home until I led them back.

The Commons Chamber had been destroyed by fire in the blitz on 10 May 1941. We met in the Lords Chamber, the Lords themselves being housed in the small Queen's Robing Room. Colonel Clifton-Brown, who had been Speaker in the previous parliament, was unanimously re-elected.

I was sworn in on 2 August along with many other new members. The House adjourned the next day until the 15th, when we reassembled temporarily in St Stephen's Hall, the ancient meeting place of the House of Commons. That afternoon Prime Minister Clem Attlee informed the House that 'at midnight last night the terms of the Japanese surrender were announced to the world'. Having read them he moved that the House should proceed at once to the Church of St Margaret's, Westminster, for a service of thanksgiving. There were prayers. Psalm 100 and 'O God, Our Help in Ages Past' were sung. As the Speaker left the church at the conclusion of the brief service, the bells of St Margaret's rang out in celebration of victory. Later that day we reassembled for the debate on the King's Speech, which began with tributes to the King by the party leaders. Winston Churchill declared in characteristic vein: 'Monstrous tyrannies which menaced our life have been beaten to the ground in ruin, and a brighter radiance illumines the Imperial Crown than any which our annals record.' I sat opposite him as he spoke and I noticed that, when he brought his fist down on the dispatch box for emphasis, he winced. He had forgotten that the smooth old oak dispatch box of the Commons, which was said to bear marks inflected by Mr Gladstone's signet ring, had been lost in the conflagration in 1941. It had been replaced by a new dispatch box encrusted with knobbly brass adornments which had been presented to the House by the New Zealand Parliament.

In the debate on the Address which followed, the Prime Minister paid an eloquent tribute to Churchill: 'In the darkest and most dangerous hour of our history this nation found in my Rt Hon. Friend the man who expressed supremely the courage never to yield which animated all the men and women of this country.' The Prime Minister made no express reference to the dropping of the atomic bombs on Hiroshima and Nagasaki or to the fate of their inhabitants, saying only: 'We have seen in action a new force, the result of scientific discovery, the far reaching consequences of which, I think, we find it difficult to grasp ... we shall have to make a revaluation of the whole situation, especially in the sphere of international relations.' Churchill explained how the decision to use the atomic bomb was taken by President Truman himself at Potsdam and how they had 'approved the military plans to unchain the dread, pent up forces'. The dire consequences for the future of the human race which resulted from that decision he made clear when he warned: 'The bomb brought peace, but men alone can keep that peace, and henceforward they will keep it under penalties which threaten the survival, not only of civilization, but of humanity itself.' The dead – and the stricken survivors – of Hiroshima and Nagasaki were witnesses of that.

A sombre warning was given in 1947 by the Emergency Committee of Atomic Scientists, chaired by Albert Einstein. They declared that certain facts were accepted by all atomic scientists:

1. Atomic bombs can now be made cheaply and in large numbers. They will become more destructive.
2. There is no military defence against atomic bombs and none is to be expected.
3. Other nations can rediscover our secret processes by themselves.
4. Preparedness against atomic war is futile and, if attempted, will ruin the structure of our social order.

The nature of the nuclear peril had been made known and its significance for the human race had been made clear. But awareness of the threat faded and international political life soon reverted to the usual power struggle, and the Cold War between the United States and the Soviet Union came to dominate political thinking and political passions.

I had been friendly with John Strachey before the war. His book *The Coming Struggle for Power* had a great influence on my contemporaries. When Attlee appointed him Under-Secretary of State for Air (he had been a Wing Commander RAFVR) in July 1945 he invited me to be his Parliamentary Private Secretary. This is an unpaid post which varies in its importance, depending on the relationship between the PPS and the Minister. In some cases the PPS merely 'runs little errands for Ministers of State'. In others he or she enjoys the full confidence of the Minister, is kept well informed about what goes on in Government and is a valuable link between the Minister and the back-benchers. The PPS is expected to support Government policy, which does however restrict freedom of speech in the House. One who falls too far out of line may be asked to resign by the Minister, sometimes at the instigation of the Prime Minister.

My task during the brief period in which I was Strachey's PPS was to help with the mass of applications for release from RAF personnel scattered in bases around the world. Some had been in the services for over five years. The speed and fairness with which, under Ernest Bevin's guidelines, the Government carried out demobilization of the Forces (in marked contrast with what happened after the 1914–18 War and its mutinous consequences) was a considerable achievement.

I myself was not 'demobbed' until 1 October 1945. During that summer I was sent as Judge Advocate to a murder trial in Belgium and to another in Germany. I also sat on a remarkable case in London. It was a trial in which a number of German prisoners of war were convicted of complicity in the murder of an anti-Nazi German prisoner in a POW camp. The extent and strength of Nazi sentiments as late as December 1944 (when the murder took place) disclosed at this trial was disturbing, although there was also hopeful evidence of the willingness of some anti-Nazi German soldiers to stand up and be counted. But they were in a minority.

Happily these demands on me from the Army were few, for as soon as I was elected to parliament a steady flow of letters and requests for help poured in from my constituents in Plaistow. Fortunately for many years I enjoyed the admirable secretarial services of Margaret Usborne, who was sympathetic and understanding of my constituents' problems. Helena Dightam later took over from her and helped me greatly. Housing then, as now, headed the list. Changing social patterns added to the immense housing shortage. During the first three years after the war there were 11 per cent more marriages and 33 per cent more births in the country as a whole than in the last three years before the war. Full employment and higher social expectations increased the demand for separate dwellings. 'Pre-fabs' – asbestos bungalows hastily erected on bomb sites and intended for only two years' occupation – remained in use for many years and some are still being used. Many of the families living in them kept trim little gardens with flowers and even vegetables. Our local council had a detailed points scheme in order to determine who should get a house. Their housing waiting list always contained thousands of despairing families. It was still lengthy when I ceased to be MP in 1974, despite the house building and repairs that had been done in the intervening years.

There was much poverty in West Ham. The misery suffered by the needy was relieved by the Government's National Insurance Act and the National Assistance Act of 1946. The grim winter weather of 1946–47, 'Manny Shinwell's winter' (Shinwell was the Minister of Fuel at the time), added to the hardships. Supplies of coal to industry had to be halved in January 1947. There were shortages of almost everything from school places and hospital beds to food and clothing. Bread rationing had to be introduced in 1946, and even potato rationing in November 1947.

One of my earliest Parliamentary Questions was in October 1945 to ask the Minister of Food what were the causes of the shortage of salt, particularly in West Ham. It brought back to my mind the long line of Italian peasants queuing for salt water in that remote village in the Apennines the year before. It was not until April 1948 that the gradual abolition of rationing began. It was not completed until the ending of butter rationing in May 1954, meat rationing in July of the same year and petrol rationing in 1958. Yet despite food shortages during the war and in the immediate postwar years a generation of British children in the poorest areas grew taller and stronger. What food was available was being better distributed.

I held 'surgeries' fortnightly in my constituency 'office' on the Barking road – a room in the rented house of Syd Warren, ex-docker and Secretary of my local Party. My constituents came to see me there on Saturday mornings, some after writing (and letter-writing did not come easily to many of them), others because they knew they could find me there. Some families were homeless, others were living in overcrowded conditions, tuberculous victims were in damp houses, and threats of eviction, sometimes by Rachman strong-arm methods, hung over many. There was a multitude of other problems: entitlement to social security payments, pensions, jobs, income tax, school worries, finding a bed in hospital. I became a universal aunt.

The fact that I was a lawyer brought many worried and bewildered constituents to seek my advice when they or members of their families had legal problems, such as pending criminal proceedings, accidents at work or on the roads, hire purchase difficulties or complaints by consumers (consumer protection was negligible in those days). There was only a handful of solicitors in West Ham and the idea of going to them for advice simply did not occur to most of my constituents in those days. I soon became aware of the urgent need for a publicly financed legal aid and advice scheme if equal access to justice was to be made a reality. I was PPS to Attorney-General Hartley Shawcross and was particularly pleased to assist him in 1948 in the passing of the Legal Aid and Advice Bill through the Commons. As a barrister I could not initiate proceedings on my constituents' behalf myself. Apart from giving such advice as I could in appropriate cases, when court appearances or litigation were involved all I could do was to refer my constituents to the local Citizens' Advice Bureau or to public-spirited solicitor friends in the area, particularly Neil Pollard, who were willing to take up their cases, usually without fee.

Being a West Ham MP was not all work and worry however. I enjoyed it all enormously and feel privileged to have represented the southern part of the area for twenty-nine years. It was and is a deep-rooted, neighbourly and jovial community, in which Polly and I soon established warm friendships. Rain or shine, when great occasions were celebrated, such as VE Day or the Queen's Coronation or the Silver Jubilee or West Ham winning the cup, long trestle tables piled with sandwiches and cakes, all home-made, were set up in the gaily decorated terraced streets. Neighbour competed with neighbour and street with street in the decoration of homes, inside and outside. Splendid results were achieved with coloured paper, tinsel, flags, coloured electric lights. For the coronation celebrations one enterprising butcher's assistant, to Polly's particular delight, set up a spirited re-creation of the battle of Hastings with painted cardboard along the roofs of the terraced street in which he lived.

Apart from these communal parties there were constant social gatherings run by Labour wards, Labour clubs, old age pensioners, the schools, the women's guilds, trade union branches, friends of the local hospitals, the YMCA, the Rotarians: social activities which held the community together and gave it its special quality. Everyone always sang and danced with gusto, especially 'Knees up Mother Brown'. There were famous youth and social clubs in the constituency such as Mansfield House and the Mayflower Centre, run by David Sheppard. Every church and chapel and synagogue ran its own particular social evening. So did the local British Legion branch, of which I was president.

Every summer there were flower and vegetable shows where cups and badges were passionately fought for. Even the poorest houses had well cultivated gardens, for West Hammers are dedicated gardeners. Indeed the occupant of one of them was so renowned that he was employed to produce seeds commercially in his ribbon of a back garden. In the winter the outstanding attraction was the West Ham Football Club matches in the Boleyn Ground. Complaints from constituents seemed fewer when West Ham won, greater when they lost.

The Commons were still meeting in the Chamber of the House of Lords when I made my maiden speech there on Germany, with Nuremberg very much in mind, in a foreign affairs debate on 22 October. Before I spoke, the Foreign Secretary, Ernest Bevin, made a massive speech dealing in part with the same subject and on lines with which I agreed. He said the Government was firmly of the opinion that the best approach to the peace of Europe was united effort by the four powers with the cooperation of the smaller Allies. He added: 'If this system succeeds it will lead to a general improvement in relations and a much greater confidence between the four great Allies.' Bevin, who was just as anti-Communist, had earlier condemned Churchill's Iron Curtain speech in Fulton in March 1946 as 'inimical to the cause of world peace', and called instead for a progressive strengthening of the newly born United Nations.

Unfortunately, fear and suspicion on both sides of the Iron Curtain undermined mutual confidence, the Cold War hotted up and Russian imperialism became the main thrust of Kremlin policy under the malign rule of Stalin.

The Nuremberg warning – that we would not be rid of war until the nations arrived at the greatest agreement to live together in peace and to obey the law of nations outlawing war – was ignored. What I found particularly unacceptable was the rearming of Germany so soon after 1945. I opposed it vigorously both in the House and in the press, causing Herbert Morrison, then Lord President of the Council, to suggest to Hartley that he should sack me from my post as PPS. I offered to resign. Hartley suggested that I should speak to the Prime Minister on the matter. A little later I was ushered into Attlee's room at the back of the Speaker's Chair. Without preliminaries Attlee said: 'I understand you are unhappy about the Government's German rearmament proposals.'

I said I was, adding: 'As you were good enough, Sir, to give me a year's leave of absence to prosecute the Nazi war criminals, among them the German field marshals and admirals, my views will not have surprised you.'

'No,' he replied, 'but we have our problems, you know. Think about them.'

'Do you wish me to resign as PPS?' I then asked.

'Certainly not,' he replied, and indicated that the interview was at an end. This was a characteristic Attlee interview. It lasted two minutes. I continued to be PPS to Hartley Shawcross until 1951 when he became President of the Board of Trade, and Frank Soskice, who succeeded him as Attorney General, asked me to carry on as his PPS.

The first post-war Parliament was the most exhilarating and satisfying in my parliamentary experience. Attlee, in his memoirs, wrote in 1954 that the ultimate objective of the Labour Party when it came to power in 1945 'was the creation of a society based on social justice and, in our view, this could only be attained by bringing under public ownership and control the main factors in the economic system'. He added, characteristically: 'We were not afraid of compromises and partial solutions.'

Even the Tories hardly opposed the nationalization of the Bank of England. The Coal Bill was more controversial. The mines were in a bad state and working conditions for the miners were appalling. The owners were bought out for £164 million. Other Acts followed later, taking into public ownership electricity, railways and canals, gas and, after some delay, the iron and steel industries. Civil aviation was reorganized. These were the years when we sang the 'Red Flag' in the division lobbies. Most of these measures were in fact largely based on findings (and often on recommendations) of Conservative-dominated investigation committees. 'The principle of nationalization is accepted by all provided proper compensation is paid,' said Churchill. It was – to excess, especially in the case of the coal mines. Vast financial resources were released to the private sector while the nationalized industries were saddled with a burden of debt which added greatly to their problems.

Despite the country's economic difficulties the national income by 1949 was almost twice its 1938 figure and the general level of production increased substantially. There was little unemployment. In the late 1930s there had been two million people out of work. Francis Biddle, the former American Attorney General, wrote in 1948, in his book *The World's Best Hope*, that Labour's record

> is not bad for a country still bleeding from the terrible onslaught of the war.... Under these conditions the suggestion that the experiments of government rationing, allocations and other controls result in an equality of misery and that they should be discarded in favour of the 'incentives' of free enterprise is ... a glib impertinence .... The alternative to Communism in Europe is not Capitalism but some form of Socialism. Europe will not return to free enterprise in the sense that most Americans attach to that phrase. Europeans will not go back to their old order.

We were determined not to return to the old social order. By 1950 an irreversible change had taken place in the social climate of Britain and in its social values. It had become accepted that it was the responsibility of the State to provide security against unemployment, sickness and old age for every citizen. 1948 saw the start of the National Health Service designed, as the Act setting it up described it, 'to secure improvement in the physical and mental health of the people of England and Wales and the prevention, diagnosis and treatment of illness'. It was a major social innovation and, as I soon found in my constituency, brought immense benefit to the people of Britain. It responded to and expressed a mass of need. One example was the supply of spectacles to three million people within six months of the operation of the scheme.

National Assistance began in 1948 as part of a comprehensive insurance system. The principle of universality in social benefits took the place of the means test. The Legal Aid and Advice Act brought equal access to justice nearer. The school leaving age was raised from fourteen to fifteen and more people were able to attend schools and universities than ever before in our history. The standard of life continued to rise and most of the direst poverty was ended, although it was still a period of shortages, rationing and austerity. Creation of the welfare state and the attack on poverty were given real priority in the work of Attlee's government. When he left office, Britain's social services were among the best in the world.

Rehousing made progress, but very slowly. I spoke, on the adjournment of the House in November 1948, about the critical housing shortage in West Ham which was causing misery to thousands of families there. A few months later I raised the inadequate allocation of steel to the blitzed areas. A scheme for a new health centre for West Ham, badly needed because of the destruction of so many doctors' surgeries in the blitz, was rejected because it would involve the use of forty tons of steel. While shortages of materials was real, in my view failure to give higher priority to housing needs was one of the most serious failings of all the post-war governments, both Labour and Tory (save for the Macmillan phase). We have paid a high price for that failure in social misery and tensions, particularly racial, in the urban areas, where the failure has been most acute.

The biggest transformation was in our relations with the subject peoples of the old British Empire. I remember vividly the exhilaration we felt in the division lobbies when we passed the measures ending colonial rule in Burma and India in 1947, and Pakistan and Ceylon in 1948. What was done then was not only politically and morally right but an acceptance of the inevitable and of the logic of events. To have accomplished, without warfare, the transition from empire to a commonwealth of free nations, in which each is able to decide on its own form of government, was of critical importance in the post-war world. I was touched to note the support the British delegation had in the 1948 Conference of the Inter-Parliamentary Union in Rome from the representatives of India, Pakistan, Ceylon and

Burma when we were under fire from some of the Arab League MPs. Millions who, had we not rejected colonialism, would have been enemies had become friends.

The economic crises in 1949 led to a tough budget, devaluation of the pound and a wage freeze. In the General Election of February 1950 Labour's majority was cut from 152 to 6, although in my constituency my three opponents – Conservative, Liberal and Communist – all lost their deposits. The Conservative candidate in that election – the irrepressible Mrs Mabel de la Motte – thought she would enliven the election by touring the constituency in a coach and four with a rider blowing a hunting horn. It drew out the voters – but not for Mrs de la Motte. The response of the West Ham children was: 'Vote for Motte – That's your lot!'

The Korean War broke out in 1950 and the international situation worsened. At the end of January 1951 Attlee announced a £4,700 million arms programme and Gaitskell's budget included charges on teeth and spectacles. Bevan, Wilson and Freeman resigned. I joined them in the division lobby. The continuation of international tensions and economic problems led to Labour's defeat in the election which Attlee called in 1951 – even though Labour won more votes than the Conservatives and indeed more than any other British party before or since. But West Ham remained faithful to Labour.

There is a heavy price to pay for the privilege of being an MP: hardly any time to give to your family and to the upbringing of your children.

Even precious week-ends when ordinary families can get together are taken up by constituency duties, such as 'surgeries', meetings, conferences.

By the time I got back from Nuremberg, Josephine was eight, Dan six and Elizabeth (Louli) five. They were delightful children and we tried to make up for the lost week-ends by adventurous family holidays when Parliament was in recess.

Our first family holiday abroad was in the summer of 1947, when the Polish Minister of Justice, Leon Chajn, with whom I had become friendly during my visit to Warsaw the previous year, invited us to spend a holiday with his family. We sailed to Poland on the beautiful Polish ship the *Batory*: Josephine first learned to swim in its swimming pool. The Minister met us at Gdynia and drove us to the seaside resort of Sopot. There our children quickly formed friendships with Polish children on the beach. Language was no barrier. They quickly adopted Polish manners. Josephine and Lou were curtseying to adults and Dan was prepared to bow. It even lasted for a while when we returned home.

After Sopot we drove south through Poland to Warsaw. The Minister had an armed bodyguard called Bronek. There were still armed gangs around in the forest. The children were very impressed when Bronek went into a wood and fired a round or two from his gun, apparently for practice.

The destruction we saw in Warsaw was heartbreaking. Even though our children were used to war damage they were shocked by what they saw and say they still remember it. From Warsaw we travelled overnight by train to Zakopane, in the Carpathian mountains. The train was venerable, and so was its tall, soldierly old attendant with a ferocious moustache elaborately curled at each end, looking as if he was a survivor from an imperial past. Our children, to whom he was very kind, were allowed as a great treat to watch him preparing his moustache for the night with the aid of an eight-inch curling rod and quantities of perfumed unguent. Wherever we went we were warmly greeted by peasants and townspeople alike, for the wartime bonds between our peoples endured. Twelve years later Lou, then an art student, returned to Poland to prepare a thesis on Polish peasant costume.

The following summer we had a different sort of holiday in another Catholic country, in Schull in County Cork, where we stayed in a friendly, ramshackle hotel with apparently no licensing hours. When the mackerel shoals came in we fished. We swam and we rowed in the bay where the yacht of Sergeant Sullivan, a local hero and defender of Roger Casement, was moored. We learned the many verses of 'The Daisy Blue' about a fraudulent yachtsman, his unpaid bills and the trusting colleen he took out to sea. One morning Dan went to the local market and spent his pocket money buying a small piglet which he brought back to the hotel in his arms. He was determined to take it home.

One year we rented a fisherman's white-washed cottage in Spain, in Cadaques, long before it became fashionable. A noble looking Catalonian named Mercedes Montjoya helped us with cooking and shopping, expertly examining the beans she selected (beans being a staple in Catalonia). The village girls sat in the sun making lace for their petticoats and on Sundays everyone dressed up splendidly for church. Every day the town crier, in faded but splendid livery, paced through the village ringing his bell, announcing the news, the state of the weather and articles lost and found.

We rented a wooden chalet one August from a Norwegian artist in Balestrand, on the Sognfjord, along with a little jetty, a rowing boat and fishing gear. She had thoughtfully left behind a Norwegian cookery book and a Norwegian/English dictionary. Dan and Louli and my nephew Christopher, Gwyn's son, came with us. We rowed the boat out each evening and set our net, tying each end to rocks on the shore. A local fisherman showed us how to do it. The very first morning when we pulled in the net we found that we had caught a fine salmon. This triumph encouraged us to repeat the operation every evening. Lou proved to be determined and competent with the oars. Although we never caught another salmon we caught plenty of cod, which became our principal diet. Really fresh cod has a taste which cannot be equalled. Christopher was always busy with his camera and insisted on taking photographs even when standing in a rocking rowing boat. Christopher, in due course, became the only member of the Jones family apart from myself to become a lawyer, establishing a good practice as a solicitor in Lincoln's Inn.

The house was of varnished wood. In the evenings Polly liked to sit at the big window overlooking the fjord trying to capture the changing light of the sky and sea with pastels and sketch book. Nobody ever locked a door in the village and postmen left letters and parcels outside the garden gate. Nothing was stolen. We fell in love with the Norwegians and left with regret.

One summer Paul Strouzer, an old French doctor friend of Polly's from her student days, lent us his house in the rue de la Fontaine Basse in Gordes in the Vaucluse, warning us to be careful of scorpions. Gordes was then practically unknown except to a few artists. The old stone house was built into the side of a ravine, its many floors linked by twisting stone steps and with no handrail. Many trades had flourished and then died in Gordes through the centuries. At first sandal making, then cultivation of silk worms, and after that production of the red dye for French military uniforms. When khaki killed that trade the village was abandoned, to be discovered after the First World War by painters Léger and Chagall.

The view across the ravine from the verandah where we ate our meals was so breath-taking that Polly slept out there one night to watch the sun rise. Dan, who at that time had a passion for insects, secretly caught a scorpion and kept it hidden from us in a match box. When the children found excellent clay nearby and brought a lump back, Dan made fine life-sized models of his scorpion, so beautiful that Polly decided to take them back to England and have them cast as earrings. Unfortunately there was no kiln to fire them in and they were broken on the way back.

One year, Madame Paul Eluard lent us her flat in Saint-Tropez, which Polly remembered as an unspoilt and poor little fishing village.

Welsh holidays, especially in Pendine, familiar to me from my youth and then still unspoiled, were greatly loved. Polly went out with the dragnet fishermen on Pendine beach one night. All they caught after a hard night's work were a few dabs. We picked blackberries and hazel nuts from the hedgerows as we had done when I was a boy. Our daughters and son still say that these holidays were the happiest memories of their childhood.

10

The Nuremberg Trial

I had just begun to find my way around Parliament and the Temple when the Attorney General briefed me in August 1945 to appear as Counsel for the Prosecution in the Nuremberg Trial. My involvement in National Socialism since 1934 was now to reach its climax. Men like Goering and Streicher, who up until then had been sinister but unseen, I was now to meet face to face in what Norman Birkett described as 'the greatest trial in history'.

I consulted the officers of my constituency Labour Party, realizing that acceptance of this historic brief would keep me away from Parliament and my constituency for some time. They agreed that I should go. West Ham was one of the worst blitzed areas in the country. They thought it right that their MP should take part in the prosecution of, among others, Goering, head of the Luftwaffe, which had killed so many of my constituents and destroyed their homes in 1940 and 1941.

When I came into the case, the governments of the United States, the Soviet Union, France and the United Kingdom had just signed the charter setting up the Nuremberg Tribunal. Many other governments belonging to the United Nations also adhered to it. The Tribunal was invested with power 'to try and punish persons who had committed Crimes against Peace, War Crimes and Crimes against Humanity' as defined in the charter.

I had no knowledge then of the negotiations that had been taking place for two years between the British, American and Russian governments on the question of whether there should be a war crimes trial at all, or of the fact that the original proposal of Prime Minister Churchill in June 1944 was that the major enemy war criminals should be declared world outlaws and that any Allied officer of the rank, or equivalent rank, of major general should have authority to shoot them as soon as they were captured and their identity was established. In this he was strongly supported by the Lord Chancellor, Lord Simon, who initialled a minute dated 1 June 1944, that the major war criminals should not be tried. It read: 'fancy trying Hitler! His fate is a political, not a legal question. There would be endless difficulties about the Tribunal and the indictment – even if these were got over, you could not really leave their guilt to a posse of jurists.' Throughout the discussions on the war crimes issue he continued to be reluctant to depart from what he called the 'Napoleonic precedent', favouring political rather than judicial action.

A preliminary list of war criminals was prepared by the Foreign Secretary Anthony Eden. Clem Attlee, then Deputy Prime Minister, criticized Eden's list in a memorandum to the Cabinet dated 26 June 1944:

> Field Marshal Keitel is the only member of the German armed forces included. I consider that those responsible for planning and ordering major criminal acts, such as the unprovoked murder of the peaceful inhabitants of Rotterdam, should be placed on the list. It is undesirable that those who have broken all the rules of conducting warfare previously accepted by members of an honourable profession should escape punishment on the plea that they were only acting under orders of the German Government. Officers who behave like gangsters should be treated as such.
>
> I think it is wrong that the big business men who financed Hitler should escape. The group of men in the heavy industries sought to use the Nazis for their own nefarious ends. Some should be executed as an example to the others. All should be deprived of their property.

Churchill in a letter to the Foreign Secretary on 11 July 1944 described the persecution of the Jews as 'probably the greatest and most horrible crime ever committed in the whole history of the world ... It is quite clear that all concerned in this crime who may fall into our hands, including the people who only obeyed orders by carrying out the butcheries, should be put to death after their association with the murders has been proved.'

Had the views of Churchill and his colleagues in the War Cabinet prevailed, Hess, von Schirach and Speer, who were all on Eden's death list, but whose lives were spared at Nuremberg, would have been put to death.

Surprisingly, Stalin thought that Hitler and company should not be shot without trial. On 22 October 1944 Churchill wrote, 'in the air above Alamein, of blessed memory', a letter to Roosevelt noting that on major war criminals Stalin 'took an unexpectedly ultra-respectable line. There must be no execution without trial; otherwise the world would say we were afraid to try them. I pointed out the difficulties in international law, but he replied that if there were no trials there must be no death sentences, but only life-long confinements.'

The war crimes question was long and fiercely disputed by the Americans before they decided in favour of a trial by an international tribunal with judges drawn from the United States, Soviet Russia, France and Britain. To this the other three governments ultimately acceded. To a large degree the trial depended on American initiative, organization and resources.

The decision to hold the trial had been made before I was briefed. In my opinion it was right: to take prisoners we had captured and held in custody and shoot them without trial would in my view have been to descend to the practices of the Nazi leaders themselves. Their guilt had to be brought home to them. Above all, the Nazi crimes needed to be faithfully recorded for all time so that future generations might learn the evils that can be spawned by racism and dictatorship.

The prosecution teams of the four countries worked together in London under great pressure in order to have the indictment against the defendants ready to be lodged in Berlin on 18 October 1945. The Attorney General, Sir Hartley Shawcross, led the British team, but his ministerial, parliamentary and court duties kept him in England a great deal of the time, although he kept overall command. As a result, Shawcross's deputy, the previous Attorney General, Sir David Maxwell-Fyfe, bore the brunt of the day-to-day work of the trial. I was able to 'pair' with Maxwell-Fyfe throughout the trial so that our respective parties did not suffer from our absence from the Commons division lobbies. Another counsel was 'Khaki' Roberts, an experienced criminal Silk from the old Bailey. A young member of his chambers, Roger Bushel, was one of seventy-nine air force officers from many nations who, in March 1944, escaped from the Stalag Luft III Prisoner of War Camp at Sagan in Silesia. Seventy-six were recaptured, of whom fifty were executed by the Gestapo on the direct orders of Hitler. Twenty-five of those murdered were British and Roger Bushel was one of them. Anger at Roger's murder influenced Khaki's mind throughout the trial and sometimes adversely affected his advocacy in court.

Harry Phillimore, later a Lord Justice of Appeal, in addition to taking part as counsel at the trial, conducted much of the administration on the prosecuting side. He wore the uniform of a full Colonel throughout the trial. The rest of us in the British prosecution team wore dark suits. In those days I liked to wear starched winged collars of the type worn by

Welsh preachers. Harry Phillimore used to call them 'Elwyn's-come-to-Jesus collars'. Maurice Fagence, one of the journalists covering the trial, reported that Goering was heard to say to a fellow prisoner that my collar wings were so large that he expected me to take flight at any moment.

The Junior Counsel – Harry Phillimore, Mervyn Griffiths-Jones, Harcourt Barrington and myself – all shared in the court work. There were other able lawyers on our staff and the Prosecution had immense help from Sir Patrick Dean of the Foreign Office, Colonel Gerald Draper, the Foreign Office librarian Jim Passant (who had lectured to me at Cambridge) and Wing Commander Peter Calvocoressi. Hersch Lauterpacht, the international lawyer, added to our strength.

The preparation of the indictment in London made us aware of the immense task which confronted us in bringing to trial twenty-four defendants representing the Nazi regime. As Mr Justice Jackson stated in opening the case: 'Never before in legal history has an effort been made to bring within the scope of a single litigation the developments of a decade covering a whole continent, and involving a score of nations, countless individuals and innumerable events.' The evidence available to us was overwhelming. Allied investigators in the wake of the Allied armies unearthed, in salt mines, in holes in the ground, in secret places behind false walls, in hastily abandoned headquarters, in ancient castles, the secrets of the Third Reich.

Never were there such meticulous record-keepers, diarists, letter-writers, minute-keepers as the defendants and their confederates. They made no general order for the destruction of their documents as the war ended. As a result we had in our document room at Nuremberg the personal diaries of Frank and Jodl, the Rosenberg papers, minutes of Hitler's most secret conferences, the secret records of the German Navy, Army and Air Force – and even of the SS and Gestapo. Our searchers kept on discovering new caches of documents even while the trial was taking place – as I was soon to discover.

Recent apologists for the Nazis have tried to cast doubt on the numbers exterminated in camps or who died after being shot or tortured by the SS, SD or the Gestapo. However the archives kept by the Nazis were detailed and voluminous. Our estimate at Nuremberg was that not less than twelve million men, women and children of many races were killed in cold blood.

At the trial it was not the eloquence of Prosecuting Counsel or the accusations of those who gave evidence that damned the defendants but their own records, which were generally unchallenged and unchallengeable.

The massive and carefully preserved Nazi archives we studied in London disclosed to us even before we heard the evidence of witnesses that the crime which fell to the prosecution to expose was on a scale and of a kind without parallel in history. It was also unique in that it was carried out by the state itself as deliberate state policy. It included 'genocide' – a new word to describe a crime which lawyers had never set out to expose and punish before – namely the deliberate attempt to destroy whole races and nations. Rudolf Hoess, Commandant of Auschwitz Concentration Camp, confessed to Colonel Gerald Draper, of the British War Crimes Group, to the murder of three million people in that camp alone.

In our lengthy London conferences some differences inevitably arose between the delegations. The Soviet Chief Prosecutor Rudenko, a small, determined man always in close touch with Moscow, insisted, in the face of the opposition of the other Prosecuting Counsel, on the inclusion in the indictment against the defendants of the massacre in the Katyn Forest of thousands of Polish officers and threatened to withdraw from the case if it was not included. To prevent this happening it was agreed that the Soviet delegation should have sole responsibility for dealing with this at the trial, which they did. The final judgment of the Tribunal did not mention the Katyn Massacre at all – it was an eloquent silence. The French caused some delay by wanting to include almost to the last bottle the exact quantity of champagne the Nazis had pillaged from France. In due course they reluctantly agreed to the round figure of 87 million bottles.

Finally the indictment, containing four counts, was made ready for signature in Berlin in October 1945. It was a truly international document and the four prosecution teams all took part in the preparation of it. The first count charged the defendants with taking part in a common plan or conspiracy to commit crimes against peace, war crimes and crimes against humanity. This count set out the steps by which the Nazi Government developed its plan in the political, economic, diplomatic and military field, listing the wars of aggression which were also wars in violation of international treaties, agreements or assurances. Count two charged the accused with crimes against peace in their planning, initiation and waging of wars of aggression. Count three was the war crimes charge alleging violations of international conventions, internal penal laws, and the general principles of criminal law as derived from the criminal law of all civilized nations. Count four alleged crimes against humanity.

The Nuremberg Charter, in providing for the first time that the deliberate murder of hundreds of thousands of innocent people was punishable as an international crime, was not making a revolutionary step. Those acts were contrary to the laws of every civilized nation. Nevertheless, recognition of the concept of crimes against humanity was a valuable contribution of Nuremberg to international law.

We flew to Berlin on 5 October. I had known the city in the 1930s as Hitler's seat of government and as a city of fear for many of my friends who were then living there. It was now a pulverized shambles, destroyed by Allied bombing and Red Army shelling. I walked through the eerie remains of the nearby Reich Chancellery : a few loose sheets of chancellery papers fluttered in the breeze coming through its gaping walls.

The next day, the chief prosecutors handed the indictment to the judges of the Tribunal in Berlin. Two days later I addressed them for the first time when I submitted that Hitler should not be included in the indictment as the evidence showed that he was dead. Our intelligence advisers had collected conclusive evidence about Hitler's suicide in his bunker and the burning of his body in the garden. Curiously the Russians did not make available to us the evidence they had, clearly identifying the body and skull that were found as those of Hitler. The judges accepted my submission. Twenty-four other names were listed in the indictment. The trial was fixed for 20 November in Nuremberg. Before it opened the effective number of defendants was reduced to twenty-one. Martin Borman had disappeared : we thought he had been killed in the battle for Berlin, but in the absence of proof of this his name remained in the indictment ; Robert Ley, leader of the Nazi Labour Front, had hanged himself in his prison cell ; Gustav Krupp, the cannon king, against whom the prosecution laid a formidable case, was too ill to be tried.

My colleagues and I flew to Nuremberg in mid-October. It was the first of many flights to that tormented city. From medieval times Nuremberg had been a great commercial and cultural centre, the home of Albrecht Dürer, Viet Stoss and the Meistersingers. Allied bombing and shelling had reduced it to rubble. Broken church spires and shattered stained glass windows, wrecked houses and broken bridges were all that remained. But long before our bombs had laid waste the city, Nuremberg had suffered spiritual death. Julius Streicher had perverted its spirit. Brutish and degenerate, he destroyed more than synagogues. He poisoned a whole generation. It was Nuremberg, controlled by Streicher, which gave its name in 1938 to the decrees by which Jews were finally deprived of their rights as German citizens. It was also the city of Hitler's party rallies.

The trial began on 20 November. It continued for the following ten months in the heavily curtained and floodlit courtroom. Its distinguishing feature was its international character, symbolized by the Old Glory, the Red Flag, the Tricolor and the Union Jack unfurled behind the Judges' Bench. Seated below the eight judges were their marshals and assistants and the shorthand writers. Opposite them were the black or purple gowned German Defence Counsel, and behind them their clients, the defendants, on two long wooden benches, Goering foremost in the front row, wearing his grey Luftwaffe uniform but shorn of his badges of rank and his many stars and medals. Prosecuting Counsel sat to the left of the Bench at four long tables, one for each delegation. Then came the world press and behind them the public. In the gallery were the visiting VIPs. Eminent citizens from all nations attended various stages of the trial. There were also small rooms ingeniously erected in the walls of the courtroom for camera operators, radio commentators, artists, tape-recorders. The trial was world news.

The President, Lord Justice Lawrence, opened the proceedings in a way which set the tone for the rest of the trial. He pointed out that a copy of the indictment had been in the defendants' possession for more than thirty days and that they were all represented by Counsel who had been supplied with the documents on which the prosecution relied 'with the aim of giving to the defendants every possibility for a just defence'. He added:

> The trial which is now about to begin is unique in the history of the jurisprudence of the world and it is of supreme importance to millions of people all over the globe. For these reasons there is laid upon everybody who takes part in this trial a solemn responsibility to discharge their duties without fear or favour, in accordance with the sacred principles of law and justice. The Four Signatories having invoked the judicial process, it is the duty of all concerned to see that the trial in no way departs from those principles and traditions which alone give justice its authority, and the place it ought to occupy in the affairs of all civilised states.

How not to conduct a trial was shown, to the embarrassment of the defendants, in a documentary film Goebbels produced for Hitler of the trial in a Nazi people's court of senior German army officers implicated in the attempted assassination of the Fuehrer in July 1944. In it the presiding judge, Roland Freisler, hurled abuse and insults at the defendants whenever they tried to address him. To humiliate them their belts and braces had been removed. When the Freisler film was shown in evidence, the contrast with the dignity and the restraint of the Nuremberg Trial and the correct treatment of the defendants in court had a devastating effect.

The trial was conducted in four languages: English, French, Russian and German. This necessitated simultaneous interpretation, which was made possible by an IBM translator system used for the first time in a trial. On the whole it worked well, though it was disconcerting to question a gauleiter or a tough SS general and sometimes to receive his answers through headphones in the southern accent and soft high voice of one of the American women interpreters.

Although it was called a military tribunal, all eight judges were civilians, one judge from each of the four countries, each with an alternate member. Sir Geoffrey Lawrence, an English country gentleman with great judicial experience as a trial judge and then Lord Justice of Appeal, presided and dominated the proceedings with courtesy, tact and authority. Sir Norman Birkett, a famous QC before he became a High Court judge, was his alternate. Both were greatly assisted by John Phipps of the English Bar. The erudite Francis Biddle, a former United States Attorney-General and once private secretary to the great writer Oliver Wendell Holmes, represented the Americans, with John Parker, a reassuring and friendly circuit judge from North Carolina, as his alternate. They were advised by eminent American lawyers such as James Rowe, Herbert Wechsler and Adrian Fisher. The French judge was Professor Donnedieu de Vabres (commonly known as Nom de Dieu at the trial). He intervened rarely in the proceedings but whenever he did say anything it was to good effect. He had a twirled moustache and a colossal sneeze which from time to time rocked the Court. His alternate was the diminutive Conseiller Falco. The Soviet judges were the courteous Major General of Jurisprudence I.T.Nikitchenko and his alternate Lieutenant Colonel A.F.Volchkov. Six of the judges wore black gowns; the French with their traditional white stocks were straight out of Daumier. Nikitchenko felt black gowns were 'too medieval', so the Russian judges wore Red Army uniforms, maroon and gold epaulettes and all.

After the indictment had been read, the President called upon each of the defendants in turn to plead guilty or not guilty to the charges against them. Goering was the first to be called, and firmly declared himself not guilty. A shrewd and immensely vain man, he constantly sought to display in court his authority and rank as former Reichsmarshal. Next to Hitler he had been the most powerful man in the Third Reich. At times he looked benign. One American counsel compared him to Byron's pirate:

> The mildest mannered man
> Who ever scuttled ship or slit a throat.

It was Goering who developed the Gestapo and created the first concentration camps in Germany in 1933 and 1934. His object was to crush all opposition by terrorizing opponents of the Nazi regime; he made his own countrymen the first victims of the Hitler dictatorship. Goering commanded the Luftwaffe in the invasion of Poland and throughout the war. He demanded from Himmler inmates of concentration camps to work his underground aircraft factories and used prisoners of war from many countries for the same purpose. In July 1941 he sent a decree to Himmler and Heydrich, the head of the Security Police, ordering them to bring about 'a complete solution to the Jewish question in the German sphere of influence in Europe'. He denied the charges brought against him eloquently and proved the most formidable of the defendants in the witness box.

The black-browed Rudolf Hess, Hitler's right-hand man and involved in all his doings until he flew to Britain in 1941 on his own initiative, was a forlorn figure in the dock. He screamed 'No' when asked whether he was guilty or not guilty. He had a strange, disorientated appearance. Most of us in Court thought that he was mad, but the doctors who examined him found him fit to plead. From time to time he rocked his body to and fro, holding his stomach as if in pain. He refused to take medicines, believing there was a plot to poison him.

Joachim von Ribbentrop, looking grey and world-weary, pleaded 'not guilty' in a low voice. Former Foreign Secretary and Ambassador to Britain, he was Hitler's willing collaborator throughout. When he went to Italy in August 1939, three weeks before the outbreak of war, the unlamented Count Ciano, Mussolini's son-in-law, recorded in his diary: 'I asked Ribbentrop while we were walking in the garden, "What do you want? The Corridor or Danzig?" He answered, "Not any more," and he stared at me with those cold Musée Grevin eyes and said, "We want war."' Ribbentrop played an active part in all the Nazi aggressions, from the occupation of Austria to the invasion of the Soviet Union, and assisted in the criminal policies carried out in the invaded territories.

Field Marshal Wilhelm Keitel came next, pronouncing himself not guilty with much emphasis. He was chief of the High Command of the Armed Forces from 1938 on and was involved in some of the worst Nazi actions. On 16 September 1941, commenting that human life was less than nothing there, he ordered that attacks on soldiers in the East should be met by putting to death fifty to one hundred Communists for every one German soldier killed. It was Keitel who signed the 'Night and Fog' (*Nacht und Nebel*) Decree in December 1941. When General von Falkenhorst tried to save the lives of British commandos captured at Stavanger in November 1942, Keitel told him they had to be shot. They were not even interrogated.

Ernst Kaltenbrunner, an Austrian lawyer born near Hitler's birthplace, was next on the indictment. He suffered a cerebral attack before the trial and did not enter the dock until later. After heading the ss in Austria, he became Chief of the Security Police and head of the Reich Security Head Office in succession to Heydrich. The defence witness Gisevius said that 'perhaps the impulsive actions of a murderer like Heydrich were not as bad as the cold legal logic of a lawyer who was handling such a dangerous instrument as the Gestapo'. He was directly responsible under Himmler for the extermination units which killed the Jews. Kaltenbrunner had a sinister appearance, accentuated by a deep diagonal scar across his left cheek, which so distressed the typists that when he gave evidence they asked for their seats to be moved further away from him.

Alfred Rosenberg, a woebegone figure in the dock, the Nazi Party's pretentious ideologist and author of the unintelligible *Myth of the Twentieth Century*, became Reich Minister for the occupied eastern territories, the scene of the worst Nazi crimes.

When unashamed ss General von dem Bach-Zelewski gave evidence of a plan by Himmler to exterminate thirty million Slavs, he was cross-examined by Rosenberg's Counsel: 'Do you believe this was simply Himmler's idea or was it part of the Nazi attitude to life?' 'I think today', the General answered, 'the logical consequence of the Nazi attitude was just such a plan as this.' Further pressed, Bach-Zelewski added: 'When for years, for decades, you preach that the Slav race is inferior and that the Jew is not even human, then such a result is inevitable.' His statement angered Goering so much that he hissed abuse at him. What Bach-Zelewski said was the key to the German tragedy. As French Counsel François de Menthon commented, 'The original sin of Nazism was its doctrine of racial superiority – from that source sprang the organized and vast criminality of the Nazis.' This emerged clearly not only in the record of the individual defendants but also of the indicted Nazi organizations.

The conquest of Poland enabled Nazi racialism to be carried out on a more ferocious scale. The next defendant to plead not guilty – Hans Frank – brutal in office, penitent in Court behind the dark glasses he wore throughout the trial – had set out as Governor General of Poland to achieve its complete destruction as a nation. Thousands of Poles were killed and over a million were deported to Germany as slave labourers. Frank also directed a programme to exterminate millions of Jews. At the start of his testimony he said: 'We have fought Jewry for years and we have allowed ourselves to make utterances and my own diary has become evidence against me in this connection – utterances which are terrible. . . . A thousand years will pass and this guilt of Germany will still not be erased.' In a sense this was the climax of the trial. Whatever else the apologists for the Nazis might say afterwards, here was one of the most fanatical Nazis confessing his guilt before a world court and a world public.

I shall never forget handling the immaculately bound report which ss Brigadier Stroop proudly sent to his superiors on the destruction of the Warsaw ghetto by the ss in 1943. On its title page it bore the words: 'The Jewish ghetto in Warsaw no longer exists.' Stroop recorded that 'the resistance put up by the Jews and bandits could only be suppressed by energetic action of our troops day and night' and that this action 'eliminated a proved total of 56,065 people. To that we have to add the number of those killed through blasting, fire, etc., which cannot be counted.'

In June 1946, during a brief break in the trial, I saw the devastation in Warsaw myself when I went with the Attorney-General on the first British ministerial visit since the war. I asked a member of the Polish Government who accompanied us what their plans for the city were. He said,

> We shall of course rebuild it, though it may not be possible to complete it in my lifetime. Indeed we don't notice the ruins any more. You see we Poles have a history of struggle. From East and West we have been invaded for centuries. We stand at the cross-roads of Eastern and Western Europe. Now there are only twenty-four million of us left but we live – and for us to live is to struggle.

By the time of my visit a great deal of reconstruction had already begun in Warsaw. The ghetto ruins had been cleared and a simple memorial had been erected in memory of its Jewish inhabitants who, in April and May 1943, had fought to the death there. It was inscribed: 'Here lie the people who died in an unexampled fight for the dignity and freedom of the Jewish people, for the people of Poland and for the dignity of Man.' I went back to Warsaw many times after this. Rebuilding it brick by brick in exact reconstruction of the old city was one of the most moving acts of faith in post-war Europe.

Wilhelm Frick was a lawyer, as were Kaltenbrunner, Seyss-Inquart and Frank. Although he used any who were willing to serve him, not surprisingly Hitler did not like lawyers. He called them 'traitors to the nation and idiots'. Frick was German Minister of the Interior and largely responsible for the legislation which ruthlessly suppressed the German trade unions, the churches and the Jews. He knew that insane, sick and aged people – about 275,000 of them – 'useless eaters' as the Nazis called them, were being systematically put to death in nursing homes, hospitals and asylums, which were under his jurisdiction. When he became Reich Protector of Bohemia and Moravia thousands of Jews were transferred from the Terezin ghetto in Czechoslovakia to Auschwitz to be murdered.

Julius Streicher, coarse and depraved, was despised by the other prisoners in the dock, who treated him like an outcast. From 1925 to 1940 he was Gauleiter of Franconia. He published the obscene newspaper *Der Sturmer*, which had a circulation of 600,000. Week after week in his articles and speeches he spread the virus of antisemitism. He had the Nuremberg synagogue destroyed and he publicly supported the Jewish pogrom of 1938. He called for extermination of the Jews and continued his propaganda of death when the 'final solution' was being murderously carried out.

Walther Funk, a miserable, crumpled figure, pleaded not guilty almost tearfully. He had been the key link between the Nazi Party and the German industrialists and financiers who backed Hitler and was in Goebbels' Propaganda Ministry. From 1938 on he was Minister of Economics, President of the Reichsbank and 'Chief Plenipotentiary for War Economics'. He agreed with Himmler that the Reichsbank should receive gold and jewels and currency from the SS and instructed his subordinates not to ask too many questions. The SS loot came mainly from the dead victims of the concentration camps: their gold teeth and fillings, spectacle frames, wedding rings, jewellery, watches, brooches and necklaces. He presented himself at the tribunal however as a small man with no power in the Nazi state – 'often at the door, but never let in'. After listening to his evidence I wrote in my notebook:

Dead men's bodies tell no lies
Nor the relics and rings of a mother who dies
The blood that was shed was red.
Seek not now to mock the dead
With faint denial, lame apology.
You trod that road of shame. No eulogy
Of Strauss, no tears for martyred Jew
Can save you now. You knew
The sin your creed engendered
The tears of blood when your minions tendered
Gas vans, death vans as red flames burned.
You cast your bitter bread. It has returned
On tides of justice and deep waters of compassion.

Disdainfully turning his back on his fellow defendants, Hjalmar Schacht came next. One of his critics in former days said that the only clean thing about Schacht was his high collar. A former President of the Reichsbank and Minister of Economics, he supported the Nazi Party and raised funds for it from industrialists and bankers. He organized the German economy for war and Germany's massive rearmament. Schacht claimed that he parted from Hitler when he realized war was inevitable. The Gestapo arrested him after the attempt on Hitler's life in July 1944 and imprisoned him in concentration camps for the rest of the war.

The two 'not guilty' pleas of the Naval chiefs – Admiral Karl Doenitz, a commanding figure, and Raeder, the political admiral – followed.

In sharing out the work in Court, Maxwell-Fyfe allotted to me the presentation of the prosecution case against Raeder, who was charged with planning and waging aggressive war and with war crimes. Unlike Rommel, who burned it as soon as he read it, Raeder issued to the German fleet Hitler's order that commandos should be handed over to the SD to be shot on capture. Two British commandos were put to death by the German navy in Bordeaux on 10 December 1942 as a result of the order. The German Naval War Staff commented that 'this was in accordance with the Fuehrer's special order but is nevertheless something new in international law since the soldiers were in uniform'.

Admiral Doenitz was in charge of German U-boat warfare. His importance to the German war effort was proved when Hitler appointed him to succeed Raeder as Commander in Chief of the Navy in 1943. On 1 May 1945, after Hitler's suicide, he became Head of State. While Doenitz was Commander in Chief of the Navy he permitted the commando order to remain in force. Guilt was also attached to him for employing thousands of concentration camp prisoners in naval shipyards.

Baldur von Schirach, well groomed in his dove-grey suit, had been 'Leader of Youth in the German Reich' with control over youth education. He confessed at the trial: 'The guilt is mine that I educated the youth of Germany for a man who murdered by the millions.' He had also been Gauleiter of Vienna and, as he had himself written, drove 'tens of thousands upon tens of thousands of Jews into the ghetto of the East'.

When Fritz Sauckel, who had the disadvantage of looking a little like Streicher, was charged he said with much passion: 'I declare myself before God and the world and particularly before my people, not guilty.' In fact as 'Plenipotentiary General for the Utilization of Labour' he was in charge of a programme which involved deportation to Germany for slave labour of millions of people, many of them under terrible conditions of cruelty and suffering. Many agencies were involved in this: the Nazi occupation authorities, the German railways, the Ministers of Labour and Agriculture, the German Labour Front and various industries such as Krupp and I.G. Farben.

Field Marshal Alfred Jodl, a rigid and able general staff officer, was Chief of the Operations Staff of the High Command of the Armed Forces. 'What I have done or had to do, I have a pure conscience before God, before history and my people,' he said, pleading not guilty. He took a key part in the invasion of Austria and Czechoslovakia. After Munich he wrote: 'Czechoslovakia as a power is out. . . . The genius of the Fuehrer and his determination not to shun even a world war have again won victory without the use of force.' He was actively involved in all Hitler's aggressive wars and in many of the war crimes and crimes against humanity set out in the indictment. He was with Hitler in March 1941 when the Fuehrer told the German High Command that the destruction of Yugoslavia should be carried out 'with unmerciful harshness' and the decision was taken to bomb Belgrade without declaration of war. On 7 October 1941 Jodl signed an order stating that Hitler would not accept an offer of surrender of Leningrad or Moscow but insisted that they be completely destroyed. A million Soviet citizens died in the siege of Leningrad.

The next five defendants – von Papen, Seyss-Inquart, Speer, von Neurath and Fritzsche – each in turn pleaded not guilty. Franz von Papen, an aristocrat like von Neurath, who lent apparent respectability to the Nazi regime, was Chancellor of Germany in 1932. He accepted the post of Minister to Austria on 26 July 1934, the day after Dollfuss was assassinated by the Nazis, and knowing also that his recent political friends like von Schleicher and von Bredow had been killed on 'the night of the long knives'. 'The Silver Fox', as he was called, used both intrigue and bullying to bring about the Anschluss, the union between Germany and Austria.

Arthur Seyss-Inquart, a former Viennese attorney who looked the acme of respectability, was the man whom Hitler had forced Chancellor Schuschnigg to accept as Minister of the Interior at Berchtesgaden. It was the death knell of pre-war Austria. When Seyss-Inquart became its Governor in March 1938, political opponents of the Nazis were rounded up by the Gestapo and sent to concentration camps, where they were tortured and often killed. Jews were subjected to pogroms and plunder and deported to the death camps in the East. Seyss-Inquart had a similar record of oppression and violence when he became Deputy Governor General in Poland and later in May 1940 Reich Commissioner for the Netherlands.

Albert Speer, tall and professional, was a powerful figure at the heart of the regime. He was Hitler's architect and personal confidant. He became a driving force as Minister of Armaments and War Production and took a major part in the slave labour programme. As a member of the Central Planning Board he told Sauckel how many workers were needed. Sauckel rounded them up and allocated them to the various industries nominated by Speer. In August 1942 he was instructed to supply Speer with 'a further million Russian labourers for the German armament industry' by the end of October.

Baron Gustav von Neurath, the experienced diplomat of aristocratic bearing who for so long gave his skills and name to the services of Hitler, had been his Foreign Secretary and Ambassador to Great Britain. He agreed to become Reich Protector for Bohemia and Moravia when they were occupied by military force in March 1939 and remained in office there until September 1941. During that time Czech democracy was destroyed, the free press, political parties and trade unions were abolished and anti-semitic laws were introduced. When war began thousands of Czechs were sent to concentration camps and many died there as a result of ill-treatment.

The last and least important of the accused was Hans Fritzsche, former head of the Home Press and Radio Division subject to Dietrich, the Reich press chief, and to Goebbels. He was in the dock more as a symbol of the role of the media in the Nazi conspiracy than as a major war criminal himself (and because the Russians had captured him).

In addition to the defendants themselves the key Nazi groups were indicted as criminal organizations: the Reich Cabinet; the Leadership Corps of the Nazi Party, the Gauleiters; the SS, including the SD (the security corps) and the Gestapo; the SA (the Stormtroopers) and the General Staff and the High Command of the German Armed Forces. I was allocated the preparation of the case against the SS, an elite corps under the command of the Reichsfuehrer SS Himmler.

In many ways the SS was the most powerful organization in the Nazi State. Over 24,000 of its members were in the WVHA (the SS Economic and Administrative Head Office), which ran the concentration camps. The Waffen SS was its combat arm, subject to Himmler's jurisdiction. Their combined task was to carry out the plan of genocide. This was not limited to the extermination of the Jewish people but extended to the neighbours of Germany: to the east, Poles and Russians; to the south-east, Yugoslavs, Czechs and gypsies; to the west, the non-German inhabitants of Alsace-Lorraine. Dutchmen and Norwegians were deemed by the Nazis to be akin in breed to the Germans and of value for Germany's breeding purposes, but Dutch and Norwegian patriots in the resistance movement were ruthlessly killed.

The evidence of the mass slaughter of the innocents (most of the victims were civilians with no part in the war) became almost unendurable until one reached the point of being almost insensitized against emotion. Maxwell-Fyfe spoke for us all when he said at the trial:

> Those of us who have been engaged day in and day out for nine months have reached the saturation point of horror. Shakespeare attempted to picture that sensation:
>
> 'Blood and destruction shall be so in use
> And dreadful objects so familiar
> That mothers shall but smile when they behold
> Their infants quartered with the hands of war;
> All pity chok'd with custom of fell deeds.'

The showing of documentary films – some made by the Nazis themselves – was a dramatic feature of the trial. When the courtroom was darkened to show a film the British Army shot of the liberation of the Buchenwald camp, with the spectacle of mounds of naked corpses and the emaciated survivors, there was a hushed silence in the crowded courtroom.

One incident haunted me. A Jewish father was asked in the witness box what had happened to his family. He slowly pulled out of his wallet a faded photograph of his wife and three children. 'This', he told the judges 'is all there is left of them.'

The perverted depths to which those running the concentration camps descended was symbolized in one of the exhibits at the trial. It was the shrunken head of a young Pole with the skull bone removed, mounted like a sculpture on a block of wood and used as an ornament. It was found at Buchenwald along with specimens of tattooed human skins used for lamp shades or to bind books at the camp. When the shrunken head was first brought into court and placed uncovered beside a typist's table she fainted.

The ss were given full facilities to present their defence. But usually the evidence which condemned them was irrefutable, for it consisted largely of their own documents. I had one vivid experience of this as counsel. One of the ss witnesses was Wolfram Sievers, who gave evidence on oath to one of the tribunal's commissioners that the Ahnenerbe, the ss Ancestral Heritage Association, concerned itself 'with research on the philosophy, cultural history and geography of the European nations on a scientific basis' and that 'its entire framework was one of intellectual research'. 'How many people', I asked him, 'do you estimate were murdered in connection with Dr Rascher's and other experiments carried out under the guise of Nazi science?' He replied that he could not say because he had no knowledge of these matters. I was not able to take the cross-examination further.

Shortly after I returned to my room in the Nuremberg courthouse an American lawyer, Captain Sandy Hardy, rushed in and showed me a file of ss documents relating to Sievers which had been brought down from Berlin, where they had just been discovered. They revealed that Sievers was at the very heart of the Nazi human experiments in the camps. I applied to the tribunal for Sievers to be called before them for further questioning. They agreed. When he appeared in the witness box some weeks later he had changed his appearance and wore a beard.

I asked him first about letters he had written relating to a skeleton collection in Strasbourg University. He said it was just a piece of academic research. A letter dated 9 January 1942, which he admitted was signed by him, had been sent to Brandt, Himmler's adjutant, with a report from Professor Dr Hirt, 'Director of the Institute for Scientific Research for Scientific Purposes' in the Ahnenerbe Office. The report read:

> Subject: Securing of skulls of Jewish-Bolshevik commissars for the purpose of scientific research at the Reich University, Strasbourg.
>
> We have a nearly complete collection of skulls of all races and peoples at our disposal. Of the Jewish race, however, only very few specimens of skulls are available, with the result that it is impossible to arrive at precise conclusions from examining them. The war in the east now presents us with the opportunity to overcome this deficiency. By procuring the skulls of the Jewish-Bolshevik commissars, who represent the prototype of the repulsive but characteristic subhuman, we have the chance now to compile good, scientific documents.
>
> The best practical method for obtaining and collecting this skull material could be handled by directing the Wehrmacht to turn over alive all captured Jewish-Bolshevik commissars to the Field Police.... This special delegate, who will be in charge of securing the material... will be required to take a previously established series of photographs, make anthropological measurements and, in addition, determine as far as possible other personal data of the prisoners.
>
> Following the subsequently induced death of the Jew, whose head should not be damaged, the physician will separate the head from the body and will forward it to its proper point of destination in an hermetically sealed tin can, especially made for this purpose and filled with a conserving fluid.

A further letter from Sievers to Brandt dated 2 November the same year stated that 150 skeletons of Jewish prisoners were required 'which are to be supplied by the K.L. Auschwitz. The only thing that remains to be done is that the RSHA [part of the SD] receive an official direction' from Himmler. Brandt then wrote to Eichmann of the RSHA asking that Professor Dr Hirt should be furnished with everything he needed. ... 'SS Obersturmbann Sievers will get in touch with you to discuss the details.'

I asked Sievers: 'How many human beings were killed to create this collection of skeletons?' He replied 'One hundred and fifty people are mentioned in this report.... I had nothing to do with the murdering of these people. I simply carried through the function of a postman.' That was a frequent defence during the trial by those actively involved in these crimes.

I then showed Sievers the letter sent by him as 'Reich business manager of the Ahnenerbe Society, Institute for Military Scientific Research' to Eichmann on the subject of 'Establishment of a Collection of Skeletons'. It stated that the doctor who was in charge of the project broke off his experiments at K.L.Auschwitz on 15 June 1943, because of the existing danger of epidemics. 'Altogether 115 persons were experimented on. ... Seventy nine were Jews; thirty were Jewesses, two were Poles and four were Asiatics.' I asked him 'What sort of experiments?'

'Anthropological measurements.'

'Before they were murdered they were anthropologically measured. That was all there was to it, was it?'

'And casts were taken.'

On 5 September 1944, when the Allied armies were advancing towards Strasbourg, Sievers asked Himmler what was to become of the collection of skeletons. He wrote:

> Because of the vast amount of scientific research connected therewith, the job of reducing the corpses to skeletons has not yet been completed.... The collection can be stripped of the flesh and thereby rendered unidentifiable. This however would mean that at least part of the whole work had been done for nothing and that this collection, the only one of its kind, would be lost to science, since it would be impossible to make plaster casts afterwards.... The flesh parts could be declared as having been left by the French at the time we took over the Anatomical Institute.

A note from Himmler's file for Dr Brandt dated 26 October 1944 read: 'During his visit at the Operational HQ on 21 October 1944, SS Standartenfuehrer Sievers told me that the collection in Strasbourg had been completely dissolved ... ' They managed to destroy the skulls and the bodies, but overlooked the incriminating letters, which showed the extent to which the scientific spirit had been distorted by Nazi racial theories.

I confronted Sievers with further documents showing his involvement with other human experiments in the camps: immersion of victims in icy water until they froze to death; deadly high altitude experiments in pressure chambers; lethal experiments in coagulation of the blood. One letter from a Dr Ad Pokorny, 'specialist on skin and venereal diseases, University Doctor of Medicine', concerning research into the use of medicine for sterilization, contained the sentence: 'The thought alone that the three million Bolsheviks now in German captivity could be sterilized so that they would be available for work but precluded from propagation opens up the most far-reaching perspectives.'

The scientific value of these experiments was of course nil. They were performed by depraved sadists with professional medical qualifications who were authorized, as Sievers' correspondence showed, to indent on Himmler for as many victims as they wanted, as if they were ordering groceries.

Throughout this historic trial we were acutely aware of our heavy responsibility as Counsel in presenting to the world the true facts of what the invading Nazis had done to the Austrians, the Czechs, the Poles, the Yugoslavs, the Greeks, the Dutch, the Belgians, the Norwegians. Of course the Jews had no counsel of their own to speak for them at the trial, but we were greatly helped by lawyers from their countries who joined us at Nuremberg. Old anti-Nazi friends from the pre-war days turned up again, for instance the Czech Dr Ecer, who had worked with me in Austria in 1934 and who later became a member of the International Court of Justice in the Hague. Our personal relations with our American, French and Russian colleagues were cordial and I formed many friendships at Nuremberg which, with the unhappy exception of the Russians, who did not respond to letters, have survived the passing years.

The trial was strenuous and harrowing. The court sat from Mondays to Fridays and occasionally on Saturdays as well, and for longer hours than is customary in British courts. After court hours there would often be conferences with our colleagues and most nights, particularly when our sections of the case came up, documents had to be studied and court submissions prepared.

The strain of the long trial was relieved to some extent by hospitality, often given at the Grand Hotel Nuremberg, a former Nazi Party guesthouse, its marble halls incongruously preserved amid the ruins of the city. The delegations also entertained each other frequently in their respective billets. The large corps of journalists from many countries gave cheerful hospitality in 'Stalag Stein', as they called Stein Castle where they were billeted. Maxwell-Fyfe gave a memorable Burns Night dinner with flown-in haggis, American Robert Burns cigars, Scotch whisky and a huge Scottish piper in full Highland dress loudly intoning native laments on his bagpipes – to the awed astonishment of the international guests, who were startled to see eminent British lawyers and their wives painstakingly threading their way through Scottish reels.

Some week-ends we were able to get out into the lovely Bavarian countryside where Harry Phillimore and Mervyn Griffiths-Jones were able to supplement our PX and NAAFI larder with game in the winter and, in the spring and summer, trout from the River Pegnitz. Our wives were allowed a very occasional visit and we ourselves were granted brief home leave three or four times during the trial, which enabled me to keep in touch with my constituents and my family. On one occasion when Polly and I flew back to London we ran into a violent thunderstorm and the plane was running out of petrol. The pilot had to land on an abandoned RAF air strip near Gravesend. Polly had visions of our children being orphaned and has resisted flying ever since.

The spring and summer months of 1946 were taken up with the defendants' cases. They all gave and called evidence and speeches were made on their behalf by their counsel, who included some of the ablest in Germany. There followed the final speeches by each of the four chief prosecutors. Mr Justice Jackson stressed that while the defendants were unable to deny the crimes that had been committed, most of them sought to shift the blame on to others – principally Hitler, Himmler, Heydrich, Goebbels and Bormann – all of whom were dead or missing. Their own personal responsibility they denied. He ended his speech dramatically: 'These defendants stand before the record of this trial as bloodstained Gloucester stood by the body of his slain King. He begged of the widow, as they beg of you – "Say I slew them not" – and the Queen replied: "Then say they were not slain. But dead they are." If you were to say of these men they are not guilty, it would be as true to say that there has been no war, there are no slain, there has been no crime.'

Hartley Shawcross then dealt with the main issues of law in the case. In pinning individual responsibility on to the defendants he said: 'The state is not an abstract entity. Its rights and duties are the rights and duties of men. Its actions the actions of men.... It is a salutary legal rule that persons who, in violation of the law, plunge their own and other countries into aggressive war, should do so with a halter around their necks.' He emphasized that it was a fundamental part of the trial to establish for all time that international law has power inherent in its very nature both to declare that aggressive war is criminal and to deal with those who aid and abet its commission. As to the war crimes charges, the murdering of millions during the war was clearly a war crime. As to the novelty of the proceedings, the first man to be tried for murder may also have complained that no court had tried such a case before. The only innovation the Nuremberg Charter introduced was to establish long overdue machinery to carry out the existing law.

Final speeches on the cases against the indicted organizations followed from their counsel and from the Prosecution. On 31 August the President informed each of the defendants that if he wished he could make a statement to the tribunal. Each elected to do so, doubtless realizing that these were probably the last public words he would utter. Goering spoke with the arrogant self-assurance he had displayed throughout: 'I wish to state expressly that I condemn utterly these terrible mass murders.' Then, despite the massive evidence to the contrary, he sought to dissociate himself from them. It was a characteristic defiance.

Hess made a lengthy and incoherent statement. He spoke of visitors when he was in prison in England 'with strange, glazed and dreamy eyes'. Goering and Ribbentrop tried to stop him. Hess shouted 'shut up' and rambled on until, after twenty minutes, the President called him to order. Hess concluded: 'I was permitted to work for many years of my life under the greatest son whom my country had brought forth in its thousand-year history. Even if I could, I would not want to erase this period of time from my existence.'

'I am held responsible for the conduct of a foreign policy which was determined by another,' Ribbentrop declared, unrepentantly. '... When I look back upon my actions and my desires I can conclude only this: the only thing of which I consider myself guilty before my people – not before this Tribunal – is that my aspirations in foreign policy remained without success.'

Keitel spoke gravely and impressively:

> I want to present frankly the avowal and confession I have to make today. In the course of my trial my defence counsel submitted two fundamental questions to me. The first was: In case of a victory would you have refused to participate in any part of the success? I answered: No, I should certainly have been proud of it. The second question was: How would you act if you were in the same position again? My answer: Then I would rather choose death than allow myself to be drawn into the net of such pernicious methods. From these two answers the Tribunal may see my viewpoint. I believed, I erred, and I was not in a position to prevent what should have been prevented. That is my guilt. It is tragic to realize that the best I had to give as a soldier, obedience and loyalty, was

exploited for purposes which could not be recognized at the time and that I did not see that there is a limit set even for a soldier's performance of his duty. That is my fate. From the clear recognition of the causes, the pernicious methods, and the terrible consequences of this war, may there arise the hope for a new future in the community of nations for the German people.

The sinister Kaltenbrunner placed all responsibility for the crimes of the ss on to Himmler and Muller, the chief of the Gestapo. While declaring that 'the anti-semitism of Hitler as we understand it today was barbarism', he denied his own part in it. 'I am accused here because substitutes are needed for the missing Himmler.'

Rosenberg asserted that his conscience was completely free from any complicity in the murder of peoples.

Frank, who apparently had undergone religious conversion during the trial, looked up to the courtroom ceiling as he made his final statement: 'Over the graves of the millions of dead of this frightful Second World War rose this International Trial, this epilogue of the war ... and the spirits of the dead have passed accusingly through this courtroom.'

'To have acted differently would have been a breach of my oath of allegiance and high treason,' lawyer Frick, Hitler's Minister of the Interior, said. He had a clear conscience about the indictment.

Ignorance was the banker Funk's only defence:

Horrible crimes have been revealed here in which the offices under my direction were partly involved. I learned this here in Court for the first time. I did not know of these crimes and could not have known them. ... I was completely deceived and imposed upon by Himmler.... The existence of extermination camps of this kind was totally unknown to me.... How was I to suspect that the ss had acquired assets by desecrating corpses?'

It was the line youth-leader Schirach took. Although he had earlier accepted responsibility for poisoning the minds of the youth of Germany, he said he knew nothing of the atrocities committed by Germans.

Sauckel, Director of Slave Labour, said:

I have been shaken to the very depths of my soul by the atrocities revealed in this trial.... Because I am a worker, I never thought of making slaves of foreign human beings. ... I myself am prepared to meet any fate which providence has in store for me, just as was my son, who fell in the war.

Schacht protested that he was 'a fanatical opponent of war and tried actively and passively, by protests, sabotage, cunning and force, to prevent it. My political mistake was that I did not realize the extent of Hitler's criminal nature at an early enough time. But I did not stain my hands with one single immoral act. The terrorism of the Gestapo did not frighten me. . . . At the conclusion of this trial I stand shaken to the very depths of my soul by the unspeakable suffering, which I tried to prevent with all my personal efforts.'

Contemplating Germany's disaster Admiral Doenitz concluded that 'the Fuehrer principle must be wrong, wrong because apparently human nature is not in a position to use the power of this principle for good, without falling victim to the temptation of this power.' And the diplomat von Papen declared that the power of evil was stronger than good and drew Germany to catastrophe.

Speer said that:

> from March 1945 onward Hitler intended deliberately to destroy the means of life for his own people if the war was lost. . . . The German people remained loyal to Adolf Hitler until the end. He betrayed them with intent. He tried to throw them definitely into the abyss. . . . Hitler not only took advantage of technical developments to dominate his own people – he almost succeeded, by means of his technical lead, in subjugating the whole of Europe.

Speer concluded:

> As a former minister of a highly developed armament system it is my last duty to say the following: A new large scale war will end with the destruction of human culture and civilization. Nothing can prevent unconfined engineering and science from completing the work of destroying human beings, which it has begun in so dreadful a way in this war. Therefore this trial must contribute towards preventing such degenerate wars in the future, and towards establishing rules whereby human beings can live together.

Admiral Raeder said: 'If I have incurred guilt in any way, then this was chiefly in the sense that, in spite of my purely naval position, I should perhaps have been not only an officer, but up to a certain point even a politician, which however was contrary to my active career and the tradition of the German armed forces.'

Field Marshal Jodl stated: 'I believe and avow that one's duty towards one's people and Fatherland stands above every other. 'May this duty be supplanted in some happier future by an even higher one, by the duty towards humanity.'

Seyss-Inquart, former Nazi Governor, claimed that he did not carry out the order which was issued to him to destroy Holland. To him Adolf Hitler remained 'the man who made Greater Germany a fact in German history. I served him and remained loyal to him. I cannot today cry "Crucify him" when yesterday I cried "Hosanna."'

'My life was consecrated to truth and honour, to the maintenance of peace and the reconciliation of nations, to humanity and justice,' said von Neurath, declaring 'that truth and justice will prevail before this Tribunal'.

The final defendant who spoke was Fritzsche, Goebbels's assistant: 'After the totalitarian form of government has brought about the catastrophe of the murder of five millions I consider this form of government wrong even in times of emergency. I believe any kind of democratic control would have made such a catastrophe impossible.'

After a four-week recess in which to prepare its judgment the tribunal reassembled on 30 September. The judgment dealt first with the organizations alleged to be criminal. The Nazi Corps of Political Leaders – including the Gauleiters and the other Nazi bosses – was declared criminal. So were the Gestapo, the SD and the SS. The Reich Cabinet and the General Staff and High Command were found not to be criminal, on the ground that they were too small to justify a general charge of criminality, and the SA because it was of little significance after 1934. The Soviet judge Nikitchenko dissented from all the acquittals.

As for the members of the General Staff and High Command, the unanimous judgment of the tribunal was that they had been:

> responsible in large measure for the miseries and sufferings that have fallen on millions of men, women and children. ... Many of these men have made a mockery of the soldier's oath of obedience to military orders. When it suits their defence they say they had to obey; when confronted with Hitler's brutal crimes, which are shown to have been within their general knowledge, they say that they disobeyed. The truth is that they actively participated in all these crimes, or sat silent and acquiescent, witnessing the commission of crimes on a scale larger and more shocking than the world has ever had the misfortune to know. This must be said. Where the facts warrant it, these men should be brought to trial so that those among them who are guilty of these crimes should not escape punishment.

Later several of these men were in fact tried, convicted and sentenced by military courts in the different Allied zones.

The next day, the 218th day of the trial, there followed the judgments on each of the defendants. Schacht, von Papen and Fritzsche were acquitted, but all the other defendants, including Martin Bormann, who had been tried *in absentia*, were found guilty on one or more counts in the indictment.

The tribunal reconvened on the afternoon of 1 October to pass sentence on the defendants. After the judges took their places on the Bench, the defendants were brought in one by one through the door at the back of the prisoners' dock. The tense atmosphere tightened when Goering entered and advanced confidently to the microphone placed in the centre of the dock. The President pronounced solemnly: 'Defendant Hermann Wilhelm Goering, on the counts of the indictment ...' At this point Goering lifted his arms with a smile and said that he could not hear a word. Everything was held up while a GI technician hurried into the dock to correct the fault, taking with him a new set of headphones. The GI tested them: 'Testing one, two, three ...' then in a ringing voice: 'It's OK, Mr President.' During this anti-climax Goering stood calmly waiting to hear his fate, which the President then pronounced: 'Defendant Hermann Wilhelm Goering, on the counts of the indictment on which you have been convicted, the International Military Tribunal sentences you to death by hanging.' Goering turned abruptly on his heels and left the dock quickly in silence. Nineteen days later he outwitted the security precautions and killed himself by biting a phial of potassium cyanide.

Hess came next. He was sentenced to imprisonment for life. He appeared totally bewildered as he left the dock. The next ten prisoners – Ribbentrop, Keitel, Frank, Streicher, Sauckel, Jodl, Kaltenbrunner, Rosenberg, Frick, Seyss-Inquart – and the absent Borman were all sentenced to death by hanging. They received their sentences without flinching and in silence. Funk and Raeder were sentenced to imprisonment for life, Docnitz to ten, Schirach and Speer to twenty and von Neurath to fifteen years' imprisonment. Judge Nikitchenko published a dissenting opinion, disagreeing with the three acquittals and with the decision of the other judges not to sentence Hess to death.

The judgment displayed the judicial care with which the judges performed their task of analyzing and weighing the evidence in the case of each of the defendants, applying the presumption of innocence, imposing on the prosecution the burden of proof of guilt and requiring proof of guilt beyond reasonable doubt. Of the twenty-one who were charged on what was believed to be reliable evidence, three were acquitted when that evidence was put to the judicial test.

The death sentences on the ten condemned men were carried out on 19 October 1946. Their bodies and that of Goering were cremated in Munich and their ashes thrown into the river Isar and borne by the Danube to the Black Sea. Nothing of them was left to become a shrine and focus for any possible Nazi revival.

11

Postscript to Nuremberg

The Nuremberg Trial was the only international trial of Nazi war criminals. There had been one important omission: not a single German industrialist or banker had been indicted, despite their key role in the Nazi state.

Before the main trial began, Mr Justice Jackson, with the support of the representatives of France and the Soviet Union, had applied unsuccessfully to the Tribunal for Alfred Krupp, Gustav's son, to be tried in his father's place. Hartley Shawcross, concerned that to make this amendment would further delay the trial, opposed this and added: 'This is not a game in which you can play a substitute if one member of the team falls sick.' However, the chief prosecutors had agreed that there should be a second international trial in which Alfred Krupp and other industrialists should be tried.

On 20 November 1945, the day the international trial began, the representatives of Britain and France published a joint declaration 'that the French and British delegations are now engaged upon an examination of the cases of other leading German industrialists with a view to their joinder with Alfred Krupp in an indictment to be prosecuted at a subsequent trial'.

The Attorney General, Hartley Shawcross, and our Nuremberg team therefore were committed to holding a second international trial of the industrialists. Preparation of the evidence against the principal potential defendants continued while the main trial was proceeding. The French gave priority to Hermann Roechling, the leading coal and steel magnate of the Saar. The Americans recommended the inclusion of two leading directors of the IG Farben chemical combine: Hermann Schmitz and Georg von Schnitzler. The British proposed Kurt von Schroeder, a leading banker, industrialist and SS brigadier, in whose home in 1933 Hitler and von Papen reached the understanding which led to Hindenburg designating Hitler the Chancellor.

First priority had of course to be given to completion of the main trial, which, far from ending by Christmas 1945, as had been hoped, continued inexorably into the next year with many months of work still ahead. In April 1946, however, the chief prosecutor set up a four-power committee to examine and report on the second trial proposal. General Telford Taylor, General Zorya and Charles Dubost were the American, Russian and French representatives, while Pat Dean and I were the British delegates. We held several inconclusive meetings in which we discussed the choice of defendants, the location of the trial (the Russians urging Berlin as the most suitable) and who should be its president. From the beginning it was evident that the American and British Foreign Offices were cool about the trial proposal.

At the second meeting of the four-power committee on 6 June there were two absentees: General Zorya, who we were told by our Russian colleagues had killed himself accidentally when cleaning his revolver, and Pat Dean, who had left for a senior post in the Foreign Office. Colonel Pokrovsky, the friendliest and ablest of the Russian delegation, succeeded Zorya and I succeeded Pat Dean as the British representative on the committee. We agreed upon the five defendants we had earlier chosen tentatively – Alfred Krupp, Roechling, Schmitz, von Schnitzler and von Schroeder – and that the trial should take place in Germany; the Russians favouring Berlin, the rest of us Nuremberg. As to who should preside over the second trial, Telford Taylor urged that as the international trial had proceeded with 'remarkable smoothness' under a British judge it was best to leave well alone.

However, British Foreign Office resistance to a second trial became apparent soon after this meeting. In a letter of 21 June Sir Orme Sargeant expressed the fears of the Foreign Office that the evidence might not suffice to secure a significant sentence on the industrialists, and might well 'deteriorate into a wrangle between the capitalist and communist ideologies'. The letter concluded: 'in short, if it were not for the undertaking given last November we should be opposed to the holding of any second trial before the International Military Tribunal but the existence of the undertaking makes it difficult for us to take the lead in refusing to take part.'

After the third meeting of our committee the French urged that a second trial should be held. Colonel Pokrovsky also supported a second trial. So did I. General Taylor recommended that in view of the attitude of the other three delegations the United States should agree to participate in a trial of not more than six to eight defendants.

On 25 July Hartley Shawcross wrote to Mr Justice Jackson that 'the British are to some extent publicly committed to a second trial' and that 'we should make as early a declaration as possible that we are prepared to participate in a second trial involving the five defendants whose names have been agreed and I feel little doubt that the Government will adopt this view'.

This, at the time, seemed to the Attorney General and to me to be the case. Indeed, he offered me the leading brief for the British prosecution in the event of a second trial taking place. I was worried about my further absence from my constituency. The Attorney General explained my problems to Ernest Bevin, who asked Morgan Phillips, the General Secretary of the Labour Party, on 20 July to write to my divisional party in West Ham 'expressing the view that it is in the public interest that Elwyn Jones should undertake the conduct of the second trial. . . . You could naturally quote me as attaching importance to their member continuing to carry on if, which is not yet decided, there has to be a second trial.'

Morgan Phillips sent the letter and Dick Windle, the Labour Party's Assistant National Agent, met my local party representatives. 'They are undoubtedly very fond of you,' he wrote to me, 'and anxious to protect you and proud of the work you are doing. They passed a unanimous resolution agreeing to your continuing the work.' It was a reassuring gesture of confidence.

What neither Hartley Shawcross nor I knew was that Ernest Bevin, on advice from the Foreign Office, had already decided to approach the US Secretary of State James Byrnes to get an agreement with the Americans in order to prevent an international trial taking place. Byrnes did not need much convincing. As he confided to Bevin, there was vehement opposition by American business leaders to the trial.

By September it had been agreed between the British and American Foreign Offices that six industrialists, including Alfred Krupp, should be extradited from the British zone to stand trial by Americans in the American zone. When I heard of these developments I wrote to the Foreign Secretary on 17 October urging that as the Ruhr was in the British zone and British investigators had collected much evidence of criminality against Krupp, they should be tried by a British court. I added: 'I do not think that it is enough simply to hand Krupp, Schroeder, etc, who are in our custody, over to whichever of our Allies cares to try them. Quite apart from the fact that the acquittal of Schacht [this had been announced at

Nuremberg on 1 October] and the subsequent political agitation in Germany and elsewhere has underlined the need for HM Government to demonstrate its belief in the criminality of the Nazi industrialists, I think severe criticism will follow if the British zone, in which so much Nazi industry was concentrated, were to be the only zone in which industrialists were not to be tried.'

Hartley Shawcross suggested that the American request for Krupp should be rejected 'until we get a clear decision whether there is to be either a second international trial or a trial of industrialists in the British zone'. He insisted that any decision should be made by the Prime Minister personally. Sir Orme Sargeant sent a memorandum against prosecuting the industrialists to Attlee, who in 1944 had urged that some of 'the group of men in the heavy industries who sought to use the Nazis for their own nefarious ends . . . should be executed as an example to the others'. Attlee, however, accepted the Foreign Office view. By 1946 the political alignment in Europe had changed. The Iron Curtain had fallen – and the second international trial became the trial that never was.

Ironically, in the event, it fell to the most powerful capitalist country in the world – the United States – to call the German industrialists and bankers to account. They did so in several trials at Nuremberg under the skilled and determined leadership of General Telford Taylor, who was appointed to succeed Mr Justice Jackson as United States Chief Prosecutor. At Nuremberg the American judges conducted three economic trials: firstly of Friedrich Flick and his fellow steel magnates, secondly of forty-two of the directors of IG Farben, and finally of Krupps, the arms kings. Pleiger, a leading figure in the management of the German coal industry, was another defendant in these American trials, as was the banker Rasche, head of the Dresdner Bank. Emil Puhl, Vice-President of the Reichsbank, charged with receiving and disposing of concentration camp loot from the SS, was also indicted and convicted.

I attended some of those subsequent proceedings on the invitation of Telford Taylor. In his opening speech for the Prosecution in the IG Farben trial, Telford Taylor declared:

> In this case we come to the very heart of the guilt for the unspeakable crimes which the Third Reich committed against civilization in this last and most terrible of wars. In a very real sense these IG Farben defendants – and others like them – not the half mad Nazi fanatics and street fighting thugs are the principal war criminals. And what is more important, these defendants will, if their guilt is unexposed and unpunished, be an immeasurably greater threat to the future peace of the world than would Hitler, were he alive today.

Prosecuting Counsel stressed in all the industrialist trials, however, that the defendants were being indicted 'not because they are industrialists or because they exercised great power and controlled great wealth'. As Telford Taylor said in opening the Flick case:

> The Tribunal is not a forum for debate over the relative merits of different economic systems. ... The charge against the industrialists was that 'they joined in the enslavement of millions of unfortunate men and women all over Europe, that they greedily plundered the resources of neighbouring countries over-run by the Wehrmacht and that they supported, joined in and profited by the foulest and most murderous policies and programmes of the Third Reich.'

In his powerful summary, Telford Taylor declared that Hitler's dictatorship

> was founded on the unholy Trinity of Nazism, militarism and economic imperialism. To industry Hitler held out the prospect of 'stable' government, freedom from labour troubles and a swift increase in production to support rearmament and the re-establishment of German economic power in the world. To the military he promised the resurgence of German armed might. Both groups, industrialists and militarists, pressed money and arms into Hitler's eager hands – and with a few notable exceptions, backed him to the last, until their power collapsed with his in the shambles of defeat.

Most of the accused industrialists who were tried were convicted and sentenced to substantial terms of imprisonment. I saw several of them in 1949 in their prison cells when I went to take evidence in the Manstein case. They were in the Landsberg Prison fortress in Bavaria where Hitler had been imprisoned in 1924 and where he wrote *Mein Kampf*.

Few of them served their sentences in full, however. Krupp was sentenced to twelve years' imprisonment, the Court having found that he employed 70,000 foreign workers who were torn from their homes, forced to work for Hitler and treated with organized brutality. Slave workers from Auschwitz camp were employed in Krupp's automatic weapons plant in sight of the crematoria and the gas chambers. But Krupp in the event only served five years of his sentence. As Airey Neave stated bitterly in his book *Nuremberg*, 'the Western Allies then restored him to his inheritance.'

In Tokyo the major Japanese war criminals were also tried by an international military tribunal of eleven judges. The Attorney General invited me to appear in it. I declined as it would have kept me away from my constituency even longer than did Nuremberg. The Tokyo judgment in due course restated and confirmed the Nuremberg principles.

A large number of war crimes trials also took place in courts in each of the zones and in the courts of some occupied countries. British military courts conducted the Belsen trial and the trial of the SS and Gestapo men who murdered the Air Force officers who escaped from Stalag Luft Three. I was one of the prosecuting counsel in one of the last war crimes trials in the British zone: that of Field Marshal von Manstein. He was convicted in 1949 of neglecting to protect civilian life as his army advanced into the Crimea accompanied in the rear by the firing squads and portable gas chambers of the SS Einsatzgruppe (Special Action Group), for which the army provided transport, supplies and intelligence. He was sentenced to eighteen years' imprisonment, later commuted to twelve.

This trial took a remarkable course. The Russians had asked that Manstein should be handed over to them to be tried. When the British authorities, who held him captive, refused the Russians would not cooperate in his trial in Hamburg. In the early stages of preparing the prosecution case the Polish authorities readily assisted me when I went to Warsaw to take evidence from some Polish survivors of Nazi atrocities. However, after the trial had started the Poles withdrew their support, possibly under pressure from Moscow. We had to prove our case against von Manstein – as we did – mainly from captured German documents.

Allied interest in continuing with further Nazi war crimes trials ended in 1949. By then the four-power administration of occupied Germany had virtually collapsed, and Western Europe's attitude towards Germany and the Germans changed.

A new chapter in the war crimes story then came to be written by the Germans themselves. They brought to trial some of their own compatriots and even today war crimes charges are still being dealt with in courts in the German Federal Republic. The truth about the Nazi tyranny has also been exposed by the Germans themselves, many of whom were its first victims.

The crime of genocide was introduced into the German Penal Code in 1954 when Federal Germany ratified the 1948 United Nations Genocide Convention. The twenty-year Statute of Limitations on criminal proceedings for war crimes was extended first in 1969 and then in 1979 for a further ten-year period.

Since Nuremberg there has been a searching of conscience outside Germany also. Why was little done to rescue the many victims? In 1963 Rabbi Joachim Prinz, who was a leading Berlin rabbi during the

Hitler period, made a moving speech at the end of the civil rights march to the Lincoln Memorial in Washington. He said:

> When I was a Rabbi of the Jewish community in Berlin under the Hitler regime I learned many things. The most important thing that I learned in my life and under those tragic circumstances is that bigotry and hatred are not the most urgent problems. The most urgent, the most disgraceful and the most shameful and the most tragic problem is silence. A great people which had created a great civilization had become a nation of silent onlookers. They remained silent in the face of hate, in the face of brutality and in the face of mass murder.

Was this guilt of silence solely that of the people of Germany? I fear not.

My own abiding disappointment about the Nuremberg experience has been the subsequent failure of governments to build upon the principles it enunciated. I did not regard the conviction and sentencing of the defendants found guilty there as completing the purpose of the trial, necessary as I believe that to have been in the conditions of post-war Europe. Our hope was that out of Nuremberg's outlawing of aggressive war, and its formulation of the concept of crimes against humanity, an internationally accepted legal precedent had been created by which all governments would regard themselves as bound. At the beginning of the trial Mr Justice Jackson had stressed that while the law making statesmen responsible in law was being first applied against German aggressors 'the law includes and if it is to serve a useful purpose it must condemn aggressions by any other nation, including those which sit here now in judgment.'

Early international response to the judgment had been promising. In December 1946 the United Nations General Assembly adopted a resolution which reaffirmed the principles of the Charter and the judgment of Nuremberg. This made them part of International Law, which every civilized nation was under a duty to respect and apply. They were formulated by the International Law Commission in 1950 into six principles applicable to all states and governments. Regrettably 'aggressive war' was not defined in the Nuremberg Judgment and the UN Assembly seminars became bogged down for decades in attempts to define it.

Proposals to establish a permanent international criminal court which were mooted at that time ended in futility. They came before the UN General Assembly in December 1950. The report on the Assembly's deliberations recorded depressingly: 'As an ultimate objective an international criminal court would be desirable, but its establishment at the present time would do more harm than good.'

Since then the Nuremberg principles have been infringed time and again in every continent. There have been over a hundred wars since the

Second World War ended, and few governments in the world could now come to the seat of judgment with clean hands. The experience has not, however, invalidated the Nuremberg principles; on the contrary, it has made their implementation even more urgent.

A further tragedy in the post-Nuremberg world has been the persistence of racial persecution and even genocide in Asia and Africa, and the revival of anti-Semitism in the Soviet Union, France and elsewhere. In London *Sieg Heil* salutes and racist shouts disturb the terraces of some of its major football clubs.

Nuremberg gave clear warning that racial incitement and racial hatred endanger not only the threatened minorities but also the societies in which they live. As has been said, 'Evil only triumphs when good men do nothing.' We must not again become mere spectators.

Awareness that whatever was possible should be done to prevent a recurrence of the monstrous assaults on human rights in the 1930s and 1940s led to a strong resolve in governments when World War II ended that the protection and extension of human rights should be in the forefront of political and legal action. Steps were taken to try to achieve this through the United Nations and through regional organizations like the Council of Europe. As a result, there developed what Paul Sieghart in his *International Law of Human Rights* has called a 'revolution in human affairs comparable with that of 1789, 1848 and 1917, namely the birth of international human rights law'. The old legal doctrine was that the way a sovereign state treated its own citizens was a matter solely and exclusively for its own sovereign decisions. After the many treaties and conventions solemnly entered into when the war ended – like the United Nations Charter of 1945, the Universal Declaration of Human Rights of 1948, and the numerous United Nations covenants and regional conventions (particularly the European Convention on Human Rights) – this is no longer the case. The individual person, wherever or whoever he or she may be – Jew or Arab, Protestant or Catholic, black or white, Asian, African or American – is no longer a mere object of compassion: he has rights recognized by international law.

Laws, however, are not always easy to enforce, especially international law, whose authority governments, while formally accepting the rule of law, are ready to ignore or reject.

Here, in our multi-racial society in Britain, juries have been reluctant to convict in cases of incitement to racial hatred. What is the remedy? Above all, I believe, education. The whole community, children and their parents, can take part in this and through toleration and friendship enrich each other.

12

From Aberaeron To Addis Ababa

As PPS to the Attorney-General from 1946, sharing his room in the Commons, I was able to follow closely the cases in which Hartley Shawcross represented Britain at the International Court of Justice in the Hague. On 22 October 1946, when two British destroyers were sailing in Albanian waters through the North Corfu Channel, they struck mines which had been laid in the channel. The destroyers were damaged, forty-four British sailors lost their lives and forty-two were injured. It was the kind of incident that could have led to war. The British Government's response was to seek reparation in the International Court of Justice. The trial which followed was a critical step in the development of the Court : it was the first dispute submitted after the war, and it was a serious test of the ability of the Court not only to deal with a mass of conficting testimony but to establish responsibility for such a grave international incident in time of peace.

The Court overruled the contention of Albania that it had no jurisdiction to try the case. It found, by a majority of eleven to five (the dissenters being the Soviet, Brazilian, Yugoslav, Czech and Egyptian judges), that the mines could not have been laid in the Corfu Channel without the knowledge of the Albanian Government. Under international law it was its imperative obligation to notify the existence of the minefield and to warn the approaching British warships of the danger. Albania did neither and did nothing to prevent the disaster. 'These grave omissions', added the court, 'involve the international responsibility of Albania and Albania is liable to pay compensation to Britain.' The damages were assessed at £843,947. They have never been paid. The inability to recover the damages could not be blamed on the court. Its charter provided that if any party to a case failed to perform the obligations incumbent upon it under a judgment of the court, the other party might have recourse to the Security

Council. Unhappily the failure of the Security Council to maintain its essential unity largely destroyed the machinery for enforcing the court's judgments. It was one of the many casualties of the Cold War.

I saw the court in action later, in 1951, when I accompanied the then Attorney-General, Frank Soskice, to the hearing of the dispute between Iran and the Anglo-Iranian Oil Company. This case was a precursor of many oil conflcts, and projected the court once more into a storm centre of world politics. The Iranian Government refused to acknowledge the court's right to deal with the dispute, and the table reserved for the Iranian delegation remained empty.

In 1949 I was again briefly involved in the international legal scene. I was appointed by the Foreign Office as the British representative on a proposed commission to examine the charges being made by the United States and three Commonwealth governments against the Hungarian, Bulgarian and Romanian governments for breaches of the human rights clauses in their respective treaties, a procedure for which the treaties provided. The Soviet satellites refused to appoint nominees and the commission never met. It could have been an interesting precursor to the European Commission of Human Rights.

I combined a growing practice at the Bar with my parliamentary work in the post-war period, especially during the thirteen years of Conservative rule from 1951 to 1964.

One of my earliest post-war cases was at Chester Assizes before Lord Chief Justice Goddard. The Director of Public Prosecutions instructed me to prosecute a motorist aged eighty who had been committed for trial by a coroner's court on a charge of motor manslaughter. When I studied the evidence I formed the view that there was no prospect whatsoever of the prosecution succeeding. The Director agreed and I went off to the Assizes to offer no evidence against the defendant. The defendant's Counsel however asked for a formal verdict of not guilty from the jury, to which he was entitled. The Lord Chief Justice ordered: 'Very well, let a jury be sworn.' Unfortunately, there were not enough jurors present to form a jury of twelve.

The Lord Chief then said to me: 'I take it that you pray a tales.' I had not the least idea what a 'tales' was. I felt like one of the stout countrymen of his day of whom Defoe said they would fight to the death against Popery without knowing whether Popery was a man or a horse. I whispered anxiously to the row of counsel sitting on each side of me: 'What is he talking about?' No one could help me.

'My Lord,' I said, 'I am afraid I am not with your Lordship.'

'Not with me,' he replied: 'Are you against me?'

'No, my Lord, but I regret I am not clear as to what is in your Lordship's mind.'

'Have you not read your *Pickwick Papers*?' he said.

'Yes, my Lord,' I replied weakly, finding that clue totally unhelpful.

'Well,' said the Lord Chief, 'you don't seem to have made yourself familiar with the career of Sergeant Buzfuz.' I had entirely forgotten that when Mr Pickwick was tried at Guildhall for breach of promise Sergeant Buzfuz too had to 'pray a tales'. I made a leap in the dark and said obediently: 'My Lord, I pray a tales,' still without knowing what the consequences would be. Everyone in court was enjoying this except me. The moment Lord Goddard explained that by ancient custom if there were not enough jurors, *tales de circumstantibus* – such persons as are standing about – may be sworn in to complete the jury, it all came back to me.

Enough barrister's clerks were found to complete the jury, which then, on the direction of Lord Goddard, found the defendant not guilty. I thanked him for reviving in Wales a medieval practice we had long forgotten. He liked this and always gave me a good run in court thereafter.

I had already appeared in a number of cases on the Wales and Chester Circuit before the war. It was a lively, friendly circuit with a high level of advocacy – and many cases with a special rural, Celtic flavour.

One such in March 1946, which arose from an information brought by the Minister of Food against the Clerk to the Aberaeron Justices, who was also a farmer, alleged that he 'caused a pig to be slaughtered for human consumption'. The Aberaeron Justices who tried the case accepted the submission of Mr Jessop, the Defendant's Solicitor, that he had no case to answer.

The Minister of Food referred that decision by 'case stated' to the High Court, where Lord Chief Justice Goddard testily questioned the fitness of the Justices to administer justice. No lesser personages than the Lord Chancellor and the Home Secretary then followed the trail of the slaughtered pig and ordered an inquiry into the conduct of the Bench. This had the distinction of being conducted in Aberaeron by Lord Tucker, a Lord of Appeal. I was briefed by the Treasury Solicitor to act as counsel to the tribunal.

Lord Tucker concluded that the decision of the Bench was not due to dishonesty or conscious bias in favour of their Clerk and attributed his acquittal to the advocacy of Mr Jessop. The Aberystwyth College Law Society invited the several lawyers who had taken part in the inquiry to dinner. As Lord Tucker led us in, the students sang with emotion '*Y Mochyn Du*', a traditional Welsh lament about an old black pig that died.

One of the several 'characters' on the circuit was the tubby, ebullient, immensely eloquent junior counsel, Jenkin Jones of Swansea. His audacity was unbounded. At one Assize at Carmarthen, Jenkin found himself constantly interrupted by Mr Justice Hallett. Jenkin could stand it no longer. He turned his back on the judge and addressing himself to the ranks of the public at the back of the court he declared with emphasis: 'There is too much talking in this court.'

He appeared before me once for the defence of an alleged burglar when I was Recorder of Swansea. A police officer gave evidence that he had seen the accused through a shop window trying to force open the shop till. He said he was able to see and identify him clearly with the aid of his torch. Jenkin's first question to the police officer in cross-examination was: 'Have you brought your torch with you?' The witness answered no. 'What? Not brought the torch with you – the most important evidence in this case?' There followed a series of questions about the torch: its make, its age, the size and illuminating capacity of its beam, what experiments as to its effectiveness through the shop window had been made, etc. The poor witness – the principal witness against the accused – was unable to answer any of the questions. However, there was a good deal of other evidence as well. Jenkin brushed this aside as trivial. He never let go of the torch and his closing speech to the jury dealt with very little else. He called the non-availability of the torch 'the Achilles heel of the prosecution case'. The tactic worked. The accused was acquitted. When Jenkin went back to the barristers' robing room after his brilliant and unexpected victory he was cheered.

Many tales are told about Welsh juries. It used to be said of them that they were against crime but they were not dogmatic about it. My experience of them was that they took their duties seriously and responsibly. However, sometimes the English language presented difficulties in some of the remoter Welsh-speaking places. The genial Mr Justice Stable was about to begin a jury trial in mid-Wales one morning when a juror put up his hand and said, 'I would like to be excused from being on the jury today.' The judge asked him what was the trouble. He replied, 'My wife is going to conceive this morning.' The Judge said sympathetically: 'It may be that what you are seeking to tell me is that your wife is going to be confined this morning. But whether you are right or I am right, it would seem to be an occasion at which you should personally be present.' The juror was allowed to go home.

I appeared before Mr Justice Stable once for a sheep farmer who had a bitter dispute with his neighbour about the respective boundaries of their pasturage (their *cynefin* as it is in Welsh) on Cader Idris. The pasturage boundaries were not always clearly defined but it was said that the sheep knew them and how to keep within them. The judge asked an old farmer I called how this came about. 'Well,' he said, 'in the spring when we do bring the lambs up to the mountain from the valley we spread a lot of sugar in the centre of the *cynefin* and ever after the lambs take care not to stray too far from it.'

'You are pulling my leg, aren't you?' the judge asked.

'Just a bit, my Lord,' admitted the witness.

In 1948 I renewed my links with Africa. I was briefed by Barnett Janner to conduct a criminal appeal on behalf of a Czech company director in Ethiopia. I flew out in a Sunderland flying boat from the sparkling waters of the Solent to a spectacular landing on the River Nile in Cairo. I had time to see the pyramids and the Great Sphinx.

The next day I left the desert airfield outside Cairo for Addis Ababa in a scarlet dawn. We flew for hours over the turquoise waters of the Red Sea and the burnt wastes of the Arabian Desert and soared above the jagged wall of mountains that separate Eritrea province and Ethiopia from the desert.

Semitic, Hellenic and early Christian civilizations each in turn had prevailed over Ethiopia. The character of this ancient African kingdom, whose Emperor Haile Selassie proudly claimed direct descent from the union of Solomon and Sheba, had changed little from those ancient times until in 1935 Mussolini imposed modern civilization in the shape of bombers, tanks and mustard gas on this land of Coptic Christians. Mussolini's fascists killed the country's educated class: its natural administrators and technicians, civil servants, engineers, teachers, lawyers. As a result the Emperor was obliged to rely heavily on Armenians, Canadians, Swedes and the British who, aided by the Allies and Ethiopian partisans, had liberated the country in 1942.

The Attorney General of Ethiopia was a friendly Swedish lawyer, Baron Leijonhufvud, who took me for a drive to the lovely Lake Bishoftu, about sixty miles from Addis in glorious mountain country. Oleanders, sycamore and tall eucalyptus trees abounded. In the lake where we swam were all kinds of wild fowl: leisurely pelicans, small white herons, snake-necked black cormorants, wild duck. On the banks were flashing green lizards. And on the way to the lake we saw scattered 'tukuls' – the single-roomed circular wattle and daub huts where whole families lived.

When I reached Addis Ababa Prison to confer with my client, a Coptic priest in black beard and long black robe arrived at the prison gates. When later I asked the Governor of the prison whether the presence of the priest had any special significance, he replied: 'Yes, we were carrying out a death sentence today.' I asked him how it was done. He said it was by electric chair, a gift of UNRRA, the United Nations Relief and Rehabilitation Agency: surely one of the most grisly forms of rehabilitation in history.

The President of the High Court of Ethiopia was an English lawyer, Mr Justice Abbott. I met him again years later when he had become Speaker of the Bermuda Parliament. My case was an appeal from a judgment of his to the European Imperial Court, presided over by the Afa Negus, 'the mouth of the King', sitting with another Ethiopian judge and a young judge from Sweden.

To reach the Supreme Court I was driven past the palace of the Emperor, 'the conquering lion of the Tribe of Judah', as the proclamation of the penal code described him. Appropriately lions were roaring in a cage at the palace gates. The approach to the law courts was by a rocky lane between juniper trees. Patient litigants, robed in spotless white, were waiting by their tethered donkeys for their turn to enter the courts. The Ethiopian litigant had to learn to wait: some cases were bequeathed from father to son. Outside the court buildings scribes were seated at wicker tables writing out letters and applications for illiterate litigants. They were frowned upon by the judges and lawyers, but many litigants still used them – they were cheaper than lawyers.

The courtroom I entered was animated and crowded. Litigation was apparently the natural pastime of Ethiopia. As soon as I arrived, I was offered a number of briefs (which I refused) payable in the handsome coinage of the country: silver Maria Theresa thalers, much preferred by the Ethiopians to the paper dollars printed in the USA.

The Ethiopian Penal Code under which the fraud proceedings in my case were brought had been codified in 1930. It was founded on custom and tradition, and was derived from Mosaic law and an ancient code called the Fetha Negast. The code preface said modestly: 'It is necessary to establish a law for our people as a result of their treading the path leading to civilization.' Much of the code was based on the Gospel. Its central core, set out in the preface, stated: 'Our Lord has said in the Gospel that he who knows much shall be punished much but he who knows little shall be punished little.' There followed an elaborate assessment of degrees of culpability and of mitigation.

Thus the poor man who was unable to know the law 'by reason of his poverty and different mode of living' had four-tenths of his sentence remitted, the 'stranger from a foreign country' had five-tenths remission, those aged from nine to twelve years nine-tenths, the woman 'who had not learned the law and does not go out to the Courts' six-tenths remission. Ethiopian women were in fact the most emancipated in Africa. Unlike the Moslem wife, who in law was but a chattel, the Ethiopian wife had had legal status as part owner of the household for a long time.

After Ethiopia's liberation in 1942 the judicial system was remodelled by the introduction of English procedure into the higher courts. I made a minor innovation myself. During the hearing of the appeal, my Ethiopian junior, angered by an intervention by Counsel for the Prosecution, jumped up, referred to him by his surname and in effect called him a liar. I told him when he sat down that in England it was the custom of counsel to refer to each other in court – even their opponents – as 'my learned friend'. He responded indignantly: 'Are you saying that I should call that man my learned friend?' 'That is exactly what I am saying,' I answered. He reluctantly accepted my guidance and I gather that Ethiopian lawyers have been 'learned friends' to each other ever since.

Our proceedings were well interpreted and conducted. I found that fraud as defined in their penal code had the same essential element of dishonest intent as it has in our law. When in due course the Court announced its decision, our appeal was allowed and the prisoner was set free. By way of celebration my learned junior invited me to lunch in his home. In his garden I saw an apple tree and a lemon tree both in blossom and bearing fruit as well. They gave two crops a year. We enjoyed a long lunch of many courses of meat cooked in various ways. After lunch my host's six children were brought in one by one, all smiling, the eldest dressed, the youngest naked. The Ethiopians were dignified and courteous, bearing no malice even to the large numbers of Italians still living in their midst.

To Polly's delight I brought back from Ethiopia a treasure of popular art which has adorned our home ever since. It is a coarse rectangular canvas picture six feet by three, divided into forty-four squares, painted in four basic colours illustrating the traditional Ethiopian version of the legend of Solomon and Sheba, ending in the crowning of the Emperor Menelik.

A series of domestic public inquiries in which I appeared after the Ethiopian visit and which gave me a close insight into the organization and work of our police forces, arose from the Police Act 1946 in which Parliament enacted that in the interests of efficiency it was desirable to put an end to the existence of small police units. The inquiries related to a number of Home Office proposals to amalgamate police forces, and were approved on the grounds that serious crime was on the increase, that criminals were becoming increasingly mobile and travelled over large areas and that, subject to some maximum size of force, co-operation between separate forces could not be as effective as unified control.

The civil cases in which I appeared on the Wales and Chester Circuit involved all aspects of life: divorce; will disputes (always bitterly contested); accidents on the road; accidents at work, in factories and on farms. One tragic case was of a boy who had just left school and was paralysed when his father's bull, which he was leading, turned on him and gored him. His father's insurers had to pay the substantial damages that were agreed. I learned later that the boy made good progress thanks to the skills of the doctors and nurses at Stoke Mandeville Hospital.

I represented many trade unions in cases brought by their members arising from industrial accidents: engineers (AEWU), electricians (ETU), transport workers (T&GWU), firebrigaders (FBU), steelworkers (ISTF), and coal miners (SWMF). Coal mining cases were particularly worrying and often strongly contested in South Wales by the National Coal Board.

There were many mining accidents in those early days before industrial safety had become a priority. I remember the anxiety I felt in advising a widow, whose husband had been killed by a fall of roof at the coal face, whether to accept an offer by the Coal Board of compensation much less than she could receive if she won; if she lost her case she would get nothing. Happily she won. Sometimes the cases turned on small but disputed questions of fact, for example, whether enough pit props had been erected at the coal face and not too far from it. The need for a system of liability without fault was evident in these cases.

The gravest of the NUM cases, in which I appeared with Alun Davies instructed by Cyril Mosley, arose from a disastrous explosion which occurred on the 22 November 1956, at the Lewis Merthyr Colliery, Trehafod, 328 yards below the surface. Fire damp (methane gas) in a thirty-feet high cavity ignited; the cavity, the roof and sides of which had not been secured, had become a reservoir in which gas collected and from which falling material could gain enough momentum to produce a spark, cause an explosion and generate the deadly flames.

Nine men lost their lives in this disaster. Two were killed outright. Seven others, who were caught in the flames, died of shock and toxaemia. Several of the survivors were seriously burned. The evidence of the bravery and suffering of the men involved in the tragedy – the colliery manager, the overmen and the colliers – moved everyone deeply. There was a tense hush in the courtroom when I opened the case.

The National Coal Board denied liability for the disaster. The trial of the action lasted several days until two mines inspectors gave evidence that the method adopted by the NCB in filling the roof cavity was 'totally unacceptable'. At that point the trial judge, Mr Justice Arthian Davies, indicated firmly to Counsel for the NCB that to try to persuade him to come to a different conclusion from that arrived at by the mines inspectors as experts, would be 'a formidable task'. He added that the case would go on a long time and that costs were mounting up.

Faced with this clear indication of the judge's views, the NCB, while denying the allegations of negligence and breach of duty against them, consented to pay damages to the victims' widows and the injured survivors.

I particularly enjoyed fighting medical negligence cases, sometimes for patients, sometimes for doctors and hospitals, for like so many Welsh people I had always been interested in medicine. The cases arose out of varying misfortunes such as failure to observe and treat the onset of gangrene in the foot of a footballer injured in a match, and wrong treatment of an eye injury resulting in loss of the eye. In one case I appeared for a dentist whose receptionist, in error, gave his patient, a farmer's wife who had come to have a tooth out, an appointment card of another patient who was to have all her teeth extracted. The farmer's wife found, on recovering from the anaesthetic, that the dentist had taken out all her teeth. It cost his insurers a substantial sum.

It was fascinating to be involved as Counsel in battles between eminent consultants disagreeing with each other completely about diagnosis or appropriate surgical techniques or prognosis. In my early days at the Bar medical reports were not exchanged between the parties and one always had to be ready for the unexpected.

In the 1950s and 1960s massive development plans were being promoted in British cities and towns and huge fortunes were being made. The first time the planners were called to public account arose from the initiative of the Civic Trust in the Piccadilly Circus inquiry.

Piccadilly Circus itself was ripe for development and in 1959 property developer Jack Cotton applied for planning permission to erect a thirteen-storey, 172-foot high building on the Monico site in Piccadilly Circus to be used for shops, offices, restaurants and, above all, illuminated advertisements. A crane for changing electrical signs with an arm extending to ninety-three feet was to be a permanent architectural feature on the roof. The London County Council were in favour of granting the application. The developers, however, made the disastrous error of publishing a drawing of the proposed new development. It was to include five illuminated advertising panels, each 156 feet high, providing no less than 18,000 square feet of advertising space. The illustration of the main front panel displayed a slogan 'SNAP plom for VIGOUR' above a mammoth wine bottle labelled 'PLOM'. Other panels on the front and sides of the building displayed similar illuminated advertisements.

This was widely reproduced in the press and immediately aroused public disquiet and parliamentary concern. Henry Brooke MP, then Minister of Housing and Local Government, recognizing 'that the public, not only in London but throughout the Country and indeed the Commonwealth, had a particularly close interest in the redevelopment of Piccadilly Circus', issued a direction to the LCC to refer the application to him for decision. He appointed C.D. Buchanan, an eminent planning authority, to conduct it.

The Civic Trust decided to act. It resolved that the outcome of the Piccadilly Circus inquiry would be of crucial importance for British town planning and for the future face of British cities, and that it should, therefore, intervene in the inquiry and oppose the granting of planning permission. I was briefed to represent the Civic Trust, who provided me with a powerful advisory team. I was helped as the inquiry proceeded by occasional discreet meetings with Duncan Sandys (the Chairman of the Civic Trust), then Minister of Defence.

The inquiry, which lasted thirteen days in December 1959 and January 1960, aroused immense public and international press interest. I was able to call leading architects, designers, planners, surveyors and critics to give evidence against the proposed development. They all roundly condemned the proposed building. One critic called it 'a ribald monstrosity'. Another described it as 'a greedy, tasteless, lumpy, clumping, squat tower on an amorphous podium'. The proposed advertisement areas in particular were attacked as too large and too high. They could even be seen from the bedrooms in Buckingham Palace.

The objectors complained not only about the unsuitability of the building but that the Monico development was to be an initial instalment of extensive changes proposed for the very heart of London at a time when England was occupying a new and important position in the arts, including architecture. They urged that a master plan for the whole of Piccadilly Circus should be agreed and that any proposed building should conform to the principles set out in the plan.

During the inquiry I cross-examined Captain Higgins, the developers' illuminations consultant. The *Daily Telegraph* reported: 'The exchanges between Elwyn Jones and Captain Higgins were more in keeping with the sparkling gaiety of Piccadilly than the mass of rather tedious technical discussions which occupied most of the second day of the Inquiry.'

My first question in cross-examination was: 'Am I right in gathering that this building is the answer to the illuminant consultant's prayer?'

Captain Higgins: 'Exactly. I have been waiting for it for years.'

I then asked: 'It will be the biggest this country has seen, 156 feet of it? You could have at the top of it the biggest aspidistra in the world?'

Captain Higgins: 'Yes, you could write songs about it.' Next day the press reports were headlined: 'The biggest aspidistra in the world.'

Mr Buchanan, the Inspector, concluded in his Report that the design of the proposed building had not attained the standard which should be expected on the Piccadilly site and that 'the present project and the planning purposes with which it was associated did not make the best of the opportunity which was now unfolding for Piccadilly Circus'. The Minister agreed with the Inspector and refused permission for the proposed development. He stressed the need for a comprehensive plan of the Circus and expressed the hope 'that it may be possible to enable a building to go ahead on this site without further prolonged lapse of time'. It was a hope that, over twenty years later, is still unfulfilled.

There were fiercely fought planning cases on the Circuit too. I appeared for the Cardiff City Council in one planning inquiry in which Tasker Watkins and I successfully resisted an application by Prince Littler to demolish the New Theatre, then the only living theatre in Wales. It became the home of the Welsh National Opera Company.

Another case of which I have happy memories arose from an inquiry into the proposal of the Tenby harbour authorities to increase very substantially the harbour dues they charged on the monks of Caldey Island for bringing their produce – sheep, vegetables, perfume, flowers – to Tenby Harbour, by then so heavily silted that it was almost unusable. The silent order of Cistercian monks on the island, for whom Philip Owen and I appeared, had a representative on the mainland to look after their interests there. He was Brother Thomas, the nicest of men. He was so popular among the people of Tenby that when he died they created Brother Thomas's Garden in his memory.

Shortly after my return from Ethiopia the Home Secretary, Chuter Ede, appointed me Recorder of Merthyr Tydfil. The Recorder had to preside over Quarter Sessions, try indictable offences with a jury and hear appeals from the magistrates. Merthyr Tydfil itself was as law-abiding as any South Wales town and many of the cases I tried came from outside the borough. I felt at home in that warm-hearted, long-suffering little town. It was to come into my life again twenty years later when, as Attorney-General, I opened the Merthyr inquiry into the Aberfan disaster.

13

In Opposition

After Labour's defeat in the 1951 election, I sat on the Opposition benches for thirteen years. The Conservative victory presented Churchill with the challenge of leading his first peace-time administration. He was then aged seventy-seven and had already suffered two strokes. Few of us in the House thought that he could stay long as Prime Minister and as time went by it became clear that his faculties were diminishing. However, he loved Parliament and liked the premiership and managed to hold the reins of office successfully until the 1955 election. Winston then went to sit on the Front Bench below the gangway. For a while Members referred to him during debates but as deafness sadly made him unable to hear the compliments being paid to him it became an embarrassment as he sat silent and uncomprehending. He continued to attend the House until he had a fall in the summer of 1962.

The 1951 to 1955 Parliament was a quiet one. The incoming Tory governments for the most part accepted Labour's post-war settlement based on full employment and the Welfare State. Winston Churchill said in 1953: 'We abhor the fallacy, for such it is, of nationalization for nationalization's sake. But when we have it, as in the coal mines, the railways, air traffic, gas and electricity, we are determined to make a success of it, even though this may somewhat mar the symmetry of party recrimination.' Churchill's discreet approach was to conciliate the trade unions. His choice as Minister of Labour, Walter Monckton, proved to be the most successful holder of that office in the post-war period, and did much to further this. Economic conditions between 1952 and 1955 improved and perversely the Korean War caused a boom in world trade from which our economy benefited.

I was not in the inner counsels of the Labour Party at that time. It was not until 1959 that I was invited to speak on the Opposition Front Bench:

to oppose the Government's Street Offences Bill, not exactly a major piece of legislation. However, even in those days, before the setting up of various select committees of the House to examine closely the work of government departments, the procedures did provide opportunities, at Question Time and in adjournment debates at the end of each day's sitting, for the MP to raise constituency and other matters of concern for which there was ministerial responsibility.

Much of the MP's constituency work is done by letters to, or occasionally interviews with, Ministers. Each local 'surgery' I conducted was followed by letters to Ministers (and to the local council, particularly its housing department) about problems and grievances raised by my constituents. Parliamentary Questions (PQs) are a more public and sometimes more effective form of pressure and protest, allowing difficulties to be raised and expressed on the floor of the House and to receive publicity in the local press – a useful means of bringing MPs' activities to the notice of their constituents.

I raised complaints about such matters as delays in the school building programme, difficulties in setting up health centres, unemployment in the ship-repairing industry, delay in payments of compensation to the hundreds of victims of the recurring floods, and the need for better distribution of coal. On a broader canvas, foreign affairs and colonial policy, at a time when the structure of Britain's overseas possessions was under challenge, was also a fruitful field for PQs.

Some ministers are better than others at the technique of answering questions in the House, which are often a test of their competence and adroitness – and that of their questioners. Usually ministers have the whip hand. In most matters departmental briefs make them better informed than the questioners and often provide them in advance with answers to the likely supplementary questions. They also have the advantage of the last word.

Ministers are sometimes reluctant communicators of departmental information. Gwilym Lloyd George, recounting travelling in Wales with his Permanent Under-Secretary (PUS) when he was at the Home Office, used to tell how they had once got lost in the mists of Snowdonia and asked a countryman, 'Where are we?' 'You are in a motor car,' he replied. The PUS observed: 'That is the perfect answer to a Parliamentary Question – it is true, it is short and it gives away no information that was not previously available.'

A ballot of Members wishing to initiate the half-hour adjournment debate at the end of the Commons day is held and enables the MP to question a minister in greater depth than a PQ. I found this most useful. Additionally, debates on government legislation and motions before the House give the Member the opportunity to speak if he or she can catch the Speaker's eye. More than once I raised the urgent need to review the flood defences of the Thames, an old anxiety. Happily the Thames barrage is at last complete. I took part in many debates on the need for further help for the blitzed towns; of particular concern to my own constituency. I was also very interested in safety in employment, in the light of my experience in trade union cases which revealed the grim consequences of lack of adequate safety precautions in most workplaces in those days.

My political activity in the post-war period was not confined to parliament and the constituency. I maintained my close links with the Polish people through the British–Polish Society. Then for a short time in 1951, at the request of Kingsley Martin, I succeeded him as Chairman of the Union of Democratic Control. Founded by Norman Angell, author of *The Great Illusion* and Nobel Peace Prize winner, it advocated open diplomacy and 'open agreements openly arrived at' instead of secret treaties. The society published vigorous pamphlets by Basil Davidson and others and held some successful public meetings. I especially remember one in 1952 addressed by Pastor Niemöller, the courageous anti-Nazi, and Lord Stansgate, the staunch radical and parliamentarian with whom I became friendly when he was President of the Inter-Parliamentary Union.

Amnesty was another useful body I supported and I was a trustee of its Prisoner of Conscience Fund. It later grew into an international body, intervening wherever prisoners of conscience were imprisoned for their beliefs and opinions. Another society, Justice, developed as the all-party British Section of the International Commission of Jurists. I became a founder member and Treasurer in 1957 and was actively involved in its work until I became Attorney General in 1964. The Society of Labour Lawyers, which I chaired in 1957, contributed greatly to the preparation of Labour's programme of law reform, later implemented during the Lord Chancellorship of Gerald Gardiner.

Of all the parliamentary associations, it was the Inter-Parliamentary Union which gave me the greatest pleasure and satisfaction. I was a member of the Executive Committee of its British branch for many years and between 1953 and 1972 I attended its international conferences in Washington, Vienna, Warsaw, Belgrade, The Hague, Rome and London. It was a meeting-ground of parliamentarians from across the world: Soviet Russian; American; Arab and Israeli; black and white. We had many serious and often frank debates at our conferences, and many valuable friendships were established across the political frontiers. It was not always plain sailing, of course. During the 1953 Conference in Washington the Chairman of the British delegation and I were stopped at the foot of the steps of the Capitol by a determined American woman armed with a sheaf of papers.

'Who are you?' she demanded.

I replied jauntily, 'We are British Members of Parliament.'

'If I had my way,' she shouted, 'I would have you hounded out of Washington.'

'I'm sorry, madam,' I replied mildly, 'but I am not aware that our paths have ever crossed before.'

'Paths crossed before,' she thundered. 'You set fire to this place in 1814!' (In 1814 a British force under Admiral Sir George Cockburn invaded Washington. The Capitol and the White House were burned down on the Admiral's orders.) She was not appeased when I assured her that we had not been personally present. That evening President Eisenhower, who had opened the conference, gave a reception for the delegates in the White House. No alcoholic refreshment was served, which was unique on such occasions, especially in America. I noticed, affixed to the lower part of the brick wall by the fireplace, there was a plaque reading: 'This is all that was left of the White House to which the British set fire in 1814'. The sins of our forefathers were indeed being visited upon us.

The 1955 General Election brought about many changes. Churchill retired, to be succeeded by Anthony Eden. The Report of the Parliamentary Boundaries Commission recommended the merger of my constituency Plaistow with Silvertown. In a selection conference to choose between Dr Comyns, the respected Member for Silvertown, and myself, the support and greater numerical strength of the Plaistow delegation resulted in my being chosen as the candidate for the new seat of West Ham South.

In the new Parliament the Conservative administration was faced with far more difficulties than its predecessor and soon ran into heavy weather. The country's economy suffered a two-year recession. The Commonwealth scene became more explosive. Africa was in a ferment during these years. There were outbreaks of violence in Cyprus and the British Government ordered the deportation of Archbishop Makarios to the Seychelles in March 1956. I questioned the legality of sending him to what I eloquently but mistakenly described as 'a Pacific *oubliette*'. Unhappily, the Seychelles are in the Indian Ocean, as several sailors in the House were quick to point out to me.

Ghana, Cyprus, Kenya, Nigeria, Sierra Leone, Malaysia and some of

Tin-plate workmen at Old Castle Works in about 1900: my father is seated third from the left in the front row of chairs

My family in about 1910: *(left to right)* Idris, me, my mother, Winnie, Gwyn and my father

As a young barrister

Polly

My brother Gwyn

My brother Idris

In Llanelli during the war: (*left to right*) a young evacuee, Polly holding Josephine, Margit and my mother

Daniel, Josephine holding 'Daddy doll' and Louli in the garden at Stansfield

Stansfield painted by Mrs Beebee, who lived there later

With my fellow gunners and our Lewis gun on the roof of Aggie Weston's, Devonport, 1940

Celebrating my election victory in West Ham

Cross-examining Carl Sievers at Nuremberg, with *(left to right)* Maxwell-Fyfe, Hoare Belisha (a visitor) and Griffith-Jones at the table behind

With Josephine in India, 1970

In the countryside near Salisbury, Rhodesia

Press conference in Sydney, 1965: Polly, who had helped me by answering one of a flood of questions, was being rebuked by a cub reporter

During the Rhodesia talks on HMS *Tiger*: me, the Captain, the Prime Minister and the Secretary for Commonwealth Relations

Starting the 'hip, hip, hip, hurrah' at the Queen's Silver Jubilee celebration in Westminster Hall

Harold Wilson's 1974 cabinet: *(back row: left to right)* Fred Mulley, Bob Mellish, Harold Lever, Merlyn Rees, William Ross, Peter Shore, Eric Varley, Roy Mason, John Morris, Fred Peart, Malcolm Sheperd, Reg Prentice, John Silkin; *(seated)* Shirley Williams, Michael Foot, Denis Healey, me, Edward Short, Harold Wilson, James Callaghan, Roy Jenkins, Anthony Crosland, Tony Benn and Barbara Castle

Greeting the Speaker of Congress during the American bicentennial celebrations at the Capitol, Washington

Presentation of Polly's pearly mug and plate to the Lord Mayor of London, Sir Ronald Gardner-Thorpe, at the Mansion House

the West Indian islands were accorded independence. It fell to both Tory and Labour Governments to divest Britain of most of her old colonial empire under the increasing pressures of nationalist movements and to do so on the whole with less bloodshed and more dignity than occurred in the dismantling of the French, the Portuguese and the Belgian empires.

One disastrous reversion to the old colonialism was 'Operation Musketeer', when in 1956 on Guy Fawkes' Day, British and French paratroopers landed at Port Said. It coincided with the advance of Soviet tanks into Hungary and the crushing of the uprising in Budapest, and diverted world attention from that aggression. The Commons reaction to the Suez war (or 'armed conflict' as Anthony Eden preferred to describe it) was stormy. Exchanges across the Floor became so heated and disorderly that the Speaker suspended the sitting of the House until we cooled down.

I was involved in one angry incident. When Rab Butler, though personally less than enthusiastic about the Suez action, was trying to defend it in the House (Eden being sick and Selwyn Lloyd in New York) Ungoed-Thomas, the former Labour Solicitor-General, and I questioned its legality. (I learned later that neither of the Law Officers – the Attorney General and the Solicitor-General – at the time had been consulted about it.) Rab remarked icily: 'I do not know why honourable and learned gentlemen opposite should desire always to denigrate the actions of their own country.' I protested. Rab said he did not impugn any wrong motives to me. Ungoed-Thomas persisted in the questioning. The furious debate continued. My daughter Josephine (then a schoolgirl) was sitting in the Gallery that night and I caught a sudden sight of her anxious face during these exchanges in which I was involved. (My personal relations with Rab Butler mended. Years later he asked me to succeed him as President of the Mental Health Foundation, whose work we both admired.)

The Suez action, intended to reclaim the Suez Canal, recently nationalized by Nasser, resulted in nothing but misfortune for Britain. The canal was made unusable. Polly, travelling to China in a British cargo ship through the canal four years later, found it entirely controlled and directed by Russian engineers: a result Anthony Eden had certainly not foreseen. World opinion and the United States Government in particular condemned the secret military conspiracy in which we had taken part. The Tory Government's willingness and ability to mount secretly the military, naval and air force actions behind the back of Parliament and without informing it was a startling revelation of governmental power and parliamentary ineffectiveness.

A serious casualty of the Suez adventure was Eden himself. The decline in his morale and his health which must have clouded his judgement was plainly visible to us as the crisis developed. He had begun his premiership so promisingly, sustained by the public admiration he had enjoyed ever since he resigned as Foreign Secretary in protest at Chamberlain's appeasement of Hitler.

He was succeeded as Prime Minister by Harold Macmillan, a skilful if theatrical performer at the dispatch box, who both impressed and infuriated the Opposition Benches. While he was succeeding in healing the wounds in the Tory Party (earning the nickname of 'Super Mac') the Labour Party continued to suffer dissensions and clashes between right and left in the party. The 1959 election resulted in Labour's third successive defeat and gave the Conservatives a majority of 107. My constituency remained loyal to Labour. I secured 28,017 votes against 5,188 for the Tory candidate and 4,020 for the Liberal.

An important issue in which I was concerned arose in 1959 when we debated the European Human Rights Convention, which had come into force six years earlier. Although I did not believe that the Convention should be incorporated into our law, I urged recognition of the right of the individual British subject to petition the European Commission and Court of Human Rights if his or her rights under the Convention were being infringed. The charter of the United Nations had already affirmed 'faith in fundamental human rights, in the dignity and worth of the human person, in the equal rights of men and women of all nations, large and small'. Similar ideas had been expressed in the North Atlantic Treaty of 1949. In turn the statute of the Council of Europe required that every member 'must accept the principles of the rule of law and the enjoyment by all persons within its jurisdiction of human rights and fundamental freedoms'. As a result of these and other developments in international law the individual acquired everywhere a new status whether, as I said in the debate in the House on 25 June 1959, she or he was travelling on the Clapham omnibus or a detainee in Nyasaland, a prisoner in the Hola Camp in Kenya, or a political prisoner in Spain or in Hungary. The Tory Government, however, refused to recognize the right of individual petition. Already by July 1955 six European states, including the Federal Republic of Germany, had accepted it. (It was not until 1966 that the right was conceded – by the Labour Government.) We reverted to the human rights issue in December 1959 in a debate on a motion that the House 'declares its strong disapproval of racial intolerance and discrimination'.

The issue arose again in 1961 when the Sharpeville killings in South Africa, which had taken place a year before, and the subsequent inquiry, which I attended, came up for discussion. Among the victims of the South African police were five British protected persons who were killed and seventeen injured. I raised the fact that no compensation had been paid to the victims or their families.

Massacres in Angola were discussed in July 1961. While I condemned atrocities that had taken place in Angola I pointed out, in the light of my visit there, that in a community suffering political oppression, people of spirit and courage with no lawful opportunity for lawful protest would fight and they would fight with arms if necessary, to assert their rights.

Rhodesia (now Zimbabwe) was debated in November of the same year when the Southern Rhodesia Bill was introduced. This made Southern Rhodesia more than a colony but something less than an independent sovereign state, with the result that the British Government became answerable internationally for what went on there. It was a problem which was to preoccupy me for twenty years.

I had taken part as Vice-President in the work of the International Voluntary Service in the 1950s and 1960s. In a debate on aid for under-developed countries I urged the Government to do more to support its excellent work in disaster areas and in the ever-growing number of refugee camps. It was a splendid opportunity for our young people to work with, learn the problems of and make friends with their contemporaries in the poor parts of the industrialized nations and in the Third World. My own son Dan worked with IVS in West Africa, Morocco, Calabria and the slums of Pittsburg during school vacations.

The year 1963 saw the merger of West Ham and East Ham into the one borough of Newham. My agent and friend Terry Macmillan, a most able and genial West Hammer, became the first Mayor of Newham. He and his devoted wife Elsie did much to make the shotgun marriage of the two boroughs a success. I relied greatly on Terry's judgement of local affairs and the priority he gave to the needs of the young in education, in sport (he was so pleased when Terry Macmillan Stadium was named after him) and in hospital services. Alas, he died all too soon.

Home Office affairs occupied much of the House's time during this period. Concern about British treatment of aliens increased owing to the number of cases which came up, and in particular the Soblen case, in which I appeared. The etiquette of the Bar prevents an MP barrister from discussing in Parliament matters arising in a case in which he or she has appeared professionally. However, in the debate on the Expiring Laws Continuance Bill in November 1963 I urged the need for a Royal Commission to carry out a fundamental reappraisal of our alien law, to review its administration and make provision for judicial review of decisions of immigration officers and of the Home Secretary.

The Campaign for Nuclear Disarmament grew into a powerful movement in the 1960s, particularly among the young. Dan and Louli both took an active part in the Aldermaston marches, Louli when she was at St Martin's School of Art and Dan when he was at Leighton Park, the Quaker School (its headmaster, Mr Ounstead, also marched), and later at the Imperial College of Science. So did Polly, who marched with the Quakers.

I only spoke once at a Labour Party conference. In 1962 three members of the party – Canon Collins (then Chairman of CND), Lady Barbara Wootton and Bertrand Russell – sponsored a World Congress for General Disarmament, organized by the World Peace Council. This was a proscribed organization. The party constitution rendered ineligible for membership of the party those who were 'members' of such organizations. In an angry speech George Brown, as Chairman of the Labour Party's organizing committee, proposed an amendment to the constitution which inserted 'or associated with' after the words 'members of'. McCarthyism in America had demonstrated the perils to democracy of the concept of 'guilt by association'. I opposed the amendment as illiberal, vague and uncertain. After Charles Pannell had made a long and maladroit speech in support of the amendment to the accompaniment of a slow handclap from Conference, Stan Newens MP moved 'Next Business'. This was carried by a large majority. It terminated the debate and killed the amendment.

These years saw major changes in the political scene. Aneurin Bevan died in July 1960. Hugh Gaitskell, the leader of the Parliamentary Labour Party, only survived him by three years.

Nye was the finest debater in the House. Even his slight stammer when he was emotionally moved seemed to add to his oratorical power. His passionate conviction that democratic socialism alone could save England and the world sustained him throughout his turbulent career in the House of Commons. There he was a determined champion of Parliament as an institution and as the means by which democratic socialism could be achieved. The Health Service will remain his finest and lasting achievement.

14
Murder on Trial

In 1952 I appeared in several cases before Mr Justice Pearson (later a Lord of Appeal in Ordinary). At the end of the Assize in Chester he told me that it was high time I applied for Silk. A silk gown is the robe of a QC (a Queen's Counsel). In those days a QC could not appear in the courts without a junior, who would be entitled to a fee equivalent to two-thirds of his leader's fee. It would therefore become more expensive to brief me as a QC than on my own as a junior: taking Silk is something of a gamble for all applicants. A Silk has to be very good to succeed. It was a sad warning to see one or two briefless elderly Silks on my old circuit who should never have taken the plunge.

One of my colleagues on the circuit approaching the Silk stage himself told me I would be ill advised to take Silk. Others were more encouraging. Polly, of course, declared she would back me fully if I decided to apply. My old solicitor friend Gordon Lawrence urged me to do so. I duly applied and was junior Silk among seventeen Silks that Lord Chancellor Simmonds appointed that year. They included Quintin Hogg, John Megaw, Eustace Roskill, Fenton Atkinson and others who later distinguished themselves on the Bench.

When Judge George Clark Williams the highly respected, retired county court judge who came from my home town Llanelli and who had always encouraged me, learned of my appointment as Silk he asked me to tea in his home in Swansea and invited me to try on his full-bottomed wig. It fitted me excellently. So did his Silk's frock coat and waistcoat. He then presented them to me. His gift brought me good fortune. In due course I wore his wig on the Woolsack (the large rectangular seat upholstered in wool on which the Lord Chancellor sits in the House of Lords, a symbol of the wool trade in the Middle Ages) – which I think would have given George Clark much pleasure to see.

Shortly after I took Silk the leading QCs on the circuit, Arthian Davies, Glyn Jones, Edmund Davies, and Vincent Lloyd-Jones – all outstanding lawyers with large practices – were made High Court judges. This released a mass of work for new Silks.

In 1953 I was appointed Recorder of Swansea – a busier Quarter Sessions court than Merthyr Tydfil, which I left with regret, for everyone there had been kind to me. I enjoyed the work of the Bench and my two years as a Judge Advocate during the last years of the war had already given me useful judicial experience. I sat at Swansea until 1959, when I was appointed Recorder of Cardiff, the senior recordership of the Circuit. Those years when I was on the Bench at Quarter Sessions were happy, hard-working and fulfilling.

When I practised on the Wales and Chester Circuit it used to be said that Wales always had the best murders. At a Law Society dinner in Swansea I was once introduced by the Chairman announcing, as if conferring an accolade upon me, that 'Elwyn Jones and I defended the last man to hang in Swansea Prison.' In fact murder was less prevalent in the principality than in most other parts of the United Kingdom, but we seem to have had more than our share of dramatic murder cases.

In the days when murder carried the death penalty, trials always attracted large numbers of morbid sensation-seekers as well as the merely curious. They would queue for admission to the court as for a play in a theatre, which in a sense every such trial was. A trial for life introduced a new dimension of drama and emotion, of anger and sometimes of pity. This charged the atmosphere of the court in most of the death penalty cases in which I appeared. I remember it prevailing particularly in the 1954 trial of Michael Dennis McCarthy at the Shire Hall, Carmarthen, at which I appeared with Alun Davies for the defence. McCarthy's trial followed immediately after that of Harris, who was convicted of murdering his aunt and uncle and burying them in a field of kale. The whole community where the victims lived had joined the police in the search for their bodies.

McCarthy's defence to the murder charge was that he was drunk and that, on his way home from a pub, the man he was accused of murdering came up to him, assaulted him sexually and invited him to commit a homosexual offence. McCarthy said he was so provoked by this and so much under the influence of drink that he lost his self-control, knocked the man down and bumped his head on the stony road, fracturing his skull in several places. The defence submitted that in those circumstances the proper verdict was manslaughter, not murder.

When the jury returned to deliver their verdict after Mr Justice Havers had summed up the case, the foreman of the jury was instructed by the Clerk of Assize: 'Look upon the face of the Prisoner and say whether he is guilty or not guilty of murder.' The foreman stretched out his arm dramatically and, pointing at the accused, said: 'The decision of the jury is that he is guilty of *murder*.'

There followed the grim procedure of passing the death sentence. The learned judge placed the black cap on his head over his wig and the judge's clerk proclaimed: 'My Lords, the Queen's Justices do strictly charge and command all persons to keep silence while sentence of death is passed upon the Prisoner at the bar.' The judge then declared to the prisoner:

> The Jury have found you guilty of murder. It was a cruel murder and the violence which you used to this man was terrible, causing dreadful injuries which resulted in his death. The sentence of the Court is that you be taken from this place to a lawful prison and thence to a place of execution and there suffer death by hanging and that your body be buried in the precincts of the prison in which you have last been confined before your execution. And may the Lord have mercy on your soul.

Then the chaplain standing at the judge's side said, 'Amen.'

Whenever I heard this grim ritual performed I felt that the death penalty was as degrading to those who had to pronounce it as it was to those who had to carry it out and that the procedure for passing it was a kind of blasphemy.

McCarthy appealed to the Court of Appeal against his conviction. The appeal was dismissed. Lord Chief Justice Goddard in his judgment said: 'Apart from a man being in such a complete and absolute state of intoxication as to make him incapable of forming the intent charged, drunkenness which may lead a man to attack another in a manner which no reasonable sober man would do, cannot be pleaded as an excuse reducing the crime to manslaughter if death results.' McCarthy did not hang, however: the sentence of death was commuted to life imprisonment.

In 1954 I defended in another Welsh rural murder case, which came to be known as 'the murder without a body'. The accused, Onufreczik, was a former Sergeant-Major in the Polish Army who, along with his Polish partner Sykut, settled in a small lonely farm in the heart of Carmarthenshire after the war. Sykut suddenly disappeared and his body was never found. All sorts of wild stories circulated in the county about the man's disappearance. One was that the accused had fed him to the pigs on the farm. In fact there were no pigs on the farm.

The accused's evidence was that at 7.30 one night three Poles arrived at the remote farm in a large dark car. One of them had a revolver. They forced Sykut into the car at gunpoint and drove him away. Onufreczik never saw Sykut again. One of the Poles, he claimed, was named Jablonski. We searched for him in vain. There was no evidence as to how Sykut met his death.

The case for the prosecution, put with devastating effect by Edmund Davies in his cross-examination of the accused, was that Sykut had given Onufreczik notice terminating their partnership, that he had not the means to purchase Sykut's half share and that this was the motive for killing him. Having killed Sykut, the accused had to embark on a trail of falsehoods to explain his disappearance and to conceal the fact of his death.

Added to the circumstantial evidence, said the prosecution, was the fact that on the wall around the kitchen fireplace a number of minute human blood spots were found and in one of these was a fragment of bone. Onufreczik's explanation of this was that Sykut had cut his hand in the field on one of the tractors and that on coming inside he must have shaken his hand at the fireplace and splattered some blood on to the wall.

Mr Justice Oliver's powerful summing-up could have left no doubt in the minds of the jury that the judge believed the murder charge was fully proved. The jury returned a verdict of guilty and Onufreczik was sentenced to death.

He appealed to the Court of Appeal. Lord Chief Justice Goddard in dismissing the appeal said: 'It would be going a long way, especially in these days when we know what can be done with acid [the Haig murder case had been tried some years before], to say that there cannot be a conviction without some proof of a body.' He added that, 'When the circumstantial evidence in a case is so powerful that a reasonable jury could properly accept it as proof of the killing of the victim and when the evidence points beyond reasonable doubt to the guilt of the accused he can be properly convicted of murder.'

However, Onufreczik did not hang. The Home Secretary, Gwilym Lloyd George, commuted the death sentence to life imprisonment. He was afraid, he told me, that if Onufreczik had been hanged and someone beyond the Iron Curtain was put forward on the radio claiming to be Sykut there could have been trouble. Onufreczik served many years' imprisonment and was eventually released on parole. He did not die of natural causes, however, but as a result of a road accident in Bradford in 1967.

The Assize Court in the little town of Ruthin, the heart of some of the loveliest country in Wales, was the scene of several murder trials. In one I was led by Vincent Lloyd-Jones QC for the Crown. The accused was a young soldier who was convicted of murdering a farmer's wife by stabbing her. It was a chance killing; he had never met her before. One day at the trial a young girl was sitting just below the dock watching the proceedings. Suddenly the accused sprang up and managed to get his hands round the girl's neck. There was a fearful struggle before the two warders in the dock succeeded in releasing his grip on her throat. He escaped the death penalty because of his youth.

In the Ruthin murder trial which was described in the British press as the 'mummy in the cupboard' case, I was led by Sir Jocelyn Simon QC, MP, then Solicitor-General, for the prosecution. The accused woman, Mrs Harvey, owned a guest-house in Rhyl. When she went into hospital her daughter and son-in-law decided to spring clean the house for her. In the stair cupboard they found the mummified body of a woman. The police were called in and established that the woman had been a paying guest at the house and was the estranged wife of an Eastbourne solicitor. They had been separated for about twenty years. During that time, through the Magistrates' Court in Rhyl, he had been paying her a weekly separation allowance of thirty shillings, all of which had been 'collected' by the accused over these twenty years. (I was told after the trial that when the accused went to get the money she was asked from time to time 'How is the old lady?' Her invariable answer was 'Oh, she's keeping very well.')

The pathologist who performed the post mortem on the deceased found a slight groove round her neck with the trace of a lisle stocking in it. The prosecution case was that the stocking was a ligature and that the accused, having procured from the deceased an authority to draw her weekly allowance, strangled her and hid her body in the cupboard. By the use of strong-smelling disinfectants, she had contrived to conceal its presence from the other guests in the house.

The defence was that the deceased had died of natural causes and that finding her dead, the landlady decided to hide the body in the cupboard in order to avoid distressing the other guests with the knowledge of her death. Drawing and keeping the weekly allowance was merely part of the concealment of the fact of the deceased's death from her guests and the deceased's husband.

Although the mummified body had been quite well preserved the critical portions of the neck and throat had so deteriorated that when the pathologist called for the Crown gave evidence the difficulty in proving the alleged strangulation became more and more apparent. Eminent pathologists and medical specialists who had examined the body on behalf of the defence – Lord Cohen of Birkenhead among them – were of the opinion that the deceased had been suffering from multiple sclerosis when she died and that she could have died of that disease. In these circumstances the Solicitor-General and I came to the conclusion that it would not be safe for the jury to convict the accused should they be of a mind to do so. We so informed the judge. The prosecution was withdrawn with the judge's approval and the accused was acquitted.

She did not emerge unscathed, however: she was convicted by the magistrates and sentenced to a short term of imprisonment for misappropriating the allowances sent by the deceased's husband, who in turn successfully sued for recovery of the money he had paid for her over the years.

The trial at the Swansea Guildhall of Mrs Alice Millicent Roberts of Talsarnau, Merionethshire (which came to be known in the locality as Talarsenic) on a charge of murdering her second husband by arsenical poisoning was the *cause célèbre* of my time on the Circuit.

I was led for the defence by Edmund Davies QC on the instructions of Cledwyn Hughes, MP for Anglesey, a busy solicitor before he became a cabinet minister and Secretary of State for Wales. In those days it was a tradition that the Attorney General always prosecuted in arsenic murder cases. In Mrs Roberts' case that task fell to Sir Lionel Heald QC, a distinguished patent lawyer with little if any experience of criminal trials. That the body of her husband (and that of her dog) were found on exhumation to contain arsenic was not in dispute. The crucial question was whether the arsenic had been administered by Mrs Roberts. She admitted buying the substance from chemists' shops but said that she required it as a weedkiller for her garden, which was being choked 'by a persistent binding creeper hard to eradicate'.

There was no evidence that Mrs Roberts had administered arsenic to her husband; no tell-tale traces of it in anything she was known to have prepared. She strongly denied the charge, shedding tears into her lace handkerchief as she mentioned her husband. Her son by her first husband, Owen Hughes, who stood by her throughout, gave evidence in her support, describing her as 'the dearest mother in the world'.

After a trial which filled the packed court and the press for several days the jury, after three hours' deliberation, returned a verdict of 'not guilty'. There were cheers from the assembled public as Edmund and I left the Court. (Mrs Roberts was Treasurer of the Labour Party in her locality and after her acquittal at Swansea Jim Griffiths, the MP for neighbouring Llanelli, congratulated Cledwyn and me 'on a good Labour win'.)

There remained for decision, however, the inquest into the death of Mrs Roberts' first husband, John Hughes, a blacksmith's striker. When his body was exhumed from the churchyard in Anglesey, it too was found to contain arsenic. I was briefed to appear for Mrs Roberts at the inquest. I had the assistance of the eminent pathologist Dr Francis Camps. He and I drove through the night from London to Holyhead, seeing on our grisly journey a beautiful dawn breaking over the foothills of Snowdonia.

When the inquest began, stampeding women broke through a police cordon in their efforts to see Mrs Roberts. Poisoning cases, particularly arsenic, always stirred up deep emotions. The inquest was conducted with meticulous fairness by the Anglesey Coroner Ditton Jones. Dr Camps gave evidence that the arsenic found in the body of John Hughes could have seeped into his coffin with rainwater from the damp cemetery and that his death was quite consistent with death from natural causes. Dr Roche Lynch, the Home Office expert, disagreed. He expressed the opinion that the amount of arsenic in Hughes's remains could not be accounted for by contamination from external sources after burial and that the administration of arsenic had accelerated his death.

Mrs Roberts admitted to the coroner that she bought a tin of weed-killer. 'I signed the poison register for it. I have nothing to hide.' She denied administering poison to her husband. She declared she had diluted the poison with water and sprayed it on a garden weed which was choking the small trees in the garden. It had a small bell-shaped flower and it wound itself 'like a snake' round other plants. Owen Hughes again stood by his mother. When details of the condition of the exhumed body of his father were given, both mother and son broke down and wept.

The coroner's jury returned an open verdict on John Hughes, adding that arsenical poisoning accelerated his death, though they could not say how it came to be in his body. Mrs Roberts was allowed to go free.

After the inquest Mrs Roberts said, 'Now the ordeal is over.' She was, however, prosecuted for continuing to draw a widow's pension following the death of her first husband and after she had married the second. She was sentenced to a short term of imprisonment by a Magistrates' Court chaired by Lady Megan Lloyd-George.

Just as the inquest was ending, the police handed me a telegram which shocked me greatly from my sister Winnie in Llanelli saying that my brother Gwyn had been killed in a car crash near Milan. He was Unilever's representative in Italy and was living in Milan with his wife

Doris and son Christopher. He had not long returned from representing the company in Brazil. The police thoughtfully waited until I made my final speech and the jury were out before telling me.

While I was working on the Roberts case I read the proceedings in an earlier arsenic murder trial on the Circuit: that of the Kidwelly solicitor, Harold Greenwood, who was charged with the murder of his wife. He was defended by Sir Edward Marshall Hall, the most sought-after criminal Silk of those days. How different was forensic advocacy then before the Bar came to rely more on persuasion than emotional appeal, on argument rather than rhetoric, although in Wales a little *hwyl* is never out of place. Marshall Hall's final address to the jury ended dramatically with the words of Othello before he strangled his wife Desdemona:

> ... once put out thy light,
> Thou cunning'st pattern of excelling nature,
> I know not where is that Promethean heat
> That can thy light relume ...

He added: 'Are you by your verdict going to put out that light? Gentlemen of the Jury, I demand at your hands the life and liberty of Harold Greenwood.' Greenwood was acquitted. (Marshall Hall's peroration at the trial of Mme Fahmy – who was also acquitted – ended: 'Open the gate and let this woman go back into the light of God's great western sun.')

Those were the days of the death penalty for murder and Marshall Hall based much of his eloquence in murder cases on the fact that juries were reluctant to convict the accused for that reason.

In these days, when juries are better informed and more hard-headed, they might well react to such eloquence by asking themselves, 'Does the way in which Othello murdered his wife help us to decide whether the accused in our case murdered his?' Judges too might well put that to the jury. Indeed some judges deflated counsel's eloquence even in Marshall Hall's time. Mr Justice Shearman, in beginning a summing-up after a concluding speech by Marshall Hall, said: 'I am always pleased when Sir Edward refers to the well-known blind figure of Justice because it means that he has come to the end of his speech.'

15

Political Trials

The law and politics have always been intermingled in my career. Before the war I tried to help, by my advice and presence at their trials, some of the brave men and women who resisted totalitarian oppression on the Continent. After the war, appeals for help, answered by the International Commission of Jurists, Amnesty International and others, came from victims of Stalinist governments in Europe, of apartheid policies in South Africa and of colonial rule – British, Portuguese and Belgian – in different parts of Africa. As a lawyer I could not remain indifferent where fundamental principles of justice were being violated.

I became involved in several international human rights cases, some of which remain vividly in my memory.

In July 1955 I was asked by Sullivan Kaufman, an able and dedicated solicitor, for my help in the case of Dr Ernst Singer, who was serving a twelve-year sentence in Lipotvar Prison in Slovakia. He was a lawyer from Bratislava, head of the Jewish Community there and a noted oriental scholar. He had been arrested in October 1951 along with about sixty-five other leading Jews in an anti-Semitic action by the then Stalinist Czechoslovak Government. Wounded on active service in the First World War, during the Second World War he fell into the hands of the Nazis in Hungary and as a result of torture lost an eye. The other eye was deteriorating and he was in danger of becoming blind. His mother, aged eighty-six, lived alone in Bratislava. Three of her children had been murdered in Nazi concentration camps.

My friend Dr Barnett Stross MP, Chairman of the British–Czechoslovak Society, and others had made representations to the Czech authorities on Dr Singer's behalf, but in vain. It was thought that because of my Nuremberg links with the Czechs I might be able to persuade their

Ministry of Justice to release Dr Singer on compassionate grounds. I approached the Czech Ambassador in London, who was sympathetic and arranged a visa for me to go to Prague.

When I arrived there on 22 September, I was met by Dr Jablonsky, Secretary of the Czechoslovak Union of Lawyers, and through him I had meetings with several other lawyers who were also well disposed. But my attempts over several days to be received at the Ministry of Justice failed.

The day before I had to fly back to London my fortunes changed. I was sitting alone in the forbidding lounge of the Alcron Hotel in Prague when there appeared out of the blue a Belgian parliamentary delegation on their way back home from a visit to Moscow. The delegation included Senator Henri Rolin, with whom I had collaborated after the war on a number of human rights questions. He was a distinguished international lawyer who had pleaded before the International Court of Justice on many occasions and had acted for the Czech Government in various cases. I told Rolin the Dr Singer story and of my inability to get to the Ministry of Justice. He was appalled and immediately telephoned the Ministry to say he wished to see the Minister or his Deputy. This was then arranged for the afternoon. Rolin took me with him without notifying them that I was coming and left me in the ante-room when he was ushered in to see the Vice-Minister, the Minister being away. A few minutes later the Vice-Minister came hurrying out of the room, very nearly embraced me and said how terrible it would have been, after all I had done at Nuremberg, if I had not been received. I then took him over Dr Singer's case with some effect, in Rolin's encouraging presence. The Vice-Minister assured me that the case was being considered with a view to the exercise of clemency and that it would be brought to a favourable conclusion before the end of the year. Dr Singer was in fact released on parole two months later and was able to return to his home on Christmas Eve. I doubt whether this would have happened but for my chance meeting with Rolin.

This was not the end of the story. Two years later I was again asked to help. Dr Singer had in the meantime been allowed to live in one room of the house which had been his before it was expropriated, and to share it with his mother. But he and his mother had been refused permission to leave the country so that they could join other members of Dr Singer's family in London. Once again there was a happy coincidental meeting: in September 1957, when the Inter-Parliamentary Union Conference was held in London, I was a member of the British delegation. There was a Czech delegation of three MPs and the Secretary-General of their National Assembly. When I put Dr Singer's case to them they said they were willing to help, as once again was the Czech Ambassador in London, and I was allowed to accompany them on their flight back to Prague.

At Prague Paul Grey, our Ambassador, undertook that, if the Singers received emigration permits, he would do all he could to ensure that there would be no British visa difficulties. I travelled to Bratislava to meet Dr Singer. I found him to be a man of courage, his spirit unbroken after a trial which was a travesty of justice and by his years in prison. He told me that the first two years in solitary confinement in the Security Police Prison had worried him most as he had no idea about his fate.

Another round of approaches to various Czech ministries followed with the help of my IPU Czech colleagues, culminating in an interview with Dr Blacek, the Deputy Minister of Foreign Affairs. This approach on the parliamentary level through the Foreign Office fortunately proved effective. Dr Singer and his mother were allowed to come to England in August 1958. The family gave a celebratory lunch in London which I had great pleasure in joining.

Dr Sullivan Kaufman also instructed me in a dramatic case with very different political undertones. It arose out of the bitterness which followed the refusal of the British Government, as the Mandate Power, to allow Jewish survivors to enter Palestine and the deportation back to Europe and to Germany itself of Jews who had succeeded in reaching the quayside at Haifa. Four members of Irgun Zvai Leumi were charged with attempting to dynamite a British train in the British zone in Germany. All four were sentenced to death in December 1947. Victor Durand and I, then both juniors at the Bar, were briefed to appear for them at their appeal hearing. The conviction of the two prisoners for whom Durand appeared was quashed for lack of evidence. The two prisoners I represented had pleaded guilty to attempting to blow up the train and my speech was in mitigation of their crime. The outcome was that the death penalty in each case was changed to twenty years' imprisonment.

I understand that the result of the appeals was a great relief to our Foreign Office. The carrying out of the death sentences at that time would have led to serious reprisals. In the event it was the only Irgun terrorist action attempted outside Palestine.

After the hearing of the appeals, Victor Durand and I were taken on a long drive in the night to a displaced persons' (DP) camp in the British zone. It was the first time I heard what was to become the Israeli National Anthem – the 'Atikva' – emotionally sung on this occasion in a crowded camp of uprooted people torn from their homes by war and oppression.

The two prisoners I represented were released from prison quietly a few years later after the State of Israel had been created.

On 28 June 1956, 16,000 workers in the Zispo factory in Poznan, Poland, where the International Fair was being held, marched out of the factory to the centre of the city. They carried banners demanding 'bread and freedom'. The rest of the people of Poznan joined them. The march became a riot and public buildings were attacked, the main target being the headquarters of the UB – the Polish Secret Police. Fifty-three people were killed and several hundred wounded. Three months later the trials of those accused of taking part in the riot began. How they were conducted was a critical test for the rule of law in Poland and had important implications for its Communist neighbours.

I was invited by the Polish Association of Jurists to join Alfred Legal, Professor of Penal Law at Montpelier University, and Jules Wolf, Chairman of the Belgian League for the Defence of Human Rights, as observers at the trial. The night before the trial began we travelled to Poznan by car, along the road on which Napoleon had marched to Moscow. About fifteen miles from the city we saw a detachment of Polish soldiers hurrying to join the troops who were ringing the city.

Next morning, to get to the courthouse in the centre of Poznan I had to pass through two lines of blue-uniformed soldiers, some with sub-machine guns at the ready. My pass was checked four times by aggressive security men before I could enter the packed courtroom. There was an air of tension in court when everyone stood up as the young presiding judge, in black and purple robes, entered with two lay assessors, one a mechanic, the other a carpenter. There is no trial by jury in Poland nor, I believe, in any Communist-governed country.

The initial impression of a police state in action did not last long. Indeed, seldom has a criminal trial been more openly conducted. In the small courtroom there were rows of press correspondents – Poles, Russians, Americans, French, Chinese, British – and television reporters and photographers. There were live broadcasts of the proceedings to the Polish public. Zofia Wasilkowska, the Polish Minister of Justice, was present, as were Dr Jerzy Jodlowski, the liberal-minded and able Chairman of the Polish Lawyers' Association, and my old friend Professor Sawicki from the Nuremberg Trial. Three trials were prepared at Poznan. Two began that morning.

One was the only murder trial that was to be launched, even though fifty-three people had been killed. It arose from the lynching of a UB corporal who had been kicked and trampled to death in the June violence. There were three youths in the dock, the oldest a pale and defiant brewery worker of twenty, then a metal turner of eighteen with a trembling chin, the third a young postman. Each defendant was represented by two black-gowned lawyers.

The indictment alleged in one count that the defendants had been incited to violence by 'capitalist radios' and 'imperialist countries' but this was not pursued. In fact the trial became a trial of the secret police on the broad allegation of terrorizing the people. The Polish authorities had already conceded that the grievances which led to the riots – high prices, desperate living conditions, low wages – were valid. Indeed, prosecuting counsel, Alfons Leman, said that 'the problem revealed by the grievances of the Poznan workers needed to be seen to and the first step towards improving wages and living conditions has already been taken.' The Polish authorities, emboldened by Khrushchev's denunciation of Stalinist misrule at the 20th Congress of the Soviet Communist Party earlier that year, did not seem reluctant to allow the hated secret police to be brought before the bar of public opinion. Julian Wojciak, a Communist defence lawyer, said in court that 'the crowd concentrated all their hatred on the secret police and on its building. The UB was for them symbolic of the crimes of the Stalin period.'

On the very first day of the trial the prosecuting counsel electrified the court by admitting that the police had beaten up the defendants after their arrest. There was a murmur of approval in the court when he added that four policemen would be tried for the assault and that several police officers (including the Poznan Commander) had been dismissed. The following day the judge underlined the court's disapproval of the police conduct by excluding all evidence taken in the pre-trial proceedings against two of the defendants who said they had been beaten.

The prosecution was conducted with moderation and fairness. One defending counsel told me that the way the lawyers had done their work at the trial would do much to improve the reputation of the Polish Bar, adding, 'We should be the spokesmen of justice.' Defending counsel were given a free rein in their pleas for the defendants. 'We want justice for the accused, truth for history,' said one. Another, Hejmowski, pleaded for 'this tormented generation of youth who have known only war, the horror of Nazi occupation and the kind of example our security authorities set them afterwards'.

The Polish press also seemed to have acquired a new confidence and, although censorship continued, vigorous comment got through. It reported a Communist Party meeting in Kielce on 17 September, attended by the Minister of Justice and the Public Prosecutor, at which 'concern was expressed that the former leadership of the Communist Party ordered about the organs of the administration of justice'. The whole crux of the issue of legality in the Communist countries, Soviet Russia no less than Stalinist Poland, was involved in those words.

The three accused were in due course found guilty, but not of murdering the UB corporal as charged, only of assaulting him, and not, as the judgment emphasized, because he was a UB man but because they had thought he had murdered a woman and child. Two of the youths were sentenced to four and a half years in prison and the other to four years. Much harsher sentences had been expected.

In a second trial, nine defendants were charged with stealing arms and firing on the secret police headquarters. In the third trial ten young men were also charged with taking part in the attack on the UB headquarters and of capturing a tank and disarming the police. The defendants in the trials were a cross-section of Poznan youth. Some had a criminal past, others were idealistic young students. Some came from the slums of Poznan, others from middle-class families.

An article which I wrote at the time expressed my reactions to the historic Poznan trial. 'A new wind is blowing through Poland. The people whose cavalry officers charged Nazi tanks on horseback in 1939 and who in 1945 resolved to rebuild a great new capital city on the pulverised wasteland which was all that the Nazis left of Warsaw are now throwing themselves with the same daring into the struggle for democracy and the rule of law.'

In July 1958 I was briefed in an entirely different political context to appear in Belfast for the defence of two young men from Coalisland who were charged with the murder of Police Sergeant Ovens of the Royal Ulster Constabulary. They were alleged to have made a telephone call to the police station which lured Sergeant Ovens to a deadly trap in a disused cottage near Coalisland, where 'a most devilish contrivance', as the trial judge described it, had been set up to kill the Sergeant. It came to be known as the 'Booby-Trap Murder'.

In order to appear as counsel in Northern Ireland I had first to be called to the Bar there. I was given every assistance to do so by Lord Chief Justice MacDermott, the Attorney General Brian Maginess and by the Bar of Northern Ireland. I knew the Lord Chief Justice as a fellow bencher of Gray's Inn and he wrote to say that if I wanted to appear as a Silk he would 'have much pleasure in making the necessary recommendations to his Excellency the Governor of Northern Ireland' and that there should be no difficulty in arranging my call as a junior and as a Silk on the same day. This was done in the Royal Courts of Justice in Belfast where I received rapid promotion in the same morning. I was first admitted as a junior, wearing a junior's gown and bob wig. I then left the court and was readmitted wearing a silk gown and full-bottomed wig, to make the ancient declaration that 'well and truly I will serve the Queen as one of her Counsel learned in the law ... and sue the Queen's process after the Courts of the Law and after my cunning.'

The trial before Lord Justice Black and a jury lasted seven days. The Attorney General led for the prosecution with impeccable fairness. Swearing in the jury took some time, Prosecution and Defence both exercising their power of peremptory challenge of persons about to be sworn. The Crown challenged people with names like O'Flaherty and O'Driscoll when they were called to be sworn. My instructing solicitor challenged the Smiths and the Joneses. It was the Northern Ireland divide in action. Ultimately a jury of twelve men was duly sworn.

On the second day of the trial I received an unsigned typewritten letter headed 'Ulster Loyalist Commando Group (Belfast Headquarters)'. It read:

> Sir, you have undertaken a task, your handling of which we intend to follow with careful attention. You came here as an utter stranger to the prevailing situation. ... There is a very thin thread of tolerance left and you could be the man to cause it to break. We therefore advise you to be very careful in your handling of this dynamic case. We are not threatening you in any way but ask you just to be careful ...

The police investigated the matter but no evidence of the existence of the 'Ulster Loyalist Commando Group' was found. Despite the tension that already prevailed in Belfast, I suffered no personal hostility during the trial either in court or out of it. On the contrary, I was treated with the utmost courtesy.

It was common ground at the trial that the evidence against the two accused, Kevin Mallon and Francis Patrick Talbot, rested almost entirely on statements made by them to the police and the main issue in the trial turned on whether those statements had been given willingly or only after the defendants had been 'grilled'. Lord Justice Black directed the jury that the first thing to be considered in dealing with confessions was whether they were satisfied that these were made voluntarily, without compulsion, threats, duress or violence. If they were not satisfied, they should be given no weight at all and disregarded. He told the jury that 'confessions had been made for all kinds of motives that could not be understood and sometimes for no motive at all'. The judge's summing up leaned more towards acquittal than conviction of the accused.

I was unable to stay for the jury's verdict for, after they retired to consider it, I had to leave Belfast in order to attend Quarter Sessions in Cardiff as Recorder. My instructing solicitor telephoned the result to me. Both accused were acquitted. But it was not the end of the sombre story. Mallon later became an active member of the IRA. He is now serving a sentence of ten years' penal servitude passed upon him in Dublin for aiding and abetting in the attempted murder of Gardai while resisting arrest, having been convicted previously for various IRA offences. While serving a sentence for one of these he escaped by helicopter from Mountjoy Prison, Dublin, along with Seamus Twomey.

Years later it fell to me as Attorney General and Lord Chancellor to be much involved in the administration of justice in Northern Ireland. No one bore a grudge against me for having in the course of professional duty defended Mallon and Talbot.

The overthrow of Portuguese colonial rule in east and west Africa took a long time to accomplish. In west Africa the Angolan struggle was supported by liberal-minded white Portuguese both in Portugal and in the colony. In 1960 many of the activists had been held in custody in Angola for long periods of time on charges of widely defined 'high treason' and 'subversive conduct' and a major trial of fifty-seven men and women was due to take place. The situation in the Belgian Congo was reaching its climax and in South Africa the endless treason trial in Pretoria and the inquiry into the Sharpeville massacre were taking place.

In May 1960, at the request of the International Commission of Jurists (ICJ), I visited all three storm centres. My first port of call was Lisbon, where I met Dr Manuel Joal da Palma Carlos, a lawyer who was to go to Luanda in Angola to defend in the big trial there. He had himself been sentenced to imprisonment in Lisbon under the Salazar dictatorship for his conduct of the defence in a criminal trial. On appeal the prison sentence was commuted to a fine which the Portuguese Bar paid as they felt it was an attack on their independence as a whole.

Dr Carlos was cheerful and courageous, with a high sense of the duty of lawyers to combat injustice. He gave me the Luanda address of two Portuguese lawyers even more imperilled than he was by undertaking the defence in political cases. One was a busy middle-aged practitioner; the other lawyer was defending an architect, one of the seven whites out of the fifty-seven accused in the pending sedition trial. Some had been in prison awaiting trial for over a year. The gist of the charges against them was that they had written and distributed four leaflets calling for an independent Angola. The fact that there were any whites in the dock was a remarkable feature of the case. Previously, the political prisoners had all been Africans. I learned that all the accused had suffered ill-treatment by the Portuguese police in the first days of their detention, particularly by the 'statue' punishment. They had to stand absolutely still for hour after hour while six or seven police interrogators worked on them. The defence lawyers to whom I spoke did not expect any acquittals from the military court which was to try the accused. As one lawyer told me: 'Their function is to condemn, not to judge.'

The British Vice-Consul in Luanda was sympathetic and helpful. He arranged for me to meet Dr Miranda, the Deputy Governor of the Colony, the Governor himself being away at the official opening of the Kariba Dam. I made representations to Dr Miranda about the complaints of ill-treatment of the accused, their long detention in custody without trial and the sufferings of their families, who were receiving no public relief or assistance of any kind. He dismissed this last complaint by saying there were charities which could help them.

The defence lawyers assured me that my visit had been of value not only by demonstrating that they and their clients had not been forgotten but by warning the Portuguese authorities that their treatment of political prisoners was under international scrutiny.

Later I learned that Dr Carlos had been prevented from leaving Lisbon to attend the sedition trial.

From Luanda I flew to Leopoldville, a fine modern city, the capital of the Belgian Congo. Sir Ian Scott, British Ambassador there, met me off the plane and took me, after a quick change, to a sumptuous banquet attended by the Belgian General commanding the colony's armed forces. The General spoke with confidence about the loyalty and ability of his troops, the *force de frappe*, to contain any trouble in the country. However, within a few months Belgian rule had collapsed. Most of the Belgian administrators and professional people – lawyers, doctors, teachers, engineers – had fled. The tragedy was that they had not trained Congolese men and women to succeed them. The Belgians left a political void which was filled by many conflicting tribal loyalties.

The Ambassador's residence where I stayed overlooked the Stanley Falls on the River Congo. A statue of the explorer Stanley in gumboots showed the little Welshman peering over the Falls named after him. There was some excitement the day I arrived. A large python had been discovered in the beautiful tropical garden of the Embassy. The Ambassador was planning a party to mark the Queen's Birthday and a problem arose about finding a suitable band to play at the reception. He asked the conductor of the local Salvation Army band if he could help out. The conductor, who was, if I remember rightly, an insurance representative from Liverpool, said he would be happy to oblige and suggested some hymn tunes, including his favourite 'We are drifting to our doom'. Some months later I had a letter from Sir Ian saying that they were still drifting to their doom but at that moment the crew were busy belabouring one another instead of the passengers.

My first objective in South Africa was to attend the treason trial, which was being held in Pretoria in a deconsecrated synagogue. It was then in its fourth year. Public interest in the proceedings had long since evaporated. There was only one person present in the vast public gallery upstairs. Ex-Chief Luthuli, a defendant, was being cross-examined in the fifth week of his evidence when I arrived. He was ill and could not testify for more than two hours a day. All the defendants were in custody under emergency regulations. During the lunch break I was able to speak a few words to some of them. Their spirit was unbroken.

The trial, initially of ninety-two South Africans – fifty-eight Africans, sixteen Europeans, eighteen Coloureds – had begun in July 1958. Gerald Gardiner and Fred Lawton (later Lord Justice) had each attended as observers earlier in the proceedings. When the trial ended, the indictments against sixty-one defendants were quashed, and another thirty were acquitted.

The Sharpeville inquiry at Vereeniging had reached the last stages of the evidence when I attended it on 23 May. The South African Government had already pronounced its own verdict on the killing by South African police of sixty-seven Africans demonstrating peacefully against the pass laws. Their information service, in flagrant contempt of the Court of Inquiry, issued a statement that 'the disturbances at Sharpeville were the result of a planned demonstration by some 20,000 Bantu in which demonstrators made a deliberate attack on a police station with assorted weapons, including firearms.' Every allegation in that statement was challenged by Sidney Kentridge and other counsel appearing for the victims' families at the inquiry.

While the hearing of the inquiry was proceeding I heard singing and cheering from friends of fifty detainees who had been brought to the adjoining court at Vereeniging in two wire-enclosed lorries for trial. They were on charges of 'public violence' at Sharpeville on the day of the massacre: the very matter the inquiry was investigating. When I later taxed the South African Attorney-General Claasens and Dr Greef of the Ministry of Justice about this apparent pre-empting of the inquiry's conclusions, Claasens said he did not think the cases impinged on the terms of reference of the Sharpeville inquiry. In fact the summonses against the fifty Africans were based in terms of the police version of the Sharpeville incident. Dr Greef did admit that the circumstances might 'give some slight cause for misgiving'.

At the hearing an African witness of the massacre testified that when the police came to arrest him they took away two of his books, *Cry the Beloved Country* by Alan Paton and *Up from Slavery*, Booker T. Washington's famous classic. Alan Paton's prophetic words spoken by Msimangu in *Cry the Beloved Country* came to mind: 'He was grave and silent and then he said sombrely, "I have one great fear in my heart, that one day, when they are turned to loving, they will find we are turned to hating."'

I attended another court during my South African visit: the Native Commissioner's Court at Forbsburg. One barefooted African who was charged with breach of the Pass Laws said from the dock: 'I am a miner. I was discharged on Friday and arrested on Saturday. I am going to another mine.' 'See you get your papers in order,' commanded the magistrate. In an adjoining court another magistrate was also hearing the degrading pass cases.

A black hospital sister I met at Forbsburg told me that two things distressed her most: 'One is the Bantu education system. They are teaching our children just enough to keep them as menial servants. The other is the pass system. It is a torture and a humiliation, made worse by the way it is enforced. A young policeman will stop an elderly African and say: "Kaffir, where is your pass?" He will strike him in the face if he is slow in producing it.'

One bright light in this racialist darkness was the presence in the back of each of these courts of two quiet white women each wearing a black sash. In 1952, when the right to vote was taken away from the Coloured (Indian and mixed race) community, a group of white women mounted a silent protest vigil, each wearing a black sash as a sign of mourning at the death of this civil right. Their public protest at their country's racist laws has continued despite the scorn and anger they had to face. Apart from attending the pass courts in dignified silence, the Black Sash women set up advice centres throughout the country to provide help to any people harassed by the complex race laws.

The Nationalists had come to power in 1948. They regarded an independent judiciary as an unfortunate legacy of nineteenth-century British colonial rule, and there was frequent conflict with the courts during the 1950s. This was intensified by new emergency regulations introduced in 1960 which declared that the courts could not entertain any application arising out of the detention of any individual. Not only was the protection of *habeas corpus* ended but a proclamation stated that no person who had been arrested and was being detained under the emergency regulations would, without the consent of the Minister or person acting under his authority, 'be allowed to consult with a legal adviser in connection with any matter relating to the arrest or detention of such persons'. The grip of a police state was tightening on blacks and whites alike.

The Malawi political leader, Henry Aloysius Chipembere, was the son of a black Anglican clergyman educated in Anglican mission stations on the shores of the beautiful Lake Nyasa, where, as he told me, 'I lived with some very kind and generous European missionaries, some of whom paid my school fees when my father was unable to do so.' He then went to a secondary school in Southern Rhodesia and finally to the University College of Fort Hare in South Africa, where he graduated. There he developed very strong feelings against the injustices in South Africa, the cruelties of apartheid and 'the ruthless suppression of peaceful attempts by Africans to resist unjust laws'. He added, however, that 'practically all the Europeans who were my masters during my fairly long academic career were very kind and helpful to me.'

After a short period in the Nyasaland Civil Service Chipembere became a member of the Legislative Council of Nyasaland on a platform of immediate independence for Nyasaland and secession from the Rhodesian Federation of Southern and Northern Rhodesia and Nyasaland created by the British Government in 1953.

After violent disturbances in February and March 1959, in which forty-eight Africans were killed by gunfire and three by bayonet or baton and seventy-nine were wounded, a state of emergency was declared. Dr Hastings Banda, later to be Prime Minister, was arrested and Chipembere was among the first to be detained.

In July 1959, Lord Devlin led an inquiry into the disturbances and the events leading up to them. It found that opposition to the Federation was deeply rooted and almost universally held, the opponents wanting 'above all self-government for the black people of Nyasaland much as they have seen happening in other parts of Africa'. It concluded that Nyasaland was, 'no doubt only temporarily, a Police State' and that 'unnecessary and therefore illegal force was used in making a number of arrests'.

After Chipembere was arrested, he was locked up first in Gwelo Prison in Southern Rhodesia and then in Kanjedza Prison, without trial, for nineteen months until his release in September 1960. He had become an even more embittered opponent of the regime than he was before.

Nyasaland was not a colony. It had been proclaimed a protectorate by virtue of voluntary treaties entered into by various chiefs with the British Government, on the basis of ward and trustee: not of governor and governed. The imposition of the Federation on Nyasaland, in which, as Chipembere described it, 'the European settlers were the masters and the Africans the servants – the hewers of wood and the drawers of water', left him embittered and betrayed.

These feelings he aired in the powerful and highly emotional speeches he made in November 1960 in Rumpi and Zomba. It was these which became the subject of charges of sedition and incitement to violence and resulted in his being brought to trial in Blantyre.

When I received a copy of the Chipembere indictment in London, some of the extracts from the speeches it purported to contain were so extreme in character that I expected them to be challenged at the trial as an incorrect record of what was actually said. I raised this question with my learned juniors Saeranie and Orton Chirwa as soon as I reached Blantyre. They had a recording of the Rumpi speech taped by a Malawi Party official at the meeting. When this was played to me the words complained of came out loud and clear, particularly the criticized passage, which read: 'Kamuzu [the title given to Dr Banda, the leader of the Malawi Party] has appealed to us for non-violence. Otherwise in my own heart, as I came from Gwelo Prison, I had good mind to ask my friends in Malawi to slaughter a thousand Europeans. But they are lucky, because Kamuzu has said to keep the peace and we are so loyal, he is so mighty, that we can't disobey him.'

At the trial, held in a small courtroom packed with supporters of Chipembere, the police produced a tape recording they too had taken at the Rumpi meeting. For some reason, perhaps because the tape had previously been used for recording the 'St Louis Blues', when it was played in court a steady drum beat accompanied Chipembere's words and the African audience began to beat time with their feet on the wooden boards until the magistrate stopped them. However, the violent words spoken by Chipembere came out clearly.

The defence case was that Chipembere's speeches, considered in their totality and not in isolated extracts, praised Dr Banda as a man of peace and not of violence and encouraged the audience to accept Dr Banda's advice and direction.

Danny Brabin QC, who came out to lead for the prosecution, made a powerful address, quoting Shakespeare to good effect. He said that Chipembere in his speeches had the same intention as Mark Antony in his oration after the assassination of Julius Caesar. After saying to the crowd:

> ... let me not stir you up
> To such a sudden flood of mutiny

he did so and when the crowd had been stirred to violent action declared:

> Now let it work: mischief, thou art afoot;
> Take thou what course thou wilt!

The evidence in the case revealed that while Chipembere's speeches were received by his huge audiences (there were 30,000 at Zomba) with enthusiasm, the crowds did not in fact react violently but dispersed peacefully when the speeches were over.

The outcome of the case was that Chipembere was acquitted of incitement to violence but convicted of sedition. He was sentenced to three years' imprisonment. (The maximum penalty for sedition was five years.) Later he left Africa and I believe settled in the United States.

During my stay in Nyasaland I was able to see something of its superb scenery, its great lake and its mountain cataracts. I was happy to meet many of its friendly people, both African and European. I was received amiably by Dr Hastings Banda, at his residence, and he bore me no ill-will for defending his opponent Chipembere. He spoke nostalgically of his experiences as a young doctor in practice in the East End of London from 1945 to 1953.

In November 1961 Salem Shita and Mukhtara Ducali, two Libyan trade unionists well known in international Labour circles, were charged with inciting workers in public utilities to strike and with 'endangering the safety of the State'. They were leaders of the Libyan General Federation of Trade Unions, a post-war development encouraged by, and a member of, the International Confederation of Free Trade Unions (ICFTU).

Desmond Hirshfield for the ICFTU asked me if I would appear for the accused and, duly instructed by Victor Mishcon, I flew to Tripoli via Tunis, where I met Tunisian trade unionists who also had been trying to help in the Libyan case, which had aroused great interest in the Arab world. It was a very different scene from the French-dominated Tunis I had known when I was there in Army days in 1944, as I soon learned when I was taken to a meeting in a vast and packed cinema addressed by the Tunisian President Bourguiba. He sat regally on a high stage in what looked more like a throne than an armchair. Sustained by ceremonial sips of fruit juices and by intermittent orchestrated choruses from his adherents of 'Bour-Gui-Ba', he harangued the audience in emphatic tones for over two hours.

When I arrived in Tripoli, I called on the Nazir of Justice of Tripolitania. He told me he could not give me permission to appear for the defendants at the trial and that this would require the consent of the Governor of Tripolitania, Fadel Ben Sickri. The British Embassy helpfully arranged for me to meet the Governor, who received me courteously but said I could not have leave to conduct the case in court because a number of 'unacceptable' lawyers from other countries had applied for permission to come to Libya to defend 158 Ba'athists who were on trial there. Their only purpose, he said, was to make propaganda against the Libyan Government and, if I was given permission to appear, they would cite this as a precedent. However, by way of compromise, I was allowed to attend the trial as an observer and to assist an able and courageous young lawyer, Ezzedin Abou Rawi, in the conduct of the defence.

Unhappily the trial was adjourned for several days. This worried me because I had accepted a brief for the defence in a murder trial at Cardiff Assizes, about the date of which I was unsure. I cabled to my clerk, Eric Cooper, in London to let me know the date. The next morning I had an anxious call from our Embassy in Tripoli, aware that cables were being intercepted, asking, 'What on earth is going on? A cable has arrived for you which reads: "Cable received. Murder fixed for Wednesday. Eric."' I explained the circumstances and the Embassy reassured the Libyans. However, security police continued to trail me throughout the visit, even following me when my Libyan friends took me to see the great Phoenician ruins in Leptis Magna.

The trial took place in a courtroom too small to accommodate all the supporters of the defendants. The overflow listened intently in the courtyard outside the open windows. I sat at counsel's table. The trial was well and fairly conducted without dramatics. It ended with the acquittal of the defendants on the fraud charges, largely on the strength of the evidence of the director of the Labour Office himself. The accused were convicted on the incitement charges but subsequently they appealed successfully against that decision. It was a notable victory for free trade unionism in the Arab world, however short-lived it proved to be.

The proceedings in England in the case of Dr Robert Soblen, which became an international *cause célèbre*, began at midnight on 6 July 1962 in Mr Justice Mocatta's dining room in St John's Wood, London. The judge had already left the Law Courts that evening when Dr Sullivan Kaufman instructed me to apply to him for a writ of *habeas corpus* on behalf of Dr Soblen, who was due to be flown to the United States early next morning on a deportation order from the Home Secretary. The famous writ is available to anyone, alien or not, who is detained within our shores. It requires those detaining him or her to show if the detention is justified by law. The application for the writ takes precedence over all other proceedings and can be applied for at any time to a High Court judge. Thus, after urgent phone calls, my instructing solicitor, my learned junior and I were received at the judge's home late that night. The dining room had been cleared and rapidly turned into a court room for the occasion. After a careful hearing – for Mr Justice Mocatta did not exactly rush his decisions – he ruled that a *prima facie* case had been made out and ordered the writ to be issued to the Home Secretary. The Home Office was at once informed and Dr Soblen was kept in Brixton Prison pending the hearing of further proceedings.

Dr Soblen was born in Lithuania and practised medicine there until 1941, when he went to live in the United States. In November 1960 he was convicted of conspiracy to commit espionage on behalf of the Soviet Union in 1944 during the Second World War and sentenced to life imprisonment. He denied the charges. That conviction could not be challenged in the proceedings which arose in the High Court in London. Several American lawyers of standing were of the opinion that the trial of Dr Soblen was a miscarriage of justice and that he had been wrongly convicted.

He made an application in America for a new trial, and at that hearing four witnesses who had worked in the Office of Strategic Services (a branch of American intelligence) gave evidence on his behalf. On hearing that his application was refused he jumped his bail and flew to Tel Aviv. From there the Israeli authorities, anxious not to quarrel with the Americans, forced him on to an El Al plane bound for New York via London, placing him in charge of Chief United States Marshal McShane.

Before the plane landed at Heathrow Dr Soblen inflicted severe injuries on himself with a knife with the object of being grounded in England. A doctor and an ambulance were waiting when the plane landed on 1 July 1962. An immigration officer, who had with him a notice to Dr Soblen of refusal of leave to land, accompanied the doctor on board the plane. The doctor advised that Dr Soblen might die (he was also suffering from leukemia) if he was not taken to hospital at once. The ill man was accompanied to hospital by a police constable. The notice of refusal to land was served on him there two days later.

He was detained as an alien, transferred to the prison hospital and would have been flown to New York early on 7 July but for the decision of Mr Justice Mocatta.

The *habeas corpus* application was heard by the Divisional Court on the 17th. Lord Chief Justice Parker ruled that Dr Soblen was an alien to whom leave to land had been refused and that he could be lawfully detained under the Aliens Order 1953. That decision was affirmed by the Court of Appeal nine days later. Dr Soblen wrote to me from Brixton Prison on 8 August: 'It is very hard to take these constant beatings when you know you are innocent.'

It was the next stage of the case that gave rise to legal issues of high constitutional importance, and caused my colleagues and myself grave concern. The Home Secretary, Henry Brooke, issued directions under Article 8 of the Aliens Order 1953 to the Israeli airline El Al requiring them to remove Dr Soblen to the United States. In the meantime much fierce opposition to Dr Soblen's deportation had grown in Israel and El Al refused to carry out these directions. The Home Secretary then made an order under Article 20(2)(b) of the Aliens Order 1953, which authorizes the making of a deportation order against an alien 'if the Secretary of State deems it to be conducive to the public good' to do so. This order directed that Dr Soblen should be deported to the United States. Once again Peter Solomon, Louis Blom-Cooper and I were instructed by Dr Kaufman to challenge the order through the *habeas corpus* procedure. This application was heard by the Vacation Judge Mr Justice Stephenson.

By now much public interest had been aroused in the case. On 8 August *The Times* reported that an American Embassy official had made representations to the British Government that the United States wished very much to have Dr Soblen returned and requested the Government to do everything possible to facilitate this. The report ended: 'In Washington, Reuter reports, the State Department said it had "emphatically" reiterated to both Britain and Israel that the United States wanted Dr Soblen returned to America.'

The main ground of Dr Soblen's challenge to the Home Secretary's order was that it was an abuse of executive power on his part. Deportation was limited to expulsion or banishment of an alien from the country, whereas the Home Secretary's action was directed primarily not to getting Dr Soblen out of England but to returning him into the hands of the

American authorities. We maintained that the power to deport did not confer a power of removal to a particular place. That power required the authority of an extradition order, with all the safeguards to the applicant which extradition procedures provided. Espionage was not an extraditable offence. Deportation was being used to circumvent the fundamental rule that a political offence is not extraditable.

I quoted Lord Castlereagh's statement in 1816: 'there could be no greater abuse of law than to allow it to be an instrument of inflicting punishment on foreigners who had committed political crimes only ... it is due to the firm attitude of Great Britain, Switzerland, Belgium, France and the United States that the principle has conquered the world.' Section 3 of the Extradition Act 1870 gave statutory effect to the rule by providing that 'a fugitive criminal shall not be surrendered ... if the offence is of a political character.'

At the hearing before Mr Justice Stephenson a subpoena was served on a representative of the Treasury Solicitor addressed to the Home Secretary requiring him in the light of *The Times* and other press reports to produce before the court all written communications to the British Government from the United States Government requesting 'the delivery up of the body of Dr Soblen'.

This was resisted by the Attorney General, who claimed Crown privilege for the communications. He produced a certificate from the Foreign Secretary Lord Home (later Prime Minister Sir Alec Douglas Home) that, on grounds of public interest, no evidence, oral or documentary, ought to be admitted as to whether there were any communications because disclosure would be injurious to good diplomatic relations. We could not challenge that certificate from the Foreign Secretary and at that time it was conclusive. (This was before the decision of the House of Lords in *Conway v Rimmer* in 1968. Since then the Court no longer accepts a minister's claims as final and conclusive and can order the production of the documents for which Crown privilege is claimed.)

The outcome of the hearing was that Mr Justice Stephenson dismissed Dr Soblen's application for a writ of *habeas corpus* as later did the Court of Appeal. In his judgment there the Master of the Rolls, Lord Denning, conceded that it was open to the court to inquire whether it was the Home Secretary's purpose to surrender Dr Soblen because the United States had requested it, which action would be unlawful, or whether the purpose was to deport, which was not unlawful. It was a power of inquiry which the Foreign Secretary's refusal to disclose any of the relevant documentation went far to nullify.

The hearing of the appeal ended on a curious note. Lord Justice Donovan asked me after the appeal was dismissed whether I had not forgotten to apply for legal aid taxation. This is the procedure which enables legal aid fees to be paid to counsel and solicitor. In fact Dr Soblen had been refused legal aid for the appeal and I had the pleasure of informing the Court that my junior colleagues, our instructing solicitor and I were appearing *pro Deo* – the ancient formula for appearing without fee.

The dismissal of the appeal did not end the matter. McShane, the marshal, who had been waiting patiently in the wings to take his captive back to prison in America, was in the end frustrated by the last sad chapter in the Soblen story. After the Court of Appeal dismissed his appeal Dr Soblen swallowed a quantity of tablets as he was being taken to the airport. According to his widow it was a further desperate attempt to prevent or delay his return to the United States and not suicidal in intent. This time the combination of the drugs and the leukemia from which he suffered killed him. It was one of the least glorious chapters in the history of those who have sought the safety of our shores.

I appeared in the Singapore High Court in August 1963 for the defence of almost all the Opposition members of the Singapore Legislature. It was a unique experience, made easier by the assistance of my learned junior Tan Wee Tiong, who knew the local scene well. I had already been instructed in some other cases in Singapore by my friend David Marshall, one of the country's ablest practitioners, but none of his cases had come to trial.

The twelve leaders of the Barisan Socialis Party of Singapore, led by its Chairman Dr Lee Siew Chok and its flamboyant, bearded legal adviser T.T.Rajah, filled the dock of the High Court. It was a spacious court in the fine colonial City Hall of Singapore. Unfortunately it had no air conditioning then and Singapore was very hot.

Eight of the Barisan defendants faced the serious charge, carrying a term of seven years imprisonment, of 'attempting to overawe by show of criminal force the Prime Minister and other Ministers with the intention of compelling them to refrain from exercising their lawful powers'. There were further charges of unlawful assembly. Four of the defendants were charged with aiding and abetting the others.

The atmosphere in the crowded court was highly charged despite the unshakeable calm and courtesy of the trial judge – Chief Justice Wee Chong Jin. When T.T.Rajah, an energetic Tamil, charged with abetting the alleged offences, was asked whether he pleaded guilty or not guilty, he replied, spelling out the words letter by letter, 'NOT GUILTY', adding:

'Not guilty and Lee Kwan Yew [the Prime Minister] is the traitor.' The Chief Justice rebuked him severely. During the lunchtime adjournment I warned him and the other defendants that if there was any repetition of such disorderly behaviour from the dock I would leave the case. Thereafter during the rest of the long trial he and the other defendants behaved with the utmost propriety.

Rajah was in fact acquitted at the end of the prosecution case on my submission that he had no case to answer. I still have the little silver ashtray he gave me, a reminder of his acquittal triumphantly inscribed upon it.

The case for the prosecution, which was conducted with moderation by the Solicitor-General, Kulasekaram, was that the Barisan Socialis Party planned a procession for which they did not have the requisite police permit. They were instructed by the police that in those circumstances the proposed procession would be contrary to law. In defiance of the ban, on Monday 22 April at 1.40 pm a procession of fifty or sixty people marched towards the City Hall carrying political placards and slogans. They distributed handbills containing a copy of a letter addressed to the Prime Minister which they intended to hand him that afternoon. This letter protested against alleged 'inhuman treatment of political detainees', 133 of whom were being held without trial, some in the notorious Changi prison.

When it reached the City Hall the procession came to a halt. Ong Chang Sam, one of the defendants, told Deputy Superintendent Lawrence, who had six other policemen with him, that they wanted to see the Prime Minister. Lawrence went in to see the Prime Minister's secretary, who informated him that Lee Kwan Yew was not in. He reported this message to Ong Chang Sam.

According to the prosecution, suddenly and spurred on by shouts from the defendants and others taking part, the crowd charged up the steps of the City Hall. Despite the resistance of the police they invaded the premises and reached the foyer of the Prime Minister's office on the second floor. There some of the leaders made speeches. Order was quickly restored when police reinforcements arrived. Assaults on the police were alleged. Emphasis was placed by the Solicitor-General on the fact that to the knowledge of the defendants the Cabinet usually sat on Monday afternoons in a room on the second floor and that they expected and believed the Prime Minister to be there.

The case for the defence was that what had been a comparatively minor incident involving a breach of the peace had been inflated into a big state trial by laying grave charges not remotely justifiable by the facts of the case. The prosecution case indeed crumbled as the evidence unfolded. The outcome of the trial, which lasted fifteen days, was that the Chief Justice acquitted all the accused on all the charges. I returned home with an armful of lovely Singapore orchids which some of the defendants presented to me at the airport when I left.

16

Missions Abroad

My parliamentary and legal activities took me abroad to many conferences and missions during Parliamentary recesses. One of the most memorable was my visit to China in 1956.

Dr Johnson had stressed to Boswell the distinction which would attach even to the children of a person who had gone to view the Great Wall of China. I accepted with alacrity the invitation from the Association of Political and Juridical Sciences of China to visit the country in April 1956 with three other lawyers from Britain, five from Belgium, one from Germany and three from France, including elegant Madame Pons de Poli from Marseilles, whose stiletto heels were to present problems later in the paddy fields of China.

Our delegation assembled in East Berlin, a grey, sad city still largely in ruins, whence we flew to Moscow in a Russian plane. Its forward cabin was furnished like an Edwardian sitting room in mahogany, with an ornate brass lamp, a red silk lampshade and a samovar. We were well received in Moscow and taken on a tour of the Kremlin. Although by the time of our visit Khrushchev had already denounced Stalin, his statues and portraits had not yet been removed. Near the mausoleum in Red Square, the ashes of Vishinsky, whom I had known at Nuremberg, had been allotted a place in the Kremlin walls with other Soviet leaders.

During the Moscow visit I tried unsuccessfully to make contact with General Rudenko, the Soviet Chief Prosecutor at Nuremberg. I was, however, allowed to meet Alexander, the twelve-year-old 'pen pal' of my son Dan, whose father had been killed in the war. Polly had suggested this exchange when she visited Russia as a journalist in 1952. In those days the Soviet authorities seemed to encourage such foreign contacts, no doubt carefully vetted.

Our flight via Sverdlovsk, Novosibirsk and Irkutzk took us over Lake

Baikal, bordered by great snow-capped mountains, orange bright in the early morning sunlight. The lake, one of the largest in the world, was frozen solid. Four years later Polly made the reverse journey by train on the trans-Siberian railway. Lake Baykal was then liquidy blue in the spring sunshine.

We arrived at Ulan Bator, the capital of Mongolia, at nine o'clock in the morning; at the small airport a military band was assembled. I asked the officer in charge if the band would kindly play us a tune. 'Not until ten o'clock,' he replied firmly. While we waited, a train of heavily laden camels came down the snow-covered hills in the charge of three men in sheepskin coats and fur hats. They waved to us cheerfully. The minutes passed. Our enquiries about our departure evoked no response save that we would have to wait. (Twenty years later, when I was Lord Chancellor, I read a dispatch from our representative in Ulan Bator reporting that 'magash' was a favourite Mongolian word meaning much the same as 'mañana' but without the same sense of urgency.)

Nothing happened until 9.45, when a lorry bearing a banner proclaiming 'Long live the fraternal friendship of the Russian and Mongolian peoples' rattled down the mountain. A few minutes later a convoy of Soviet limousines appeared bearing a general and a number of Mongolian functionaries in homburg hats and heavy black overcoats. Three little girls appeared in national costume carrying red bouquets. Clearly a VIP was expected. Finally at 9.55 a plane descended from the blue sky. We were immediately hurried into the plane which had brought us. The band at last struck up. It was not until we reached Peking that we learned that the VIP was Mikoyan, the Soviet Deputy Prime Minister. I hope he enjoyed the band.

Our plane flew over the vast Gobi Desert and then over mountains on whose crests we glimpsed the Great Wall of China, on which I later had the pleasure of walking.

At Peking Airport we were met by leading Chinese lawyers accompanied by their spouses, and students who greeted us with bunches of spring flowers. My hotel room overlooked the yellow roofs of the Forbidden City. That evening the Vice-President of the Chinese Association of Political and Juridical Sciences announced at the welcoming dinner that 'In China the guest is the master of the house' and that we could meet and see anyone and anything that we wanted. Apart from Professor Jim Gower's request to see some American prisoners from the Korean War held incommunicado, our requests were all granted.

We visited some of the glories of Peking: its temples and beautiful gardens, and I remember a wonderful lunch in the Hall of the Golden Oriole. Everywhere there were lots of friendly schoolchildren. The children took us for Russians for they had seen few other visitors with white faces. One little lad shook my hand and enquired, 'Molotov? Stalin? Malenkov?'

Great gusts of dust blew in from the Gobi Desert as it has done from time immemorial and many Peking citizens wore dust masks over their noses and mouths. Rows of young trees were being planted all over Peking, to protect the city from the threatening desert. In Bahai Park there were propaganda posters proclaiming 'Taiwan is our territory. Taiwan must be liberated.' In the gardens we saw the massive ceramic 'screen of the nine dragons'. That afternoon we were shown some of the treasures of the Forbidden City, its great courtyards, marble terraces and stone pekinese-faced guardian lions.

We were also taken to some of the new industrial developments, including the first motor car factory in China. Everywhere loads were mostly still being pulled or carried by human labour: there were not many lorries, tractors or cranes. This traditional harnessing of the people's strength and energy was evident everywhere we went. When we came to Hankow, where they were building the first bridge over the Yangtse River, about five thousand workers were employed on the project. They were carrying building materials in wicker baskets, some acting as human pile-drivers hauling at ropes on a pulley to lift a heavy stone to a considerable height and then letting it crash down with a great shout.

At Wuhan I saw thousands of labourers raising the height of the dykes in order to curb the age-old, disastrous floods. The 1931 floods, I was told, caused the deaths of 700,000 people.

We had long, illuminating talks with our hosts about the state of the law in China. They explained to us that there was very little declared law in existence after the revolution. The old legal codes had been repealed and work was proceeding on new penal and civil codes. The key person in the administration of justice with responsibility for enforcing the law in the courts was the Chief Procurator, who had an office with 2,000 branches throughout China. Every arrest had to be reported to it. Our hosts stressed the importance of this and told us that Khrushchev himself had pointed out that the absence of this control in the time of Stalin was one of the factors that made possible the cruel denials of justice in Russia. As yet there was no *habeas corpus* in China, they admitted, to enable the citizen to say to the authorities 'I am being detained unjustly. Let me be brought before the court and let those holding me prove that they do so lawfully.'

One of the trials to which I was taken was the hearing of a divorce case in the village of Nan Yuan outside Peking. The white-washed courtroom was crowded with villagers who had left their fields of cotton and maize to hear the proceedings. Facing the Court and seated next to each other on a small wooden bench were the nineteen-year-old wife (with long black plaits and indigo cotton jacket and trousers) and her husband, five years older. In China if both parties wanted a divorce they could have one. If only one applied a representative of the village council tried to bring the parties together. If that effort failed the matter came before a court of three villagers, one of whom in Nan Yuan was a woman. Neither husband nor wife had a lawyer.

To achieve reconciliation was still a primary object of the proceedings. In this case the wife complained that her husband and father-in-law would not let her take part in social activities or go to night school or attend village meetings, and that they had beaten her. This the husband denied. The Chairman told them: 'You should try and help each other and not rush into divorce on impulse. We all have our shortcomings. Examine and criticize yourselves. Will you try again?' The wife was unmoved. She simply said, 'If I go back I shall be beaten.'

The judges – a professional judge and two assessors – left the courtroom to consider their decision. When they came back the wife's petition was dismissed, but 'if after further thought and effort you still have bad feelings towards each other you may have your divorce.'

I attended two criminal trials, the first in the High Court in Peking. The accused was a peasant charged with murder and with being a Japanese agent. The judge sat with two lay assessors. The accused was defended by a lawyer, which was then the exception rather than the rule. Although the principle was accepted that accused persons on serious charges should be legally represented there were not enough lawyers to go round. The accused was convicted but, surprisingly, only sentenced to three years' imprisonment. The trial was conducted with dignity. The judge, wearing no special robes, elicited the evidence and did most of the questioning of witnesses. Counsel had a secondary role.

The second trial I attended took place in the great city of Nanking. The accused, an electrician, was charged with causing malicious damage in a factory. Members of the public were present as well as the friends and relations of the accused. The drama of the courts clearly had great appeal to the Chinese. I noticed that there were court scenes in two of the three splendid Chinese operas I saw. However, I saw no press reporters at any of the trials I attended.

There was a good deal of drama in the Shanghai High Court in an appeal by a prisoner who had been sentenced to death on conviction of being a colonel in the army of Chiang Kai-shek and having landed secretly from Formosa to organize a counter-revolutionary group in Shanghai. His death sentence was quashed after an eloquent plea for mercy and the assurance of future good behaviour given by Counsel on his behalf. He was sentenced instead to eight years' imprisonment.

When the judges left the court, I asked a law student who was there why he was attending the trial. He replied, 'To see whether our civil rights are being protected.' I asked him what particular civil rights he had in mind. He answered: 'The protection of our people so that they may live in security and safety.' Individual liberties and rights were not his concern at all – only social rights and obligations. Emphasis on the duty of service was, I was told, of the essence of the old Confucianism. So was the conception that everyone could be made to realize his or her duty to the community.

This was the theme of the directors of the two prisons I visited in Peking and the 'Loafers' Camp' in Shanghai. The basic principles were reform by hard work, learning a trade and 're-education' by constant indoctrination. The first prison I saw was in effect a stocking factory, the second a large brickworks. In each the prisoners worked for nine hours a day. They received no regular wages, only small financial rewards and remissions of their sentences for good work and behaviour.

I asked some of the few British businessmen remaining in Shanghai amid the ghosts of the famous old foreign enterprises on the Bund, what the impact of the Chinese revolution had been on law and order. They told me that the contrast between the banditry, lawlessness, corruption and prostitution of the pre-revolutionary days and the prevailing high standards of both public and private morality and honesty was dramatic. I had one small experience of this in Hankow. I took something out of my wallet in a crowded street. After I had walked on for some yards, a Chinese boy of about eight ran up to me and handed me a ten-cent note saying I had dropped it. Through my interpreter I invited him to keep it. He firmly refused.

Confucian respect for the old had continued. I noticed in Peking a policeman stopping the traffic (which was not allowed to exceed twenty miles an hour) to help an old woman who was hobbling across the road, on her tiny bound feet. Footbinding has long been forbidden and only some very old women suffer from this relic of the past.

Religious observance still appeared to play a significant part in Chinese life. I attended a Protestant church in Shanghai one Sunday morning in a congregation of over 500 young and old people. Colleagues in our delegation told me that the two big Roman Catholic churches they attended were crowded for Mass. Buddhist temples and a mosque I observed had many worshippers. The temples played an important social part in the everyday life of China just as in English villages the church is the social centre. Several times I saw little processions of mourners with white mourning sashes carrying sacrificial bowls of rice and corn to the burial mounds of their ancestors.

Although atheism was and is the Communist Party doctrine, the religious communities of China were holding fast to their beliefs. Indeed I was told at the Protestant Institute of Theology in Nanking that the churches were increasing rather than losing their influence. This was before the Cultural Revolution and during the period of the Culture of a Hundred Flowers.

Most of our contacts during the visit were with judges, lawyers and professors. The only political event was a call on Peng Chen, the impressive Secretary-General of the National Peoples' Congress and Mayor of Peking. At that time, on the insistence of its United States members, the Inter-Parliamentary Union was refusing to admit China to membership of the IPU despite the efforts over the years of Lord Stansgate (then its Chairman), and others of us, to have the decision reversed. I handed to Peng Chen a letter from Lord Stansgate. His comment was: 'The Americans do not believe we exist. But they will learn. It may take ten, twenty or a hundred years. How long does not matter. We can wait. They will learn.' Peng Chen himself fell into disgrace during the reign of the 'Gang of Four' but he was reinstated on their downfall.

The Chinese farewells to us the night before we left Peking for home were touching. Our hosts presented personal gifts to all of us. During our travels they had discovered that my wife was an artist, that I had two young daughters at school, that our son Dan was passionately interested in insects and that I was fond of gardening. They presented me with drawing materials for Polly, charming Chinese prints for Josephine and Lou, a neatly packed bamboo plant for me and for Dan a little box containing silkworms' eggs. But the weather had became warm and next morning at Peking airport when the customs officials examined the little box they found that the eggs had hatched out. They had to be confiscated. They also refused to allow the bamboo plant to be taken on board as I had no export permit for it. However my colleague Robert Pollard, who returned to England after the rest of us, was given a new supply of silkworm eggs for

Dan and a licensed bamboo plant for me. The eggs in due course hatched in Dan's school where, however, there was no mulberry tree to provide proper sustenance. But the adaptable Chinese silkworms thrived on lettuce leaves until the end of term when Dan brought them home and left them with Polly, who fed them with leaves from our mulberry tree. I carefully planted the bamboo, which I hope still flourishes in our old garden in Cranford.

I had hoped to visit Israel ever since my meetings early in the war with Dr Chaim Weizmann, who had played such a great part in its foundation. Polly and I were happy to accept an invitation to accompany George Thomas MP to Israel in 1957. We stayed in Jerusalem and Tel Aviv, Haifa and Beer-sheba. We met the Mayor of Beer-sheba, a former student of philosophy in Vienna, in his modest home set in a lovely garden in the Negev Desert.

They called Beer-sheba 'the pressure cooker'. Not only was a green oasis being created in the arid desert but also a fusion was being attempted of immigrants from different levels of civilization with different social patterns of behaviour. Ringleted Jews from the Yemen mingled with university-trained professional people from the troubled heart of central Europe. Settlements such as Boker, where the then Prime Minister David Ben-Gurion made his home, thrived in the desert. Revivim, Mash-abbé-Sadé and Eilat itself were further advances on the road to making the Negev bloom as it did centuries ago when the Nabataeans ruled it from 'rose-red Petra'.

We drove long distances over sandy tracks : there were fewer roads then. Black goat-hair Bedouin tents like crumpled umbrellas were scattered about. Water was the over-riding concern. Hydrologists were working out ways of bringing water to the Negev and learned historians were studying how the armies of ancient Rome had survived there. It did sometimes rain in a sudden deluge and the problem, they told us, was how to retain and save this precious life-giving water and how to cultivate plants which could survive on little of it. Great advances have been made since then. If Israel and her neighbours could only live in peace together, the experience and skill of the Israelis in making the desert bloom could transform vast desert areas of the Middle East and enrich the lives of all its peoples, Arab and Jew alike. I remember Golda Meir, then Israel's Foreign Minister, asking when I met her in Jerusalem, 'Must our children continue to be brought up in our frontier areas in trenches and under the shadows of guns?' Golda Meir, direct and unpretentious, gave us the impression of a wise grandmother determined to hold her family together in difficult circumstances. She was one of the most impressive women I have met.

Jerusalem stirs emotions unlike any other ancient city: the holy places, the olive garden at Gethsemane, the steep cobbled alleys between ancient stone walls, the crowing of a cock on Easter morning. The past is alive there and will not release you.

During my visit I addressed a gathering of lawyers in Tel Aviv. I described how deeply moved I had been looking out from my bedroom window in the St David Hotel in Jerusalem at the holy places I had learned about as a child in Tabernacle Chapel, Llanelli. When I sat down the Chairman of the meeting said genially that they knew King David was a great king but until I spoke they had not realized that he had been canonized by the Church of England.

The function of the Commonwealth Parliamentary Association is to promote close links between parliamentarians of the Commonwealth. In May 1959 I accompanied the delegation from the British branch to the celebrations in Kaduna of Northern Nigeria's attainment of regional self-government. Nigeria had become a federation in 1954.

In the middle of a pitch black African night we arrived at the ancient walled city of Kano, where the desert trade routes converged. On the floodlit tarmac we were greeted by a herald of the Emir of Kano mounted on a doleful camel and blowing mournful blasts out of a horn about ten feet long. There was also an emissary from the Emir welcoming us to the ancient emirate of Kano, which the Hausa dynasty had ruled for about 800 years.

We then flew to the regional capital, Kaduna, 'the place of the crocodiles', where I stayed with the Solicitor-General, Malcolm Lewis, who was the grandson of the Rev. Elvet Lewis, one of the great Welsh Nonconformist preachers I had known at Aberystwyth.

Our first official engagement was to present a copy of Erskine May, the Bible of parliamentary practice and procedure, to the House of Assembly in Kaduna. We were welcomed by the handsomely robed Premier Alhaji Sir Ahmadu Bello, the Sardanna of Sokoto, a man of great charm and presence. Earl De La Warr addressed the House of Assembly first. I followed, presenting Erskine May as a symbol of the link between the many peoples of the Commonwealth who had chosen to adopt the parliamentary system of government, which I commended as the most sensible, the most practical and the most just way for civilized and free people to conduct their political affairs. The Premier expressed similar sentiments.

The governing parties in north, east and west Nigeria all formally adopted western-style parliamentary democracy. Tragically it did not last. In January 1966 a group of majors seized power. The Federal Prime Minister, the Federal Minister of Finance, the Premier of Northern Nigeria (our host at the Durbar), the Premier of the Western Region and most officers above the rank of major were assassinated. Nigeria was plunged into a civil war which lasted for many years. There was no inkling of the problems to come at the self-government celebrations in Kaduna, where the mood was one of total optimism.

The highlight of the celebrations was the spectacular pomp and pageantry of a great Durbar. Thousands of men and horses in provincial contingents had travelled to Kaduna by road, rail or canal or on camel or horseback. Some riders had been in the saddle for five weeks before they reached Kaduna. Each contingent sought to outshine the others, bringing a magnificent array of costumes, accoutrements and musical instruments of many kinds with them. Some came from the Plateau Province – 'the Province of Tin' – some from Kabba province and its main town, Lokoja (the town, we were proudly told, which Charles Dickens in *Bleak House* called Borrioboola Gha, where Mrs Jellyby exercised her missionary zeal). The Duke and Duchess of Gloucester presided over the event from their brightly coloured canopied dais.

The Durbar opened dramatically with a thunderous charge of hundreds of horsemen galloping at breakneck speed towards the dais, pulling up their rearing horses only when they were within a few feet of it. Then followed a magnificent procession of emirs and chiefs; the emirs riding majestically on richly decorated camels beneath their ceremonial umbrellas, the chiefs on horseback. Each emir was preceded by a mounted herald proclaiming like a town crier his titles and virtues. In the midst of lines of richly caparisoned horses – some of their riders in crusaders' coats of mail, others carrying spears and shields of buffalo skin – swayed a twenty-foot high white-sheeted man on stilts. One contingent was preceded by two attendants leading muzzled hyenas on chain leads. There were tumblers, dancers in cowrie shell masks and troops of dancing girls in flowing robes. A dozen military and police bands gave rhythm to the procession.

We managed to see something of the life of the country. One visit was to a British medical unit researching sleeping sickness – a major scourge of the area at that time. (There were others working on leprosy.) The Scottish director, one of the dedicated British medical personnel working hard to eradicate tropical diseases in west Africa, showed us around the laboratories, which included a visit to a carefully sealed-off room containing samples of live tse-tse fly, carriers of the disease. A notice on the wall warned: 'Flies must not be allowed to escape.' As we moved around in the heat with rolled-up shirt sleeves I noticed a fly had landed on the bare arm of one of our delegates, William Deedes. I remarked how reassuring it was that it was not a tse-tse fly. However, the Director corrected me: 'I am sorry – but it *is* a tse-tse fly. Don't worry, it will not harm you.' This did not wholly reassure us and we hastened to a less hazardous part of the premises. Happily, Deedes came to no harm; he is now editor of the *Daily Telegraph*.

I had made plans to accompany my parliamentary colleagues to other regions of Nigeria after the Durbar when I received the sad news from home that my father had died. I flew back at once in time for his funeral in the Box Cemetery in Llanelli, which was attended by a large gathering of his friends of all ages. My father was over ninety when he died. He had no enemies.

Reports of large numbers of arrests of political opponents of the regime of Dr Nkrumah in Ghana having reached Justice and the International Commission of Jurists, I was invited to go there in May 1961 to make representations about this.

I flew to Accra, where I met several of the leading lawyers of the country. Most of them were pessimistic about the state of civil liberty in Ghana and thought it was moving increasingly towards authoritarian rule. I learned that forty-three detainees – most of the leadership of the Opposition Party – had been arrested in November 1958 and were still in custody after two-and-a-half years. Since then there had been about 200 further arrests by the use of emergency powers. No ill-treatment of detainees was alleged.

While I was in the capital I was invited to address the Ghana Law School. John Lang, its head, impressed me, as did the academic standards he was maintaining in the school.

After a few busy days in Accra I flew to Kumasi, the capital of the historic Ashanti province, where I gave a lecture to the Kumasi Bar Association on 'The Obligations of the Advocate'. This was attended by the local judges and lawyers, including the bubbling Joe Appiah, the son-in-law of Stafford Cripps. I had heard him in frivolous form speaking in Ghana's somewhat disorderly Legislature the day before, where scant attention was being paid to the rulings of a weak Speaker.

The member of the Ghana Government about whom I heard most criticism when I was there was its Attorney General, Geoffrey Bing QC. He had been a junior whip in Attlee's government and when he was in Opposition in the Commons he made skilful use of the procedures and devices of the House to make life difficult for the Conservative Government. He was an able if unpredictable lawyer but in Ghana it was thought that he used his undoubted talents to promote President Nkrumah's illiberal measures.

I flew from Accra to Freetown, the fine capital of Sierra Leone once known as 'the white man's grave'. Sierra Leone is unique in having a former Lord Chief Justice of England as a national hero: when Lord Mansfield gave judgment in 1772 in 'the Case of James Somersett, a negro', he declared that slavery was contrary to the law of England and ordered Somersett to be given his freedom. Another national hero there is the nineteenth century campaigner against slavery, William Wilberforce.

I addressed the law students at Fourah Bay University College, headed by a brilliant principal, Dr Nicol, which had contributed so much to the education of Africans on the west coast.

The Prime Minister, Sir Milton Margai, received me in his home. He practised medicine and was a pioneer in the efforts to stop the painful and damaging initiation rites carried out upon the young women of his country. He invited me to a reception he gave to delegations from the United Arab Republic and from the West Indies. Twenty Susu girls and a group of Bundu women, under the Prime Minister's personal direction, danced to the music of xylophones and the beat of drums.

On my return flight from Freetown to Dakar our plane stopped for two hours at Conakry Airport in Guinea. The waiting passengers were mostly Russians and Czechs, some with their wives and children. They looked like working technicians. I gathered that they and 150 Chinese had filled the gap created when the French pulled out of the country precipitately. They had left as little as they could behind, destroying office records and causing a breakdown in the administration. It was not an unfamiliar story in the colonial aftermath.

In May 1964 the Colonial Secretary, Duncan Sandys, invited me to join a British team of four observers of the referendum in Malta on the question: 'Do you approve of the Constitution for independence?' There was concern that pressures might be exercised on the electorate by the powerful Catholic Church there and that this could prejudice the 'No' campaign of the Malta Labour Party and unfairly benefit the Nationalist Party.

We had a fascinating week in the gallant George Cross island of Malta, witnessing the clash between the powerful personalities of Catholic Archbishop Michael Gonzi on the one side and Dom Mintoff on the other.

On one occasion the Archbishop received us in his palace wearing the magnificent robes of his office. Complaints had been sent to us that absolution was being denied to individuals unless they promised not to vote for the Labour Party. The Archbishop responded by drawing our attention to a circular letter he had ordered to be read in every church in Malta indicating that the referendum was an entirely political matter and that all Catholics were free to vote according to their consciences.

The outcome of the referendum, the administrative arrangements for which were in our view excellent, was that 65,714 electors voted 'Yes' and 54,919 'No'. There were 9,016 invalid votes, which we thought were intended as a vote against independence. It left the future of Malta in a state of division and uncertainty.

17

The Corgi of the Community

The 1964 General Election produced one of the closest results in Britain's electoral history: the Labour Government had a working majority of only four. The Government remained in office on its slender lead until the 1966 General Election gave it a large working majority.

The new Prime Minister, Harold Wilson, announced the names of the senior members of the Cabinet on the night of Friday 16 October.

He had given me no indication of his intention to give me an appointment. However early on the Saturday evening, after further ministerial appointments had been announced, a private secretary at No 10 telephoned me to ask if it would be convenient for me to come there at noon next day.

On that sunny, chilly Sunday morning Polly and I walked from Gray's Inn, where we lived, to St James's Park. I left Polly there on a bench reading the Sunday papers and went to Downing Street. A mass of television and press reporters were waiting outside No 10. As I approached the door at two minutes to twelve, one of them came up to me and demanded brusquely, 'Who are you?' 'Jones,' I said. At a press lunch I attended some time later, they told me that when the reporter joined his colleagues and was asked who I was he told them: 'Some geezer called Jones.'

When the policeman admitted me into the hallway of No 10, one of the Prime Minister's Private Secretaries, who was waiting for me, said: 'I'm afraid there's been a mistake. After we called you last night we found the time-table had gone wrong. We tried to ring you again at Gray's Inn but got no reply. You are not needed until twelve-thirty.' I then remembered that after the phone call on Saturday night Polly and I had strolled across the lawn to the Walks of Gray's Inn, where a scene from an American movie was being shot, starring Kim Novak, as an unlikely Moll Flanders, being driven down the Walks in a wobbly stage coach. Thus I had missed the second phone call.

I knew there was a back entrance to the building and I asked the Private Secretary if I might leave and return that way to avoid the press. He agreed and so I ambled back to Polly in the park, where she was sitting patiently in her heron's nest of Sunday newspapers.

She asked, 'What have you got?' 'Absolutely nothing,' I replied and explained about the second phone call. At twelve-thirty I made my back-door re-entry into No 10. When I entered the Cabinet Room the Prime Minister greeted me cheerfully with, 'Good morning, Mr Attorney.'

Harold Wilson then announced that he had a surprise for me: he proposed to appoint a solicitor to be the Solicitor-General. I knew that a solicitor could not appear as Counsel in any of the higher courts nor sign Counsel's opinions. I explained this to the Prime Minister, but characteristically he brushed it aside: 'You can always hire a QC to do that sort of thing.' I did not press my objections at once but before leaving the building I asked if I could speak to George Dudman, then Legal Secretary to the Law Officer's Department. I explained Harold Wilson's proposal to him. He said it was quite impracticable and would mean that the new Solicitor-General would be unable to carry out some of the most important duties of the office and that I would be obliged to take on his work as well.

I asked to see Harold Wilson again and explained this to him. He then divulged that he had in mind to make Eric Fletcher MP (who was a solicitor) Solicitor-General and to appoint Dingle Foot QC, MP as a minister to handle our law reform programme in the Commons. Clearly he contemplated an early flow of law reform legislation: unhappily such reforms do not come as easily or as quickly as that. He then decided that the best solution was for him to appoint Dingle as Solicitor-General and Eric as Minister without Portfolio. Relieved, I went off to tell Polly the news. It was to change our lives considerably.

The following day I made my call on the Law Officers' Department in that endearing Victorian extravaganza, the Royal Courts of Justice in the Strand, which was to be my workplace for six years. It was within walking distance of our flat in Gray's Inn and an easy run to the House of Commons. The car which came with the office of Attorney was a black hearse-like Austin Princess, relieved, however, by the cheerfulness of my admirable driver Miss Green and after her Joe Gladstone.

My first formal duty was to be sworn in as Attorney General by the new Lord Chancellor Gerald Gardiner, tall, austere, kind, and to receive from him my Letters Patent and Writ of Attendance at the House of Lords. This ancient writ read:

> Whereas by the advice and assent of Our Council for certain arduous and urgent affairs concerning Us the State and defence of Our United Kingdom and the Church We have ordered a certain Parliament to be holden at Our City of Westminster on the third day of November next ensuing and there to treat and have conference with the Prelates Great Men and Peers of Our Realm We strictly enjoining COMMAND you that (waiving all excuses) you be at the said day and place personally present with Us and with the rest of Our Council to treat and give your advice upon the affairs aforesaid And this in no wise do you omit.

Like many matters pertaining to the offices of Attorney General and Lord Chancellor, the Writ of Attendance has a very long history. For the first few centuries of his existence the function of the King's Attorney was to maintain the Crown's interests before the courts. In 1461, however, when the modern title of 'Attorney General' was first used, the Crown's principal law officer was called upon to go to the House of Lords to advise upon legal matters. Ever since the Attorney General has been served with the Writ of Attendance, although in practice Law Officers ceased to attend the Lords in the seventeenth century.

In the early days of the office the Attorney General was called 'the Bulldog of the Crown'. (When I was made an honorary freeman of my home town of Llanelli, Roderic Bowen QC described me as 'the corgi of the community', the corgi being Welsh and the Queen's favourite dog.)

Traditionally the Recorder of the Royal Borough of Kingston-on-Thames has been the Attorney General of the day. It is now a purely honorary office. The Recorder has no judicial functions and apart from attendance at occasional civic events the office involves no other duties. At my installation as Recorder I was given the traditional gift of 'two sugar loaves', massive cones of solid crystallized sugar. Dan got busy with a knife and mallet and carved them into Gothic royalties which lit up his Stepney sitting-room until like snowmen they gradually melted away.

In my time the outstanding function and main duty of the Attorney was to be the legal adviser of the Government as a whole and of the various government departments. Naturally the Lord Chancellor sometimes expressed an opinion about legal matters which came before the cabinet. Sometimes he might be asked by the Prime Minister to advise on some problem of particular difficulty or weight – but it was not the Lord Chancellor's job to advise government departments, indeed it would be inconsistent with his office as head of the Judiciary. Lord Gardiner was meticulously careful about this. My relations with him throughout our years in office were excellent and when very occasionally the need arose he was my staunch defender, as I was his. Gerald had never been a member of the House of Commons and gave me a free rein as his spokesman there.

I was not a member of the Cabinet. The last Attorney General to be so was Sir Douglas Hogg (Lord Hailsham), the father of Quintin. Since then it has been considered more appropriate that the independence and detachment of the office of Attorney General should not be blurred by inclusion in a political body which may have to take political decisions on the basis of his legal advice. I found this an advantage because I was spared from the heavy burden of reading cabinet papers, save those about which I was specifically consulted. However, I attended cabinet meetings frequently to advise on legal or constitutional matters; more often than not concerning the problems of Rhodesia and Northern Ireland.

I was also a member of several cabinet committees, to which much decision-making was delegated, by-passing the Cabinet. They were and are a crucial part of the machinery of government. It was only when the members of the committee failed to agree that the matter before them would be brought before the full Cabinet. The Home Affairs Committee, for instance, dealt with proposed legislation in the home affairs field and with problems concerned with policy decisions which departments considered to be of sufficient importance to be referred to it.

The Legislation Committee was one of the key committees and met in the Treasury Board Room in the Cabinet Office in Whitehall. It provided the final opportunity to examine a bill before it was published and it was there that any still outstanding points of law were dealt with and the advice of the Lord Chancellor and Attorney General obtained. Ministers were allowed to bring one of their departmental civil servants with them to be available for consultation at the committee's meeting.

All government legislation is drafted by parliamentary counsel, who, oddly enough, are under Treasury control, not the Lord Chancellor's. They are a team of skilled lawyers in full-time employment of the Crown. There are over a thousand barristers and solicitors in other branches of the government legal service. It is to their departmental solicitors and legal advisers that ministers turn first for legal advice. While the Attorney General is properly described as the legal adviser to the government, his advice is normally only sought where some problem arises which is of special difficulty or importance; either because of the complexity of the legal problem in question, cr because of the political, international or financial importance of the decision which turns upon that advice. In my time failure to consult the Law Officers on one or two such problems led Harold Wilson to issue a sharp reminder to ministers of the importance of consulting my department, especially before action was taken which might give rise to difficulty in the courts, and particularly when important policy issues were involved.

This is not to suggest that an Attorney General's advice is or was infallible! Indeed I was on the losing side in some notable cases in which I led for the Crown – particularly in 1968 in *Conway v Rimmer*, the House of Lords decision which imposed important limits on Crown privilege, and *Dorset Yacht Co v The Home Office*, which established Home Office liability for damage caused by borstal boys on the run from an open borstal. Final reference of a legal question to the Law Officers' Department does, however, enable fresh thinking to be given to it and at a level when the best advice can be obtained from Treasury Counsel and the Bar. I was fortunate during my term of office to have two oustanding Treasury 'devils' to advise me: Nigel Bridge, who became a Lord of Appeal in Ordinary, and Gordon Slynn, a High Court judge who became Advocate General to the Luxembourg Court of Justice of the European Community.

The Law Officers' Department is headed by the Attorney General and the Solicitor-General. The Solicitor is the Attorney's deputy and can exercise all his powers when he is not available. He has no special powers or responsibilities special to him alone. Theo Mathew described it thus: 'What is the difference between the Attorney General and the Solicitor-General? Broadly speaking the difference between a crocodile and an alligator.' The Solicitor-General is not a solicitor and so far as I know a general has never held the office. This eccentricity of title is not unique in our constitution. When Rab Butler was Lord Privy Seal he took pleasure in announcing that he was neither a lord nor a privy nor a seal.

Dingle Foot, who was my first Solicitor-General, was a unique, witty and irrepressible character of high international reputation for his work in Commonwealth and colonial cases. Few were the leaders of the newly independent Commonwealth countries for whom Dingle had not appeared, usually in sedition cases. He was succeeded in 1966 by the tall Scot Arthur Irvine, an experienced and able Silk, who unfortunately suffered from serious heart trouble during the latter part of his term of office. This added considerably to my burdens.

The job of Attorney General is highly demanding. Francis Bacon described the office as 'the painfullest task in the realm', and a few centuries later Sir Patrick Hastings noted that to be a law officer was to be in hell. I certainly did not find it so; in fact I enjoyed it most of the time although it was extremely hard work – as indeed most of my life has been. Fortunately I had an immensely able (though very small) staff under the leadership of

Tony Hetherington, now the Director of Public Prosecutions. He had a good nose for problems which needed extra careful handling.

Although not a member of the Cabinet, I was made a Privy Councillor within a few days of my appointment. I made the Affirmation of Allegiance along with three or four cabinet ministers in the elegant Privy Council office in Whitehall in the presence of the Queen. We did so on bended knee on a low cushion, some keeping a steadier balance than others.

All discussions 'on Privy Councillor terms', in particular at cabinet meetings, carry an obligation of secrecy. Sadly it was an obligation not always complied with even at cabinet level. In our media-dominated age, unrestricted 'freedom of information' – the right to tell as distinct from 'the right to know' – is regarded in some quarters as more important than the confidentiality vital to many policy decisions. From time to time it was suspected by those of us who sat in Cabinet that at least one of our number was taking careful note of what was being said, with a view to publication. On one or two highly secret matters the Prime Minister expressly asked the cabinet members not to take a note of what was being discussed. Attempts by the Lord Chancellor, the police or the Civil Service itself to trace the source of cabinet leaks always proved unavailing. During my term as Lord Chancellor I was not asked to make such an inquiry. Gerald Gardiner was: he found no deliberate leakage of information about cabinet business and apparent leaks frequently appeared to be no more than inspired guesses by experienced journalists.

Both Gerald Gardiner and I favoured extended 'freedom of information', in the sense of making more classified documents more readily available. In 1967 we steered through Parliament the Public Records Bill to provide wider access to information sealed up in Whitehall. It reduced from fifty to thirty years the period during which public records, subject to certain exceptions, were closed. There is however an important field of public policy in which I think confidentiality is essential. I have in mind such matters as defence, security intelligence, police activity and economic and financial proposals, premature disclosure of which could endanger security and public safety, profit the unscrupulous and disrupt markets. Mutual trust and courtesy between colleagues also call for restraint in disclosure of what is said in the privacy of the Cabinet.

The Government considered the rules and conventions governing ministerial use of official material otherwise than for current official purposes in September 1967. Gladstone had stated the constitutional doctrine clearly: 'In Cabinet differences of view can be stated and if need be argued and then advisedly surrendered with a view to a common conclusion.

Soundness of Cabinet government depends on mutual confidence – its basis can be eroded by the disclosure of what has passed within the confidential relationship.'

Harold Wilson appointed me to a small committee consisting of two lawyers (the Lord Chancellor and me) and three non-lawyers (Roy Jenkins, Patrick Gordon-Walker and Frank Longford) to consider the question of memoirs by ex-ministers. We agreed on the classic principles stated by Gladstone. But there was no unanimity on the question of whether ministers should be asked, as the lawyers proposed, to give an undertaking to accept, after discussion, any changes which the Secretary of the Cabinet thought it necessary to make in any manuscripts they wrote. The non-lawyers thought that it would be unreasonable to expect ministers to undertake to accept, in advance, what would amount to future censorship in circumstances which could not be foreseen. In his published diaries, Dick Crossman disclosed the two-hour discussion in the Cabinet of the committee's divided report. Cabinet opinion was also divided and the vexed issue was pursued no further.

My duties as Privy Councillor were limited to attendance at occasional meetings of the Privy Council. When Parliament was sitting, these normally took place at Buckingham Palace or at Windsor, wherever the Queen was in residence. Usually four Privy Councillors were in attendance on these brief formal occasions when the Queen would be invited to approve orders in council or charters or state documents requiring royal assent. We would all remain standing.

In the parliamentary recesses, when the Queen was out of London, Privy Councils were held at Sandringham and Balmoral and once at Arundel, in the drawing-room of the Duke of Norfolk's house during the Goodwood Races. Balmoral has been as carefully preserved as it was when Queen Victoria lived there: the same wallpaper and furnishings, Landseers in abundance, including *The Monarch of the Glen* and *The Stag at Bay*.

At Balmoral the members of the Council were invited to an informal Royal Family lunch. That was where I first had the great pleasure of becoming acquainted with Prince Charles, then a schoolboy, and began the friendly association with him which has been happily maintained over the years. His investiture as Prince of Wales in Caernarvon on 1 July 1969 was a tremendous Welsh spectacular staged within the medieval walls of the great castle.

As Attorney General I was apprehensive about the Investiture for security reasons. The trial at Swansea Assizes of six members of the Free Wales Army had reached its fifty-third, and final, day on the eve of the ceremony. That day a time bomb exploded in a post office in Cardiff, the fourth in the city within three months. Although there was one small explosion near the castle at the start of the proceedings, happily no one was hurt. The Investiture was joyously celebrated in Wales and the Prince, who had taken pains to speak the Welsh language convincingly, was enthusiastically welcomed throughout the principality. Afterwards the members of the audience were allowed to buy the orange and gilt chairs in which they were seated at the Investiture. They decorate many a sitting room in Wales, and beyond.

I flew to Balmoral for one highly important Privy Council after a unique Cabinet meeting held in the Royal Hotel, Brighton, in October 1966 during the Labour Party Conference. The Privy Council was to obtain the Royal Assent to an order to bring into force Part IV of the Prices and Incomes Act and introduce a total wage freeze.

Unlike other ministers, as Attorney-General I was not directly responsible for the introduction of legislation. While I could be questioned in the House about the enforcement of the criminal law, for which I had overall responsibility, it was the Home Secretary who was entrusted with the criminal law itself and for keeping it up to date. I was, however, the spokesman in the Commons for the Lord Chancellor. In the Commons the Solicitor-General and I handled the bills which were the Lord Chancellor's responsibility in the Lords. Some of these had been planned before we took office. In 1963 Gerald Gardiner and Andrew Martin had edited *Law Reform Now*, to which I and several other members of the Society of Labour Lawyers contributed. It became the blueprint of the Labour Government's law reform programme and it was our good fortune that Harold Wilson was enthusiastically committed to it. Not only did the programme identify many areas of the law urgently needing reform, but it also called for the establishment of a law commission.

There already existed two standing committees – the Law Reform Committee and the Criminal Law Revision Committee – and many important law reform statutes, both criminal and civil, have resulted from their work. These committees were composed of extremely busy judges and lawyers meeting at intervals, usually after court hours.

We thought that what was needed was an independent statutory body of lawyers working full-time on law reform. This was achieved in 1965 by the passing of the Law Commissions Act. This act established the Law Commission of England and Wales and the Scottish Law Commission, each with the duty 'to take and keep under review all the law with which they are respectively concerned with a view to its systematic development and reform, including in particular the codification of such law, the elimination of anomalies, the repeal of obsolete and unnecessary enactments, the reduction of the number of separate enactments and generally the simplification and modernization of the law'. It was an ambitious programme, which, as experience has shown, will take many years to realize, for at the time the Act was passed there were about 4,000 Acts of Parliament in force, over 350,000 reported law cases and about 100 volumes of delegated legislation.

The first chairman of the Law Commission for England and Wales, Sir Leslie Scarman, and the four founder commissioners, Neil Lawson, Norman Marsh, Andrew Martin and Jim Gower, tackled their task with skill and enthusiasm. The methods of work they adopted have proved effective: a preliminary working paper, wide consultation and then the final stage of a report to the Lord Chancellor usually accompanied by a bill drafted by the Commission's parliamentary counsel. By mid-1980, out of fifty-six reports containing law reform recommendations, thirty-nine had been implemented by legislation in whole or in part. Important statutes such as the Criminal Law Act 1967, the Divorce Legislation of the early 1970s, the Criminal Damage Act and the Animals Act, the Unfair Contract Terms Act 1977 and many others were largely products of the commission.

So was a flow of Statute Law (Repeals) Acts (repealing obsolete acts) and Consolidation Acts. The latter are dealt with by a joint committee of both Houses and are not debated on the floor of either House (as is the case with ordinary reform bills). For them the scarcest of all parliamentary commodities – time – has to be found to get them through both Houses. The result has been failure so far to implement many useful law reforms proposed by the Law Commission. Only a limited number of days are available each session in the House of Commons for the consideration of 'optional' bills after essential finance and appropriation bills have been dealt with. Departments naturally give priority to bills forming part of their own programmes, and the Lord Chancellor has to fight hard to find a place for law reform bills, for which there is rarely any popular appeal. Often progress on these bills depends on the willingness of Private Members to take them up and steer them through the House in the limited time available for Private Members' Bills. Although since 1965 we have had a statutory scheme for the systematic and continuous review of our law, we have not yet found the administrative and parliamentary solutions to make it effective.

Gerald Gardiner had one notable success in the contest for parliamentary time with the Law Reform Bill of 1969, which I took through the Commons. This gave effect to the Latey Committee Report on the age of majority, and the Russell Committee Report on the law of succession in relation to illegitimate persons. The bill lowered the age of full legal capacity to eighteen, reflecting the social reality of our time.

The choice of twenty-one for coming of age had no magic about it. It was originally linked with the ability of a knight's son to sustain a heavy suit of armour or lift a lance or sword. A peasant's son came of age at fifteen, a merchant's son came of age when he could count pence and measure cloth. It was also thought necessary in Victorian times to protect from the clutches of money-lenders young men who were said by the *Law Journal* of the time to be 'prone to horse-flesh, dog-flesh, cigars, sparkling drinks, swell attire, betting and making presents to ladies who are sometimes fair and often fragile'.

The evidence before the Latey Committee was that now the vast majority of young people were more mature and more responsible than they had ever been and their conclusion was that it was about time that our laws recognized the fact. The Bill did so by enabling persons of eighteen (of both sexes) to hold and dispose of property, to make binding contracts and to make wills. It also made eighteen the age of 'free marriage', marriage not needing parental or court assent. Getting the vote and eligibility to do jury service came in separate legislation. Another part of the 1969 Bill gave a better deal to children born out of wedlock. Now, whether a specific provision has been made or not, the illegitimate child is no longer excluded from all benefit of her or his parents' estate.

The Protection against Eviction Bill was an early measure of social reform which Dick Crossman and I handled in the House. It was directed against forcible eviction of tenants by unscrupulous landlords. It made it a crime for a landlord to evict a tenant without previously obtaining a court order, and it granted to county courts the power to stay the execution of an eviction order for twelve months.

In addition to Law Commission bills, the Law Officers were involved in bills introduced by other Ministers or by Private Members which had a substantial legal or constitutional content or raised legal questions about which the House would wish to know the views of the Law Officers.

The first constitutional matter with which I had to deal as Attorney General was the Machinery of Government Bill. Its main purpose was to provide the structure for three new departments of state – the Ministries of Land and Natural Resources, Overseas Development and Technology – which were to be charged with carrying out important aspects of Labour's programme.

Increasing the salaries of judges was never a popular measure in the House. By 1966 the salaries of the High Court judges had been left behind to a point where recruitment of the best of the Bar to the High Court Bench was imperilled. The Lord Chancellor found it necessary to remedy the position. The Judicial Salaries Bill, which I introduced as his spokesman, faced some eloquent opposition.

Two important law reform measures on which I spoke were passed in 1966: the Criminal Appeal Act and the Criminal Justice Act. The former implemented most of the recommendations of the Donovan Committee, of which I was a member. It abolished the Court of Criminal Appeal and transferred its powers to a criminal division of the Court of Appeal, which had higher status than the old court. This act also extended the grounds for allowing an appeal against conviction to cases where, under all the circumstances of the case, the court concluded that the verdict was 'unsafe or unsatisfactory'. The court lost its power to increase the sentence on the appellant when it refused his or her appeal. (This had made appeals a risky undertaking.) Another liberal change was to reckon the time during which the appellant had been in custody as part of the sentence, unless the court gave a specific direction to the contrary.

The Criminal Justice Bill was an important measure of reform. It simplified time-consuming committal proceedings. It introduced majority jury verdicts, which have proved of great value in avoiding retrials without, in my opinion, doing harm to the jury system. The Bill abolished the sentences of preventive detention and corrective training, which in fact had not been used for years. It also ended corporal punishment and the use of the 'cat' in prisons (although none had been confirmed since 1962). Overcrowding in prisons was already considered serious even then, when there were 35,000 prisoners in British jails. It was to rise to 44,000 by the 1980s. The Bill aimed to keep out of prison those who, from the point of view of the protection of the public, did not need to be there. To reduce prison numbers the power of justices of the peace to restrict bail was itself restricted. Suspended sentences were introduced. Unfortunately a big increase in crime and in the number of those convicted frustrated these attempts to reduce the number of men and women behind bars in increasingly deteriorating prison conditions.

Major changes in the administration of justice were introduced in the Administration of Justice Act in February 1970. The massive increase in the number of cases, both civil and criminal, coming before the courts called for detailed review of our arrangements. This was carried out by Lord Beeching. He estimated that a quarter of judicial time was wasted because assizes had to be held quite unnecessarily in towns, often no more than large villages, which had been selected for the purpose in the reign of King John. Beeching recommended the overhaul of the court system and of the administration of the higher courts. It fell to the present Lord Hailsham, who succeeded Gerald Gardiner as Lord Chancellor, to carry through Beeching's proposals.

One significant change which marked the importance our society attaches to the place of the family was the creation of a new family division of the High Court out of the old Probate, Divorce and Admiralty Division.

Some important developments affecting the citizen's rights and privileges took place outside the court system. A mass of tribunals were set up to meet the needs of the Welfare State and to deal judicially with claims against the administration.

The liberal tradition of the Labour Party was reflected in the setting up in 1967 of the office of Ombudsman – the Parliamentary Commissioner for Administration – with the object of giving MPs a valuable instrument for protecting the citizen from injustice through maladministration. We had the benefit of the work of Justice and of the Whyatt Committee in this initiative. The Ombudsman was given the power to examine complaints against a government department submitted to him by a Member of Parliament, on behalf of a constituent claiming to have suffered loss or damage as a result of maladministration. It gave the Ombudsman access to all departmental documents relating to the case, including its internal minutes, and the authority to publish his reports to Parliament. The resistance of one or two departments and of some MPs, who feared that the Ombudsman might reduce their importance as 'grievance chasers', was overcome and has proved to be unfounded. Much injustice in many individual cases has been put right as a result of the Ombudsman's intervention.

One parliamentary issue in the legal field which gave rise to the stormiest Commons battle I faced arose out of the War Damage Bill, to amend the law as laid down by a majority of the Law Lords in the case of the *Burmah Oil Co v Lord Advocate*. Three of the five Law Lords had sustained the Burmah Oil Company's claim of £84 million damages for the blowing up, on the orders of the British military commander, of their oil installations in Burma in 1942 in order to deny their use to the advancing Japanese Army. Prior to the Lords' decision it was generally thought to be the law that there was no liability at common law to pay compensation for a lawful act done by the Crown in the exercise of its prerogative in the course of war. The Burmah Oil Company had already received £4,750,000 compensation for their loss.

Our defence of the Bill, against the fierce attack that it was unjustifiable retrospective legislation, was that a bill of indemnity arising out of wartime actions was a proper use of retrospective powers and needed to ensure that equity was done between the different victims of war. If we had met the Burmah Oil Company's claim for full compensation, how could we have justified it to the multitude of other people who had suffered ruin, the loss of their families or their limbs or faculties, and who had had to be content with the modest level of pensions which was all we were able to afford?

Tempers were raised in the debate and during a division on the bill, the former Conservative Attorney General, Lionel Heald, with whom I had previously maintained friendly relations, strode angrily across the floor of the House and abused me roundly. The bill, however, survived both Commons and Lords. Several former Conservative ministers in the Lords, including a former Lord Chancellor, Lord Dilhorne, voted for the Government Bill.

One of my parliamentary duties was to answer parliamentary questions about matters for which the Lord Chancellor and I were responsible: the courts, legal aid advice and assistance and the appointment of JPs. In the post-war period there were so many questions and so many ministers that a rota system was agreed which determined when and how frequently a minister should be questioned. The Attorney General came off lightly – to my regret – for I enjoyed greatly the cut and thrust of Question Time.

From time to time the House asks for the advice of the Attorney General on a legal problem. It was in that capacity that I sat as a member of the Committee of Privileges, one of the most important parliamentary committees. It is directed by the House to examine and report upon allegations of breaches of the privileges of Parliament by Members, the media, or whoever. As Attorney General I was called upon to do a good deal of the questioning. It was an all-party committee with a predominance of Privy Councillors. Its decisions were usually made on a non-party basis and normally accepted by the House.

The Attorney-General has further important duties as protector of the public interest, to give his name to relator proceedings brought to protect public rights. I recall doing so in one case where blasting operations in a quarry were bombarding road traffic and forcing neighbours to take cover. In another a developer was destroying trees which were protected by a preservation order.

In these relator cases the Attorney General has to consider whether it is necessary to take action in the public interest. As was decided by the House of Lords in the Gouriet case, he is not accountable to the courts for his action or inaction, unless he is shown to be acting in bad faith. As Lord Fraser expressed it, if he errs the 'error would not be an error of law but would be one of political judgement, using that expression of course not in a party sense but in the sense of weighing the relevant importance of different aspects of the public interest. Such matters are not appropriate for decision in the courts.'

This does not mean that the Attorney General is not accountable to anybody. Like every minister, he is answerable for political decisions to Parliament.

Another aspect of the protective role of the Attorney General is to intervene in charitable matters as *parens patriae*. When charitable bills were introduced into Parliament it was my duty to present a special report about them.

I had other unlikely duties. I was an *ex officio* Church Commissioner. I had to advise the Crown before the royal assent was given to legislation from the Channel Islands or the Isle of Man. I advised the sovereign whether charters should be granted : this produced a number of problems, for many institutions such as universities have royal charters and can only change their constitution by supplementary charters.

I established closer university links when in 1970 I became President of University College, Cardiff, one of the constituent colleges of the University of Wales, which has contributed so much to the principality. Under its Principal, Bill Bevan, and with a very able academic staff, the college has achieved high standards in teaching, scholarship, consultancy and research, particularly into the problems of industry. And no less than seventy per cent of the overseas students reading education in Britain in 1981–82 were at University College, Cardiff.

18

Foreign Affairs

Far and away the most intractable and most persistent problem with which I was actively concerned as Attorney General and later as Lord Chancellor was that of Rhodesia. I was a member of the Cabinet Rhodesia Committee which usually met, with the Prime Minister in the chair, around the oval table in the Cabinet Room at No 10. We faced a crisis in Rhodesia immediately after we took office in 1964. The Central African Federation of Northern and Southern Rhodesia and Nyasaland had finally broken up in December 1963 and each of those three territories had become in law a British colony until Nyasaland became independent as Malawi in July 1964, and Northern Rhodesia as Zambia a week after we took office.

Southern Rhodesia had had limited self-government and its own armed forces since 1924. In its 1961 constitution, however, only one in twenty of the population had the vote. It had two main rolls of voters: the A roll was confined to Europeans, the B roll to a small proportion of African, Asian and coloured voters. Registration as an elector – after a severe literacy test – depended on educational, property or income qualifications. The voteless Southern Rhodesian Africans outnumbered the Europeans by fifteen to one. African representation was, in practice, limited to the fifteen reserved B roll seats.

Since South Africa became independent in 1909, no British colony had been granted full independence except on the basis of universal adult suffrage: 'one man, one vote'. In April 1963 the Rhodesian Front headed by Winston Field came to office determined to acquire independence on the 1961 constitution, either legally, if the British Government could be persuaded to carry the necessary legislation through parliament, or, if not, by an illegal Unilateral Declaration of Independence (UDI). Ian Smith, who replaced Winston Field in April 1964, asserted this demand in even stronger terms.

The British Prime Minister Alec Douglas-Home and the Commonwealth Secretary Duncan Sandys made it clear that Parliament could only grant independence on the basis of proposals brought forward by the British Government. It must be satisfied 'that any basis on which it was proposed that independence should be granted was acceptable to the people of the country as a whole'. This came to be known during the long years of subsequent negotiation as the crucial 'fifth principle'.

On this the Conservative Government remained firm. The day of the British election, 16 October 1964, Duncan Sandys sent a telegram to Smith rejecting the proposal that an *indaba* (a conference) of chiefs and headsmen, nominees of the Rhodesian Government, should be the means of testing the views of the African population. He refused an invitation to send observers.

However, after the change of Government, despite a message from Arthur Bottomley, Duncan Sandys's successor at the Commonwealth Office, reaffirming the rejection of Smith's proposal, the *indaba* took place on 22 October and Smith prepared for an 'independence referendum' on 5 November. A clear warning from the British Government that UDI would be 'an open act of defiance and rebellion, that it would be treasonable to give effect to it' and that Southern Rhodesians would cease to be British subjects, was issued from Downing Street on 27 October.

Smith won the independence referendum but, when he came to London in January 1965 to attend the funeral of Sir Winston Churchill, he did not appear to regard UDI as urgent. He had been advised by his South African lawyers, he said, that, living under the 1961 Constitution and putting his own interpretation on its provisions, there need be no question of majority rule for 150 years – in keeping with his formula 'not in my lifetime'.

Two odd events occurred during Smith's visit to Winston's funeral. First Smith failed to turn up at the Queen's reception for the world leaders at Buckingham Palace, to which he had been invited. The Queen ordered an equerry to seek him out. He was found eating a steak at an hotel and informed the equerry that he had not received the invitation. Harold Wilson records that he was told later by Smith's High Commission that it was, in fact, in his pocket all the time.

The other incident was a surprising call on me in the law courts from a junior minister asking me to arrest Smith and to prosecute him for treason. I asked him whether he came with the authority of his Secretary of State. He said he did not. Of course a prosecution of Smith for treason when he had come here at Her Majesty's invitation and at the Government's suggestion was out of the question. It was the only time a minister sought to bring pressure to bear on me as Attorney General to launch a prosecution.

The 'five principles' which we insisted must be the basis of any agreement with the Rhodesian Government had by then been determined. They were:

1. The principle and intention of unimpeded progress to majority rule would have to be maintained and guaranteed.
2. Guarantees against retrogressive amendment of the Constitution.
3. Immediate improvement in the political status of the African population.
4. Progress towards ending racial discrimination.
5. The British Government would need to be satisfied that any basis proposed for independence was acceptable to the people of Rhodesia as a whole.

Gerald Gardiner and the Commonwealth Secretary, Arthur Bottomley, went to Salisbury in February 1965 for what proved to be unproductive talks with the Smith Government. There was no progress on any of the five principles.

My first visit to the Rhodesian capital was with the Prime Minister and the Commonwealth Secretary in October 1965. It began stormily. Harold Wilson had asked to talk to Joshua Nkomo, leader of ZAPU (the Zimbabwe African People's Union), and the Reverend Ndabaningi Sithole, leader of the rival ZANU (the Zimbabwe African National Union). When they arrived separately at Government House (they were hardly on speaking terms with each other) Harold Wilson discovered that neither had eaten all day and had been confined in a hot, unventilated police vehicle. Harold was very angry and lost his temper. It was the only time during the years I have known him that I ever saw this happen. He rounded fiercely on all the Rhodesians present, including the startled Governor-General, Sir Humphrey Gibbs (usually treated with respect and regard by us all), and ordered that the African leaders should be given a meal at once. He sent the British Army Colonel who was accompanying us with them to satisfy himself that Nkomo and Sithole were being properly fed. The Prime Minister was already incensed by reports we had received from British and American journalists who had seen police dogs deliberately set loose on Africans peaceably gathered at the gates of Government House to cheer their leaders on arrival.

During this visit we had meetings with many leading figures in Rhodesia's political and business life: the most memorable was the gathering of the Council of Chiefs, each gorgeously arrayed and bearing his insignia of office. It was evident from our discussions that they had no clear idea of the constitutional issues we had been discussing about amendment of the 1961 Constitution and were quite unqualified to be a representative consultative group capable of expressing the opinion of the Africans.

That evening Harold Wilson, Bottomley and I dined with the Rhodesian Prime Minister and Cabinet in Ian Smith's residence in Salisbury. Harold sat on his right, I on his left. He was sociable at dinner and talked nostalgically about his days as a fighter pilot during the war.

During dinner the Duke of Montrose, still known there as Lord Graham and thought to be the likely 'Regent' of Rhodesia if independence were declared, told a coarse story embellished by movements of his large body. When he sat down, Harold Wilson, in a voice loud enough for all the assembled company to hear, remarked, 'Now I understand what qualifications you have to have to become the Regent of Rhodesia.' An embarrassed silence followed.

During that mission we held long, difficult and inconclusive exchanges about an independence constitution based on that of 1961 but with amendments to provide guarantees for the effective fulfilment of the five principles. We got nowhere. My opposite number, dour Lardner-Burke, the Rhodesian Attorney General, was the most diehard of Smith's team.

In one of his many endeavours to break the deadlock, Harold Wilson then proposed the setting up of a Royal Commission, appointed by both governments, to make recommendations on the constitutional arrangements on which Rhodesia could proceed to independence. Our discussions went on until late that night. No agreement was reached so it was decided that Arthur Bottomley, Henry Steel of the Commonwealth Office and I should remain in Salisbury for further talks with Lardner-Burke. Once again we got nowhere.

Further abortive telephone discussions between Wilson and Smith took place in London. The end of the road was now being reached. The Smith Cabinet chose Armistice Day – 11 am on 11 November 1965 – to make the fateful decision which was to plunge Rhodesia into a bloody civil war lasting many years. UDI was declared.

At the United Nations almost every 'non-aligned' nation, headed by the Africans and supported by the Soviet bloc, demanded the use of troops by the British Government to quell the rebellion, to arrest the illegal government and to impose a new constitution based on immediate majority rule. We rejected the use of force. Rhodesia had her own well-equipped army and air force under the command of the regime's authorities. We were advised that a British military assault would be resisted. Our army would have to be supplied through Tanzania and Zambia, and the aerodrome at Lusaka in Zambia could have been put out of action easily. Many South Africans would have helped Rhodesia with soldiers, money and arms. There would have been many casualties and much physical destruction.

And there was a real danger that the use of force would escalate into a conflagration which could spread across the entire continent.

It fell to me as Attorney General to deal in the House with the legal consequences of UDI. The day after it was declared I emphasized that Southern Rhodesia was part of Her Majesty's dominions, that the Government and Parliament had jurisdiction over it and responsibility for it and that Parliament alone could grant the territory independence.

The enabling bill I moved three days later gave the Government powers to make whatever orders in council appeared to be necessary or expedient in consequence of the illegal declaration of independence. The orders (which had to be approved by Parliament) included a constitutional order invalidating any post-UDI laws passed by the Legislative Assembly in Rhodesia and also empowered the Secretary of State to exercise executive authority there and to make laws for the peace, order and good government of Rhodesia.

The most controversial order was the Oil Embargo Order, which initiated oil sanctions against Rhodesia. This, as later events showed, proved to be the most vulnerable of the economic sanctions and, unknown to me, the most successfully evaded. A few months later, in April 1966, I attended the Security Council in New York to assist Lord Caradon, our Ambassador to the United Nations, in presenting the Beira Resolution designed to plug one of the gaps. Oil tankers were unloading at Beira in the Portuguese colony of Mozambique and oil was being pumped from there by pipeline to Rhodesia. The resolution gave the British Government power to intercept tankers delivering oil, by force if necessary. Senator Goldberg, the United States delegate, who was most cooperative, congratulated the British Government on recognizing its obligations under the Charter of the United Nations and 'its respect for the decent opinion of mankind'. It was my first experience of lobbying at the United Nations and of talking with a small group here and using a little persuasion there.

Despite UDI and because of the seriousness of the position, we decided to make another attempt at an acceptable settlement. In December 1966 I accompanied Harold Wilson and the Secretary of State, Herbert Bowden, the Cabinet Secretary, Burke Trend, and the other leading officials, plus Dr Joe Stone, Harold's doctor, to the conference with Smith and his colleagues on HMS *Tiger*. Harold chose a ship, not for theatrical reasons – although he was fond of dramatic actions – but because of the need for privacy and freedom from media pressure. As I left the cabinet meeting at No 10 at which the decision to make his new attempt was reached, Gerald Gardiner handed me a note which read: 'Remember, you are our conscience.' He and others feared that the Prime Minister was so determined to achieve a settlement of the Rhodesia problem that excessively favourable terms might be offered to Smith.

We flew to Gibraltar in an RAF plane. Before we landed a message came over the radio from George Wigg, the Paymaster General with special responsibility in the field of security (which he was inclined to dramatize), instructing us, on security grounds, to run to the safety of the airport building as soon as the plane's doors were open. When we landed at Gibraltar we were faced by a heavy rainstorm. We did indeed run as fast as we could to the airport building. However, it was not George's apprehensions but the storm that impelled us.

We were driven to the Gibraltar dockside, where we boarded a small launch, which rolled and bumped over a rough sea in a force ten gale till we came alongside HMS *Tiger*. A sailor in frogman's kit stood by to get us safely from the rearing launch on to the foot of *Tiger's* gangway. The officers and men of the Royal Navy looked after us splendidly during the days we spent on board. They steered a skilful course to and fro on the restless Mediterranean between Gibraltar and the African coast.

The long conference sessions (the minutes of which have been published in Command Paper 3171) were held in a large wardroom with the delegations seated on opposite sides of a big mess table. They became bogged down in detailed constitutional differences about the franchise, the number of A roll and B roll seats and the setting up of a Royal Commission to advise whether the proposed independence constitution was acceptable to the Rhodesian people. Harold Wilson was determined to achieve a settlement if he possibly could and went far to meet Smith's demands: indeed further than I was happy to go. It was a worrying time and I had little sleep on board HMS *Tiger*.

After two days of contention, heads of agreement were drawn up which, had they been put into effect, would gradually have resulted in majority rule in Rhodesia as more and more Africans got on to the electoral roll.

To reassure the white Rhodesians Wilson proposed a new sixth principle to be added to the basic five: it would be necessary to ensure that regardless of race, there was no oppression of majority by minority or of minority by majority.

All that remained was for the two Prime Ministers to sign the agreement on the basis that they would recommend it to their respective cabinets.

We adjourned while the document was being typed and Harold, Herbert Bowden, Burke Trend, Marcia Williams (the Prime Minister's secretary) and I waited in Harold's cabin until the agreement which Smith had accepted arrived for signature. We waited and waited. Harold then sent one of our staff to find out where Smith was. He was found to be in the engine room touring the ship. We were informed that he was only willing to sign the document as a record of what had been discussed and not as an agreement which he would recommend to his cabinet on his return to Salisbury.

Smith confirmed this at an angry meeting in which Harold declared that he had only agreed to the *Tiger* talks on the strength of Smith's assurance that he had full authority to commit his cabinet. On the Prime Minister's instructions HMS *Tiger* then returned at full speed to Gibraltar, where Smith and Chief Justice Beadle, upon whom we had initially, but mistakenly, placed high hopes, made a grim departure.

A few days later the Prime Minister faced a heated debate in the Commons on a motion endorsing the decision of the Government to accept the *Tiger* Agreement, and deploring its rejection by the illegal regime in Rhodesia. This the Opposition opposed. The Prime Minister commented bitterly: 'Every one of the gentlemen opposite is more interested in trying to get rid of the legal Government here than the illegal regime in Southern Rhodesia.' A fortnight later the Government supported a mandatory resolution in the United Nations under Chapter VII of the UN Constitution, setting up a wide-ranging system of international sanctions on trade with Rhodesia: they were only partially enforced.

The growing conflict in Rhodesia was highlighted in March 1968. The then Commonwealth Secretary, George Thomson, learned that the Smith regime proposed to hang some of the prisoners who had, for up to two and a half years, been under sentence of death. George consulted me. I agreed that it would be constitutionally, and in all other respects, right for the Commonwealth Secretary to advise the Queen to exercise the prerogative of mercy in those cases. This was done but was ignored by Smith's government. The first three men named on the Salisbury death list were in fact executed on 6 March.

This action raised a storm in the Commons in a debate in which Peter Tapsell, a Conservative MP, quoted to a troubled House Winston Churchill's memorable words: 'Grass grows quickly over the battlefield; over the scaffold never.' In the United Nations there were repeated demands for tighter sanctions and calls on the British Government to quell the Rhodesian rebellion by force.

One consequence was a Security Council resolution in May 1968, banning all trade with Rhodesia. I moved the Southern Rhodesian

(United Nations Sanctions) Order in June to give effect to that resolution. In a frequently interrupted speech I stressed the fact that the Rhodesian problem had grave international aspects and that although Rhodesia was a British responsibility it was inevitable that 'the situation there, under which a small minority of European stock of about 232,000 are oppressively blocking the political advance of an African majority of over four and a quarter million, should be a matter of international concern'. We were committed to a policy of restoring Rhodesia to constitutional rule not just because the regime was in rebellion against us, but because we could neither honourably nor wisely underwrite the rebellion's objectives.

In that speech I stressed the conviction which had greatly influenced my political life, particularly since the Nuremberg Trials, that racism is one of the great evils of our time. I expressed my profound belief that it is vital to the peace and prosperity of the world that the industrialized countries of the Western world should not enrol themselves under the banner of racialism and should show themselves ready to resist racial oppression wherever it occurs. A little later, when I spoke in the House on the Race Relations Bill, I urged the use of the sanctions of the law against purveyors of racial hatred and against racial discrimination.

Feelers put out in Rhodesia in the later part of 1968 led the Prime Minister to make yet another effort at achieving a settlement with Smith. On 8 October Harold, the Commonwealth Secretary and I, together with our advisers, flew to Gibraltar to confer on HMS *Fearless*, which was moored in harbour alongside HMS *Kent*, where Smith was accommodated during the conference. On *Fearless* the quarterdeck and wardroom area we were to use had been sealed off with the impressive notice 'Conference Citadel'.

The *Fearless* discussions were more relaxed than those on board *Tiger*. They lasted thirty hours. We prepared the text of an acceptable constitutional settlement, and proposals for the return to legality. The document was handed to Smith to study after a Sunday church service on the afterdeck of *Fearless*, with the Smith delegation seated on the port side and ourselves on starboard. A free afternoon enabled me to accompany Harold (who proudly wore his naval cap as an Elder Brother of Trinity House) on a cruise in the Admiral's launch in the waters around Gibraltar, some of which were claimed by the Spaniards.

Both at the *Fearless* discussions and in Parliament afterwards we insisted that the six principles remained the key to a settlement. In the Commons debate on these latest proposals, although a number of MPs were unhappy about accepting anything short of NIBMR (no independence before majority rule) and a few favoured the use of force to impose a solution, there was substantial agreement on both sides of the House that the *Fearless* terms were right. But Salisbury rejected them. Smith nevertheless suggested that a visit by George Thomson could be helpful. He went over and stayed for many days, at the end of which he reported that there was no movement on the Smith side towards an agreement. 'Not in my lifetime' remained Smith's attitude. The doors to settlement were again closed.

The Law Officers were consulted about other international matters during my term of office. This was not new. In 1875 Sir James Jessel wrote: 'Anything that was not very clear was put into a big canvas bag at the Foreign Office and sent to the Law Officers.' We improved on that when I was Attorney General. William Dale, who was seconded to the Law Officers' Department from the legal staff of the Foreign Office, gave us great assistance. So did Francis Vallat with his vast experience in the international field and Vincent Evans, his successor as Legal Adviser to the Foreign Office.

One foreign problem on which the Law Officers were asked to advise came to a head shortly after Labour came into office. It was whether we could pull out of the open-ended treaty commitment which the Conservative administration had made with France to research and produce two Concorde prototypes. Our advice (which was revealed by Richard Crossman when he became editor of the *New Statesman*) was that quite apart from our duty to honour treaty obligations, it could prove as costly to break the treaty with France as to carry on. President de Gaulle was determined to go on with Concorde, which he regarded as a symbol of France's technical prowess. He could sue us in the International Court of Justice for breach of the treaty agreement and if he did so, we advised that he would be likely to succeed. At that time the cost of research and production of two prototypes had escalated from the original figure, estimated by Julian Amery as £150 million, to £380 million in 1964. We would have had to pay half of this if we had lost the case at the Hague, and we would have had nothing to show for it. Quite apart from this, the Foreign Office did not want a break with France on this issue at a time when the possibility of our joining the European Economic Community was being canvassed. So production of the Concorde continued.

Legal problems also arose over Gibraltar. Spain was asserting her claim to sovereignty over the Rock and imposing new travel and trade restrictions at the frontier. We resolved that if the people of Gibraltar wanted to remain with us – as they did – they should do so. We were confident that our title to sovereignty over Gibraltar was good. In furtherance of the peaceful settlement of disputes, the British Government proposed to Madrid that all the legal issues in dispute over Gibraltar should be referred to the International Court. Spain, however, had not accepted the compulsory jurisdiction of the court and refused to take up our offer.

As a Law Officer of the Crown I had a number of miscellaneous functions to perform. The Attorney General is the titular head of the Bar of England and Wales, and presides over its annual general meeting. I kept in close touch with affairs of the Bar and with its members, to whom I made myself accessible. Nomination of counsel to take part in public inquiries, or to appear for the Crown in the most serious criminal cases and in civil cases where the public interest was involved, was a frequent task, in which I was assisted by my clerk, Eric Cooper. When new Silks were appointed the Lord Chancellor sought the advice of the Law Officers.

As Head of the Bar I attended several Commonwealth and Empire Law Conferences. The first of these was in Sydney, Australia in 1965. Polly, who does not like to fly, went to Sydney by cargo ship, leaving several weeks before I did. Travelling by slow cargo ships to West Africa or the West Indies or China and writing and drawing aboard them was bliss to her. I flew to Sydney, on the way spending two memorable days in Mexico City with our Ambassador as an expert guide to some of its treasures. Then, on to Tahiti, where I was garlanded at Papete airport by Tahitian friends, descendants of Lord Bambridge, who went to Tahiti in the last century and married a beautiful Tahitian princess. They took me to their home set in a great garden where their ancestors were buried, every grave adorned with fresh flowers each day. The Tahitian calm was broken by the unwelcome presence in Papete of many members of the French Foreign Legion: the French were carrying out atmospheric nuclear tests on a Pacific atoll.

Two old friends greeted me at Nandi airport in Fiji. Ronald Knox-Mawer was a justice of the Fiji High Court and June, his wife, was writing and broadcasting. They drove me to the Governor's official residence on the western side of the island – a *bure*, its great thatched roof supported by massive gable posts in the classic Fijian style.

A feast was given in my honour and I was hailed as 'Vuni Lewa' (meaning the 'Root of the Law'), the native rendering of Attorney General. We sat cross-legged on mats feasting on turtle, crab and roasted pig. Mountain tribesmen prepared a huge bowl of kava – made from macerated roots of the kava plant – with much solemnity and ceremonial. It was brought to me in a coconut shell to be drunk in one draught. As was the custom I tossed the empty shell across to my hosts when I had consumed the spicy, intoxicating concoction, to the cheers of the company. We talked and made speeches and sang and drank and ate until midnight. Then hibiscus-garlanded dancers arrived from the neighbouring Vuda village and danced to the beat of drums and sang nostalgic songs on the moonlit lawn.

Next day I flew to the Fijian capital Suva and stayed with the genial acting Governor, Paddy Macdonald, in the white colonnaded Government House on a high wooded hill in a park overlooking the busy city.

I finally arrived in Sydney and met Polly there. As journalists fired a series of questions at me, Polly obligingly helped me out by answering one. In Australia women were expected to know their place. Polly's expression on receiving a glare of outraged rebuke from the very young male reporter who had asked the question was captured by a press photographer. It has remained one of our favourite photographs.

Polly had been exploring the Sydney docks and had discovered the sailors' small bistros on the waterfront, alcoved like old London coffee houses. There at a very modest price you could eat excellent lobsters, huge crayfish and shad, washed down by very strong Indian tea. Later she introduced Bill Dale, one of our delegation, to these delights. Thereafter he abandoned the bustle and delay of his expensive hotel to eat his lunch there, parking his bowler hat and settling down to work on conference papers, while the other customers studied their racing newspapers.

I already knew Bob Menzies, the former Prime Minister, as a popular bencher of Gray's Inn. He opened the Law Conference in characteristic style by saying that when he met the judges dressed in their robes of scarlet and ermine after the church service that morning, he had expected to savour the odour of sanctity. All he encountered was the smell of mothballs.

This, the third Commonwealth and Empire Law Conference, was attended by distinguished representatives from many of the new African and Asian countries which had achieved independence and become full participants in the Commonwealth.

The Commonwealth itself was still subject to stresses and strains. South Africa had withdrawn and racial issues were tense in Southern Rhodesia. There were even some doubts as to whether the Commonwealth could survive as a multi-racial community with enough in common to warrant regular meetings of all its members. In the event the Sydney conference, ably organized by our Australian hosts, affirmed the strength of the Commonwealth bond. (Incidentally one of these – John Kerr – was later appointed Australia's Governor-General, and was at the centre of the Commonwealth's most sensational constitutional storm when he dismissed the Whitlam government.)

Alongside the main conference another took place in Canberra attended by the Lord Chancellor, Chief Justices and Attorney Generals. Gerald Gardiner proposed the setting up of a centralized Commonwealth Court of Appeal to take the place of the Judicial Committee of the Privy Council and announced that England and Wales would consider favourably giving up appeals to the House of Lords if it would help the creation of that court. He had in mind that the court would be peripatetic, travelling to the countries accepting its jurisdiction. Unfortunately we found that the proposal had come too late and, although several of the smaller countries of the Commonwealth supported it, it was rejected by the larger countries.

The item at the conference which most attracted the world press was the speech by Chief Justice Cornelius of Pakistan in which he advocated that some criminals should be physically disabled as a punishment for their crimes. He praised the high security of property in Saudi Arabia, which he claimed resulted from the fact that the punishment for theft was amputation of the thief's hands. The Chief Justice did not go as far as that, but thought that minor surgery immobilizing a hand would suffice. No one supported him.

After the Sydney conference Polly and I snatched a blissful holiday on Hayman Island on Great Barrier Reef, where we walked on the coral strand.

I attended several conferences of European Ministers of Justice at the Hague and at Strasbourg, where I addressed the conference of the Council of Europe. The expertise of interpreters faltered even there. A reference to 'the common lawyers of the United Kingdom' was interpreted as '*les juristes très ordinaires du Royaume Uni*'.

Two other agreeable conferences come back to mind. I led the British team to the conference of Anglo-American Parliamentarians in windswept but hospitable Bermuda. It was held in their ancient Parliament House, its procedure a faithful replica of the Westminster model. I felt equally at home in Bermuda's courts of law. It was one of the friendliest communities I have known. David Wilkinson, a distinguished member of its Legislature and Bar, has become a great friend.

Another legal gathering I attended as Attorney General took place in Lahore, where they were celebrating the centenary of the Supreme Court of West Pakistan. I presented to the members of the court a silver salver bearing the coats-of-arms of each of the four Inns of Court, where generations of Pakistan lawyers had been called to the Bar.

Pakistan was suffering from a terrible drought. One of the highlights of the celebrations was a garden party in the beautiful walled Shalimar gardens. Ladies in elegant silks sat at attractively decorated separate tables. Suddenly, just as President Ayub Khan entered the great gardens the drought broke. A torrent of rain poured down upon us. The reaction of the rain-soaked guests however was one of joy, not complaint, and I was given credit for bringing the rain.

I once had another experience of a drought breaking: this time in East Africa, in Nairobi. As we flew over Kenya I could see the skeletons of giraffes and other animals which had perished in the drought. I was briefed to appear in the Kenya High Court for the defence of a Kenyan business consultant who faced a charge of perjury. The jury acquitted him. That night he invited me, in celebration of his acquittal, to dine with him and his family and to attend a performance of *The Rainmaker*. It is a play about a con man who persuades drought-harassed farmers to pay him a fee to bring the rain. Throughout the play the actors in a parched sunlit setting complain of the drought. However, just as the curtain went up at the opening of the first act, the Kenya drought broke. The rain crashed down on the hot tin roof of the theatre and it was hard to hear the words of the actors for the sound of the rain. In Nairobi, too, I was given credit for bringing the rain.

My final year as Attorney General, 1970, began with a judicial tour of India in which I was accompanied by my daughter Josephine, deputizing for Polly. The Chief Justice of India had complained to the Lord Chancellor that they were losing touch with British judges and lawyers, although Russian and other nationalities visited them. The Lord Chancellor then arranged for the Lord Chief Justice and Lady Widgery, the Master of the Rolls and Lady Denning, and Josephine and me to go. By the time I was appointed Attorney General in 1964, Josephine, our eldest child, had graduated from Cambridge, married and moved to Hong Kong, where she taught science and divinity at the Diocesan Girls' School in Kowloon. Polly visited her there and spent most of her time exploring the Chinese markets and the waterfront; her Hong Kong paintings and lithographs are now in many national collections. When Josephine returned to Europe she wrote a series of children's books about Hong Kong which Polly illustrated; they were made into a *Jackanory* television programme called 'Stories from Ladder Street', movingly read by Judi Dench. Josephine then began work as a popularizer of science, and edited a series of his papers for N.W. Pirie before joining the Science and Features Department at the BBC to work with Dr Bronowski on the series and book of *The Ascent of Man*. By then her marriage to Richard Marquand had ended. Later they both remarried.

I had visited India before, in 1959 for the conference in Delhi of the International Commission of Jurists on the Rule of Law. Pandit Nehru, relaxed and genial, had opened that conference superbly in an unscripted speech. In 1970 we attended the Supreme Court in Delhi, the High Courts in Rajasthan, Allahabad, Madras and Bombay and the District Courts of Varanasi (Benares) and Agra. Each of us made at least one speech a day.

We were impressed by the good quality of the advocacy at the Bar and the effectiveness of the Bench. We were moved by their pride in the heritage of English law, which they declared to be one of the greatest legacies the British had given to India, and by their resolve to maintain this bond.

Josephine and I were invited to stay in Delhi with the British High Commissioner and his wife, Sir Maurice and Lady James. The gardens of the residence were alive with birdsong from dawn chorus to sundown.

In Jaipur we rode on painted elephants up to the royal palace to see the mirrored walls and ceilings. Josephine remembers that I quickly picked up the mahout's song as he kept the elephant swaying up the steep hill to the Palace.

We visited Mahabalipuram, south of Madras, a site of India's early history, its temples carved out of solid rock. We had an exciting passage on a ferry boat steered by an aged ferryman to the turbulent confluence of the Jumna and the Ganges. My stock went up in Josephine's eyes when in the late Pandit Nehru's home in Allahabad she spotted my Penguin Special, *The Attack from Within*, on his bookshelf.

We were graciously entertained in Rashbrabati Bhavan, the old Viceroy's residence, by the distinguished V.U.Giri, Muslim President of India, a critical figure in the Indian educational programme and a symbol of the secular state in which Mahatma Gandhi and Nehru so deeply believed. Mrs Gandhi, the Prime Minister also received us in her home.

Only one mishap marred our Indian mission : while saying farewell to an Indian friend, Josephine was bitten by his Alsatian dog. The doctor at our High Commission gave her a tetanus injection and assured her that if the offending Alsatian did not die of rabies within three weeks, she had nothing to fear. The dog lived and all was well.

We were moved by so much that we saw and by the warmth of our welcome wherever we went and we were all sad to say farewell to India. I returned there in 1977 for the funeral of the then President, Sakhrudin Ali Ahmed.

19

Crime and Punishment

The Attorney General has important responsibilities for the enforcement of criminal law in the courts, although in practice he is involved directly only in a very small minority of the criminal cases that are tried. The bulk of prosecutions are the responsibility of the police and the prosecuting authorities up and down the country. There are, however, a number of offences where, by Act of Parliament, the prosecution cannot be brought without the fiat of the Attorney General. These include offences which come under the Explosive Substances Act, the Prevention of Corruption Act, the Official Secrets Act, the Public Order Act and the Race Relations Act among others. These are all cases where Parliament has considered that for one reason or another there may be a special risk of a prosecution being brought in circumstances which would be an abuse of proceedings or for some other reason contrary to the public interest. Sometimes the act creating the offence has had to be drafted in wide terms and Parliament has relied upon the Attorney General or the Director of Public Prosecutions to see that the provision is not abused.

The decision whether or not to prosecute in a given case is not always an easy one. The first test is whether there is a reasonable prospect of a conviction; the second whether its circumstances are such that a prosecution is required in the public interest. Sometimes there are considerations of public policy which make it undesirable to prosecute a case: youth or old age or infirmity or mental illness of the offender for instance, or the staleness of the offence. Or perhaps to prosecute him would make the offender seem a martyr.

While the decision whether or not to prosecute was my responsibility, I usually had, in addition to the statements of witnesses and a police report, the advice of the Director of Public Prosecutions – and sometimes the advice of senior counsel as well. Party political considerations did not influence my decisions. In a few cases of public importance and one where a Member of Parliament was prosecuted I informed the Prime Minister of my decision to authorize a prosecution. Harold Wilson was meticulous in not seeking to influence any of my decisions, nor did I solicit his advice or that of any other minister. I never referred any of my cases to the Cabinet, nor was I asked to do so. The decision is a quasi-judicial decision which the Attorney General must make himself.

Which cases Attorney Generals themselves should prosecute is for them to decide. They no longer prosecute – as was the practice before the Homicide Act 1957 – in all murder poison cases, but they do occasionally prosecute in murder cases which may be of great public importance – as I did in the 'Moors Murders Case' and the trial of the murderers of three policemen in Shepherds Bush. They normally prosecute in serious cases under the Official Secrets Act.

The spy cases brought under the Official Secrets Act between 1965 and 1968 in which I led for the prosecution had the same motivation. The men on trial who had sold highly secret official documents to Soviet agents were not disloyal for ideological reasons. They betrayed their trust entirely for money, and comparatively little money at that. All were in deep financial trouble. One – Bossard – had fallen into the hands of moneylenders. Early in their dealings with the Soviet agents (their 'controls') some of them signed receipts for the money they received. After that they were trapped.

Soviet espionage techniques in these cases ranged from the sophisticated to the curiously amateur. The accused were given money to buy the best cameras with which to photograph documents, plans and designs. Sometimes they received their instructions in actual meetings with the Soviet agents but these, because of the risk of detection, were infrequent. Hiding places in trunks of trees, under junk left in woods or, in one case, under a telephone kiosk, were chosen in different locations outside London. At prearranged dates and times the accused would deposit in the hiding place packets of films or whatever it was they had to deliver. In addition to these 'puts' there were 'takes' – collection points where at pre-arranged times the accused would collect their money or instructions from the Soviet agents. In some cases the secret material was packed in putty to look like a stone. Messages were sometimes conveyed by the deposit of church notices or cinema advertisements. In one case the accused received his instructions via Moscow radio on specific wavelength transmissions on prearranged dates and times by means of a code based on the playing of a particular tune and the number of times it was played.

In all cases the accused were employed in positions of trust which gave them access to secrets it was their duty to safeguard. This enabled them to supply material of great value to a potential enemy.

Frank Clifton Bossard was an engineer grade one in the Guided Weapons, Research and Development Division of the Ministry of Aviation when he was approached by a Soviet agent in 1961 and told he would be paid good money for intelligence information. He photographed ministry files and was caught red-handed by our security service. In all he received £5,000 from the Russians. The last payment to him – of £2,000 in five-pound notes – was left for him in a 'take' in Blackheath. He pleaded guilty and was sentenced by Lord Chief Justice Parker in May 1965 to a total of twenty-one years' imprisonment.

This was also the fate of Donald Ronald Britten, whom I prosecuted in November 1968 shortly after I returned from the HMS *Fearless* talks off Gibraltar. Britten was a chief technician in RAF signals units in Cyprus and then at the Digby RAF Station where he was employed to intercept the radio signals of Soviet Air Force units. He had been in contact with the Russians since 1962. He passed highly secret information to a member of the Soviet Embassy in London he knew as Yuri. When he was arrested in September 1968, he was found to have extensive espionage equipment, including a camera ingeniously disguised as a cigarette case which he was able to take in and out of his base. He was married with four children and was in serious financial trouble. Several of his cheques had been dishonoured. On one occasion the Russians photographed him receiving money from an agent and subsequently used the photographs to maintain their hold over him. He pleaded guilty at his trial at the Old Bailey to five charges under Section 1 of the Official Secrets Act. He had no ideological motives. What he did he did for money: about £5,000.

Staff Sergeant Allen's case covered different ground. He was a clerk at the Directorate of Land and Air Warfare in the Army Department of the Ministry of Defence. He received £65 for selling secret documents to Middle Eastern governments. He was heavily in debt and was caught in Northumberland Avenue, London, handing over documents to the Assistant Military Attaché of the Iraq Embassy in return for £10.

The most extraordinary espionage case in which I appeared was after I ceased to be Attorney General and had returned to the Bar. I was briefed for the defence in the trial of the remarkable Mrs Bingham, who wore a different dress for each day of the trial. She was the wife of David James Bingham, a Sub-Lieutenant on HMS *Rothesay* in Portsmouth. Bingham had admitted having been in Soviet pay for eighteen months and passing secret information to Kugmin, the Soviet Naval Attaché in London, in 1970 and 1971. His pay as a Sub-Lieutenant was not enough to meet his household needs. He too had run into debt. He was sentenced to twenty-one years' imprisonment.

After her husband's trial, Mrs Bingham insisted in numerous newspaper and television interviews that it was she who made the first contact with the Soviet Embassy in London. She claimed to be the intermediary between her husband and the Russians. She deliberately brought the trial upon herself. She was sentenced mercifully to two years' imprisonment by Mr Justice Sebag Shaw (as he then was) at Winchester Crown Court in 1972. Her world had already been destroyed. The case aroused so much feeling in Portsmouth that I had the unique experience of being hissed by one or two women – perhaps naval wives who had come to Winchester for the trial – as I left the court after making my closing speech in mitigation on her behalf.

Another prosecution with which I was concerned arose from the murder in cold blood in August 1966 of three police officers going about their ordinary duty of protecting members of the public. They were investigating a suspect van in Shepherds Bush when three men each carrying guns shot and killed them at close range.

Two of the suspects – Witney and Duddy – were soon apprehended but despite the intensive police search for Harry Roberts, the third man, there was no trace of him. Detective Superintendent Chitty, who was in charge of the massive search for Roberts, assured me that they would find him in time for the trial. However, by November we decided we could wait no longer. I opened the trial of Witney and Duddy at the Old Bailey on 14 November 1966. The very next day a tent belonging to Harry Roberts was found in the undergrowth in Epping Forest. There he had lived rough and well concealed for about three months. The discovery of the tent soon led to his arrest.

We adjourned the trial of Witney and Duddy until 5 December so that Roberts could be tried jointly with them. Unfortunately one of the recurring Rhodesian crises arose just then and I was unable to do the case myself. The Solicitor-General, Dingle Foot, took my place. All three were convicted of murder and were sentenced to life imprisonment.

In the course of my practice at the Bar I appeared as counsel in various murder cases: murders for greed, murders in the heat of passion, sadistic murders, drunken murders. The 'Moors Murders' of innocent children committed by Ian Brady and Myra Hindley, between 1963 and 1965, were unique in their depravity and heartlessness.

I took the view, with which the then Director of Public Prosecutions Norman Skelhorn agreed, that it was a case of such exceptional gravity and public concern that the Attorney General should lead for the prosecution. I was admirably assisted by counsel – William Mars-Jones and Ronald Waterhouse (each made a High Court judge later) – and by Skelhorn and his staff.

The trial took place during one of the recurring Rhodesian UDI crises, so that on two days of the trial I had to go back to London and return again to Chester in the early hours of the morning, to find my loyal colleagues waiting to brief me on the day's events. We seldom got to bed before 3 am during the trial.

The case was this, twelve-year-old John Kilbride disappeared on 23 November 1963. He was last seen earlier that evening in Ashton-under-Lyne market. Leslie Ann Downey, aged ten, vanished on 26 December 1964. She had gone in the late afternoon to the Christmas Fair in Ancoats. Despite massive police enquiries, public searches and press publicity, no trace of either of the two children was found.

The secret of their disappearance was not revealed until October 1965. In the early morning of 7 October two very frightened young people, David Smith, aged seventeen, accompanied by his wife Maureen (who was Myra Hindley's sister), telephoned the Stalybridge police from a telephone kiosk. Smith was carrying a carving knife and a long screwdriver because he feared attack by Ian Brady. He made a statement to the police and as a result an immediate police action was mounted.

Brady was already known to the police. He had previous convictions for housebreaking and theft, for which he had been sent to borstal. Police Superintendent Talbot, dressed in a white overall and carrying a basket of fresh loaves hastily borrowed from a baker's van, knocked on the back door of 16 Wardle Brook Avenue, Hattersley where Brady and Hindley lived, together with Hindley's seventy-seven-year-old grandmother, Mrs Haybury. Myra Hindley came to the door. When the Superintendent told her that an act of violence had been reported to the police she said: 'There is nothing wrong here.'

Superintendent Talbot entered the house at some risk, for David Smith had told the police that there were loaded guns in the house. He found Brady writing a letter to his employer, for whom he worked as an invoice clerk. Myra Hindley was his typist. The letter said that he had been knocked down by a bicycle and could not come to work that day. The reason for this soon became clear. Brady had planned to do other work that day.

In an upstairs room Superintendent Talbot found, in polythene wrapping inside a rug, the trussed body of Edward Evans, a lad of seventeen. He had been battered to death by fourteen blows with a hatchet and a piece of electric cable had been pulled tightly round his neck.

Brady told the police that he and the deceased Evans had an argument and came to blows, that there was a hatchet in the fireplace with which he hit Evans, and that 'the situation became out of control'. He insisted that Smith had taken part in the deadly assault on Evans and that they had carried the body upstairs together. Seeking to protect Myra Hindley, who refused to make a statement to the police, he said nobody else was involved.

David Smith's version of what had happened was that he was in the kitchen when:

> All of a sudden I heard a very loud scream, very loud. Just before it died, another one followed it. Then Myra shouted 'Dave, help him.' I didn't know what was coming. I just ran out of the kitchen and into the living room on the left and I just froze and stopped dead. My first thought was that Ian had hold of a life-size rag doll and was just waving it about. Then it dawned on me that it was not a rag doll.

Outside Brady's home on the morning Superintendent Talbot entered it, the police found in his car a detailed 'disposal plan' for Evans's body. The prosecution contended that it was prepared before the planned killing of Evans and that Brady had set up this murder as part of the process of corrupting David Smith and involving him in his own murderous deeds.

The minute police search of Brady's home by Chief Inspector Tyrrell yielded the clue to the deaths of John Kilbride and Leslie Ann Downey. In the hollow spine of a prayer book (that had been given to Myra Hindley seven years before by her aunt and uncle as a souvenir of her first Holy Communion), he found a receipt for two suitcases deposited in the left luggage office of Central Station, Manchester on the evening before Evans was killed.

The suitcases contained books and photographs and two copies of a tape recording. The latter proved to be the most terrible of all the exhibits in the case.

I will never forget the shock when I heard the tape played to me before the trial by one of the detectives in charge of the case.

It began with the frantic screams of the little girl Leslie Ann Downey.

Her screams were repeated several times. Then followed the child's sobbing voice pleading, 'Let me go,' and begging for her mother. Then she pleaded, 'Please God, help me.' Myra Hindley's voice could be heard saying: 'Come on, shut up.' When Leslie Ann was being gagged, Myra Hindley's voice was again heard instructing the child: 'Put that in your mouth again packed more solid.' Then the child's voice was heard no more. The silence on the tape merged into the Christmas music of 'Jolly Old St Nicholas' and the drums of 'The Little Drummer Boy'. It was Boxing Day 1964.

The horror of the tape was augmented by nine pornographic photographs taken by Brady of Leslie Ann, her mouth sealed by a man's scarf tied behind her head. She was naked except for her shoes and ankle socks.

Another photograph taken by Brady furnished the detectives with a vital clue. It was of Myra Hindley with her small dog in her arms, gazing down almost reverently at a disturbed patch of earth on Saddleworth Moor. The police tracked down the spot. In a shallow grave they found the body of John Kilbride. Earlier they had found John Kilbride's name written by Brady in an exercise book found in his home.

A photograph Brady had taken of another otherwise unremarkable patch of disturbed ground on Saddleworth Moor proved to be the grave of Leslie Ann Downey. The moor had also been intended as Edward Evans's graveyard, but in his case the 'perfect murder' went wrong. David Smith had gone to the police. Before Evans was murdered, according to David Smith, Brady had told him: 'I have killed three or four. I will do another one, but I am not due for another three months.'

The trial began on 26 April 1966 in the Assize Court in Chester Castle. The dock in which the two accused sat had been given extra protection on three sides with splinter-proof glass panels.

At the trial I sought the direction of the judge as to whether the fearful tape should be played in camera or in open court. The judge ruled: 'There has been so much talk that in my opinion we have no right to exclude the public. Anyone who wishes not to listen should leave now. During it I request complete silence. The Attorney General will beforehand read out the transcript, at dictation speed.' I did so as dispassionately as I could, for the passions which could have erupted in that anguished courtroom might have been uncontrollable. It was the worst ordeal I have ever had to carry out in court.

After I finished reading the transcript the tape was played. It lasted seventeen minutes. When the tape ended the only persons unmoved in the court were the two accused.

In my cross-examination of Brady I asked him why he had preserved this tape.

He answered, 'Because it is unusual.'

When I questioned him about his shameful photographs of Leslie Ann Downey, I asked him: 'Do you think they are horrible?'

'Not necessarily,' he replied.

I have wondered why Brady did not destroy the tapes and photographs, which, if discovered, were bound to lead to his doom. It may be that he was proud of them as evidence of how far he had gone down the de Sade road.

I asked Myra Hindley had she not been cruel to Leslie Ann.

'Yes, I was cruel,' she said.

'And pitiless?'

'I was cruel.' She did not admit to having been pitiless. Throughout the whole trial, neither she nor Brady showed the slightest trace of compassion or remorse.

Early in my cross-examination of Brady he in effect admitted murdering Edward Evans. To the other charges he and Myra Hindley both claimed that Leslie Ann had left the house safely after the photographs had been taken and that they knew nothing at all about John Kilbride. The two accused blamed David Smith for what had happened to Leslie Ann. Brady claimed David Smith had brought her to his house and even suggested that the little girl had agreed to pose for pornographic photographs for ten shillings. He said it was David Smith who took her away safely afterwards. Myra Hindley claimed she was a reluctant spectator. The fatal tape nailed these lies. David Smith's voice never appeared in the recording. There was no doubting the voice of Myra Hindley.

Both Hindley and Brady persisted in lying when they gave evidence. Both kept their self-control. They were relaxed in the dock and were alert to every move at the trial.

During cross-examination I showed Hindley her flat checked slippers, the outside blotched with Evans's blood. She denied that she was wearing them on the evening of the murder, insisting that they simply happened to be in the sitting-room. I asked her what she was wearing. She said the ones she had on in the witness box. She took off a spotless white shoe and offered it to me for inspection. I asked her to note that there was no blood inside the slippers, which there well might have been had they been lying empty in the living room when Evans's skull was being battered. She examined the linings carefully with the apparent detachment of an expert witness. No, she persisted, she was not wearing them that night.

Brady lost his self-control only once. During a trial within the trial the defence challenged the admissibility of a statement he had made on the grounds that it was not voluntary and that the police had used improper means to obtain it. When I questioned Brady about the truthfulness of his allegations against the police he went wild with rage like a trapped animal and almost leaped out of the witness box as if to try to get at me.

I thought he might have been moved to anger when I questioned him about his collection of sado-masochistic and pornographic books. Instead his only comment was: 'You'll find much worse collections in Lords' manors all over the country.' Brady, twenty-five years old at the time of the first murder, had acquired this corrupting library over the years and indoctrinated Myra Hindley (four years younger than himself) and to some extent David Smith (ten years younger) with its contents. De Sade was one of his favourite authors and he was well acquainted with one particularly sinister passage which was read out at the trial:

> Is murder a crime in the eyes of nature? Doubtless we will humiliate man's pride in reducing him to the ranks of other productions of nature, but nevertheless he is merely an animal like any other, and in the eyes of nature his death is no more important than that of a fly or an ox.... Destruction is nature's method of progress, and she prompts the murderer to destruction, so that his action shall be the same as plague or famine.... In a word murder is a horror but a horror often necessary, never criminal, and essential to tolerate in a republic.

Pamela Hansford Johnson, who followed the trial closely, asked in her book *On Iniquity* whether it was inconceivable that this passage may have given Brady just that rationale, that self-justification, he needed for the acts festering in his mind. His 'library' included fascist and Nazi writings – Heinrich Himmler, *The Mark of the Swastika* and *Mein Kampf*. He introduced both Myra Hindley and David Smith to this literary poison to which he became addicted. Myra Hindley kept in her room a photograph of Irma Grese, who was hanged for her war crimes after Belsen was liberated.

One important decision we had to make at the trial was whether to call David Smith as a witness for the prosecution. Although our case was very strong without him, we decided that he had to be called. Brady and Myra Hindley both tried to shift blame on to him, particularly for the murder of Leslie Ann Downey. He was, we knew, a vulnerable witness. He was Myra Hindley's brother-in-law, he had been a close friend of the two accused and he himself had previous convictions for violence. He had also admitted being present when one of the murders was committed. We also discovered that he had been offered sums of money from a newspaper for his story.

When I learned about this I protested strongly to the Press Council. I expressed my misgivings that such payments might lead to the colouring of David Smith's evidence and that a long process of newspaper questioning of witnesses might prejudice the proper conduct of the trial. As a result the Press Council made a 'Declaration of Principles' condemning such practices, and it appeared to have some effect on the press, until the mischief recurred again during the trial of Jeremy Thorpe.

Despite the serious criticisms which could be made of David Smith, there was one outstanding fact in his favour. It was he who brought the criminal activities of Ian Brady and Myra Hindley to the notice of the police. Had he not done so there would have been more lonely graves on Saddleworth Moor. When he was asked why he had gone to the police he said: 'I could not have lived with myself if I had not done so.'

In my final speech to the jury I submitted that the evidence had disclosed eight trade marks of murder which pointed to the conclusion that the same pairs of hands had been involved in the killing of three of the discovered victims.

The jury were out for two hours and twenty-two minutes. Brady was convicted of all three murders, Myra Hindley of two. She was acquitted on the Kilbride charge, but found guilty of receiving, comforting, harbouring and assisting Brady knowing that he had murdered the boy. Brady was sentenced to three concurrent terms of life imprisonment, Hindley to two such terms plus a concurrent seven years.

There was no death penalty in force in 1966. In sentencing them Mr Justice Fenton Atkinson, one of our most experienced judges, said they had been found guilty of 'calculated, cruel, cold-blooded murders'. When I spoke to him immediately after the trial it was obvious that the trial had affected him deeply – as indeed it had affected all of us engaged in the case. When the judge sentenced the two prisoners to imprisonment for life I believe he meant for life – and not for any lesser term. It was also my view.

Some years after the trial a suggestion was made, and has been repeated since, that the defence was at fault in not raising the defences of insanity and possibly *folie à deux* or diminished responsibility, which could have reduced the crimes from murder to manslaughter. The alleged defence of *folie à deux* has not, to my knowledge, ever been raised in this country, but has been considered in France and the USA. As its basis, apparently, the defence would have had to establish the insanity of Brady and the 'referred insanity' of Hindley, arising solely from her infatuation with him. Such criticism does less than justice to the able defence counsel in the case: Emlyn Hooson, QC, and David Lloyd-Jones for Brady and the late Godfrey Heilpern, QC, and Phillip Curtis for Myra Hindley. These matters were, in fact, carefully considered, for both accused had the benefit of expert psychiatric examination long before the trial – Dr Neustater examined Brady and Dr Finkleman examined Hindley. The advice given to the defence by these two eminent psychiatrists must have accorded with the medical advice that the prosecution received: that there were no medical grounds on which to raise such defences. Their responsibility in law for what they did was clear.

Associated with the Attorney General's duties to enforce the criminal law is the responsibility for dealing with contempt of court. To maintain a balance between on the one hand the right of a person to a fair trial and on the other the freedom of the press to report and comment on matters of public interest is not easy. As Attorney General, I was often urged to bring contempt proceedings against newspapers. In fact I did so only once: against the *Sunday Times*, for a serious but inadvertent contempt it published shortly before the trial of 'Malcolm X' on a charge brought under the Race Relations Act.

It referred to him as a former brothel-keeper, procurer and property racketeer. The editor, Harold Evans, knew nothing about the contempt and had devised a system to prevent it happening. But happen it did, through no fault of his. No penalty was imposed on him but Times Newspapers were fined £5,000. Up until then no contempt cases had been brought against the company for 150 years.

20

A Chapter of Disasters

One of the duties of the Attorney General is to represent the public interest in inquiries into disasters or major accidents giving rise to public disquiet: not only because of the circumstances of the accident itself and the loss of life involved, but also because of the need to take all necessary steps, including legislation, to prevent similar accidents in the future.

I opened four such inquiries, among them the inquiry into the disaster at Aberfan, and subsequently the wreck of the *Torrey Canyon*.

On Friday 21 October 1966, 144 men, women and children of the small mining village of Aberfan in South Wales were killed by being buried alive under an avalanche of wet coal waste from a huge tip halfway up the steep mountainside. One hundred and sixteen of the victims were children, mainly between the ages of seven and ten. Most of them were killed as they began their lessons that morning at the Pantglas Junior School, Aberfan. Five of the adults who died were teachers in the school. In addition, twenty-nine children and six adults were injured, some of them seriously.

The whole nation was stunned by the news of the disaster. Messages of sympathy were received from all parts of the world. Donations to the Aberfan Disaster Fund poured in: £1,750,000 was received from more than forty countries.

Before a week was out, resolutions were passed in both Houses of Parliament to establish a tribunal of inquiry into the causes of and all the circumstances relating to the disaster. Lord Justice Edmund-Davies, born in Mountain Ash only a few miles from Aberfan, was appointed chairman. It was an admirable choice for he was a distinguished judge (later a Lord of Appeal in Ordinary) with great experience as counsel in mining cases. Sir Harold Harding, consulting civil engineer, and Vernon Lawrence, former Clerk to the Monmouthshire County Council, sat with him.

I nominated a powerful team of counsel to assist the tribunal in the ascertainment of the facts and the presentation of the evidence. It consisted of Tasker Watkins, VC (later a Lord Justice), the late Breuan Rees and Ronald Waterhouse, assisted by the staff of the Treasury Solicitor.

I soon became worried about some of the television and press reporting, not because I wanted anything withheld but because I was afraid that the work of the tribunal might be prejudiced and that public confidence in it might be undermined before it had even started. I was not alone in my concern. The Lord Chancellor, Lord Gardiner, criticized 'mini-trials'. The Cabinet was anxious. I consulted the Chairman of the tribunal. We both took the view that a reminder to the media and the press about the law of contempt of court was desirable. We hurriedly drafted a statement in Lord Justice Edmund-Davies's room in the Law Courts and I made it that afternoon in the House of Commons.

In retrospect, I think that although a statement was needed it was badly drafted. It read:

> The tribunal having been established with wide terms of reference, it is highly undesirable that any comments should be made either in the press or on the radio or on television on matters which it will be the express function of the tribunal to investigate. Apart from their manifest undesirability, such comments may have legal consequences which are, perhaps, not at present appreciated. Just as comments on the subject matter of a pending trial may constitute contempt of court, so also the tribunal would have to consider whether such comments amounted to such an interference with their highly important task as to necessitate the chairman certifying that it called for an investigation by the High Court as to whether there had been contempt of the tribunal. The possible consequences call for no elaboration by me.

The statement was immediately criticized in the Commons. Sir John Hobson, a former Conservative Attorney General, thought it went too far in stifling comment. I replied in terms which stated more clearly what the Chairman and I had in mind: 'There is a certain danger in examination of potential witnesses on television and in the press, when the best means of ventilating opinion and passing on information now, if we are going to get the most effective result from this Inquiry, is by communication with the Tribunal itself.' In reply to further questions I said: 'The important thing is that there should not be either prejudicing of the issues or such interference – if that is not too harsh a word – with witnesses as to embarrass their future position as potential witnesses before the Tribunal.'

This did not satisfy the press. The statement was assailed as politically motivated and meant to protect a nationalized industry from exposure of its responsibility. I received several abusive and some wounding letters alleging that I was engaged in a cover-up to protect the National Coal Board and was indifferent to the fate of the children. So hostile and widespread was the criticism that I was determined that none of it should be directed against the Chairman of the tribunal and I did not disclose that he and I had drafted the statement together. Had I done so perhaps the alleged political motivation of the statement would have been less readily believed. The issue became more political when the Prime Minister decided to answer Ted Heath's attack on me in the Commons.

I was touched by a speech by Jim Griffiths, himself a former miner, when he said:

> As one who has known the Attorney General all his life and knows his family, may I say how deeply I was hurt, knowing his character, by what was said and rumoured about him. May I assure my Right Honourable and Learned Friend, who knows and who is attached to his people and who has served Merthyr as Recorder, that I believe he will apply his full power to make this the searching inquiry we all want.

At the preliminary meeting of the tribunal on 7 November, the Chairman announced that, at his request, counsel acting for the tribunal were headed by the Attorney General. He said: 'The Attorney General, a South Walian and an advocate with great knowledge of the South Wales coalfield and its people, would be able to assist us to an extent that could not normally be expected of the head of the Bar, however zealous.'

The tribunal opened on 29 November. In the opening speech I said:

> The mining community of South Wales is not unfamiliar with disasters in the mines, but the tragedy of this death of almost a whole generation of the children of Aberfan is of a magnitude no words are adequate to describe and no sympathy adequate to console. Our duty now is to probe into every aspect of this dreadful disaster....
>
> To the north of the school ... the mountain rose in a sharp gradient on which was a farm and higher up no less than seven coal refuse tips, testimony of the long existence of the Merthyr Vale Colliery ... around which the life of Aberfan has for so long revolved.
>
> At nine o'clock on that Friday morning, when the children were assembling in the Junior School, there was nothing particularly to distinguish that day from any other autumn day, apart from a belt of mist which hovered low upon the mountainside and upon the village. The mist ... hid the tips from those below who were going about their usual tasks that morning. The air was still for there was no wind and as the younger children in the Junior School were busy with their lessons the older ones were making their way to the Senior School to begin their classes at half past nine.
>
> At about a quarter past nine four of the older boys who were making their way

> to the school ... heard a sound which Thomas Davies, aged 13, described as though loose trams were running down an incline. In fright he ran back towards his home in company with another boy.
>
> In the agony of that moment the remaining two boys chose to go on. They were soon buried and killed by a wide, fast moving, deep avalanche of wet colliery rubbish. This had travelled about 500 yards from Tip No 7, the disaster tip. It filled the old canal; it crashed over the railway embankment, engulfed the Junior School and a number of dwellings, part of the Senior School and the highways round about at a pace which one boy described as much faster than running pace.
>
> The local hairdresser was making his way to his shop in Moy Road when all this happened. He was struck to the ground but soon rescued. He tells us that after the tip fell everything went quiet. You could not hear a bird or a child.

I found it hard to go on at this point in my opening. To have broken down in a hall full of parents and friends of the dead children would have been dreadful.

When news of the disaster spread, desperate and immediate attempts were made to release the victims. Essential services were brought to the village and there began the unprecedented and Herculean task of recovery. People came in their hundreds from far and wide to lend their hands, while the officials and the sturdy, experienced colliers hurried from the local colleries to use their strength and skill as never before. But despite the heroically sustained efforts of so many of all ages and occupations who rushed to Aberfan from far and wide, after 11 am that day nobody buried by the slimy wet mass was rescued alive.

My opening exposed in detail the evidence disclosed in the full records, documents and plans which had been made available by the National Coal Board, their predecessors Powell Dyffryn & Co, the Merthyr Tydfil Corporation and many other concerned bodies and organizations. Nothing was withheld.

The key to the disaster was soon revealed by the records, and by the preliminary view formed by the experts who advised the tribunal. In their opinion the primary cause of the slip of No 7 Tip was due to the fact that the area, containing streams and springs, was unsuitable for the purpose of tipping. The whole behaviour of the Aberfan tips since they were created (particularly the very similar accident at Tip No 4 in 1944) clearly demonstrated this. Between 1952 and 1965 severe flooding occurred on at least eleven occasions and probably more, in the Pantglas area of Aberfan. The information on proper drainage measures which would have obviated the disaster was available to the officials of the National Coal Board the whole time.

From 1963 on a series of letters emanated from the National Coal Board and the Merthyr Tydfil Council bearing the sombre title: 'Danger from coal slurry being tipped at the rear of Pantglas Schools'. The Merthyr Vale Ward Labour Party in a letter to the Council of 16 December 1964 wrote:

> This week's flooding of Aberfan, which still continues ... is a source not only of great inconvenience but very real danger, particularly to children. The tons of shale and slurry that have blocked water courses and drains proves very conclusively the responsibility of the National Coal Board in this matter and drastic action, even if it means prosecution, should be taken to convince them that they have a civic responsibility to the residents of the neighbourhood.

My speech was followed by an address by Phillip Wien QC (later a High Court judge), counsel for the National Coal Board. He said: 'The Board's view is that the disaster was due to a coincidence of a set of geological factors, each of which in itself is not exceptional, but which collectively created a particularly critical geological environment.' No responsibility on the part of the NCB for the disaster was admitted. Indeed, referring to my opening address he observed: 'When it is said, as it has been said, that one of the questions before the Tribunal is whether the National Coal Board should have considered the slides or slips that had occurred in the past, such lessons as could have been learned from those slides would not have led to the discovery of anything that could have prevented the disaster.'

Philip Wien was followed by Desmond Ackner (later a Lord Justice of Appeal), counsel for the parents and residents of Aberfan. He spoke of 'the folly and neglect which appear at this stage to be the irresistible inferences to be drawn from the facts which the Attorney General has opened'.

Despite this, the tribunal had to sit for no less than seventy-six days: the longest inquiry of its kind in British legal history. The evidence pointing the blame at the National Coal Board mounted with each week that passed. Nevertheless it persisted through its counsel until the very end in maintaining that a slide of the tip could not have been foreseen. It was not until day seventy-four of the inquiry that the Board's counsel said in his closing address that the plain answer to the question 'why did it happen?' was that 'Tip 7 should never have been allowed to go over unsuitable ground without proper investigation. That is a much better way of putting it than saying the primary cause of the disaster was geological.' That is how it had in fact been put on behalf of the Board on the second day of the inquiry.

Indeed the tribunal's report commented that 'it was really nothing short of audacious for the Board to tell the Tribunal, as it did on Day 74 in the closing speech of its learned counsel, that: "It was already clear by Day 1, when the Attorney-General opened his case, that tip safety arrangements were inadequate and it really did not require Lord Robens to come here and tell the Tribunal so when it was perfectly obvious."' (Lord Robens, Chairman of the National Coal Board, two days after the disaster had, without technical advice, told a television reporter: 'It was impossible to know that there was a spring in the heart of this tip which was turning the centre of the mountain into sludge.')

The introduction to the report, and the report itself, were trenchant and devastating. It said that it was its

> strong and unanimous view that the Aberfan disaster could and should have been prevented. The Report which follows tells not of wickedness but of ignorance, ineptitude and a failure in communications. Ignorance on the part of those charged at all levels with the siting, control and daily management of tips; bungling ineptitude on the part of those who had the duty of supervising and directing them; a failure on the part of those having knowledge of the factors which affect tip safety to communicate that knowledge and see that it was applied.

The tribunal held that 'the legal liability of the National Coal Board to pay compensation for the personal injuries (fatal and otherwise) and damage to property caused by the slide of Tip 7 is incontestable.' They concluded that:

> the clear blameworthiness of the National Coal Board as a body is by no means founded solely upon their own belated admission. They, like others, fall to be judged against the background of events occurring over a period of some years before the disaster. ... There was a total absence of tipping policy and this was the basic cause of the disaster. In this respect, however, the NCB were following in the footsteps of their predecessors.

What of those who had been responsible for the tragedy? In its report the tribunal referred to 'the vastly disagreeable task of censure' which the sense of public duty of its members obliged it to carry out:

> Whether or not named or adversely referred to in this Report, there must be many today with hearts made heavy and haunted by the thought that if only they had done this, that or the other the disaster might have been averted. Of these, some will blame themselves needlessly; others, while blameworthy in some degree, will condemn themselves with excessive harshness; yet others must carry the heavy burden of knowing that their neglect played an unmistakeable part in bringing about the tragedy.

In the Commons debate on the report on 26 October 1967, the House accepted the conclusion of Cledwyn Hughes, the Secretary of State for Wales, approving the Report: 'There, in my view, the matter might now be allowed to rest.' As Attorney General, I had come to the conclusion before the debate that the facts disclosed by the Report did not justify the institution of criminal proceedings.

The tribunal's report included a series of important recommendations to avoid another Aberfan disaster. The Government and the National Coal Board took early steps to implement them. Immediately after the disaster the Board ordered an inspection of all tips, active or disused, in its ownership. This disclosed potential instability in several tips and remedial action was taken at once.

First priority was given to safety. A National Tip Safety Committee, as recommended by the Tribunal, was appointed to advise ministers on problems affecting the stability of tips. In 1968 the Mines and Quarries (Tips) Act filled the gaps in legislation which the tribunal had identified. Disregard of the provisions of the Act was made a criminal offence. Powers were given to local authorities to obtain information, to enter land and to carry out tests and determine whether a tip, by reason of its instability, constituted a hazard. A Derelict Land Unit was set up by Cledwyn Hughes in the Welsh Office in Cardiff to work with the local authorities in preparing schemes of rehabilitation and scores of derelict sites were cleared.

The Welsh Development Agency, which came into being in 1976, continued the work of reclamation and brought thousands of acres into use for industry, housing, playing fields and public open space. The massive dumps of industrial filth which led one poet to describe South Wales almost romantically as '*Gwlad y pyramidau*' (the land of pyramids) were being dealt with at last.

As for Aberfan itself, the disaster pit No 7 was virtually removed by the NCB in the months after the disaster and the area of the hillside over which the avalanche poured was cleaned up and sown with grass. The tops of the uppermost tips, Nos 4 and 5, were removed and their sinister, dominating presence was ended.

Out of the horror of Aberfan some good did emerge and what had once been the green valleys of South Wales were at least made safer for its people. A poignant cluster of small white gravestones on the Aberfan hillside remains as a warning to all.

When Polly and I were spending a restful Easter week-end in 1967 in Toppesfield, in the heart of Essex, I was suddenly summoned by the Prime

Minister to a 'beach battle Cabinet' of six ministers at the RN Air Station in Culdrose in Cornwall. In broad daylight and perfect weather, the *Torrey Canyon* had been making a short cut to catch the tide at Milford Haven with a cargo of 117,000 tons of Kuwait crude oil. The ship had struck a reef on the Seven Sisters, eighteen miles west of Land's End, at a speed of seventeen knots and was held fast on the reef. It proved impossible to pump the oil out into other vessels: the danger of an explosion made it impracticable to install on the *Torrey Canyon* the generating equipment which would have been required to do this. The Chief Salvage Officer of a Dutch salvage team was killed aboard the ship and other members of his team were injured as a result of an explosion on 21 March. Five days later heavy seas broke the ship's back. It became one of the biggest wrecks in modern maritime history. Seepage of oil began to pollute a hundred miles of the Cornish coast and the coast of Brittany, creating a major ecological disaster. Thousands more tons of oil remained in the intact ship's tanks and the problem was how to deal with it.

Much conflicting advice was offered. When the matter was debated later in the Commons, Tony Greenwood, then Minister of Local Government, quoted the Cornish proverb: 'Everybody knows what to do with a kicking horse except the man who is in charge of it.' The advice we received from Sir Solly Zuckerman, the Government's scientific adviser, was to set the oil on fire by bombing the ship. I was asked whether we were entitled to do this as a matter of law. I had no law books with me but I took the view that this action was justified for the protection of our shores and to mitigate the damage the oil pollution was causing.

Two days later aircraft of the Fleet Air Arm bombed the *Torrey Canyon* and set the oil on fire. The fire was maintained by RAF aircraft and a Navy helicopter dropping tons of aviation fuel, napalm and sodium chlorate on the wreck, to feed the fire. Further bombing attacks were necessary to destroy the remaining tanks. As a result 40,000 tons of oil were set on fire.

There followed litigation to recover damages from the owners and time charterers of the *Torrey Canyon* for the damage, loss and expense incurred as a result of the escape of the oil from the vessel. One of our difficulties was to find assets belonging to the Barracuda Company, which owned the ship. Happily a sister ship of the *Torrey Canyon* – the *Lake Palourde* – sailed into Singapore harbour for a minor repair and Admiralty agents were able to nail a writ on the mast of the ship – to use the old expression – and to hold the ship until a bond in the sum of £3,000,000 was forthcoming.

The French authorities also brought proceedings in respect of damage resulting from the pollution. After much negotiation the claims of both countries were settled on payment by the defendants of the £3,000,000, which we agreed to share equally with the French. I took the view that it was a fair settlement bearing in mind the uncertainties, delays and expense of litigation, which would have had to be conducted in Singapore, the complex and unique questions of law which arose in establishing liability and the difficulties in quantifying and proving damage. In addition to the £3,000,000, the owners agreed to make £25,000 available as compensation to individuals and firms whose property was damaged. When I announced the settlement in Cabinet, to whose proceedings the cautionary advice of the Attorney General rarely brought cheer, it was well received. My reward was a glass of sherry from the Foreign Office when the French Ambassador and I went to receive drafts of £1,500,000 for our respective governments.

Another disaster with which I was concerned came nearer home. Early in the morning of 16 May 1968 my agent Terry Macmillan ('Mac') – who always kept me in close touch with my constituency – phoned to say that Ronan Point, a high-rise apartment block, had collapsed and perhaps as many as fifty of my constituents might be buried in the rubble. I rushed down and saw that the whole south-east corner of the twenty-two-storey block had collapsed. The immediate cause of the accident was an explosion following a gas leak in an eighteenth-floor flat. The explosion blew out the large pre-fab concrete panels which formed part of the load-bearing flank wall of the block. This led to the progressive collapse of the corners of all the flats. Mercifully it happened at a time of day when the inhabitants were in the parts of the flats which remained secure, although sadly four people died in the falling rubble, including a husband and wife.

A tribunal of inquiry under the chairmanship of Hugh Griffiths QC, as he then was, was appointed which attributed the collapse to the inherent design faults in the building and not to faulty workmanship. They found that the disaster which had occurred was unique in the Ronan Point type of building. They recommended that the existing blocks over six storeys high which were constructed in the same way should be structurally appraised and where necessary strengthened. The gas supply was cut off in buildings with a collapse risk. Confidence in high-rise blocks of flats has never been quite the same since.

21
Encounters at Home and Abroad

While I was naturally disappointed when Labour lost the 1970 General Election and that my job as Attorney General had come suddenly to an end, my future course was clear. It was to continue in the political battle in the Commons (my faithful constituency had once again re-elected me, this time with a majority of 13,477) as Shadow Attorney General on the Opposition Front Bench, and to resume my practice at the Bar.

I had, of course, kept in close touch with my constituency during my years as Attorney General, holding my regular 'surgeries' in the constituency office on the Barking Road and attending to the many problems of my constituents. In this work, which I always enjoyed, I was greatly assisted by Councillor Bill Dunlop, who became my agent afer 'Mac' died. Bill lives in Silvertown and works as a bus driver, his wife Elsie (until her retirement) working as conductor on the same bus. Bill is 6′ 3″, burly, genial and interested in everything – photography, gardening, housing and especially horses. Together with Elsie and their two daughters, Bill set up a riding school in Silvertown with an ex-cavalry officer to teach the youngsters. It has been a particular godsend to handicapped children from local schools.

Bill's sitting-room became a whirlwind of activity during elections, in which his two enormous labradors and the Dunlop parrot joined.

In the House of Commons Sam Silkin and I put the Opposition case on Law Officers' and sometimes Home Office matters when they overlapped. We questioned closely the Emergency Powers legislation which was brought forward in December 1970 by the Government as a response to the first official national dock strike since 1926. The impact of economy cuts introduced by the Heath Government gave rise to several questions in the House about their effect on my constituents – such as the provision of school milk and why cuts had been ordered in the expenditure on school projects in

Newham. The increase in unemployment in Newham was already giving cause for concern. The fiercest political and legal battles were fought on the Industrial Relations Bill, which led to bitter confrontation with the unions.

Some of the legislation that came through, for instance the Courts Bill, which gave effect to the Beeching Royal Commission Report on Assizes and Quarter Sessions, was a continuation of work begun when we were in office. Other useful law reforms reported upon by the Law Commission included the Criminal Damages Bill in 1971, which strengthened provision for compensation for the victims of crime.

In the international field acute legal and constitutional questions continued to arise from the Rhodesian conflict. I opposed the sale of Wasp helicopters to South Africa and condemned the French nuclear tests in the Pacific.

1971 was a sad year for my family. Not long after the death of my sister Winnie, a much loved schoolteacher, magistrate and centre of the family after the death of my mother, my brother Idris died. Idris, who was my closest friend and confidant, had never married and was the perfect uncle to my children. While he is best remembered in Wales as a Welsh rugby international and captain of the 1925 Welsh team, his standing as a scientist was high. After seven years with ICI at Billingham, he became Research Manager of Powell Dyffryn in 1933, when Wales was in the depth of the economic depression, and later Director-General of Research of the National Coal Board. He was passionately devoted to the way of life, the language, literature and music of Wales. I always remember the happy day when Idris and I, garbed in white robes, along with Cledwyn Hughes, Geraint Evans, Hugh Griffiths and Emlyn Hooson, were admitted as bards into the Gorsedd Circle during the National Eisteddfod at Aberavon in 1966. Idris was an active vice-president of the University College of Wales, Aberystwyth, where his scientific and athletic career began. His last years were spent reading, writing and listening to music in the village of Llandaff, near its beautiful cathedral.

My practice at the Bar, in which Idris had always been interested, acquired an even more international flavour after I had been Attorney-General. Then I had appeared for the Indian Government in its proceedings in the English Courts for the extradition of Teja, the Indian shipping tycoon, who was wanted for trial in India on serious fraud charges. It may have been the publicity attached to that case which led to my being briefed for the much publicized Americans Robert Vesco and later Howard Hughes, in extradition proceedings brought against them in the Bahamas by the American authorities, alleging fraud charges. The evidence brought in support of the allegations failed to substantiate them and the Bahamas magistrate dismissed the extradition applications in both cases. Howard Hughes continued his strange, reclusive existence and I never saw him.

Another international commitment outside my usual range of work was the brief for the Moroccan Government in the case brought against it by the Occidental Petroleum and Holiday Inn Companies claiming payment for hotels they had built. The defence was that they were of a quality and rating far below what had been contracted for. The dispute was referred to international arbitration by the International Centre for the Settlement of Investment Disputes under the auspices of the World Bank.

Work on the case involved brief but entertaining visits to the ancient Moorish citadel of Rabat, to Casablanca, an uneasy architectural blend of ancient and modern, and to hearings in Paris.

So lengthy were these preliminary proceedings that I had to leave the case in the competent hands of my juniors, Anthony Lester and Maurice Mendelson, when I became Lord Chancellor. The case was settled by agreement some years later.

Libel actions are often occasions for airing important issues of public policy. Robert Shulman, Counsel for the Church of Scientology, in opening its case against Geoffrey Johnson-Smith, a Conservative MP, called the trial 'the religious freedom trial of the century'. It was one of the many extravagant claims made by him and was in keeping with his remarkable though short-lived career at the Bar.

The libel action arose out of a BBC television interview given by the MP in which he agreed with the decision announced in the House of Commons by Kenneth Robinson MP, then Minister of Health in the Labour Government, to impose restrictions on the entry into the United Kingdom of alien scientologists intending to work at their world headquarters, known as St Hill Manor. This was situated in East Grinstead, the MP's constituency, and many of his constituents had complained to him about the activities of the Scientologists.

Kenneth Robinson gave evidence at the trial that by April 1967 he too had received a considerable number of complaints, that he had taken medical advice about them and that convincing evidence showing the dangers to mental health of scientology techniques had accumulated over a period of eighteen months. In his television interview Johnson-Smith spoke in similar terms about his own correspondence and approaches from his constituents. He put himself at risk in doing so because at that time the deliberate policy of the Scientologists was to issue writs for libel against those who criticized them.

One of Geoffrey's purposes in his broadcast was to dispel the fear that it was dangerous to criticize the Scientologists. His case was that the facts he referred to in the broadcast were justified and that his comments on those proved facts were fair. It was a poignant, often painful trial, which lasted for five weeks. The outcome of the trial was that the jury rejected every complaint made by the Scientologists against the MP and that they were ordered to pay his costs. He was fully vindicated.

It was not the first time that libel proceedings in this country proved to be more dangerous to the party bringing them than to the party sued. Oscar Wilde learned this bitter lesson; so too did Sir Oswald Mosley when he recovered a farthing damages from a trade union leader, and Harold Laski when he sued the *Daily Express* and had to sell his library to pay his costs. Sometimes people, particularly those in public life, do have to take the risk of taking proceedings in order to clear their reputation when they have been libelled. Sir Leslie Plummer MP, for whom Stanley Waldman and I appeared, did so in the successful libel action he brought in 1962 against the odious John Tyndall and other members of the National Front Party, which was conducting a scurrilous campaign against him in his constituency.

Like most public men I, too, have been libelled on occasions, although generally the press has been kind to me. I have never brought a libel action, but I did succeed in securing retractions from both the *Sunday Express* and the *Spectator* when they printed untruths about me.

One remarkable libel action in which I appeared for the plaintiffs with Bryan Rees (whose lamented death by accidental drowning deprived the Bar of a junior who would have gone far in the profession) was brought by the family of an old lady in Cardiganshire who had owned a cottage by the sea. This she rented in the summer to a distinguished artist, who was the subject of a BBC television 'Monitor' programme, during which it was stated that she had cut off one of her husband's hands. She had died long before the programme appeared and the general rule that you cannot claim damages for libelling the dead appeared to apply. But her family was appalled at what they claimed was a totally unfounded story. The ingenuity of Bryan Rees produced a statement of claim alleging that the family had been libelled, for so horrific an alleged action by the grandmother was calculated to bring her family to hatred and contempt. At the trail of the action at Swansea Assizes the case was settled, the family being content with a withdrawal of the allegation by the BBC and a contribution towards their costs.

I think there is much to be said for the recommendation of the Faulks Committee on Defamation that for a period of five years beginning with the date of her or his death, near relatives of the deceased should be entitled to sue the person responsible for the publication of a statement defamatory of the deceased; not for damages, but for a declaration that what is complained of is untrue. The court should have power to grant an injunction and costs, as it thinks fit.

A case of considerable parliamentary and professional importance was the libel action brought by the Beach brothers, solicitors practising in partnership, against Reginald Freeson, a Member of Parliament. Freeson sent letters in identical terms to the Secretary of the Law Society and to the Lord Chancellor setting out complaints by one of his constituents alleging that the plaintiffs had grossly mismanaged his affairs and also the affairs of his relations. The MP did not dispute that the letters were defamatory but claimed that publication of the letter was protected by qualified privilege. The solicitors alleged that Freeson was actuated by express malice.

The case was heard before Mr Justice Geoffrey Lane (who later became Lord Chief Justice). Citing earlier cases he held that when a complaint is received from a constituent about the conduct of a public official acting officially in the constituency, the MP has a consequential interest or duty in passing the complaint on to the proper quarter. Complaints about the conduct of professional people in their calling are on the same footing as those about public officials.

The gist of the plaintiffs' case was that the MP had no duty of any sort to complain to the Law Society as he knew that his constituent was himself approaching it. The judge rejected this: 'It will be a sad day when a Member of Parliament has to look over his shoulder before ventilating to the proper authority criticisms about the work of a public servant or a professional man who is holding himself out in practice for the benefit of the public, which he honestly believes to merit investigation ...'

The further question was whether the Lord Chancellor had an interest, social or moral, in the complaints levied against the solicitors. If he had, then the MP would have the corresponding interest, or possibly duty, to communicate with him.

I had called Sir Dennis Dobson, Permanent Secretary to the Lord Chancellor's Department, as a witness on these matters. (He was my principal and valued adviser when I became Lord Chancellor.) The judge concluded that while the nature of the interest of the Lord Chancellor may be difficult to define

> he is sufficiently concerned in the proper behaviour of solicitors; in solicitors as potential holders of judicial office; in the expeditious prosecution of litigation and in ensuring that litigants are honestly and conscientiously advised, to give him the necessary interest to protect the communication on occasions such as this with qualified privilege.

The judge held further that the plea of malice was not made out and gave judgment for the MP.

One of the most remarkable cases that ever came before the High Court in London was the action brought in 1971 by the Banabans (the Ocean Islanders), whom I represented, against the British Phosphate Commission and the Attorney General (as representative of the Crown). It became 'litigation on a grand scale' as the judge, Vice-Chancellor Megarry, later described it.

Ocean Island (or Banaba) is a rocky coral island less than three miles in circumference, a mere speck just south of the Equator in the immense Pacific Ocean. Until 1900 the few hundred Banabans who inhabited it lived by deep sea fishing and cultivating food-bearing trees: coconut, pandanus and almonds. These grew between the pinnacles of coral thrown up from the ocean bed in ancient convulsions. Recurrent droughts always threatened the survival of the Banabans. But they did survive and evolved a culturally rich life.

Their entire wealth was land, 1,500 acres of it in all, divided among them in small plots. Men and women had equal rights of ownership of land and indeed equality of all other rights. On marriage a woman retained her own name.

The history of the case began in 1900 when the ss *Archer* arrived bringing Albert Ellis, a New Zealand phosphate chemist, and other representatives of the Pacific Islands Company. Ellis acted with confidence, for the chairman of his company was Lord Stanmore, who was a former High Commissioner of the Western Pacific, Private Secretary to a Prime Minister and an ex-Colonial Governor. Ellis was in search of new sources of phosphate which the farmers of Australia and New Zealand needed to fertilize their land. He found Ocean Island to be immensely rich in the substance. There were millions of tons of it just below the surface of the land or deep down between the vertical coral pinnacles. The Banabans of course had no inkling that it had any value.

Ellis recorded his first impressions of Ocean Island on 3 May 1900:

> A line of surf breaking on the reef, behind which was a thirty-foot rampart of rough coral limestone cliffs crowned with groves of coconuts and other dense, bright foliage on sloping ground rising to a moderate height. The whole constituted a picturesque scene soon enlivened by numerous shapely canoes dashing through the surf and in a short time *Archer*'s decks were crowded with strapping, excited natives clad in a short skirt made of coconut leaves tanned brown. They brought aboard numbers of shark fins and shark swords, some fruit and vegetables for bartering purposes.

The chemist wasted no time. The very day he arrived he signed a purported 'agreement' on behalf of his company with 'the King and natives of Ocean Island'. In fact there was no king. Neither of the two islanders, Tamati nor Kariatobewa, who each placed his mark on the document, had authority to sign it nor any understanding of its meaning. When the islanders learned what it meant they repudiated it. The 'agreement' purported to concede the sole right to raise and ship all the rock and alluvial phosphate on Ocean Island for and on account of the company. The company agreed to pay the natives fifty pounds per annum or in trade to that value in the goods in the company store. The agreement was to be in force for 999 years. It would not have stood up in a court for a minute. E.C. Eliot, Resident Commissioner of the Gilbert and Ellice Islands from 1913 to 1920, in his book *Broken Atoms*, described it later as an 'iniquitous document'.

This was the beginning. The next step was that on 2 October 1900, after some correspondence between the Pacific Islands Company and the Colonial Office in Downing Street, a licence in the name of Queen Victoria, executed by the Secretary of State for the Colonies, was granted to the company, giving it the sole lease to raise and export phosphate from Ocean Island for twenty-one years from 1 January 1901, and to display the British flag in token of the occupation. Ellis had in fact without authority already hoisted the British flag two days after he had signed the agreement.

Within four months, representatives of the company landed and started to mine and export the Ocean Island phosphate.

The history of what happened thereafter was told by the Vice-Chancellor in his judgment in the case in 1977, reported in 240 pages of the Chancery Division Law Reports of that year and in *Treasure Islands* by Pearl Binder (Polly).

Already by 1909, 240 acres of Ocean Island had been mined and two million tons of phosphate had been exported. The mined land was denuded, stripped of its food-bearing trees and left a desert of pointed coral rocks. Only 960 acres of land were left on which food could be grown for the island's several hundred inhabitants.

By then the Banabans had decided not to sell another square yard of their land to the company. According to E.C. Eliot, his predecessor Captain Quayle Dickson had already made the strongest representations to the Colonial Office in favour of the oppressed landowners. The company brought pressure to bear for his removal from office. The Colonial Office obligingly posted him to the Falklands.

When Eliot succeeded him, he was given two tasks. One was to turn the protectorate of the Gilbert and Ellice Islands (he called them the Gilbert and Sullivan Islands) into a colony. The other was to obtain more land on Ocean Island for the company to mine. He succeeded in both. The new status of the Gilbert and Ellice Islands as a colony cleared the way for 85 per cent of the phosphate royalties to be paid to the administration of the Gilbert and Ellice Islands and only 15 per cent to the Banabans. Eliot wrote: 'With no knowledge of the iniquitous past history, I eventually managed to persuade the younger generation on Ocean Island that the terms which I had to offer would turn them into a rich community, and the Company was given enough land to continue their operations.'

In 1920 the British Phosphate Commission (BPC) was set up by the governments of the United Kingdom, Australia and New Zealand, with a commissioner from each country. The British Phosphate Company was bought out for Australian $3,500,000 for their Ocean Island and Nauru undertakings. The BPC brought great benefit to the farmers of Australia and New Zealand by selling the phosphate not at market price but at cost price, to the detriment of the Banabans.

In 1923 the BPC sought the approval of the Colonial Office for acquiring another 150 acres of land. The Banabans were firmly opposed to this. However in July 1927 the Colonial Office, the Western Pacific High Commissioner, and Arthur Grimble, then Resident Commissioner on Ocean Island, agreed that the Banabans should be asked for another 150 acres. Prolonged negotiations took place. At one point the Banabans did agree to what was proposed but then changed their minds and renewed their opposition to the offer of an inclusive price of £150 sterling an acre for land and trees.

A week later, on 5 August 1928, Arthur Grimble sent an ultimatum in the native language, which he knew well, to the people of Buakonikai, a village in the centre of the island. A postscript to his letter reads:

> You will be called to the signing of the Agreement by the Resident Commissioner on Tuesday next, the 7th August and if everyone signs the Agreement, the Banabans will not be punished for shaming the Important Chief [the British King] and

their serious misconduct will be forgiven. If the Agreement is not signed consideration will be given to punishing the Banabans. And the destruction of Buakonikai Village must also be considered to make room for mining if there is no Agreement.

One of the island's leaders, Pastor Tito Rotan, lived in Buakonikai village and cultivated his land there. It was regarded by the Banabans with special reverence. As the judge said at the trial, 'with every allowance made, it is impossible to read that letter without a sense of outrage.'

Worse was to follow. On 18 September 1928 a new mining ordinance provided that the royalty to be paid for minerals extracted was to be such 'as the resident Commissioner may prescribe'. It was he, Arthur Grimble, who had sent the threatening letter to the people of Buakonikai. He did in fact prescribe the royalty in 1931. The judge had strong things to say about this in his judgment, while stating that neither the Colonial Office nor the High Commissioner knew about the Buakonikai letter.

In spite of these humiliations, when the Second World War came the Banabans raised no less than £12,500 for British war funds. They stood by Britain loyally throughout the war, suffering much by doing so.

The continued destruction of their homeland led the Banabans to petition to the Secretary of State in 1940 for permission to buy a second island for themselves somewhere in the Fiji group so as to be under the same Western Pacific High Commissioner but with easier access to him. They made it clear that they did not intend to give up Ocean Island and wanted to be free to come and go between the two islands, both of which would be their property.

In April 1942 in the middle of the war, Rambi, an island in the Fijian group, was bought for the Banabans with their own money for £25,000. It went cheaply because Lord Leverhulme, who had acquired and planted it for the cultivation of coconuts for his soap and margarine industry, was convinced that the Japanese would overrun it.

At the end of August 1942, the Japanese invaded Ocean Island. By 1945 most of its inhabitants had been either killed or deported to other islands to grow food for the Japanese troops. Of the 150 Banabans still on the island after Japan surrendered, all but one were killed by the Japanese. The survivor, Kabunare, who had hidden in a hole after feigning death, came to London to give evidence at the trial.

Ocean Island was recaptured by the Australians in 1945. The remaining Banaban exiles were collected from the scattered islands and brought to the island of Tarawa in the Gilberts in charge of Major Kennedy, who had the task of 'diverting the Banabans from their wish to return to Ocean

Island' and persuading them to be taken instead to Rambi: as the BPC had been urging. The High Commissioner for the Western Pacific minuted that 'the removal of the Banabans and the settlement of the Banaban question is even more to the essential benefit of the BPC than the Government'. On the BPC undertaking that the Banabans could return to Ocean Island whenever they wished but not immediately because it was still 'uninhabitable', the Banabans agreed to try out Rambi for two years. Meantime the BPC were actively recruiting hundreds of Gilbertese for phosphate mining on Ocean Island.

Major Kennedy took 1,030 people to Rambi: 337 men, 297 women and 396 children. Three hundred of them were Gilbertese. They had been shown idyllic summer-time photographs of Rambi, taken when it had belonged to Lord Leverhulme and had been well maintained. Since then it had fallen into total neglect.

When, in mid-December 1945, the Banabans were disembarked in Rambi the camp prepared for them consisted of 150 tents and twelve army pre-fabs. It was the cold rainy season. As Polly wrote in *Treasure Islands* (from the testimony of Banabans who survived):

> The Banaban people never have and never will get over this disastrous beginning. They had been promised an Eden for which they had paid with their accumulated savings over many years. Now they found themselves sleeping, or rather not sleeping, on soaking wet stretchers in tents swimming with rain. Inevitably, outbreaks of influenza led to pneumonia etc. ... Forty of the old and many of the young died that winter on Rambi. All the rest were ill.

They believed God had abandoned them. It was Pastor Tito who gave them the will to live.

What was to happen to Ocean Island was still to be resolved. Negotiations, suspended after the Japanese occupation of Ocean Island, were resumed in Rambi in 1946. By then a Fiji ordinance had established a Rambi Island council. Pastor Tito Rotan became its chairman.

Negotiations about acquiring further mining land on Ocean Island continued into 1947. They related to the purchase of two parcels of land; a total area of 671 acres. This would take nearly all the workable phosphate left on Ocean Island and consume over two-fifths of the entire island.

Far from encouraging the Banabans to get the advice they needed, the Western Pacific High Commissioner in a letter of 25 March 1947 to Major Holland, whom he had appointed to look after the Banabans, wrote: 'You should, of course, take no part whatever in Mr Maynard's [the BPC negotiator] land negotiations with the Banabans, making it clear to them, if necessary, that those negotiations are wholly between them and the British Phosphate Commission.'

The outcome was that in the 1947 agreements the Banabans, as the judge put it, 'were disposing of phosphate which would take well over a century to work, at a rate of royalty which was fixed and invariable, no matter how long the extraction took'. From 1947 to 1973 the Banabans tried to get better terms than those fixed in 1947. 'These attempts achieved some success, but far less than the Banabans considered right.'

In 1967 the British Government offered a once-for-all ex gratia payment of £80,000 to the Banaban Development Fund. The Banaban requests for independence for Ocean Island, for limitation of the rate of phosphate extraction and for an increased share of the phosphate payments were all rejected. A reference of the case to a Select Committee in Parliament to which the Banabans could present their case was turned down. In 1971, with confidence still in British justice, the Banabans decided to take their case to the High Court in London. The Banabans had been economizing for years to accumulate funds for the case and a sudden rise in the price of phosphate finally enabled them to undertake it.

Pastor Tebuke Rotan (Tito's able son) came to London knowing no solicitors there. Someone he befriended recommended the small family firm of Davies, Brown and Co of Wimbledon to him and it fell to them to handle the mammoth case. When I came into the case, John Macdonald, one of the ablest juniors at the Chancery Bar, had already been briefed and the writ in the action had been issued against the BPC and the Attorney-General as representing the Government of the United Kingdom.

For convenience the case was divided into two actions. In one the Banaban landowners claimed specific performances of contractual obligations to replace the mined and worked-out land with food-producing trees and shrubs which had previously grown there or alternatively damages for failure to do so. In the other action, Tito Rotan and the Banaban Council of Leaders claimed that in relation to the 1931 and 1947 transactions the Crown stood in a fiduciary position towards the Banabans. (The 1931 transaction was the compulsory acquisition for the BPC on Grimble's terms of 150 acres.) The Banabans' case was that the royalty was fixed at less than a proper figure, that there had been a breach of trust and that the Crown must pay compensation to make up the royalty payments to the amount that ought to have been paid.

As to the 1947 transaction, the agreement between the Banaban landowners and the BPC for the mining of 291 and 380 acres in return for certain lump sums for the land and royalty, it was claimed that the Crown through its agents was under a duty to make full disclosure of relevant facts to the Banaban landowners and to ensure that they received a full commercial price for the land or that they received competent independent advice. The Crown failed to discharge that duty by not revealing that the phosphate was being sold at less than its true value to Australian and New Zealand concerns for manufacture into superphosphates, and by failing to disclose what sums were being paid by the BPC to the colony from the phosphate royalties in lieu of taxation or otherwise. Nothing had been done to ensure that the Banabans had proper advice. The royalty payable under the 1947 agreement was far below the proper royalty and the Banabans were entitled to compensation from the Crown.

We had numerous conferences in London and meetings at the Foreign Office. Tebuke Rotan urged us to make an early visit to Rambi to meet the chairman and the members of the Rambi Council and to confer with their Australian and Fijian advisers on the way. This we did, flying via Sydney, where we met Mr Shrapnell and Mr Walker, the Banabans' able Australian economic advisers. From there we flew on to Suva, the capital of Fiji, to discuss the position with sympathetic representatives of the Fijian Government, who had taken the Banabans under their wing.

At Suva the more adventurous part of our journey began. We flew in a small plane to the grass landing strip in Savu Savu, its airport building a mere thatched roof on four posts. Then came a long car drive between the palm trees through the green island of Savu Savu to a sandy shore whence the small Rambi launch took us across the sea to Rambi.

The members of the Council were awaiting us on a small jetty. As I stepped on to it the Banaban band struck up 'O God our help in ages past': their favourite hymn. The chairman, Pastor Tito Rotan, made a speech of welcome. I replied with a reference to the Banaban David facing the Goliath British Government. All good Methodists, they knew what happened to Goliath. I soon discovered that the Christian religion was the centre of their lives.

We stayed in the Council's little house overlooking the ocean. The meetings with the Council, which took place in the cool conference room, were dominated by Pastor Tito Rotan, a pure-bred Banaban born in 1900. His father had been a converted Methodist pastor. Upright, dignified, always courteous, with great physical and spiritual strength, Tito Rotan led the struggle for justice for his people. When I asked him if he would come to London to give evidence at the trial he said: 'I've been waiting for that chance for fifty years.'

Rambi was an unspoiled green tropical jungle with lovely beaches from which I enjoyed plunging into the balmy sea. Tebuke, warning me against sharks, told of being confronted with one himself face to face: 'I stared at it firmly in the eyes until it swam away.'

John Macdonald began the task of interviewing the landowners; work which Bertram Jones continued. Few of them could read or write but all remembered the location of their own plots of land on Ocean Island.

On the day we left Rambi these tremendously sociable and friendly people danced and sang for us in a touching farewell. It ended with speeches of hope and encouragement from John Macdonald and myself which Tebuke interpreted to the intently listening Banabans.

As our little boat pulled away across the water the Banabans gathered on the shore sang for us in their native tongue the Maori song: 'Now is the hour / When we must say goodbye.' It was an emotional moment.

We returned to Rambi the following year on the long journey to Ocean Island, which took us via Australia and Fiji for final consultations on the case. When I went to my old bedroom in the Council house in Rambi I found on the mirror on the dressing table a cheerful illustrated message which Polly had left for me. She had spent the previous winter there living with the Banabans, collecting material for *Treasure Islands*.

The Rambi Council decided to take a number of the landowners back to Ocean Island by ship in order to refresh their memories before the trial. John Macdonald, Richard Brown and I flew to Suva, from there to the New Hebrides and then to Honiara in the Solomon Islands, with a final flight to Nauru in a Fokker plane owned by its President. Nauru Island is a former German colony which became trust territory under the League of Nations mandate after the German defeat in 1918. The island was also rich in phosphate. The Nauruans, however, had the whole benefit of it, whereas, as the judge put it in his judgment, 'the Gilbert & Ellice islands took far more of the phosphate revenue than the Banabans got for themselves from the consumption of their own property and the mining of their homeland.'

We joined the Banaban contingent at Nauru aboard their ship, in which we made the 170-mile overnight voyage together to Ocean Island. The Banaban women aboard sang with emotion their traditional rather melancholic songs. They were going home. During the brilliant moonlit night a shooting star flashed across the sky. In the equatorial dawn there appeared on the horizon a solitary whale, far larger to the eye than the shape behind it, Ocean Island.

One or two of the BPC ships were at anchor off shore waiting for yet another cargo of phosphate to be loaded efficiently with modern engineering equipment. The technical skill used in the recovery of the phosphate from the land between the steep coral pinnacles was impressive. The price paid for this mining efficiency was the total destruction of the mined area. Ocean Island had become a dangerous and desolate moonscape. When Tebuke and his colleagues showed me around, I was touched by the care with which they shepherded me as we walked and climbed over the coral pinnacles and through the hot, grim wilderness.

The Banabans with whom we had sailed endeavoured to identify their plots of land. In most cases it was impossible to do so. In some of the marginal, unmined bits of land they looked excitedly for any fruit that might still be growing and some showed me proudly the odd handful of pandanus and almonds they had picked.

There was of course no hotel on Ocean Island and we stayed in the BPC staff quarters. Even amid the utter ruin of what had been their home the Banabans contrived to keep up their spirits and we attended a spirited dancing and singing evening with them.

Much work remained to be done on the case and we flew back home as directly as we could via the Gilbert Islands. Alas, sadly, my participation in the case had to end in March 1974 after the Labour victory in the election, when I was appointed Lord Chancellor and was therefore precluded from acting as counsel. Fortunately John Macdonald remained to lead in the trial of the action against the BPC and to support W.J. Mowbray QC in the action against the Attorney General. The learned judge paid a special and deserved tribute to John at the end of the case. I was pleased to hand him his Letters Patent when he was appointed Queen's Counsel before the trial ended.

In his judgment, which was probably the longest recorded in the history of British litigation, dealing as it did with many complex issues of fact and law, the judge also referred approvingly to the tribute which John Winelott QC, on behalf of the Attorney General, paid to Tito Rotan as leader of the Banabans 'largely responsible for bringing the community through the horrors of the war'.

Tito Rotan was the principal witness for the Banabans. He reacted strongly to cross-examination, a procedure with which he was unfamiliar.

'Do not try to make us fools,' he declared in the witness box through an interpreter. 'I would only beg to remind Your Lordship that I am the plaintiff. I have been begging that I might come before the Government to show what I have deeply felt, and that our complaints might be heard in the High Court and the truth arrived at. I expected when I arrived at the court that I would be asking the questions to the court because I was the one who was robbed.'

The lengthy judgment, delivered at the end of July 1976, took a remarkable course. The judge concluded that 'the Crown was not in a fiduciary position in relation to either the 1931 transaction or the 1947 transaction . . . and that throughout, the obligations of the Crown were governmental obligations and not fiduciary obligations enforceable in the courts.' But he added: 'As must be plain from what I have said, I think there have been grave breaches of those obligations. I shall refer to two. The first was in the fixing of the royalty for the 1931 transaction . . .. The other the absence of any advice to the Banabans, or encouragement to get advice, when they were embarking on the 1947 negotiations.' He said he was 'powerless to give the plaintiffs any relief in these matters'. There followed the important directions: 'I draw the attention of the Attorney General to the matters of criticism that appear in this Judgment . . .. The Crown is traditionally the fountain of justice, and justice is not confined to what is enforceable in the Courts.'

On the replanting issue the judge rejected the claim for specific performance but made an award of Australian $75 per acre. This action was later settled out of court when the BPC offer of Australian $1,250,000 was accepted by the Rambi Council.

While a number of Members of Parliament on both sides of the House called for proper recompense to be made to the Banabans, public opinion was not fully roused until Jenny Barraclough's documentary, *Go Tell It To The Judge*, filmed on Ocean Island, was shown on BBC television. A mass of letters poured in from the public to the BBC, to MPs and to the government departments concerned, many with gifts for the Banabans. Questions were raised on the floor of the House. The government spokesman announced that Mr Richard Posnett, former Governor of Belize, would fly out for discussions with the Banabans.

In May 1977 the Foreign Secretary, Dr David Owen, informed the Commons that the three governments of the United Kingdom, Australia and New Zealand were prepared to make available, on an ex gratia basis, and without admitting liability, the sum of Australian $10 million to establish a fund to be preserved for the benefit of the Banaban community.

Negotiations continued until in April 1981 the sum of Australian $14,879,453 was handed over to the Rambi Council. In addition the British Government offered £1 million sterling for the development of Rambi and financed a resources survey of Ocean Island. Constitutional contentions about the status of Ocean Island and the Banabans' relationship with the independent state of Kiribati (the old Gilbert Islands) continued. This unhappy chapter in Britain's colonial history is still not closed.

*

On 19 March 1973 I had an SOS from Alexia Mercouris and other representatives of the Campaign for the Release of Political Prisoners in Greece, seeking help for six young Greek lawyers.

These young men had been held incommunicado for several weeks in the notorious EAK/EAS military police interrogation centre in Athens and denied access to lawyers. Amnesty International had already reported that they had smuggled this message out of prison: 'Please do what you can – the suffering is unbearable.'

The lawyers had not been charged with any criminal offence, the authorities merely alleging that they had engaged in 'subversive activities'. There had been student unrest in Athens University since the spring of 1972 when the Greek military regime appointed retired army officers to administer the university and restricted the right of students to meet and demonstrate. Seven hundred students in Athens had protested and there were allegations of police brutality in raiding the university and making arrests. Student demonstrations continued in all the main universities of Greece.

Eleven students arrested in February 1973 were tried before a three-judge civilian court. Former Conservative Prime Minister Kanellopoulos, and the Liberal leader George Mavros, besides many ex-Ministers, retired generals and professors testified on behalf of the students. Eight of the students received eight to eleven months suspended sentences for insulting the police and disturbing the peace and three were acquitted. A week later the Greek authorities arrested the six lawyers who defended them.

I agreed to go to Athens to try to help. A few days after my arrival an international commission of inquiry into the detention of the lawyers also arrived: Morris Abram of New York, for the International Commission of Jurists and the International Law Section of the American Bar Association, Bill Butler for the Bar of New York City and Professor John Humphrey of McGill University, Montreal, for the International League of the Rights of Man.

My time was limited so I made my own enquiries before they arrived. The Minister of Justice in Athens refused to receive me but I did succeed in obtaining an interview with Mr Philippos Anghelis, appointed as President of the Athens Bar Association – not by the Bar, but by the military regime. I asked him why the six imprisoned lawyers were denied access to legal advisers, why three of them had not been allowed to see their families and if he would comment on reports that the prisoners had been subjected to ill-treatment in prison.

He replied that as Greece was under martial law the military police had absolute power over them and could detain them indefinitely. I pressed my question about the alleged ill-treatment of the lawyers. He answered, 'That is a matter for the Red Cross, not for the Athens Bar Association.'

I continued my unsuccessful efforts to meet the Greek Minister of Justice. Finally I contrived to get a letter, which I had marked 'confidential', delivered to him at the ministry by a porter from my hotel telling him to be sure to get a receipt.

The porter duly returned with the receipt from the ministry. Translated it read: 'Received a letter addressed to the Minister of Justice by Mr Confidential, 6.4.73.' The same day my letter was sent back to me by the Ministry of Justice with 'Returned' typed on a slip of paper attached to it. My letter had asked four questions:

1. Have the procedures provided in the laws of Greece been complied with in respect of the six lawyers?
2. What is the nature of the charges against them?
3. Since their arrest, have they been allowed to see their lawyers?
4. There have been reports in the English Press of ill-treatment injurious to the health of the lawyers since they have been in military custody. Would Your Excellency care to comment on this?

Next day, to my surprise, the contents of my letter were disclosed in an official press release which soon hit the world press. This stated that Greece was unprepared to tolerate interference in her domestic affairs.

My American and Canadian colleagues, who stayed on in Athens until 15 April, were also refused permission to see the Greek Minister of Justice and their petition on behalf of the incarcerated young lawyers was also rejected as 'an improper interference in Greek domestic affairs and implementation of Greek justice'. They responded publicly: 'We regret that the Greek Government has rejected an opportunity extended in good faith to state its position. As a sovereign state it has that power. Lawyers and jurists have painfully developed a realm of their own called the Rule of Law. Its sovereignty reaches the highest aspirations of all men and women irrespective of their nationality; and it has sanctions of its own.'

I was distressed to learn after my return to London that George Mangakis, one of the outstanding Greek lawyers I had met, had been arrested by the military police and interrogated for seven hours.

Even more worrying was the news of the arrest and incarceration in the military police headquarters of John Pesmazoglu, a courageous Greek patriot, economist, banker and radical politician. I saw a great deal of him during my stay in Athens. The military government had exiled him for several months in 1972. I urged him not to be seen with me in public as I knew I was being shadowed by the secret police. He scorned this precaution. I remember dining with him and his wife one night in a restaurant near the Acropolis which provided a magical spectacle of the Parthenon by moonlight. He said quietly that nothing would deter him from the struggle for the liberties of his people.

He was held in custody until August 1973, when he sent me a message that he and many of his fellow detainees were convinced that the campaign waged on their behalf abroad was instrumental in securing their release. Later he wrote to me without bitterness: 'Personally I was not physically ill-treated but the whole ordeal of solitary confinement was quite harsh.' He is one of the finest men I have known, a civilized human being in the classic Greek tradition.

22

The Woolsack

The General Election on 28 February 1974 gave Labour 301 seats, Conservatives 297, the Liberals 14 and others, mainly Nationalists, 23. For the first time since 1929 no party had an overall majority. I was asked to a Labour Parliamentary Committee meeting at Transport House to consider Labour's couse of action. Ted Heath was still Prime Minister and the future was unclear. We heard of talks between him and Jeremy Thorpe which might have resulted in a coalition government.

It was an anxious and uncertain week-end, during the course of which I received a phone call from the Queen's Secretary, Sir Martin Charteris. We discussed the constitutional position, which was that until Ted Heath resigned or, if he persevered, he was defeated on the Queen's Speech, his government continued in existence. It was not until Monday evening that Ted Heath did resign. Harold Wilson was then summoned to Buckingham Palace to be asked by the Queen whether he could form an administration. He said he could. He went to No 10 that evening as Prime Minister. It was the first minority Labour Government since 1931 and one which Harold Wilson resolved should govern as if it had a majority. I was asked to No 10 that evening, to be told that he wanted me to be Lord Chancellor.

The exciting challenge of undertaking this great office had one sadness: it meant parting from my constituency, which I had represented since the war and in which over so many years Polly and I had enjoyed numerous close friendships. My new office did not break our links with Newham though. The friendships have endured. After I was appointed we had a cheerful farewell party with beer and sandwiches in the residence in the Lords and sang the old songs with West Ham gusto.

I received a generous flood of letters wishing me well from friends and colleagues I had known and worked with in many parts of the world. My namesake, Sir William Elwyn Jones, who had been in the Commons with me, sent the laconic message from Bangor: 'The Great Seal will be perfectly safe with you.' Rex Welsh QC wrote from Johannesburg: 'You are the only Lord Chancellor I have ever accompanied on the piano.' Bernard Miles advised: 'Mind you give your wig a good dusting before you put it on.' Melford Stevenson, a judicial friend who had been shaken by the Tory defeat in the election, noted: 'I cannot keep the hymn "Lead kindly light" out of my mind.' Charles Hodson, one of the Law Lords, wrote: 'My devotion to Welshmen is of long standing. We came under fire in Mesopotamia in open country and had to dig ourselves in. The ground was soft but having only a miscellaneous collection of entrenching tools we did the best we could. I should be digging still but for the fact that two Welsh miners, one on each side of me, dug themselves underground like lightning and took me with them.'

There were letters too from friends from my old Circuit, from the Mayor of Llanelli, and the Llanelli Rugby Football Club, from Tabernacle Chapel, and from many constitutents. Rab Butler once spoke of 'the chill winds that blow around the summit of politics'. On the contrary, I felt sustained by the warmth of so much goodwill.

I soon learned that my appointment as Lord Chancellor involved much ancient ceremonial, for the office has existed for over a thousand years. The first step was to take the oath of office in the Queen's presence in Buckingham Palace, 'kiss hands' and receive the Great Seal of silver weighing eighteen pounds.

The Queen touched it on the table before her in the gesture of handing it into my care. It was later taken to my office, whereupon I became the Keeper of the Great Seal, a function of the Lord Chancellor since the Middle Ages. To counterfeit the Great Seal was and still is treason.

Lord Chancellors have varied in their care of it. Lord Chancellor Nottingham comforted himself by taking the Great Seal to bed with him. Before James II left the kingdom he required Lord Chancellor Jeffreys to surrender the Great Seal to him. In the course of his flight King James threw it into the Thames so that it might never be taken over by William the Prince of Orange. But it turned up in the net of a fisherman near Lambeth and was restored to official custody. In 1784 Lord Thurlow took the Great Seal home with him for safety to his house in Great Ormond Street, where the countryside then began. However thieves broke into his house and stole it on the eve of the proposed dissolution of Parliament. A new seal was quickly cast and Parliament was dissolved the next day. The lost seal was never recovered nor were the thieves traced.

The next ceremonial step was to be sworn in as Lord Chancellor in the

Royal Courts of Justice, in the Strand. Until 1875 the Lord Chancellor presided over the Court of Chancery, described by Charles Dickens in *Bleak House* as 'most pestilent of hoary sinners'. The duty of the Chancellor to be 'Keeper of the Royal Conscience' related to his equitable jurisdiction in that court. Lord Birkenhead said he found it hard enough to keep his own. Since 1875 the Chancellor's judicial work has been almost entirely in the House of Lords sitting in its judicial capacity, and in the Judicial Committee of the Privy Council.

My swearing-in took place in the Master of the Rolls' Court in his presence and that of the Lord Chief Justice and many other members of the Judiciary. Once again I took the oath of allegiance and then the judicial oath to 'do right to all manner of people after the laws and usages of this Realm without fear or favour, affection or ill-will'.

There followed a formal session of the court over which I presided. As tradition required, I asked the Queen's Counsel present: 'Are there any motions within the Bar?' Each in turn rose, bowed and sat down. So did Junior Counsel when I asked: 'Are there any motions behind the Bar?' Finally, addressing the members of the public at the back of the court, I asked: 'Are there any motions?' expecting a similar silence. Not so. A man stood up and moved that 'the Judiciary and complaints to the Law Society should be submitted to investigation by an ombudsman'. Two similar unflattering motions relating to the Judiciary followed before he gave up.

The final formal ceremony was my introduction and swearing in as a peer in the House of Lords. Since the eighteenth century every Lord Chancellor has been a peer, otherwise he could not take part in debates in the House of Lords or answer questions at Question Time.

The choice of my title was not without difficulty. Jones is not exactly unusual as a surname. There were already many of them in the Lords. Official opinion was that I should choose a related territorial title, like Lord Llanelli. However, my wish to continue to be known as Elwyn Jones was finally accepted: provided it was hyphenated. In recognition of my birthplace and my constituency, I was duly sworn in as Frederick Baron Elwyn-Jones of Llanelli and Newham.

The introduction was an elaborate procedure in the course of which I had to lay my Patent of Appointment upon the throne with my right hand while holding the Lord Chancellor's large embroidered purse in my left hand and then, having taken up the Patent again, retire backwards down the three steps of the throne. At each opening of Parliament I had to repeat twice over this movement backwards from a kneeling position at the Queen's feet and burdened by the long train of my gold and black robe:

once after presenting the Speech to the Queen to read and again after the Speech had been read and the Queen handed it back to me. I managed to perform the feat safely on five occasions, aware that some of my old friends from the Commons standing at the far end of the Chamber would, in the friendliest possible way, have quite enjoyed seeing the Lord Chancellor fall flat on his back.

A further ceremonial, in which Selwyn Lloyd played the leading role, was his presentation in the House of Lords on his re-election as Speaker of the House of Commons. He led into the far end of the Chamber as many MPs as could find room behind the Bar of the House of Lords and announced to the assembled Lords and Commons his election by the Commons as their Speaker. I in turn communicated to him the Queen's approval and confirmation of him as Speaker. He responded with the famous traditional words: 'It is now my duty, in the name and on behalf of the Commons of the United Kingdom, to lay claim by humble petition to Her Majesty to all their ancient and undoubted rights and privileges; especially to freedom of speech in debate; to freedom from arrest; to free access to Her Majesty whenever occasion shall require; and that the most favourable construction be placed upon all their proceedings.'

I replied in the time-honoured formula: 'We have it further in Command to inform you that Her Majesty doth most readily confirm all the Rights and Privileges which have ever been granted to or conferred upon the Commons by Her Majesty or any of Her Royal Predecessors.'

Centuries of turbulent parliamentary history and constitutional struggle lay behind those exchanges.

Parliament has always maintained the right to regulate its own affairs without interference from elsewhere and in particular without interference from the Crown and from the courts. The existence of a distinct body of law and custom relating to Parliament has been recognized and acknowledged by the courts ever since the fifteenth century. Special protection for Parliament and its members was accepted as essential if it was to carry out its functions properly. This body of law came to be known as 'parliamentary privilege'. The right of Members to enjoy it and the Queen's confirmation of it were again being reaffirmed by the Speaker and the Lord Chancellor as their predecessors had done down the centuries. On the Woolsack, bearing an office older than Parliament, older than Magna Carta, I often became aware of being part of the great stream of British history.

In the course of a debate in the Lords, shortly after my appointment, one Noble Lord referred to me as 'the Noble and Learned Prelate on the

Woolsack'. While I soon realized I had to wear three hats (as Speaker, Head of the Judiciary and Cabinet Minister) I did not in fact also wear a bishop's mitre. Had the Noble Lord in question been speaking a few hundred years earlier, he would have been correct in his description of the Lord Chancellor as Prelate. Before the Reformation in England most Lord Chancellors were in Holy Orders and were often archbishops or bishops. Four of my predecessors were indeed saints: Saint Swithin and then three saintly Thomases: Thomas à Becket, Thomas de Cantilupe and Thomas More. Some Lord Chancellors were by no means saints. Some were great men of affairs like William of Wykeham, Cardinal Wolsey, Francis Bacon and Clarendon.

The name 'chancellor' derives from the *cancelli* or lattice screens of a Roman court. The *cancellarius* was the court official, the usher, who sat at the screen. He progressed to notary or secretary of the court. The office prospered in the Middle Ages. The 'chancery' became a separate establishment when the Chancellor sat in judgment as a royal councillor and issued and sealed writs. By the middle of the fourteenth century he sat in Westminster Hall exercising the jurisdiction which had formerly been vested in the full Council. He also played a leading role in Parliament from its beginning. He became a key member of the sovereign's Council and inner group of advisers.

Cardinal Wolsey's term of office marked the high point in the power and influence of the Lord Chancellor. After Wolsey, the Lord Chancellor ceased to be the monarch's personal confidant and confessor as a matter of course. In an age when the finances of the realm came to depend less on the dispositions of landed estates and more on the exploitation of commercial ventures, the skills required to raise the money the government needed were to be found elsewhere. Other officials, particularly the Secretary and Lord Treasurer, eroded the Chancellor's position. Finance came to dominate government; the Prime Minister is still sworn in as First Lord of the Treasury.

However, the Lord Chancellor still takes precedence over all ministers of the Crown, even the Prime Minister. He ranks in precedence after the Royal Family and the Archbishop of Canterbury. Although the death penalty for murder has been abolished in the United Kingdom it still applies for treason. To assassinate the Lord Chancellor while he is in his place doing his office is an act of high treason for which the punishment is death by hanging, unless the Crown by warrant under the sign manual, countersigned by a Secretary of State, substitutes death by decapitation. The medieval act providing for this has never been repealed.

The Lord Chancellor continued to convey the sovereign's will to Parliament and it was one of my duties on the prorogation of Parliament to read from the Woolsack the Queen's Speech in her absence.

Although the Lord Chancellor does not now sit frequently as a judge, as was my case, his office is the core of the administration of justice generally. It is he who recommends to the Queen the appointments of High Court judges, Circuit judges, stipendiary magistrates and recorders, Queen's counsel, masters and registrars of various kinds and over 24,000 justices of the peace. To help in the last task he has local advisory committees he appoints throughout the country. Lord Gardiner once referred to all this as 'a scandalous amount of judicial patronage'.

It is however governed by well established conventions. Although the Lord Chancellor of the day is likely to have a wide personal knowledge of senior members of the Bar and of the judiciary, especially if he has previously been Attorney-General, judicial appointments are only made after considerable consultation and careful study of the records which build up in the Lord Chancellor's office about members of the Bar.

When a High Court vacancy had to be filled, the heads of the Divisions (the Lord Chief Justice, the Master of the Rolls, the President of the Family Division and the Vice-Chancellor) were invited to my office to consider likely names. Usually we agreed as to the one most meriting appointment. Occasionally two names were equally supported. Then the choice was left to me.

After the Queen's approval of the judge's appointment was received from the Palace, the new judge came to my office to be sworn. Usually his or her family came too: husband or wife and children, sometimes parents as well and always the judge's clerk. These were happy occasions. I remember the day when James Comyn's young son Rory came when his father was sworn in as a High Court judge. Rory was impressed when I told him that since the Thames had been cleaned up it might even be possible to catch a salmon from my office window. I also told him that the Great Seal was kept in my office. After Rory had gone home he was asked what he remembered of the ceremony. He said: 'The Lord Chancellor spends his time catching fish in the Thames to feed his Great Seal.'

There was another pleasing moment when Miss Margaret Myfanwy Booth QC came to my office to learn that I proposed to put her name forward to the Queen to be appointed a High Court judge. I explained to her that I hoped she would agree to being called 'Mrs Justice Booth' and not 'Miss Justice Booth' (which would be liable to be misconstrued). I asked delicately whether she was contemplating marriage. She looked at me, smiled and said: 'Are you available, Lord Chancellor?' This confirmed my view that she was obviously highly suited to be a judge in the Family Division, as she has proved to be! A few years later she did in fact marry my old friend Joe Jackson QC.

Until the outbreak of war in 1939 the House of Lords met at 4.30 pm. This enabled the Lord Chancellor to preside over the judicial sittings of the House in the morning and afternoon. During the war, in order to enable members to get home before the air raids began, the House met at 2.30 pm. After this the Lord Chancellor was only able to preside occasionally over its judicial sittings and his role as a judge was somewhat diminished.

Nevertheless the Lord Chancellor continues to have important functions in the judicial field. One is to sustain the independence of the Judiciary. In our constitutional developments we have never achieved a clear separation between the functions of the Executive and of the Legislature, nor have we established any formal mechanism for securing the independence of the Judiciary. We have no written constitution by which the responsibilities of the different areas of government are defined or in which personal rights may be entrenched.

A written constitution, a Bill of Rights or some similar device would not in my view be necessarily a beneficial change. It would merely take political decisions out of the hands of politicians – who, in a parliamentary democracy, are answerable to the electorate – and put them into the hands of judges who have no such remit or authority. However, as no formal limit can be imposed in our constitutional arrangements on the powers of the Executive in Parliament, it is all the more important to hold to the principle that a judge is not the creature of the government of the day, nor subject to its privately expressed wishes and influence.

One feature of our constitutional arrangements always surprises foreign visitors. The House of Lords, in addition to being the Upper House of the Legislature, is also the final Court of Appeal for the whole of the United Kingdom. Its function as such is of ancient origin, stemming from its role as part of the King's Council in the Middle Ages. This role was deliberately preserved when the superior courts of England and Wales were reorganized over 100 years ago. A consequence of this is that the dozen or so judges (who are known as Lords of Appeal in Ordinary) who exercise this supreme appellate jurisdiction, are members of the House of Lords. A few other senior members of the Judiciary, including the Chief Justice, are also usually created peers and thus become members of the Second Chamber.

This arrangement, like so much else in our constitution, is made workable only by the existence of well-established conventions: the first is that no member of the House of Lords who is not a Lord of Appeal now takes part in the judicial processes of the House; the second that the Lords of Appeal in Ordinary (that is those Lords of Appeal who are appointed to the House expressly for the purpose of exercising the appellate jurisdiction) do not normally take part in the debates of the House when politically contentious matters are being discussed. As long as these conventions are observed, the mutual independence of each function of the House can be safeguarded. The arrangement has the advantage of enabling the House to have the opinion of the most senior judges in the land expressed in debate on, for example, proposed measures of law reform, and to be able to draw on their legal expertise on other occasions as well.

If judicial independence is to be preserved three things are, in my view, necessary. First, appointment to judicial office must be seen to be based on merit alone and not as a reward for political services rendered. This I believe has been broadly achieved since the last war. Secondly, the authority to correct judicial errors must be contained within the judicial system itself and not be performed by Parliament or the Government. Thirdly, the judge must be free from pressure to tailor his or her decisions to make them acceptable to the government of the day: this does not mean that judges should be immune from criticism. As Lord Atkin said, almost half a century ago: 'No wrong is committed by any member of the public who exercises the ordinary right of criticizing, in good faith, in private or in public, the public act done in the seat of justice.'

The Lord Chancellor has a delicate role to play in all this. Political colleagues should understand – as I believe mine did – that he has a fundamental responsibility which is not related to the immediate problems pressing on the Government. While he must bear his share of ministerial responsibility for the decisions of the Cabinet, he must also enjoy the confidence and respect of the judges and protect them as best he can from political interference in their judicial activities. The judges in turn must avoid encroaching on the politician's ground on controversial issues and playing politics themselves.

Ever since the Act of Settlement of 1701 High Court judges can only be removed by an address by both Houses of Parliament. Only one judge has actually been removed in this way and that was in 1830. Occasionally a motion to remove a judge has appeared on the Order Paper of the House of Commons simply for the purpose of enabling the behaviour or ability of a judge to be discussed. Parliament has, in order to avoid any appearance of interference with the Judiciary, adopted a rule that the conduct of judges and criticism of decisions of the courts may only be discussed upon a substantive motion for removal of the judge. The Speaker keeps a watchful eye on this. Such motions have appeared on the Order Paper during the years I have been in Parliament but have only rarely been actually debated.

The power of Parliament to remove members of the higher Judiciary reflects the supremacy of Parliament as an estate in the realm, a supremacy which (in the case of the House of Commons) is reinforced by the authority which it has by virtue of its democratic composition. If it is not impossible to remove judges – which would be most unsatisfactory – the power of removal must reside somewhere. The risk that our system leaves open – the possibility of removing a judge for purely political reasons unconnected with his or her ability and impartiality as a judge – has not in fact materialized since the procedure was instituted in 1701. As I said in a report to the Conference of Presidents of European Assemblies at the Hague in June 1978: 'In great measure this has been due to the understanding and respect which both Parliament and the Judges have had for each other's functions, and to Parliament's acceptance of the fundamental importance of the need for the Judiciary to be independent.'

In this process the office of Lord Chancellor has played an important part, because by combining in one person the Speakership of the House of Lords and the Head of the Judiciary, he is able to mediate between the two powers, and indeed between the Judiciary and the Executive as well when the need arises (which it did occasionally during my term of office), and in this way to forestall at an early stage incidents which might otherwise lead to serious conflict.

Circuit judges are not so fully safeguarded as High Court judges and can be removed by the Lord Chancellor for misconduct or incapacity. More than once during my term of office I was pressed both in the House of Commons and by the press to remove a Circuit judge on much more slender grounds than that. An isolated error, an insensitive remark from the Bench, or the passing by a normally sensible judge of a sentence thought to be grossly inadequate was urged as a ground for removal. Such isolated grounds for criticism would, in my view, not have justified such a step and would have been an improper interference with the independence of the judges.

However, in a few such cases I did think it right to ask the judge in question to have a private talk with me in my office about the matter complained of. Exceptionally, in one case which had caused much public concern because of its racialist undertones and in which the judge in question had departed from his usual sound standards of judgment, I informed the press that I had done so. The judge did not sit on such cases again.

The responsibility of the Lord Chancellor for judicial administration increased greatly after the recommendations of the Royal Commission set up by Gerald Gardiner and chaired by Lord Beeching were put into effect during Lord Hailsham's chancellorship. Beeching made the Lord Chancellor's office generally responsible for the administration of justice throughout the country and directly responsible for the administration of justice in the Law Courts in the Strand and of all Crown Courts and County Courts. The new Circuit administrators were members of the Lord Chancellor's staff and directly answerable to him. The system came into operation when the great increase in the number of criminal cases coming to trial was putting court administration under intense pressure. More and more judges, especially to service the growing numbers of Circuit courts, had to be appointed. More court accommodation had to be found. Saving of judicial time became imperative. While it was painful for an old circuiteer like myself to see the end of several treasured features of life on the circuit, for instance localized recorderships, the need for greater flexibility in the system was imperative.

Without the changes made in the 1970s, the continuing problems created by the growing case load would in my view have been far worse. The appointment of presiding judges in each Circuit improved matters considerably. An able and energetic presiding judge keeping in close touch with the Circuit judges and assisted by a competent Circuit administrator enjoying the confidence of the courts and the profession, brought good results.

More cases coming to trial resulted in more appeals, both criminal and civil. The number of criminal appeals rose from 1,267 at the end of March 1974, when I was appointed, to 1,682 in the following year. The number of divorce appeals also increased considerably. The position was made worse by the fact that trials and appeals were taking longer to dispose of. As a result I had to introduce an order in May 1975 to increase the maximum number of lord justices in the Court of Appeal from fourteen to sixteen.

I found improvement in the running of the Civil Division of the Court of Appeal (which had begun to show signs of an inability to cope with the increasing work pressures) was slow in coming. Proposals which were initiated in 1977 did not achieve fruition until the passing of the Supreme Court Act in 1981. In the Chancery Division too it took some years to quicken and improve the disposal of cases.

A great deal of my time as Lord Chancellor was spent in chasing between the House of Lords and No 10 Downing Street and the Cabinet office in Whitehall to attend meetings of the cabinet, and cabinet and ministerial committees. The key questions of public policy, whether domestic or foreign, were decided in Cabinet. This involved study of a mass of memoranda, minutes and reports with which ministers were deluged. About half the papers in my red boxes related to general government business, the rest to judicial administration: the business of my own department.

From time to time the Prime Minister asked me to chair special committees on questions of public policy about which there were inter-departmental differences: for instance whether we should persevere with Concorde, housing finance and other issues. I was also consulted on security questions.

Cabinet meetings took place at No 10, but there were occasional cabinet meetings at Chequers when a full day's discussion was needed for major reviews of policy. The Chequers visits provided a welcome change of scene. They also gave us longer time to talk to colleagues about our common problems.

Many important questions on economic policy, defence policy, Northern Ireland and Rhodesia were examined and often decided by small cabinet committees appointed by the Prime Minister. Sometimes this gave rise to protests in Cabinet from Ministers who were not 'in the know', particularly in regard to economic decisions and public expenditure. However without such delegation of decisions, government business could not have been got through.

Conduct of cabinet business was of course in the hands of the Prime Minister. Usually the cabinet agenda included a statement of the issues involved and supporting memoranda prepared by the staff of the cabinet office. The Cabinet Secretary, who remained silent throughout the proceedings, sat on the Prime Minister's right and, with the assistance of two other officials who were present, prepared the minutes.

The departmental minister concerned would open the discussion on any matter within his or her responsibility. Each minister was then free to intervene, but the need to finish cabinet business created a self-imposed discipline. Discussion was frank, free and to the point. Occasionally a clear division of opinion would emerge. The Prime Minister would then take a head count and the view of the majority would prevail. I have attended many committee meetings in my time, both political and professional. In few have I seen business better conducted than it was in the cabinet meetings during the premierships of both Harold Wilson and Jim Callaghan. Unfortunately the confidentiality of cabinet discussions was not always respected by one or two of those who took part in them, nor was the principle of collective responsibility.

The preparation of bills for which the Lord Chancellor is responsible reaches its fruition in the debates on the bill in the House of Lords. There the Lord Chancellor takes part as Speaker but more significantly as a minister dealing with government business within his sphere of responsibility.

The Lord Chancellor's duties as Speaker are confined to putting procedural questions to the House. His powers as Speaker and that of his twenty or so deputies who take his place on the Woolsack a good deal of the time are very limited and quite unlike those of the Speaker of the House of Commons. He has no control over the proceedings of the House, which regulates its own proceedings. He does not decide who is to speak in the Chamber nor any question of order. The latter is the responsibility of the Leader of the House or his deputy or as a last resort a whip.

The Lord Chancellor has no role whatsoever in the House of Commons and may not enter there. It was not always so. Towards the end of the Middle Ages he did attend the Commons in order to press the King's will upon it. This led to some great confrontations. In 1523 Cardinal Wolsey, the Lord Chancellor, came to the House of Commons aggrieved by the fact that, according to the biographer of Thomas More, 'nothing was so soon done or spoken in the Commons but it was immediately blown abroad in every alehouse.' This was before Hansard and the press were reporting what was happening in Parliament. Sir Thomas More described how on that occasion the Cardinal came 'with all his pomp, with his maces, his pillars, his crosses, his pole-axes, his hat and his Great Seal too'. When the Cardinal demanded a subsidy of £800,000, which the Commons complained was more than the whole current coin of the Realm, the Speaker excused himself and the House from answering. The Cardinal said: 'Here is without doubt a marvellously obstinate silence' and strode out of the Chamber. In the end, however, the King did get his subsidy.

The Lord Chancellor is no longer burdened with pole-axes or pillars, but he still has his mace, his purse and the Great Seal. Indeed he has two maces, although only one is normally used as a symbol of royal authority. The other is used only occasionally, as when the Chancellor attends the Lord Mayor's Banquet in the Guildhall.

The Lord Chancellor's large, heavily tasselled purse is of crimson velvet embroidered in gold thread and pearls with the royal arms and the lion and unicorn with attendant cherubim. It was originally used to hold the Great Seal. Now it is normally carried empty, although it is used to hold the text of the Queen's Speech at the State Opening of Parliament.

When sitting as Speaker of the Lords on the Woolsack, the Chancellor wears a black cloth court suit, silver buckled breeches, cotton and silk stockings, silver buckled shoes and overall a black silk gown with train. On his head he wears a full-bottomed late seventeenth-century wig. The wig I wore was the one Judge Clark-Williams gave me when I took Silk in 1953. The Chancellor's black tricorne is only worn on ceremonial occasions, on top of the wig. When it had to be doffed three times during the introduction of a new peer I had to take care to ensure that my wig did not come off with it. Ceremonial dress should be worthy of the office. My jabots were made of Brussels lace by our friend the designer Bill Pashley, who also made Polly's dresses for state occasions.

The introduction of a new peer is a remarkable piece of theatre. The new peer with his two sponsors (all carrying cocked hats in their left hands and wearing their red and ermine parliamentary robes) enter the Chamber in a line. On reaching the Bar of the House they bow, each in turn, to the Cloth of Estate: the position which the sovereign, if present, would occupy. The procession then advances, led by Garter King of Arms wearing his tabard and carrying his silver gilt sceptre of office. The bows are repeated as each member of the procession reaches the Table and again at the Judges' Woolsacks. At the Lord Chancellor's Woolsack itself the new peer kneels on one knee at the feet of the Lord Chancellor and presents his writ of summons to him, while Garter presents his Patent. All three return to the Table where the Reading Clerk reads the Patent and Writ, and the new peer takes the Oath of Allegiance or affirms and signs the Roll.

Garter then conducts the peer and his sponsors to the rear bench in the chamber, once the Barons' Bench. (Now all peers are equal and no places are reserved according to rank, save for the Bishops' Bench.) On the back bench, at Garter's direction, they sit, put on their cocked hats, rise, and doff their hats and bow to the Chancellor three times, the Chancellor returning their salutations. The procession then again proceeds the length of the House back to the Woolsack, bowing at the appointed places as before. The Lord Chancellor shakes hands with the new peer and the procession leaves the Chamber.

I had thought that the procedure of three bows was associated with the Trinity. Sir Antony Wagner, former Garter King of Arms, and John Sainty, the Reading Clerk in the House of Lords, in a paper to the Society of Antiquaries of London suggest an even earlier origin: that three has been a sacred or magic number in widely separated times and places, both non-Christian and Christian. The Greek funeral pyre was circumambulated three times. In Rome a formula against gout was repeated twenty-seven times. Celtic mythology is full of triads. In South Wales we still say '*tri cynnig i gymro*', three tries for a Welshman.

The Lords debated the ceremony of introduction in March 1975, when Lord Raglan proposed shortening and amending it and described it as 'very comic and absurd'. His was a lone voice. Lord Cudlipp, making his maiden speech from the Labour back benches, defended the ceremony unreservedly, making a plea for authenticity in the ceremonial, which had been performed in exactly the same way since 1621.

The Lord Chancellor's procession from his office to the Chamber which marks the beginning of each sitting of the Lords also accords with ancient practice. He is preceded by his mace-bearer and purse-bearer and followed by his train-bearer. Gerald Gardiner advised me that in formal processions it is seemly to look straight ahead. This I tried to do at the opening of Parliament in March 1974. My then small grandson Reuben, who watched the procession, said to me afterwards: 'Grandpa, why did you look so angry?' After that I relaxed my expression.

The Lord Chancellor's residence, unlike Mr Speaker's perfect Pugin house, is simply a long train of large, draughty rooms over twenty feet high (with two freezing cold bathrooms curiously contrived at the far end of a long corridor) on the second floor of the tower at the southern end of the Houses of Parliament overlooking the river and the Victoria Tower gardens. However, as the Lord Chancellor's heavy workload entails long and late working hours, I decided that it would be wise to live there, directly above the office. I thought it prudent however to keep on our flat in Gray's Inn. I had seen two Prime Ministers rendered homeless on a change of government.

Polly soon discovered that the large kitchen contained nothing in the way of cooking utensils except for a very small brush for glazing pastry and an enormous colander.

Prominent on the wall behind the traditional green baize door was an impressive glass device for summoning the servants to 'His Lordship's Bedroom', 'Her Ladyship's Bedroom', the Library, Bathroom, etc. The bells worked all right – as my grandchildren soon discovered – but there were no servants. Eventually, kind Mrs Kaye, one of the cleaners in the Commons, came to our rescue when she had finished work there. When she retired, Mrs Joan Watts and Mrs Sylvia Heathfield, who were cleaners in

the Lords, took her place to clean the acres of floor and to our great relief stayed with us until we left. I also had the good fortune of having as my driver Rene Mutimer. She married Sam Mutimer, a watchful custodian who guarded the Lord Chancellor's corridor.

Polly soon covered the expanse of wall-space in the residence with paintings, but the best picture of all was the Thames itself, always there, always changing, always marvellous, in sun, in rain and in fog, and always on view through the tall cathedral windows in each room. Completely bewitched, Polly often stayed up all night working feverishly with chalks and inks, learning the river's eddies, its moods and its lights. The most magical time of all, she used to tell me, was about 3 am, when the river became quieter and St Thomas's Hospital, Westminster Bridge and Lambeth Palace were reflected in the water like a Canaletto. The Thames affected us all. Staying with us for a few days our old friend the composer David Heneker, who was working on a musical about pearly kings and queens with Polly, bewitched by the evening lights on the river, came up with the song 'Diamonds in the Water' to Polly's lyric.

At night, especially in the quiet of Sunday night, living in the residence was curiously spooky. I do not believe in ghosts. But one of the custodians apparently did and sent me a drawing of the Lord Chancellor in dressing gown peering through a door at a headless figure at a typewriter holding his head in his right hand.

Our grandchildren, who sometimes picnicked with us there at week-ends, took it all for granted. They called the entire Palace of Westminster 'Grandpa's house' and gave each other blissful rides up and down the slippery corridor on the invaluable trolley Polly had bought. The lino-covered corridor proved to be a trap however. One morning Polly rushed to answer the phone and slipped, breaking three ribs. The Works Department quickly covered the corridor with carpet after that.

My old friend George Thomas occupied the Speaker's house at the northern end of the Houses of Parliament. The most dramatic of our many meetings together took place early in the morning of 17 June 1974. As I was having breakfast in the kitchen I heard a loud explosion and saw, through the windows, flames and smoke rising above Westminster Hall. I rushed down the long corridors, through to St Stephen's Hall into Westminster Hall, arriving at the same moment as the Speaker. We stood together in anguished silence watching the smoke and flames rising from the far end of the Hall and the fire brigade battling to control them. From the river huge jets of water were being directed on to the roof.

An IRA bomb had exploded a gas main. But for the quick response and efficiency of the fire brigade and the police on duty the great medieval Hall, the finest of its kind in Europe, begun by William Rufus in the eleventh century, would have been destroyed. When the Luftwaffe had bombed it in 1941, the air raid wardens and the firemen had to make the agonizing choice between saving the burning Commons Chamber and saving Westminster Hall. They could not save both. They saved Westminster Hall. It was saved again in 1974.

The political curtain-raiser in the new Parliament in March 1974 was the usual debate on the contents of the Queen's Speech which had set out the Government's programme for the new Session. I made my maiden speech as Lord Chancellor on home affairs.

The prospects ahead were bleak. The world economy had been gravely distorted by the oil crisis. Britain, already in massive payments deficit, had to face a four-fold increase in our oil import bill: North Sea oil did not begin to flow until a year and a half later. World inflation persisted and a world recession worse than anything known since the 1930s brought with it deepening unemployment and currency instability. Its persistence cast a blight on economic and social progress right across the world, as I found during my many foreign visits as Lord Chancellor.

In my speech I urged the need for a greater measure of social justice so that national unity could hold us together during the period of crisis we had entered. There was much to do. In many of our inner city areas there were conditions of squalor, aggravated by racial stresses, straight out of Mayhew or Dickens. At every point law and social reformers should work closely together and legal services and better access to the courts should be a key element in a comprehensive social welfare service.

The need for action was highlighted in the twenty-third Report of the Legal Aid Advisory Committee (chaired by Lord Hamilton of Dalzell), which I found in my in-tray soon after I was appointed. It contained a devastating four-fold indictment of existing arrangements. The committee declared that they had little doubt that, first:

> There are many people whose legal rights are, for a variety of reasons, at present going wholly by default; secondly, that some of these are unaware even that they possess such rights; others realize it but either do not know how to obtain help in enforcing them or lack the money or the ability, or both, to do so; thirdly, that there is a severe overall shortage of solicitors in the country and, mainly for economic reasons, their geographical distribution is very ill-suited to serve many of the poorer sections of the community; fourthly, that there are considerable areas of the law, notably those relating to housing, landlord and tenant matters and welfare benefits, where expert advice and assistance is urgently needed, but is often hard to come by.

Unhappily this exposure of the extent of the problems, which I resolved to try to remedy, came when restraint in public expenditure was pressed on ministers as a first priority at almost every cabinet meeting. I had learned from my son Dan, who was a youth social worker in Tower Hamlets, in East London, of troubles being faced in some of the law centres. These centres were largely run by public-spirited young solicitors, barristers and social workers and had sprung up through their initiative in some of the run-down parts of our big cities. Not only were they short of money; they were also being opposed in some places by local solicitors who feared that they would be competitors for a limited pool of work.

I had several meetings with the Law Society about this question. Finally they agreed to waive their professional rules against advertising so that law centres could make their availability known in their localities. The existence of the centres in fact generated a good deal of work for solicitors. It was encouraging that whereas when I was appointed there were only six law centres, when I left office there were twenty-six. Many of them received the active support of local solicitors.

Legal aid and assistance became more extensive as time went on. By the time I left office in 1979 over three million people had been granted legal aid certificates to enable them to pursue their rights through the courts.

Even though the cost of the Civil Legal Aid scheme in England and Wales rose from £500,000 in 1950 to nearly ten times as much in 1979, it was still not possible to maintain the coverage of the scheme in the face of inflation. The 1979 Act and Regulations made under it did achieve a significant improvement. At least 70 per cent of households with two parents and two children became eligible for legal aid and assistance and over a third were able to obtain it free. The proposals of my office for improvements in the administration of legal aid had to be shelved on the setting up of the Royal Commission on Professional Legal Services in 1976.

We soon began the task of putting through the programme of legislation set out in the Queen's Speech. Much responsibility for this in the Lords rested on the shoulders of our Chief Whip – Pat Llewellyn-Davies. She had a mastery of the business of the House and was admired on all sides for her competence at the Dispatch Box and her personal charm. We relied heavily on her both when we were in office and in Opposition. She should have been in the Cabinet. Her room in the Lords – summer and winter – was always filled with lovely flowers from her place in the country where she lived with Richard, her architect husband. Pat was unique in many ways. The Chief Whip in the Lords is by tradition made Captain of the Gentlemen-at-Arms. For the first time in history the Captain was no Gentleman!

The first major piece of legislation the new Parliament had to consider was the Trade Unions and Labour Relations Bill. By March 1974 there was a total breakdown in industrial relations. Victor Feather, the cheerful and dedicated former General Secretary of the TUC, who had joined us in the Lords, made a powerful attack on the 1971 Act, as did Lord Sainsbury.

In welcoming the new Bill from the point of view of an employer Lord Sainsbury said that employers were reluctant to invoke the laws. 'You cannot threaten to bring a person before the court one day and expect him to come and work for you the next ... Industrial relations', he said, 'are about human relations and cannot be placed in the straitjacket of the law.' I agree.

Lord Hailsham led the opposition to the Bill with passion and without restraint. We had one stormy passage which Lord Shinwell, not often disposed to support his Front Bench, described as 'an altercation conducted in the harshest terms' between Lord Hailsham and myself, and complimented me on not losing my temper. My relations with Quintin Hailsham cooled for a while after this exchange but were in due course restored to our normal watchful courtesy in the House and amity outside it.

IRA terrorism in both England and Northern Ireland continued to shatter our domestic peace. Following the bombings in Birmingham, we introduced the Prevention of Terrorism Bill. This proscribed the IRA, making it possible to make exclusion orders against people involved in terrorism, and gave the police wide powers to arrest and detain suspected terrorists and also to carry out security checks on all travellers entering and leaving Great Britain and Northern Ireland.

Anxiety about terrorism led to a demand for renewal of the death penalty. I opposed this in the debate in December 1974, particularly on the ground that it would increase the risk of retaliatory violence and ruthless reprisals against our armed forces. I added: 'We live in a period when there is a desperate need to restore respect for human life. I believe we need to foster a deep reverence for it. I do not believe that restoring the Death Penalty will increase that reverence.' The issue was not put to a vote.

Normally Lord Harris of Greenwich, the Minister of State for the Home Office, dealt with matters relating to criminal justice but I also assisted in the progress of major bills. I spoke in October 1974 on a Criminal Justice Bill aiming to provide more effective legal means of bringing to justice fugitive offenders in Ireland.

The Children Act, based on the Report of the Departmental Committee on the Adoption of Children, was one of our many reforms dealing with the family scene and the welfare of children. We also gave support to a Private Member's Bill on Domestic Violence and Matrimonial Proceedings, improving the remedies available to women and children who were victims of such violence and giving the police, in serious cases, a new power of arrest. Evidence given to a Select Committee showed that as many as 5,000 wives were assaulted each year.

The Inheritance (Provision for Family and Dependants) Bill of 1975 was another of the law reform proposals of the Law Commission which we enacted. It was the first instalment of much needed reform of our law of family property and dealt with the law of family provision on death. Until 1925 a person could leave all his or her property by will to a charity or an individual outside the family – to a cats' home or to a lover – leaving a surviving spouse and children destitute. The Bill increased the provision which could be made for the surviving spouse and enlarged the class of persons who could apply for maintenance from the estate of the deceased. It brought in anyone who was dependent on the deceased, whether related or not. The basic theme of the Bill was to give the court discretion to deal with each case on its merits.

Difficult legal problems were created by the suffering and handicaps caused to many children whose mothers had taken the thalidomide drug. There was some doubt as to whether a child born with a deformity could claim for damages when it could be proved on the child's behalf that the deformity was caused by some wrongful act which affected the mother's capability of giving birth to a healthy child without that deformity. The Congenital Disabilities (Child Liability) Bill removed that doubt.

I had already been involved in the thalidomide saga. I appeared, after I returned to the Bar in 1970, with Michael Burke-Gaffney for London Weekend Television in proceedings brought against them by the Attorney-General. This arose out of a programme concerning the plight of the thalidomide victims in which critical comments were made about the conduct of the Distillers' Company, who had marketed the drug in England. I asked to see the videotape of the feature. Its key scene was of a delightful family in the sunlit garden of their home. One of the children was a victim of the drug. She was evidently much loved by her family but the handicap from which she was suffering was clear to see. The scene was so touching that I asked that the videotape should be shown in the Divisional Court. I was sure that the judges would be as moved as I was. They were. The proceedings for contempt of court were dismissed.

A steady stream of law reform measures continued to flow through Parliament during my term of office: Statute Law Repeals Bills weeding out obsolete acts of Parliament; Consolidation Bills; reforms in the criminal law, particularly the law of conspiracy.

The Litigants in Person Bill enabled the litigant in person to recover the costs incurred in preparing his or her case. The Patents Act of 1977, which made major changes in our patent law, brought considerable benefits to industry, inventors and our economy by modernizing our domestic patent law and procedure and enabling the United Kingdom to ratify a number of international patent agreements. The Arbitration Act brought more arbitration work to the London courts and went far to restore London's position as a world centre for arbitration.

The Limitation Act 1975 helped persons who were injured but who only discovered that they were suffering from an actionable injury after the normal three-year time limit for the bringing of an action had elapsed. It gave the courts a discretion to override the limitation period in personal injury cases where it considered that it would be just to do so.

Another and more far-reaching reform bill was the State Immunity Act 1978, as a result of which foreign states and their agencies can no longer enjoy any immunity in respect of their commercial transactions which they undertake to perform wholly or partly in the United Kingdom.

A constitutionally interesting bill to which I gave the Government's support was the Tenure of Office and Discharge of Ecclesiastical Functions Bill introduced by Lord Hailsham to remove a doubt which had troubled constitutional lawyers as to the capacity of Roman Catholics to hold the office of Lord Chancellor. There was no legal incapacity attached to Jews, Moslems, Christian Scientists, Buddhists or atheists. The Bill received general support in its subsequent progress through Parliament.

One of my agreeable tasks in the House was to be a spokesman on Welsh affairs. The Welsh Development Agency Bill was the first wholly Welsh bill on major economic and environmental questions in the principality. Much of the natural beauty of Wales had been despoiled in the past. The Agency was given real powers to arrest that decline. The Development of Rural Wales Bill in turn created a development board for rural Wales, which had suffered severely from the flight of so many of its inhabitants from the country to the towns.

The Government's most ambitious legislative proposals were its Devolution Bills for Scotland and Wales. I addressed a number of meetings in Wales when the referendum was held on the Welsh Devolution Bill. It was one of my most unexpected political experiences : there was no enthusiasm at the meetings, indeed there was hardly an audience. We had had endless cabinet committee meetings to thrash out the proposals, both in No 10 and at Chequers. Some ministers were enthusiastic in support of the Bill, believing that it would bring decision-making closer to the people most affected by those decisions and produce greater democratic control over central government's activities in Wales. Others regarded devolution as threatening the political and economic unity of the United Kingdom, whose inhabitants had an immense bond of shared history and of shared sacrifice in war and peace. As I said in one of the many debates we had in the Lords through the long summer of 1978 : 'working in unison over the years, they have achieved far more together than they could have achieved separately.' I myself did not think that the executive devolution we proposed for Wales would damage that unity. In the event the devolution proposals failed to dispel the fears of those who thought it would and in the referendum they were decisively rejected by the people of Wales.

Direct rule from Westminster and Whitehall over Northern Ireland had, from its commencement, added considerably to the Lord Chancellor's responsibilities. This reached a high point when it fell to me to steer the Northern Ireland Judicature Bill through the House in 1978. The courts of Northern Ireland could no longer cope with the big increase in the number of cases coming before them. The Bill provided the Supreme

Court with a new administrative structure, merged the Court of Criminal Appeal with the Court of Appeal and established a new Crown Court to try criminal cases on indictment in place of the original criminal jurisdiction of the old Courts of Assize and County Courts. Finally it established a unified courts service to provide the administrative staffs for the courts.

While overall responsibility for the administration of the courts rested in the Secretary of State, careful steps were taken to make all decisions as to the siting of the courts, judicial appointments and the tenure of office of the judges the responsibility of the Lord Chancellor or the Lord Chief Justice. I gave an assurance in the House that 'I and my successors will continue to support and uphold the judges should the Executive at any time seek to encroach on judicial territory.'

The Bill also included valuable remedies in administrative law, simplifying the old procedures and making it easier to challenge the decisions of government departments.

Just as the Bill was on its way through the Lords, my friend Airey Neave DSO, MC, Croix de Guerre, who escaped from Colditz after being wounded and made a prisoner of war and then masterminded the escape of many allied pilots and prisoners of war behind enemy lines, was murdered by the IRA. A bomb exploded under his car as he was driving it out of the MPs' underground car park in New Palace Yard, in the precincts of Parliament.

Airey and I were at Nuremberg together and I had been with him and his wife shortly before the bombing at the launching of his last book: a vivid personal record of his dealings with Goering and the others as the tribunal's representative. In my tribute to him in the House I read a passage from the end of his book:

> It will be many years before we can afford to forget the Nazis. Before our eyes, the problems of race and terrorism are a frightening reminder of Hitler's example. He lived by terror and his methods appeal today to the young and rootless all over the world. Those who use terror to gain their political ends are the heirs of his Revolution of Destruction, however much they may claim to represent opposing doctrines.

He added the poignant words: 'The whole experience had a deep influence on my future life.'

I made several visits to Northern Ireland and was heartened by the notable absence of sectarianism either on the Bench or in the conduct of the legal profession there. The friendships I had established there when I was at the Bar were fortified by the collaboration I enjoyed at all levels when I was in office, from the Lord Chief Justice to the court officials and staff and the members of the legal profession.

It was perhaps fitting that the last major debate in which I took part when I was Lord Chancellor was to move the Continuation Order to renew section 2 of the Southern Rhodesia Act which I had introduced as Attorney General in 1965, enabling Her Majesty's Government by Order in Council to make such provision in regard to Southern Rhodesia as appeared necessary.

By November 1978 the violence of the civil war in Rhodesia had escalated and over 5,000 Rhodesians, black and white, were being killed each year. The tragedy had come to pass that was foreseeable when the Smith regime wantonly rejected the proposals we put forward on HMS *Tiger* and HMS *Fearless*. Had those proposals been accepted, the way would have been open to a peaceful and gradual attainment of majority rule.

Lord Caradon warned in debate that there could be nothing more serious in the world than a war in Africa between white and black, with the West supporting one side and the East the other. If we were to remove sanctions, as a minority of Tories were advocating, we would give encouragement to the Smith regime. As Lord Caradon pointed out, 'it would be a declaration of our joining in a civil war.' The Continuation Order was in fact carried by 166 votes to sixty-five.

The same month the Bingham Report disclosed how the Oil Sanctions Orders had been successfully evaded by oil companies which supplied the Smith Government with its basic requirements. As Attorney General I had caused a number of prosecutions to be brought for breaches of the sanctions orders, but none were brought in respect of the activities of the oil companies. This was not because I gave them immunity. I had no knowledge of the evasions that had been going on.

When the report was published and more recently, an exhaustive search was made at my request into both the Law Officers' Department (LOD) papers and those of the Foreign and Commonwealth Office (FCO) to discover whether I or my department was ever informed or consulted about the part played by the Shell and BP companies and their personnel and overseas subsidiaries in evading our oil sanctions during my term as Attorney General and specifically in the critical years 1967 to 1969. The search of the papers of the LOD showed no evidence of any correspondence or consultation on this matter with me or my officials during the relevant period. The FCO papers in turn gave no indication of any consultation having taken place with the LOD in the years 1967 to 1969 on the question whether the British oil companies had been, or still were, in breach of the petroleum order either by reason of the transactions that took place before the introduction of the 'switch' arrangement of early 1968 (when the

British companies worked through the French company Total) or by reason of the switch arrangement itself.

It was not the first time that Law Officers were left in ignorance of a government department's activities. The Law Officers could only act on the basis of information supplied to them by the departments. They had no intelligence sources of their own.

Alongside the Lord Chancellor's parliamentary duties a multitude of other responsibilities had accumulated around the office. One was the safeguarding of public records and access to them in the Public Record Office. Concern was expressed in the House in 1977 when Lord Denning, the Chairman of the Advisory Council on Public Records, questioned whether government departments sent to the Public Record Office all the records they should. He cited as an example the fact that the records of the Profumo inquiry, which he conducted, had been destroyed. In fact this was not so. They were and are retained in the Cabinet Office.

One of my responsibilities was for the Council on Tribunals, with which I kept in touch and which I met in an annual review of its work. I was impressed by its activity in promoting standards of justice and efficiency in the hundreds of tribunals up and down the country.

Another task with which my small but able staff had to cope was the considerable volume of complaints sent to me by Members of Parliament and the public. One woman sent me regular letters about her disappointment with her contact lenses. I still receive angry and expensive phone calls from a distant and resentful member of the public who lost his case and blames me for it because my name as Lord Chancellor appeared on the form of writ which began the proceedings. I suppose there is some advantage in having available a symbolic figure to whom the harassed citizen can blow off steam.

Members of Parliament came to see me from time to time either alone or in a deputation about current issues – a complaint about a judge, inadequate court facilities for witnesses, legal aid, siting of new courts. One deputation complained that judges were prejudiced against lesbian mothers in proceedings about custody of children. Court records showed that the judges had, in fact, been even-handed, the father being given the custody in some cases, the mother in others.

In the course of time the Lord Chancellor had become Visitor to a number of Oxford and Cambridge Colleges, including my own. With Mr Speaker he was also a joint Vice-President of Westminster Hospital.

For historical reasons the Lord Chancellor is not only a Church Commissioner and Visitor to St Stephen's Chapel, Windsor, but, surprisingly, he also possesses extensive ecclesiastical patronage. This dates in part from the Middle Ages, but more substantially from the days of the Reformation. When I was Lord Chancellor, there were still over five hundred livings the patronage of which I exercised on behalf of the sovereign. They were in places with fascinating names like Upton Snodbury with Broughton Hacket, Offord D'Arcy with Afford Cluny, Egg Buckland, and Colden Parva on the Yorkshire coast. When my Ecclesiastical Secretary, Colonel Salmon, went to the latter he searched in vain for Colden Parva Church. He was, nevertheless, solemnly greeted by four churchwardens, two of whom were the wardens for Colden Parva. When he enquired where the church was, they pointed out to sea and said that regrettably it had been washed away some two hundred years before, but that since a few acres of the original parish were still left, they thought it proper to mark the fact by continuing to appoint churchwardens.

I was advised on these ecclesiastical appointments by Colonel Salmon, who interviewed suitable candidates and consulted the local bishop, churchwardens and others. Great care was taken to try to find the right man for the right place.

In April each year the new Queen's Counsel, in full bottomed wigs and silk gowns, come to be sworn in and to receive their Letters Patent from the Lord Chancellor in the Moses Room in the House of Lords. Their numbers have grown year by year. The practice of calling Silks within the Bar has gone on over the centuries in the Palace of Westminster, where since the middle ages the courts functioned in Westminster Hall. When Peter the Great visited the Hall in 1697 he asked who were all the men in wigs and gowns. When told they were all lawyers, he said, 'I only have two lawyers in my whole Empire and I propose to hang one of them when I get back to St Petersburg.'

The first QC was Francis Bacon. Before his time the pleaders were Serjeants-at-Law. When they were appointed it was the practice for the new Serjeant to give gold rings to the sovereign and the Lord Chancellor. I assured the new Silks that the practice had long fallen into disuse.

The Lord Chancellor maintains close links not only with the Bar but with solicitors and has frequent meetings with representatives of both. Meetings of the Magistrates' Association, both nationally and with as many of its branches up and down the country as I could find time to visit, enabled me to discuss their problems with their members. I attached great importance to this part of my duties. Our system of Justices of the Peace is as unique as it is ancient. Upon the efficiency and good standing of the Magistrates' Courts, where about nine-tenths of the criminal cases in the country are tried and where people are most likely to come up against the law, confidence in the administration of justice largely depends. We owe a great deal to the unpaid magistracy and to the Justices' Clerks who advise them.

The places where some Magistrates' Courts had to sit were notoriously inadequate to cope with the continuing increase in the number of cases they had to try. Many courts were old, ill-equipped and run-down. New Crown Courts had also to be built. In the contest for priorities in public expenditure getting money for new courts was not easy. In spite of this we did make progress and I opened a large number during my term of office: always happy civic experiences.

The close links between the Lord Chancellor's office and the Lord Mayor and the City of London, particularly because of the City's responsibility for the Central Criminal Court at the Old Bailey, resulted in my taking part in many of the City's ceremonies.

Each October by ancient custom, the Lord Mayor Elect, accompanied by his wife and his fellow aldermen, attend the Princes' Chamber in the House of Lords to receive from the Lord Chancellor the Queen's approbation of his election as Mayor. The Recorder of London first presents him to the Chancellor and proclaims his virtues: in my time always in elegant and witty speeches from Karl Aarvold and his successor James Miskin. The Lord Chancellor and the Lord Mayor Elect then toast each other in two loving cups adorned with white silk bows and lilies of the valley.

This ceremony is followed soon afterwards by the Lord Mayor's Banquet to Her Majesty's Government at which the Prime Minister speaks, followed by the Archbishop of Canterbury and the Lord Chancellor. It is held in the historic Guildhall.

The 647th Lord Mayor of London, Sir Henry Murray-Fox, was the Lord Mayor at the first ministerial banquet at which I had to speak as Lord Chancellor. The theme of his Lord Mayor's Show, an annual patriotic street pantomine greatly relished by the public, was 'the Sinews of Britain'. It included the surprising presence of a Royal Marine on a camel, the Chief Accountant of the Bank of England in a bed of roses – and a solicitor on horseback.

At the banquet the Lord Chancellor's liveried trainbearer stands behind his chair to relieve him of his full-bottomed wig and cumbersome gold and black robe before the meal, place them safely on the carpet behind him and put them on again at the end of the meal before the Lord Chancellor's speech. On one occasion my trainbearer not only managed to lose his sword but also contrived to mix up my wig and robes with those of Lord Justice Scarman, and take his away from the Guildhall. There was a flurry of phone calls next day. This, however, was nothing compared with the misadventure of Lord Jowitt when he was Lord Chancellor. His trainbearer, who had also indulged in the City's hospitality, dropped Lord Jowitt's wig in a handy firebucket full of water. Murphy's Law 'if anything can go wrong it will' has universal application.

In the first of the banquets to the judges I attended, in July 1974, the Lord Mayor was Sir Hugh Wontner, Chairman of the Savoy Theatre and Trustee of the D'Oyly Carte Opera Trust responsible for the Gilbert and Sullivan operettas. At the Bar Musical Society's jubilee concert in the Middle Temple Hall in December 1978 I was invited to join John Reed, outstanding in the role of Lord Chancellor in *Iolanthe*, in singing alternate verses of

> When I went to the Bar as a very young man,
> I said to myself said I . . .

We had to sing an encore. The Queen Mother, a Bencher of the Middle Temple, seated in the front row of the audience, enjoyed the fun as much as we all did.

Gray's Inn honoured me, when I was appointed Lord Chancellor, with a house dinner, over which Hugh Francis QC, a fellow student from my Aberystwyth and Cambridge days, presided in the Hall of the Inn, faithfully reconstructed after being blitzed in the war. Apart from Lord Birkenhead and Lord Kilmuir, in the post-war period, there had been no Gray's Inn Lord Chancellor since Francis Bacon. After his disgrace for corruption towards the end of his life, Bacon retired to live in the Inn 'for quiet and the better to hold out' and to enjoy the beauty of the gardens he himself designed. His statue in South Square is a landmark for the students who pass it on the way to the Library.

Another event I enjoyed at this time was a Royal Academy banquet in Burlington House, where I was bidden to reply to the toast to Her Majesty's ministers. I told the story of the English school teacher who, tired out on a walking tour in Central France, decided to stay overnight in a village *auberge*. The proprietor Gaston showed her the guest room. She cautiously prodded the mattress – *le matelas* – which she found to be biscuit-thin and demanded : '*Je veux deux matelots, s'il vous plait.*'

'*Écoutez, mademoiselle!*' the astonished Gaston replied. '*Il faut être raisonnable. Ici nous sommes loin de la mer. Dans le village il y a un boulanger, un boucher, un garde-champêtre et le vieux curé, mais pas de matelots.*'

'*Alors je m'en vais*,' protested the weary schoolteacher, '*je ne peux pas dormir sans deux matelots*' – and off she went.

Gaston rushed down to the kitchen where his wife Marie Claire was cooking dinner to explain why they had lost the English traveller. Marie-Claire was startled. '*Vraiment? Tu dis que la dame anglaise a insisté qu'elle ne peut pas dormir sans deux matelots?*'

'*Oui, je le jure*,' insisted Gaston.

'*Ah*,' sighed Marie-Claire, '*quelle race maritime!*'

This anecdote was so rapturously received that my fellow guest, Lord Mountbatten, asked me if he could borrow it to enliven a dinner he had to address in France. Later, I was intrigued to read, in the press account of Lord Mountbatten's speech, that he began the story: 'When I was a young midshipman on a walking tour in France ...' I had hoped to find an opportunity later to ask him what he really did say. Alas he was assassinated by the IRA shortly afterwards on his yacht in Ireland. A few years later his ADC, who was present at the French dinner, told me that he had indeed used those words: 'He had a roguish sense of humour.'

The Lord Chancellor has a special role to play in maintaining amity with the Judiciary and the legal profession of the countries of the Commonwealth, the United States and Europe.

Legal links with France were strengthened each year by invitations from the French Bench and Bar to the formal opening of the French legal year in the Palais de Justice in Paris. At the ceremony two chosen entrants to the Bar declaimed orations in the old rotund style on given subjects: one of the most eloquent I heard was on the Dreyfus case.

One of my early visits abroad as Lord Chancellor was to Strasbourg, to the Council of Europe. This was followed by law conferences in New York. The Watergate crisis was still simmering. An American lawyer friend called me and asked with feigned solemnity: 'Is it true that the Queen has sent the Lord Chancellor to America to offer a pardon to her former rebellious colonists and a restoration of their colonial status?' During this visit I sat with the Supreme Court of Massachusetts in Boston. I noticed that the judges enforced a strict time limit on the length of counsel's speeches but did allow 'injury time' to compensate for their own interventions.

1975 was a year of exciting travels: firstly in February to Nigeria, where determined efforts were being made to maintain the traditions and standards inherited from generations of lawyers trained in the Inns of Court in London. In the crowded Supreme Court which I addressed in humid, tropical Lagos, counsel were dressed exactly as they would have been in the Law Courts in the Strand: in black gowns, bob wigs, starched collars and white bands. Their formalities were the same, their courtesies the same. I was very pleased to see my old colleague Chief Rotumi Williams QC in court.

In March I flew via Australia to New Zealand for their Law Society conference. I was a guest of the Governor of Victoria in Melbourne, the Governor of New South Wales in Sydney, and the Governor-General in Canberra. It was shortly before the dramatic personal clash between Prime Minister Whitlam and Governor-General Kerr which resulted in the fall of the Australian Labour Government. They were still friends when I was their guest. The formalities at Government House in Sydney made a state banquet at Buckingham Palace seem like a family gathering.

The cheerful conference of the Commonwealth Magistrates' Association in Kuala Lumpur in August 1975 was dominated by the Lord President Suffian and his wife. Our Malaysian hosts extolled the value of such conferences in broadening our horizons and preventing us from becoming a *Katak di – bawah temupurong*, a frog under a coconut shell.

The following month London became the centre of a great international gathering when the British group of the Inter-Parliamentary Union hosted the 62nd conference of the Union. Over 600 members of the Parliaments of seventy-five countries, together with their wives and entourages, assembled. The Queen opened the conference.

After the daily work of the conference there were receptions each night. The Lord Mayor received the delegates in the Mansion House, Mr Speaker and I hosted a reception in Westminster Hall, the GLC entertained them in County Hall. There were receptions also at Lancaster House, Hampton Court, the Banqueting Hall in Whitehall and Lincoln's Inn, where the band of the Royal Marines entertained the guests and performed the ceremony of Beating Retreat on the green lawn.

The programme of the conference enabled my duties and Polly's interests to coincide. It included a dress show which Polly helped to organize, aided by her colleagues in the world of fashion and textile design. James Fitton RA secured permission to stage the show in the Royal Academy and Prince Philip wrote the programme foreword. Polly's introduction read:

> Our country is rich in creative talent and our training system enables us to find and develop it. What you are seeing today is the work of our talented and highly trained young designers from all over Great Britain, some already world-famous, others just graduating from our renowned Schools of Design represented here by The Royal College of Arts in Kensington Gore and St Martin's

School of Art in Charing Cross Road, which also have the honour of training designers from all parts of the world.

The pearly queens distributed the programmes. Norman Hartnell came to cheer. The guests were served with three English wines and nine varieties of British cheeses. The show was an outstanding success.

In September 1975 Canada celebrated the centenary of its Supreme Court in Ottawa. There I stayed with the High Commissioner, Sir John Johnston, in his house overlooking the river Ottawa where the Rideau joins it. Mr Justice Byron White represented the Supreme Court of the United States and the President of the Cour de Cassation that of France. The Canadian Chief Justice, Bora Laskin, a rare and distinguished example of an academic becoming head of the Judiciary, presided over bilingual discussions. Ottawa University conferred on each of us an honorary doctorate in Law.

1976 marked the bicentennial of the United States. In June a British parliamentary delegation (with their spouses), led by Mr Speaker Thomas and myself, presented to Congress in Washington one of the original copies of Magna Carta on loan for one year and a specially designed jewelled showcase and a replica of Magna Carta as permanent gifts.

It was a great occasion. The ceremony of presentation took place in the Rotunda of the Capitol in the presence of the members of the Senate and of Congress. I delivered an address (see Appendix) which was duly recorded in the Congressional Record of the Senate. Mr Speaker Albert, of the House of Representatives, responded. Edmund Burke once referred to our bonds with America as 'ties which, though light as air, are as strong as links of iron'.

At the ceremony in the Rotunda I was seated next to Vice-President Nelson Rockefeller. The Treasury had provided me with a new gold and black robe for the occasion. As I was speaking a fragment of the gold braid fell on to the carpet. When I sat down, the Vice-President picked it up, held it in his hand and said, 'May I keep this as a souvenir?' I thought when I returned home that my grandchildren would be impressed when I told them I had given gold to Rockefeller. Not so – the name rang no bell for them.

A nostalgic item in the proceedings was the singing of the 'Ballad of Magna Carta', a cantata by Kurt Weill.

A high point of the Rotunda ceremony was the perfect drill of a small detachment of British Guardsmen who stood guard over the case in which the Magna Carta was displayed and the equally impressive performance of a detachment of servicemen from the American armed forces who took over the duty from the Guards when I had formally handed over Magna Carta to Mr Speaker Albert.

The British parliamentary delegation was later received in a special session of the Senate and introduced to its members and taken on a tour of the Capitol and of the Library of Congress. The Librarian indicated that they had a copy of almost every book ever published. Douglas Jay, testing the Librarian's claim, asked if the Library had a copy of Adam Smith's *Wealth of Nations* published in 1776. The Librarian said he would enquire. To test his claim further I asked him in fun whether they had a copy of the laws of Howel dda (Howel the good), the South Wales king who collected the laws of Wales in the tenth century. In no time at all the Librarian proudly produced a first edition of Adam Smith's book – and three translations from the Welsh of Howel dda's laws. I ventured to suggest in my speech of thanks afterwards that if I had asked to see the Ten Commandments, the Librarian would no doubt have promptly produced them on Moses' original stone tablets.

President Ford entertained our delegation in the White House: a very much larger version of No 10, but with a similar domestic flavour.

The bicentennial celebrations continued throughout that summer. The ceremonial visit of the 'tall ships' from many countries was extremely popular. Polly made her own way to Washington to enjoy the multinational folk song and dance festival on the banks of the river Potomac. To augment the solitary British contribution (a group of robust north country Morris dancers) Polly enlisted the help of our enthusiastic Ambassador, Sir Peter Ramsbotham, to bring over Mrs Rosie Springfield, the old cockney pearly queen of Stoke Newington. Dressed in full pearly regalia she flew over with the Morris dancers and delighted everyone at the festival with her husky Cockney music hall songs.

I returned to the United States in August 1976 for the conferment of the degree of Doctor of Laws, *honoris causa*, of Columbia University, New York, on Warren Berger, Chief Justice of the United States, John Widgery, Lord Chief Justice of Great Britain, and myself. Polly and I stayed with my old lawyer friend Mal Hoffman and his wife Anna, who made their old-fashioned Riverside Drive house a second home for us in New York.

From New York I flew to Atlanta for the Bicentennial Conference of the American Bar Association. Polly joined me there at the vertiginous Peach Tree Plaza Hotel with its alarming outside elevator. We received warm hospitality in Atlanta and established pleasant friendships there which have lasted.

One curiously memorable meeting which Polly and I attended was addressed by the Democratic presidential candidate, a small and vulnerable man, who announced: 'I'm Jimmy Carter. I'm standing for President.'

A special service for the conference was held at the Atlanta Episcopalian Cathedral at which I wore my full regalia. I failed to notice the order of service and when 'Jerusalem' was sung I naturally stood up to sing. Who ever sang 'Jerusalem' sitting down? When I looked round at the vast congregation I found to my dismay I was the only person standing. Everyone else had followed the order of service and kept to their seats while the choir sang the hymn. Lawrence Walsh, President of the ABA, however loyally stood up to support me.

The closing event of the conference was the giant annual dinner of the ABA at which its President, Chief Justice Warren Berger, Peter Rawlinson, Chairman of the Bar Council, and I all spoke.

It was a merry occasion. In my speech I upheld the Welsh claim that America was not in fact discovered by Christopher Columbus but much earlier by Prince Madoc of Rhos-on-Sea, North Wales. I told them of the tradition in Wales that Prince Madoc set sail from Port Madoc in the year 1170 with a fleet of thirteen ships and landed in Mobil Bay, Alabama; a belief confirmed five centuries later when the colonists coming from England found that the Madan Indian tribe living in those parts used many Welsh expressions in their speech.

The Welsh poet Ceiriog wrote a poem about it, which in my young days every Welsh schoolboy knew. I read out one verse in translation:

> Behold on a fair morning
> Thirteen small ships set sail
> On a dangerous venture
> May God preserve them from wave to wave.

When I added that it was sung to a charming tune, Polly sitting beside me urged, 'Sing it.' I told the audience of lawyers and their wives that unless they had overwhelming objection I would sing it. Encouraging shouts of 'Sing it, Lord Chancellor,' came from all parts of the room. I did so. We had all dined well. It was joyfully received.

This exhilarating visit ended with our returning home, as guests of the American Bar Association, on the *QE2* – for once Polly and I were able to travel together.

1976 was an eventful year for the country politically and for me personally. The Cabinet assembled in No 10 on the morning of 16 March for what we assumed to be an ordinary cabinet meeting. We were dumbfounded when Harold Wilson, the Prime Minister, announced without emotion in a long and carefully prepared statement that he had been to the Palace that morning and had tendered his resignation to the Queen. I asked whether his decision was irrevocable. He said that it was.

Jim Callaghan formed the new administration, in which I continued as Lord Chancellor. The pattern of my life was unchanged.

A few days after his resignation, Harold gave a farewell dinner in No 10 to the members of the Cabinet and a few of his staff. What happened has been partially recorded by Barbara Castle in her diary. After dinner the Prime Minister spoke briefly and was followed by Ted Short in what was clearly an emotionally felt tribute. A somewhat uneasy silence followed, which I broke by telling the story of Harold's last visit to Salisbury after our talks with Smith. As we left Smith's Cabinet Office Harold was escorted by the Salisbury Chief of Police, who, like him, was a 'tyke', a Yorkshire man. A number of hostile Rhodesian Front supporters in the crowd which had assembled outside shouted at the Prime Minister: 'Get back to Yorkshire, you tyke.' Harold turned blithely to the Chief Constable beside him and said: 'They don't seem to like you very much, do they?'

That Easter Polly and I were overnight guests of the Queen and Prince Philip at Windsor Castle. To entertain the guests the Librarian had a small display of historical documents of particular interest to each one of us. One selected for me was a letter dated 29 January 1818 from the Lord Chancellor to the Prince Regent proposing the appointment of Mr Best to the office of Chief Justice of Chester and the Welsh counties connected with it even though 'Mr Best, the Chief Justice, may be unable to attend occasionally by reason of gout'. Polly enjoyed a unique illuminated translation in Hindi of Queen Victoria's *Journal of our Life in the Highlands*.

Each year the Foreign and Commonwealth Secretary hosts a dinner to celebrate Her Majesty's Birthday to the High Commissioners and Ambassadors accredited to the Court of St James in different historical settings such as Hampton Court. The Royal Naval College in Greenwich is also a perfect choice for such an event. All nations east and west have chosen Greenwich Mean Time as their universal standard. Queen Elizabeth I was born and lived there. It was there that she knighted Sir Francis Drake on board the *Golden Hind*. Sir Walter Raleigh and Peter the Great were guests there. In June 1976, the Foreign Secretary, Anthony Crosland, being absent abroad on urgent Foreign Office business, could not host the dinner. I was asked to take his place. As Polly was also out of England, my married younger daughter Elizabeth (Louli) Taylor accompanied me instead. She looked stunning in a long dress of vivid blue and crimson cotton batik which I had brought back for her from Nigeria. The programme which had announced that the guests would be received by the

Lord Chancellor and Mrs Elizabeth Taylor caused considerable excitement.

In my address in the great painted hall I stressed the essential interdependence of the world's nations. No country is able fully to assure its prosperity and security regardless of the actions and policies of other members of the international community. It had been a bad year for diplomats. Some had been murdered; others had been kidnapped and held to ransom. On behalf of the Government I assured the guests that we in Britain would take every possible step open to us to maintain the safety of the diplomatic corps and its freedom and facilities.

The dinner ended with the superbly executed Ceremony of Beating Retreat by the band of the Royal Marines against the background of the quiet Thames and slow moving barges beneath the starlit sky.

In September 1976 it fell to me on behalf of the two Houses of Parliament to open the 4th Conference of Commonwealth Speakers in the Royal Gallery. Thirty Speakers attended. It came at an auspicious time. In England we were celebrating the 600th anniversary of the office of Speaker of the House of Commons. The parliamentary clerks upon whom Speakers – and, from my own experience, Lord Chancellors – are accustomed to lean, were also in attendance. Parliamentary institutions were under threat that year and in more than one Commonwealth country they had been silenced by military dictators. Parliamentary democracy is a plant of slow growth and is easily uprooted in unstable societies. It is all the more important and precious to maintain the authority of Parliament here.

That autumn an official invitation to visit his country came from Nicolas Giosan, President of Romania's National Assembly. It was a time when the Romanian Government were asserting some independence within the Warsaw Pact and a ministerial visit from the United Kingdom was thought by our Foreign Office to be timely. Polly stubbornly refused to fly, so we boarded the Orient Express in Paris. As we rightly guessed, it was not what it had been in Agatha Christie's heyday. Wisely we had equipped ourselves with a picnic, supplemented on the train by truly fearsome *ersatz* coffee served in a leaky cardboard cup. The miracle was that we did find our sleeper when we changed trains at Budapest.

Forty years had passed since my last covert visit to Romania before the war to establish contact with the young lawyers who were defending political prisoners of the corrupt regime of King Carol. In 1976 we were most cordially received. In Bucharest I had long talks with Romanian ministers and judges. The Deputy Minister of Justice escorted me to some of the courts. There was the usual throng of bewildered defendants and scurrying lawyers. These were not easy to distinguish for they wore no identifying robes. The Deputy Minister of Justice took me into court to hear some cases. One was a will dispute. Another was a bastardy case, in which the alleged father made a truly bold defence. He swore that so far from being the father of the claimant's child as she alleged, he had never even seen her before. The woman judge, who sat with two lay assessors, showed not unexpected signs of incredulity. It was like being back in my early days at the Bar.

From Bucharest we travelled to Constanta on the Black Sea coast. We were taken to the Murfatlar Vineyard and tasted its delicious wines. But the most memorable visits were to the churches, their exteriors brilliantly painted with frescoes, and to the monasteries of Moldavia built in the fifteenth century.

One monastery we visited was in fact run by an impressive and delightful Mother Superior. She told us that the greatest threat to the survival of the monasteries were the three terrible Ts: Turks, termites and tourists. We had an unforgettable lunch which lasted from one until four. The table was strewn with sweet-scented flowers. As course followed course the Mother Superior assured us that the food was all grown by her nuns on their home farm. One of the guests was the Archimandrite, a huge, genial, bearded figure who, surprisingly, was also a member of the Romanian Parliament. The Minister who accompanied us and his colleagues sang a drinking song of many verses which recounted the drinking prowess of each member of a large family. At the first verse I thought the Mother Superior was looking down her nose rather primly, but by the tenth verse she joined merrily in the chorus. I contributed the Welsh folk song about the black pig that died. My private secretary John Watherstone piped up with a verse of 'The Oak and the Ash'.

At the end of the visit I had a long televised interview with President Ceauşescu, small, energetic and very sure of himself. Shortly after our visit he paid a state visit to London – the first Head of State from a Warsaw Pact country to do so. I found the top officials in Romania refreshingly outspoken about the Soviet Union. Anti-Stalin stories were gleefully recounted.

While I was seeing politicians and lawyers, Polly was visiting folk museums and delivering lectures to several institutes and art schools.

In February 1977 I represented the British Government at the funeral in Delhi of Sakhrudin Ali Ahmed, the President of India. Prince Michael of Kent represented the Queen. There were government representatives from many parts of the world. The mother of the American President, Mrs

Carter, who had once rendered personal service to India as a nurse in a Bombay hospital, was especially fêted. I delivered one of the several funeral orations that were made to an assembly of 10,000 people inside the historic Red Fort in Delhi, including one from President Carter, read by his son.

Later in the year Prince Michael and I again flew out as mourners, to the funeral service of Archbishop Makarios in Cyprus. Villagers greeted us as we drove from Larnaca Airport to Famagusta. I sat next to Chief Justice Warren Berger in the hot and packed funeral service in the cathedral there. Professional mourners wailed both inside and outside the cathedral.

In June 1977 I flew to Vienna on the invitation of the Austrian Government as a guest of my friend Dr Christian Broda, the Austrian Minister of Justice. He was one of the Socialist prisoners who were incarcerated in Vienna after the February rising in 1934 whom I had tried to help. He took me on nostalgic visits to places like the small street near Vienna University where I lived in 1934 and the restored Gemeindehaüse, which the Fascist Heimwehr had shelled.

From Vienna I flew to Warsaw to receive the honorary degree of Doctor of Laws at a touching ceremony at the University of Warsaw. The statue of Copernicus, who opened the universe to the human race, presided over the main gates of the university, founded in 1814. I believe the honour was conferred on me because I had presented some of the Polish evidence in the Nuremberg trial. The Rector's citation mentioned the fact that I was awarded the Polonia Restituta Medal in 1946 after the trial ended. In my speech I thanked the courageous academics from the University of Warsaw who during the war obtained and analysed the V-2 rocket guidance system and smuggled the blueprint to London.

There was a simple, moving memorial in the university campus to staff and students who were murdered during the genocidal regime of Hans Frank. I heard many heroic accounts of the courage, and success, of university teachers and students during that time in keeping classes going in basements, churches and other hiding places when discovery meant death.

The Commonwealth Law Ministers' Conference held in Winnipeg in August 1977 enabled me to meet again Charles Njonjo, the Attorney-General of Kenya and a former pupil of my chambers, and then to have a brief holiday with Josephine and her family in Maine.

In September, on the invitation of the Polish Minister of Justice, Polly and I made another nostalgic return visit together to Poland on the new MS *Batory*. At Gdynia we were taken on a trip on the rough Baltic Sea in a small launch to see the new Port North, constructed to handle the largest general cargo vessels which can enter the Baltic. One of Poland's marine experts accompanied us. I teased him that all their technical skills had not yet enabled them to still the waters. He commented cheerfully: 'There are too many Communists on board.' Afterwards at lunch in Gdynia Polly, who had braved the rough waves successfully, was gallantly congratulated on being 'a true daughter of Albion'.

Later that day I laid a wreath in Gdansk (Danzig) on the war memorial at Westerplatte, a finger of land jutting out of Port Canal, which a League of Nations resolution of 1925 had permitted the Poles to occupy. In 1939 the German warship *Schleswig-Holstein* arrived in Gdansk on what was supposed to be a courtesy visit. Instead, before dawn on 1 September, the warship without warning began shelling Westerplatte. The Polish garrison of 182 men under Major Sucharski courageously resisted a massive German onslaught for many days, almost to the last man. On the third day after the invasion, Britain and France declared war on Germany. The Second World War had begun.

From the brilliantly reconstructed city, which had been destroyed during the war, we went by road to Warsaw, calling on the way at the grim Marlborg Teuton Castle which became an ss headquarters during the Nazi occupation. More agreeable was the visit at Torun to the modest home of the great Copernicus.

In Warsaw we were guests of Jerzy Bafia, the Minister of Justice. There was no hint of the impending crisis of 1981–82 which was to bring about martial law and military dictatorship to Poland. The splendid new Opera House was crowded with enthusiastic audiences. Polly was taken by her old friend Professor Wanda Telekowska to a fine exhibition of Polish posters.

We drove south from Warsaw to Katowice and passed the sombre road pointing to Auschwitz. It was a sunny morning and families dressed in their Sunday best were making their way to church. Later we climbed the hills to the mist-enveloped mountain resort of Zakopane, where we had been on holiday just after the war with our children when they were very young.

The ancient city of Cracow with its great university of Copernicus had delighted me when I visited it then. This time on display was one of the vast carpet-draped tents of the Turkish army of invaders repelled by the Poles. The Poles had successfully hidden the tent from Hans Frank when he made Wavel Castle his headquarters.

1977 was the year of the Silver Jubilee, the twenty-fifth anniversary of the Queen's accession. It was a timely boon to the British souvenir industry, Wedgwood in particular producing a gorgeous assortment of commemorative china including Polly's pearly jubilee mug, which proved popular both with the pearlies and the public. The nation-wide celebration was launched with an assembly in Westminster Hall of members of the Lords and Commons. It was my privilege to greet and thank the Queen on behalf of the House of Lords for a quarter of a century of devoted service. Mr Speaker Thomas spoke for the Commons.

In my address to the Queen I declared: 'Your courage in the face of difficulties, and sometimes dangers, commands our admiration. Your ability cheerfully to adapt to the mood of the times and yet preserve a calm continuity, is a virtue for which everyone assembled here today is grateful.'

The Queen made a gracious reply. As the proceedings came to an end I called for three cheers for the Queen with the triple naval 'Hip! Hip! Hip! Hooray'. I had been accustomed in my army experience to two 'Hips' but Black Rod – Admiral Twiss – pressed the case for three. They were enthusiastically given by all who were present.

There were jubilee celebrations everywhere as we discovered in Whitby, Cardiff and West Ham, where they were lively and cheerful despite the deluge of rain.

In the Palace of Westminster, the carefully preserved privacy of the Lord Chancellor's quarters suffered a considerable jolt very early on the morning of 14 July 1977, when a custodian telephoned me in my bedroom in the floor above my office to tell me that when he had unlocked my office door at six o'clock that morning he found a naked man asleep in my armchair wrapped in my black silk gown. The intruder was an unemployed Yorkshire man of thirty-four. He had been seen on Westminster Bridge very early that morning to undress, fold his clothes and then jump into the Thames. The Thames Division Police, who are accustomed to such dramas, searched the river for him without success, and he was presumed drowned.

Further inquiries revealed that he had been carried by the incoming tide to the river wall of the Palace of Westminster below my office. By this time his attempt at suicide had been changed by the shock of the cold water into a frantic bid for life. He had managed to grab a lightning conductor which led down to the river from the roof and with its aid he climbed up to one of my office windows. He smashed a small window pane with his fist (broken glass and blood were found on the office carpet) and having released the window catch he was able to climb in. He had no idea at all which building he had entered or where he was.

Having got into the room – my main working and reception room – the intruder was trapped, for both of its doors were locked. He thereupon wrapped himself in the only covering available, which was the official black silk robe I wore on the Woolsack, and fell asleep in my armchair.

He was later found to be suffering from mental illness and was taken to a hospital under the provisions of the Mental Health Act. The police hoped that the press would not get hold of the story because of the serious breach in security it exposed. In vain : the story appeared in the papers the next morning. I should add that the security of the Palace of Westminster and of the Lord Chancellor's office was greatly strengthened after this episode.

Jill Craigie, to whom Michael Foot is married, was adviser for the exhibition on women's suffrage (on which she is an expert) which took up the whole of one side of Westminster Hall in 1978. Polly helped with the figures and costumes loaned by the theatrical costumiers Berman and Nathan. The public flocked in and every day classes of schoolchildren came to learn. I overheard one little miss know-all, pointing to Polly (who was busy behind the ropes adjusting the widow's peak cap on Queen Victoria), whisper to her friend, 'That's Mrs Pankhurst.'

Polly's last effort in the Lords while I was still Lord Chancellor was concerned with the long overdue redecoration of the River Room (as we called the great reception room), which was in a sorry state of dilapidation. Over the years, unwise decoration and furnishing had worked havoc on Pugin's original gothic-revival creation. His hearth tiles had been smothered under thick beige paint, his walls and ceiling coated pale blue. Moreover the River Room had become a repository for unlikely white elephants : immense tattered French tapestries, a blackened Italian painting, gigantic brass fire irons guarding the gas fire, and coquettish pink and blue velvet armchairs suitable only for a suburban boudoir. Pugin had never made a mistake, yet this noble room had been made to look curiously out of proportion. Though Pugin himself was half-French, his work was deeply British. The River Room as he designed it belonged to the world of early Dickens.

Polly called in the experts to advise the Works Department on restoring the room to its original Pugin concept. There were many consultations as they put their heads together in this labour of love.

Mr Norton, the Building and Maintenance Officer of the Houses of Parliament, scratched tentatively at the beige paint with a 10p coin. Underneath, Pugin's original brilliant glazed tiles shone out in a four-variation flower design. The job had begun. That night Polly told me she now knew exactly how Howard Carter must have felt when he uncovered Tutankhamun's treasure.

High scaffolding took the skilled workers up to the ceiling where they began to scrape off the pale blue paint, revealing the original dark wood ribbed diamond patterns intersected by gold bosses. 'Look missus! Look!' they called down excitedly to Polly, far below; 'Every single boss is different!' As soon as the ceiling was restored, the noble room regained its original perfect proportions, the ceiling blending with the linenfold wall panelling and harmonizing with the cathedral windows. Pugin indeed had not made a mistake.

Books of Pugin's original wallpapers were examined, lighting and furniture were discussed. Time was pressing. An election was pending and we did not wish to leave the job unfinished. Professor John Drummond designed the new carpet, closely based on Pugin, and Nicholas Kitchener, the Supplies Officer (recently killed, alas, in a motor accident), tracked down the perfect sofas and armchairs and had them upholstered in mulberry velvet to blend with everything else.

It is I believe, essential today to give young British talent every opportunity to show what it can do. This was an excellent opportunity. Polly enlisted the talented stained-glass students of the City Literary Institute under the supervision of their teacher Amal Ghosh, who had worked on the stained-glass windows of Coventry Cathedral. They undertook to produce twenty-two stained-glass panels for the River Room windows with the heraldic coats-of-arms of twenty-two former Lord Chancellors.

John Darwin, the Resident Engineer in the Palace of Westminster, thrilled the students by telling them that the black and gold royal portraits in the Princes' Chamber had been painted over a century ago by students of the Royal College of Art. Conditions in the City Literary Institute, which runs on half a shoestring, are cramped and difficult, especially for those working in stained glass, but the students' patience and enthusiasm triumphed. My term of office ended before the stained-glass panels were fixed in the River Room windows, but later, at Lord Hailsham's opening of Parliament reception, Polly and I were happy to see them in place with the sun streaming through them.

In the spring of 1979 I was invited by Enrique Syquia, President of the International Law Association, to address its Philippines branch. I flew first to Singapore, which looked even more prosperous than when I defended the Barisan Socialis there many years before.

I then paid a brief visit to Jakarta, the capital of Indonesia, which has a population of 140 millions, nine-tenths of whom are Muslim. Before World War II began and after Japan had invaded China, I had met a charming group of Javanese students, members of the Sultan's private ballet and orchestra in Jakarta, who came to London from Amsterdam University to dance at the Phoenix Theatre in aid of the Chinese Peace Hospital. Margery Fry and Polly and I were among the sponsors of the visit. The performances at the Phoenix raised a good sum for the hospital.

President Suharto's 'new order' in Indonesia was established after the downfall of Sukarno in the mid-1960s. When I questioned the Attorney-General in Jakarta about the 11,000 people still held in detention, where they had been since the 1965 coup, he claimed that this was still necessary in the interests of national security.

In the Philippines I had talks with several lawyers, both those who supported the rule of President and Mrs Imelda Marcos and those who thought the time had come for martial law to be ended. I raised with President Marcos a number of individual cases which had been reported to me and expressed to him the concern of the British Government about the continuing infringement of human rights in the Philippines.

I had a happy meeting with the professors and students of the University of St Thomas Aquinas in Manila, which honoured me with a degree. They expressed friendly feelings for Britain and gratitude for the work of the British Council in the Philippines.

I rushed back from the Far East in May 1979 for the General Election battle which had just begun. My Labour colleagues and I had the satisfaction of knowing that despite the economic crisis Britain found herself in from 1976 on, the living standards of many of the poorest people in our country – the unemployed, the disabled, the pensioners, the lowest paid and those dependent on the new child benefit – had not only been sustained but improved.

Shortly before polling day, Polly and I gave a party in the still unfinished River Room for the staff of the Lord Chancellor's office and for those who helped us in the residence. In welcoming them, I explained that if the Labour Government won the election it would be just a thank-you party for their hard work and friendship during my five years of office. If Labour lost, it would also be a goodbye party.

Labour lost. We packed our belongings, including our cherished collection of Polynesian shells, and returned to our flat at Gray's Inn.

During my term of office as Lord Chancellor our nine grandchildren, all very dear to us, had grown up rapidly : they are all totally at ease in today's changing world of computers, videos and satellites so mystifying to Polly and me, who can remember the primitive cat's whisker radio of the 1920s.

Josephine had married Francis Gladstone (whose wife Janet was killed in a car crash when their daughter Melissa was a baby). With their son Elwyn, Melissa, Hannah and James, they made a home together in Boston, Massachusetts. Jo and Francis are working in television and films, and Jo is also writing a PhD thesis at Harvard on the nutrition and health of the combatant seamen of Britain and America during the war of 1812.

Living in Brighton (where we have enjoyed an unexpected new friendship with our neighbours Tom Lodge, his wife and family) and in London, we were able to keep in close touch with Dan's family and with Louli's.

Our son, Dan, is a youth worker in Tower Hamlets in the East End of London, where he lives with his wife Den and their three children, Davey, Sammy and Polly, in the thick of its racial and economic problems. Overworked though he is in that sadly deprived area, Dan has also become a well-known artist, interpreting what goes on around him in pictures, posters, murals and children's books with perception and a sense of humour. Den runs a popular bookshop nearby, part of the lively local arts project.

Our younger daughter Louli's talent has turned out to be in teaching. After the success of her Fortuny Exhibition in Brighton, she planned and helped to set up a unique Fashion Gallery in Brighton Museum. She lives in Brighton with her husband Joe, who lectures at Sussex University, and their two sons, Reuben and Noah, and is now enjoying her job as a lecturer at Brighton Polytechnic. Her first book, *The History of Mourning Dress*, is soon to be published.

After half a century, Polly, enthusiasm undiminished, is back again making lithographs at her old Central School of Art in London. Having assisted at the beginning of British television at Alexandra Palace before the war, she still enjoys preparing picture programmes for BBC television today.

When the new Parliament assembled on 15 May 1979, I joined my colleagues on the Labour Opposition Front Bench. It did not take long before harsh application by the Tory Government of monetary theories eroded our industrial base and brought about an even higher level of unemployment than our country had suffered in the darkest days of my youth in South Wales. Divisions in our society were sharpened. Racial and social tensions erupted in serious disorders in several of our cities, fuelled by squalid housing, racial discrimination and insecurity. The need for an attack on these conditions was imperative. Tory attempts to dismantle the Welfare State, which had been Labour's response to the people's call for a new deal when the Second World War ended, had also to be resisted.

On the international front fresh initiatives were needed to re-open the dialogue between West and East, to reduce growing international tension, to halt the nuclear arms race and to dispel the threat of nuclear annihilation. In my speech on the Address in May 1979 I stressed the wisdom of the advice contained in the Welsh *Mabinogion*: '*A vo ben bid bont*' – he who leads must be a bridge. Our country and the world sorely need such leadership.

Appendix

Magna Carta Presentation Speech in the United States Capitol

It is my honour and pleasure first to bring to this great Assembly of representatives of the American people the greetings and abundant good wishes of my fellow Parliamentarians and of the people of the United Kingdom.

It was our privilege to welcome you, Mr Speaker, and your distinguished Delegation to Westminster Hall last week, the historic centre from which the system of Common Law was taken to every quarter of the globe. It is now our privilege to be received at the very heart of your Congress, the Rotunda.

On behalf of my colleagues and myself, I would like to thank you for the warmth of your hospitality. On this historic occasion your generosity has extended to permitting Mr Speaker Thomas and myself to appear before you in the full-bottomed wig which has been traditionally worn by our predecessors for the past 200 years. We have ventured to do so, despite the firm resolution of our fellow Welshman, Thomas Jefferson, that English judicial wigs should not on any account be worn in these United States. As for our robes, I can only repeat the assurance of a certain English clergyman, who betook himself two centuries ago to a village in my native Wales called Cerrig y Druidion – Druid's Stones. The clergyman appeared in such unfamiliar garments that upon the sight of him 'a general roar of laughter shook the village'. But he was not abashed. His response was to say: 'Gentlemen, you may consider us as ridiculous as you please, but I do assure you that at home we pass for decent men.' I hope our colleagues from Westminster will be willing to give you the same assurance about Mr Speaker Thomas and myself.

One of the great precepts of friendship is 'rejoice with those who do rejoice and weep with those who do weep'. Our peoples have been borne together by the sorrows of two World Wars. Now we rejoice that we can share your Bicentennial celebrations. Peoples not familiar with our ways have thought it paradoxical for the British to be joining in the celebration of the Bicentenary of what was, after all, the loss of the American colonies. They overlook our traditions of compromise. We now regard the events of two centuries ago as a victory for the English-speaking world.

In truth there is much to celebrate in this Bicentennial Year.

There is the enduring relationship between our two countries which overcame the severance of political links between us two centuries ago. Only six years after the Declaration of Independence King George III expressed the hope to the Parliament of his day that 'religion, language, interests, affection may prove a bond of permanent union between the two countries'. And so it was to be. For two centuries now we have been linked by those bonds. Fundamental among our common values is the principle of the rule of law, expressed in the words of your President John Adams and incorporated in the Declaration of Rights – 'a government of laws and not of men'. This principle, which is basic to any free society, found one of its earliest written expressions in King John's Great Charter of 1215. Beginning as an affirmation of the privileges of the dominant classes of feudal society, it gradually became a charter of liberty for all men. It became a fundamental law against which all other laws and executive acts should be tested. The famous clauses 39 and 40 ring down the centuries: 'no free man shall be proceeded against, except by the lawful judgment of his equals or by the law of the land. To no one will we sell, and no one deny or delay, right or justice.' For centuries Magna Carta lay dormant. I don't think Shakespeare ever mentioned it, even in his play *King John*. But its finest hour was to come. The Common Lawyers of the seventeenth century used it as a powerful weapon against the absolutist claims of the Stuart Monarchy, for its main theme was that government governs under the law and is itself subject to law. 'Magna Carta', thundered Lord Chief Justice Coke, 'is such a fellow that he will have no sovereign.'

It was a formidable weapon for use at that critical time in Parliament's history. 'We are the last monarchy in Christendom that retains our original rights and constitutions,' said one English MP in the 1620s. Unless they insisted on their rights, said another, 'then farewell Parliament and farewell England'. Fifteen years later, the English Parliament was able to challenge the King and defeat him in civil war. Parliamentary sovereignty was assured. In that very time the English settlers were going across the sea to the New World, taking the message of Magna Carta and the substance and spirit of the Common Law with them, with its insistence on individual rights and its repudiation of arbitrary power in any form. They took it to Virginia in 1607, and Massachusetts in 1620, and Maryland in 1632, and Rhode Island in 1636. And when the testing time came in the 1770s it was on the principles of Magna Carta that John Adams based his first appeal to the colonists. As streams join and make a mighty river, so have our Magna Carta and Bill of Rights and your Declaration of Independence and Constitution mingled to form a common heritage and tradition which has served as an inspiration to both our countries. We can together therefore repeat the familiar lines of Rudyard Kipling: 'All we have of freedom, all we need to know: This our fathers won for us long and long ago.'

We in Britain recognize, in the Bicentennial Year, the achievements of your great nation, whose institutions, whose air of freedom, whose enterprise, idealism and courage have gained our admiration and respect. The leadership of the free world rests on the shoulders of a powerful and generous people. Your recovery from the tribulations of recent years has especially impressed us. Both at home and abroad, you have been beset by circumstances and adversities which appeared to shatter your confidence and to threaten the principles on which depends the smooth running of a great democracy; circumstances which might have broken a less resilient people. But now it is evident to all your friends that your strength is untouched and your resolution firm. Above all, your Constitution has proved its soundness and its vitality.

Britain, too, has had her serious problems. But we British are also a resilient people. I shall never forget my emotion when, at the Nuremberg Trials in 1945, I handled the text of Hitler's 'Operation Sea Lion', the order for the invasion of Britain in the summer of 1940. The first paragraph reads: 'Although the British military situation is hopeless, they do not show the least sign of giving in.' With your help we survived that threat. We shall once again resolve the problems that now face us; and, in partnership with you, will continue to stand for the freedom which our heritage has bequeathed to us.

We have accordingly thought it fitting – and you have graciously agreed – that Magna Carta should be selected as the focal point of the participation of our Parliament in your Bicentennial celebrations.

The copy of Magna Carta which we hand over today to your care is the best of the four surviving originals of the 1215 version. At the wish of Her Majesty The Queen and on behalf of the members of both Houses of Parliament, it is my honour to present to you this show case and to ask you to accept into the safe keeping of Congress, for the Bicentennial Year, the Magna Carta. May we continue to respect and defend the principles which it symbolizes and may the friendship between our countries and our peoples long endure.

Bibliography

Tony Austin, *Aberfan: The Story of a Disaster* (Hutchinson)
Francis Biddle, *The World's Best Hope* (University of Chicago)
Pearl Binder, *Treasure Islands* (Blond & Briggs)
Maurice Bond and David Beamish, *The Lord Chancellor* (HMSO)
Tom Bower, *Blind Eye to Murder* (Deutsch)
Lord Butler, *The Art of Memory* (Hodder & Stoughton)
John Davies, *David Lloyd George and the National Insurance Act of 1911: Wales and Medicine* (British Society for the History of Medicine)
J. Ll J. Edwards, *The Law Officers of the Crown* (Sweet & Maxwell)
G. E. R. Gedye, *Fallen Bastions* (Gollancz)
Martin Gilbert, *Auschwitz and the Allies* (Michael Joseph)
James Griffiths, *Pages from Memory* (Dent)
Whitney Harris, *Tyranny on Trial* (Southern Methodist University Press)
T. E. B. Howarth, *Cambridge Between Two Wars* (Collins)
H. Montgomery Hyde, *Norman Birkett* (Hamish Hamilton)
Robert Rhodes James, *Victor Cazalet* (Hamish Hamilton)
Pamela Hansford Johnson, *On Iniquity* (Macmillan)
Naomi Mitchison, *Vienna Diary* (Gollancz)
Airey Neave, *Nuremberg* (Hodder & Stoughton)
Alan Paton, *Cry the Beloved County* (Cape)
Friedrich Scheu, *Der Weg Ins Ungewisse* (Verlag Fritz Molden)
Alan Sked and Chris Cook, *Post-War Britain* (Harvester Press, Barnes & Noble)
Norman Skelhorn, *Public Prosecutor* (Harrap)
Paul Sieghart, *The International Law of Human Rights* (Oxford University Press)
Bradley F. Smith, *The Road to Nuremberg* (Deutsch)
Telford Taylor, *Sword and Swastika* (Simon & Shuster)
Raleigh Trevelyan, *Rome '44* (Secker & Warburg)
Harold Wilson, *The Labour Government 1964–1970* (Weidenfeld)

Verbatim proceedings of the International Military Tribunal, pub. HMSO, 1949

Index